Ray Charles
THE BIRTH OF SOUL

MIKE EVANS

Ray Charles
THE BIRTH OF SOUL

MIKE EVANS

OMNIBUS PRESS

London • New York • Paris • Sydney • Copenhagen • Berlin • Madrid • Tokyo

Cover designed by Josh Labouve-Untype

Cover photograph by Jean-Pierre Muller/Getty Image

ISBN: 978-1-84609-341-8
Order No: OP51348

Exclusive Distributors
Music Sales Limited,
14-15 Berners Street,
London W1T 3LJ, UK.

Music Sales Corporation,
257 Park Avenue South,
New York, NY 10010, USA.

Macmillan Distribution Services,
53 Park West Drive,
Derrimut, Vic 3030,
Australia.

To the Music Trade only:
Music Sales Limited,
14-15 Berners Street,
London W1T 3LJ, UK.

Printed in the United States of America by Quebecor World

A catalog record for this book is available from the British Library.

Visit Omnibus Press on the web at www.omnibuspress.com

Contents

*This book is dedicated to the memory of Nesuhi Ertegun,
Zenas Sears, Edgar Willis and Ray Charles Robinson.*

Acknowledgements

The germ of this book lies in an interview I conducted with Ray Charles at the Pickett's Lock Leisure Centre in Edmonton, north London, on April 20, 1975.

The tape-recorded conversation, used at the time on a local radio show I hosted in Liverpool, was facilitated with the invaluable assistance of Oliver Morse and Jonathan Morse and the kind cooperation of Ray's bass player, the late Edgar Willis.

Other interviews conducted in 1975 and 1976, for which I also extend thanks, were with Chris Barber, Nesuhi Ertegun, Zenas Sears, Horace Silver and Steve Winwood. I am similarly grateful for interviews conducted in 2004 and 2005 with John Bryant, Eric Burdon, Leroy Cooper, Ahmet Ertegun, Renée Geyer, Jack Higgins, David Hoffman, David Newman, David Redfern, Jerry Wexler and Glenn Wheatley.

Thanks also to John Conroy, Robert Gordon, Bill Harry, Trevor Hyatt, Spencer Leigh, Stuart Lyon, Johnny Rogan and Steve Turner for assistance of one kind or another, and Chris Charlesworth at Omnibus Press.

Introduction

I can't remember exactly when or where I first actually heard 'What'd I Say'. It just seems always to have been there, but I can recall clearly the revelation, the impact, and the coming together of all those musical references that had led to that point by the end of the Fifties.

The grey, wet, sometimes-sunny-if-you're-lucky landscape of the North Wales coast was about as far removed from Black America as you could get. Maybe that was why jazz and blues seemed particularly exotic and intoxicating, even more so perhaps than in the big cities of the British Isles where such things were more accessible at concert venues, basement jazz clubs and "specialised" record shops. Whatever, I was part of a small group of like-minded teenage fans who between us enthused about everything from early Louis Armstrong to the latest Adderley, with Leroy Carr and Leadbelly, Basie and Brubeck thrown in for good measure.

We were fiercely partisan of course, and puritanical in that youthful way that mellows with maturity. Jazz snobs to a man, most of us dismissed rock'n'roll out of hand as rubbish, the more liberal of us patronisingly conceding that the early stuff was OK but . . . In my modest collection of vinyl − and a few already outmoded 78s − there among the Mingus and MJQ discs were Little Richard, Fats Domino, Lonnie Donegan's 'Diggin' My Potatoes' and Bill Haley's 'See You Later Alligator'. I *was* that liberal. But even I was shocked when a jazz-loving friend declared solemnly that Elvis "could have been the greatest blues singer since Bessie Smith". Blasphemy indeed.

Then everything changed with Ray Charles and 'What'd I Say'. Suddenly the raw energy of blues-driven rock'n'roll, infused with the gospel-tinged spirit that cutting-edge jazzmen were espousing at the time, came together in two glorious sides of 7-inch plastic. Ray Charles was *soul* personified, long before the term came to represent a whole movement in popular music − of which he had laid the foundations.

Four years after 'What'd I Say', and I'd begun playing alto sax in a Liverpool rhythm & blues band. We had a two-horn line-up, the only outfit to do so on the guitar-dominated Mersey beat scene. Our repertoire included Ray Charles small-band classics like 'Hallelujah I Love Her So', 'I Got A Woman' and a raucous version of 'Tell Me How Do You Feel'. Two years later, our set list had expanded to include the new material coming out of the States – Otis Redding's 'Mr Pitiful', Wilson Pickett's 'In The Midnight Hour' and so on – and now we were calling ourselves a soul band.

That development demonstrated in microcosm the changes that were taking place in the popular music of Black America, but which now manifest themselves far beyond the borders of the United States. The impact that Ray Charles made on rhythm & blues had reverberated around the world.

In the late Fifties "soul music" referred to a back-to-the-roots movement in modern jazz partly inspired, as it happens, by Ray's music. By the mid-Sixties it had come to mean, along with the white rock music that also had its roots in Fifties black R&B, the major trend in cutting-edge pop.

When soul as a pop genre *did* evolve, it wasn't difficult to trace a lineage that went directly back to Ray's radical mix of the sacred and the secular, a fusion of parallel traditions which had previously been unthinkable. But there was much more to it than that. Ray's very delivery, his interpretation of songs – any kind of songs – invested them with a burning passion, a stylistic fervour all his own, as he used them as a vehicle to bare his emotion.

Ray's seminal blueprint wasn't just about church-derived chord sequences, down-home harmonies and gospel singing's call-and-response. From the start Ray Charles could be said to have put the *soul* into soul music, and into a lot of other areas as well. In fact the very time in Ray's career when he cast doubt on the notion of his being the premier voice in Black American music was with his album *Modern Sounds In Country And Western Music* in 1962, before soul as pop music had hardly raised its head. But in retrospect, that exercise was just one of many when he injected *his* soul into seemingly alien material. What he was saying from early on was that it's not the song that makes soul music, it's the interpretation of the song – and in Ray's hands, it seemed like almost any song would do.

That element of interpretation, delivered with a truly unique voice, is what elevates Ray Charles' art to something even greater than being the prime architect of soul music. He was one of a handful of singers – Armstrong, Sinatra, Presley are names that immediately spring to mind –

who could truly be said to have redefined popular music, whose style formed a template for much of the music created thereafter.

The parallel with Louis Armstrong, who virtually invented jazz singing, is particularly apposite. Vocally and instrumentally Armstrong defined the basics of jazz improvisation, but the changes he wrought soon transcended "pure" jazz and permeated popular music (of which jazz very quickly became a driving force in the Twenties and Thirties) on a worldwide scale. His influence was apparent not just in the styles of subsequent jazz vocalists, but with popular crooners from Bing Crosby onwards.

Likewise, Ray's vocal style has touched every bona fide soul singer, be it Marvin Gaye, Aretha Franklin, Stevie Wonder or whoever. But the soul *approach* to a song that he instigated impacted far wider, to be heard in the work of vocalists as disparate as Billy Joel, Bruce Springsteen, Elton John and Prince. In the words of David Ritz, co-author of Ray's autobiography *Brother Ray*: "Just as Louis Armstrong had taught the world that the jazz aesthetic was applicable to any song, Ray showed that soul was every bit as universal. Legions of spirited white singers, from Steve Winwood to Joe Cocker to Rod Stewart, would build careers on the essential Ray Charles style."

And, like Charles, when Armstrong took the style that *he* had invented into the popular arena himself, he was accused of "selling out" by the purists. As Ahmet Ertegun neatly put it to me: "It's just like Louis Armstrong. He appeals to a much wider audience than most jazz musicians, but when that happens people have a tendency to say 'he is no longer jazz', but that's not true. What it is, it's jazz that sells to a lot of people. Louis Armstrong sang 'Hello Dolly', and sold millions of records – but that doesn't make 'Struttin' With Some Barbecue' less of a jazz record."

Substitute Ray Charles for Louis Armstrong, "soul" for "jazz", 'I Can't Stop Loving You' for 'Hello Dolly' and 'What'd I Say' for 'Struttin'', and we're looking at the furore when Ray had his biggest-ever hit in 1962.

First and foremost, Ray Charles – like Louis, and Ray's early role model Nat "King" Cole – was a hugely successful singer who himself came out of the jazz tradition. He always referred to jazz players as his musical idols; he had developed as an instrumentalist within the jazz discipline; he made a number of very fine jazz recordings with some of the great players of the day; and as soon as he was able, he modelled his touring big band on the great swing orchestras of Ellington and Basie.

In the late Forties, however, when only the most famous big bands were able to survive financially, Ray, like most aspiring young players, worked in smaller outfits. In Ray's case it was usually trios or quartets around the nightclubs of Seattle, or cutting his teeth on the rhythm & blues circuit with the likes of Lowell Fulson. Indeed, those early R&B combos sprang out of that same post-war situation where small bands were the order of the day, usually two or three horns and a rhythm section, backing a front-line vocalist or a "honkin' tenor" saxophone star.

It was the era of Earl Bostic and Louis Jordan, hot players who set a pattern for highly successful small-band jazz (each had a string of hits to his name) that by the late Forties was starting to be marketed under the label of rhythm & blues. Instrumentally that was the model for the classic seven and eight-piece line-ups that Ray led through the Fifties – saxes and trumpet horn section, piano-led rhythm section, often not a guitar in sight.

By the mid-Fifties however, when many of his rhythm & blues contemporaries were now being promoted as "rock'n'roll" bands, Ray had instigated his unholy musical alliance of the juke joint and the church hall. His band, complete with female backing singers straight out of a revival meeting, became the model for soul pioneers like Ike & Tina Turner and James Brown, and, further down the line, the classic sound of southern soul as exemplified in Memphis and Muscle Shoals.

But by the time that particular evolution made itself manifest in the middle Sixties, Ray Charles' consummate eclecticism – and what at the time proved to be an astute commercial instinct – had led him into new areas. Thus he would never become part of the soul music revolution, despite having written its original manifesto.

When Ray Charles died in 2004, I, like many more around the planet no doubt, dusted down vinyl that hadn't been played for years and just listened; *Ray Charles At Newport, The Genius Hits The Road*, the wonderful *Renaissance*. And newer stuff on pristine-looking CDs, right up to the duets album he completed not long before his death. Then I dug deeper into personal effects that hadn't seen the light of day for ages: a programme from Ray's first British tour in 1963; a snapshot taken in New York in the Nineties, Ray's face grinning from the back of a Pepsi cola truck. And a tape cassette of an interview I conducted with Ray Charles in London in 1975.

That British visit, one of many over the years, was just about halfway through Ray's career as a working musician. He'd started gigging around

Florida as a teenager in the late Forties, and played his last live date in Alexandria, Kentucky in July 2003. During that time he fulfilled a continual brief as an on-the-road musician. That road had taken him from Harlem's Apollo Theater to the Colisseum in Rome, from wine festivals in the Australian outback to the sports stadia of South America and Japan.

It was a lifetime journey that not only reached to audiences in every corner of the globe, but left a legacy of recorded work that changed the course of popular music. This book is about that journey.

Mike Evans, May, 2005.

Prologue

Winter 1948, Tampa, Florida.

Ray Charles Robinson, known to those around as RC, is playing piano and singing in the style of the great Nat "King" Cole, filling a residency at the Skyhaven Club with the Manzy Harris Quartet.

Although the outfit is giving the 17-year-old a taste of the spotlight for the first time, it's clearly going nowhere further than the Tampa city limits. Drummer Harris and bass player Otto McQueen have ambitions no higher than holding down a steady gig in order to feed their families, while RC and guitarist Gossie McKee are getting itchy feet. There's a whole world of music out there, across the America that RC hasn't explored outside of Florida yet, including places up north where, the more-travelled Gossie assures him, it doesn't matter too much what colour your skin is.

Discussing where they might head for, blind RC asks his partner to go get a map of the United States. Ray asks Gossie to pinpoint the major city which is the furthest away from Tampa, and they home in on Seattle, up on the north-eastern seaboard in the state of Washington, not far from the border with Canada,

A few weeks later, and RC Robinson is heading out of Florida on the five day bus journey to Seattle, the first leg of a musical odyssey which is going to touch hearts and souls around the world.

October 2004, Melbourne, Australia.

Ray Charles, as RC became known universally, has been dead just four months.

I'm talking to Glenn Wheatley, a local promoter who presented Charles in Australia and New Zealand venues three times. Glenn fondly recalls Ray performing John Lennon's 'Imagine', or simply busking at the piano during sound checks, with the awe of someone who is a self-confessed lifelong fan.

Sitting in Glenn's office looking out onto the lush greenery of south Australia in springtime, discussing how Ray Charles impacted on popular music, it suddenly strikes me that from my home base of London – and from RC Robinson's roots in Georgia and Florida, thinking of Gossie McKee and his map – this is almost as far as it gets. The influence of the man dubbed The Genius, who more than anyone triggered the birth of soul, truly spanned the globe.

1

Genesis

"Do it right or don't do it at all. That comes from my mom. If there's something I want to do, I'm one of those people that won't be satisfied until I get it done. If I'm trying to sing something and I can't get it, I'm going to keep at it until I get where I want it."

– Ray Charles

It's only a hundred miles or so north from the country town of Greenville, Florida, to Albany in Georgia, but back in 1930, for a black girl from the poorest part of town, that may as well have been halfway round the world. Aretha Robinson, or Retha as she was known to her friends in Greenville, was dispatched there by her adopted family after it became obvious that the unmarried teenager was pregnant.

When her mother died a couple of years before, Aretha Williams had been taken in as the ward of Mary Jane and Bailey Robinson. As was the way in the black communities of the South, arrangements like adoption – and indeed marriage – were often "common law" rather than official, so Retha Williams soon became known as Robinson, though technically her surname was always Williams.

Bailey Robinson had moved with his mother Margaret from Albany some years before, and lived with her and his wife Mary Jane in the black quarter of Greenville known as Jellyroll. But when little Retha became pregnant, things were turned upside down in the Robinson household when it emerged that the father was Bailey. As her condition became more conspicuous, they packed the young mother-to-be off to relatives in Albany to have the baby. On September 23, 1930, 16-year-old Retha gave birth to a boy, who she subsequently named Ray Charles Robinson.

Soon after that, when Retha moved back to Greenville with baby Ray, Bailey and Mary Jane split, the former moving out of town and Mary Jane very quickly becoming Ray's "second mother" – Ray recalling years later in his autobiography that the two women "bathed me in affection". Bailey Robinson still visited from time to time, Ray remembering him as a big man who appeared just occasionally, but who apparently took little or no interest in the child's welfare or upbringing.

The two women's attitude to RC, as everyone called him, couldn't have been more different, yet they complemented each other perfectly; Retha was strict, laying down firm rules and applying corporal punishment when she felt it necessary, while Mary Jane was more lenient, spoiling Ray as much as any kid could be spoiled in those poverty-stricken circumstances.

And they were certainly poverty stricken. The Depression hit all America hard, rural America worse, and black rural America worst of all. As an unmarried mother, with a weak and often sickly constitution that rendered most physical work out of the question, Retha Robinson had it even harder, as Ray was to reflect: "Even compared to other blacks . . . we were on the bottom of the ladder looking up at everyone else. Nothing below us except the ground."

The third family member in Ray's early childhood was his brother George, who arrived before Ray was one. As they grew from babies to toddlers, they became almost inseparable, playing together in the woods and by the streams surrounding their home. Still blessed with the precious gift of eyesight, the surroundings in which he played became visual recollections of the world that Ray carried with him for the rest of his life – "the pecan, chinaberry, and pine trees, the pigs and cows and chickens" – a world filled with the glow of wonder that illuminates early childhood. "It was just a very country life, we lived in a small town with dirt streets. I had short pants and would walk around barefoot on those dusty streets. And from time to time, if someone had on the radio to a music station, you'd stop and listen to it . . ."

Ray also recalled how George was an incredibly bright child, able to tackle simple mathematical exercises at the age of three, and adept at making little toys out of bits of string and wire. In fact the skills of the youngster were a source of amazement to his mother, Mary Jane and other folk in Jellyroll.

The second child, though loved by Retha as much as little Ray, was an added burden for a woman whose frail health added to their poverty by preventing her from working in a regular situation like most of her female neighbours. Indeed she eked out a living from taking in washing and ironing from some of those neighbours who had too much to cope with in

2

their laundry services for white households on the other side of the segregated town.

To make things easier for the struggling family, George was informally adopted by Wylie Pitman and his wife Miz Georgia, proprietors of the nearby Red Wing Café, which also functioned as a general store and boarding house, and Ray recalled he and his mother also living there for a short while when things were really grim financially. But "Mr Pit", as young RC referred to him, was to figure in Ray's life for a far more fundamental reason – music.

Inside the Red Wing Café were two fixtures that became magnets for the eager child – a jukebox and a piano. The jukebox was full of blues and jazz that captivated his tender ears just as the Florida landscape impressed itself indelibly on his visual memory. "There was a jukebox that was in the little store that he owned. And people would come and put nickels in and play records, and of course I'd go and sit in the back – because I liked the music from that thing."

Years later Ray would recall the magic of the sounds that emanated from the silver machine; primitive country blues by the likes of Tampa Red and Washboard Sam, and, most impressively, boogie-woogie by the piano-pumping pioneers of the genre, players like Pinetop Smith, Cow Cow Davenport and Meade Lux Lewis. He was all ears.

But the piano itself was the real thing.

From the first time he wandered into the Café when Wylie was playing, three-year-old RC was hooked. From then on, whenever he heard Mr Pit's brand of vibrant boogie coming out of the Red Wing, he would go in and climb on a chair next to him, banging on the keys with him.

"He was a boogie-woogie pianist. Of course he could play any type of music, but he was that type of pianist basically," Ray would recall in a 1986 interview for the BBC. "That was his stock-in-trade – but he was a good one, a very good one. At least I thought so, I was impressed, it stopped me from playing out – it didn't matter what I was doing, when I heard that, that was it for me. He was the guy who started showing me how to take one thing at a time, how to take one finger and do this, then how to take the other finger and do that. And it was so impressive to me, just to press a key and hear that sound. Then he showed me how to get little melodies – and of course at that age I was always trying to sing. He was a wonderful man, and really it would be hard to imagine what might have happened to me if he'd not been around."

3

What struck Ray when he thought about it in later life was how Wylie, rather than being annoyed at the interruption to his practice, encouraged the child. "As a youngster I would jump in the chair next to him and start banging on the piano keys while he was trying to practise. And he would say, 'Oh no, son, you don't play like that; you don't hit the keys with all your fingers at one time. I'm going to show you how to play a little melody with one finger.' He could have easily said, 'Hey kid, don't you see I'm practising? Get away, don't bother me.' But instead he took the time to say, 'No, you don't do it that way.' When Mr Pitman started playing, whatever I was doing I'd stop to go in and sit on that little stool chair he had there."

From then on, for the rest of the time he spent in Greenville, Ray Charles Robinson would play on Mr Pit's piano, and absorb everything the genial Wylie taught him at every opportunity. As the singer put it to writer Robert Gordon in an interview in 1992: "I would say that that was the first music that I recall that would stop me from my playing outdoors with other children . . . I heard other music . . . I heard records, even the *Grand Ole Opry* on the radio, when my mom would let me stay up on Saturday night. But it was Mr Pitman's piano playing that was attractive because that was right there on the spot, it was live!"

Wylie Pitman wasn't a professional, although Ray always reckoned that with his powerful style of stride piano and boogie-woogie he could well have been. Whatever, in the case of little RC, he was clearly a good teacher.

"He was the guy that was there to show me, he never stopped, even as I was losing my sight, and even after I lost my sight, he was always showing me things. Because he always knew more than I knew, he could always show me something. And right up to when he passed away, he was always showing me little things to help me on the piano."

As Ray's interest in music blossomed, he became aware of the huge variety of music around him: "My first love was the music I heard in the community: blues, church gospel music, and country and western." Mr Pit's jukebox, alongside the boogie and blues, had its share of jazz records, and you could also hear the music of Duke Ellington, Count Basie, et al. on the radio. But this was the South, and country music was predominant. "The airwaves were running wild with hillbilly tunes from morning to night," Ray told David Ritz in his autobiography. "They'd make them steel guitars cry and whine, and it really attracted me." Likewise, gospel music, the sanctified music of Sunday morning prayer meetings, was omnipresent in the black neighbourhood of Jellyroll. "I was raised in a Baptist church . . . I went to revival meetings, I went to BYPU [Baptist Young People's Union] meetings on Sunday as a kid. And on Sunday you went to church in the morning, you stayed there all day, you went to church on Sunday night, and if there was a revival you went to all those things. I was around religious music, just like I was around the blues. Both had an effect on me."

With a child's innocence of spirit he accepted both blues and gospel for their similarities, rather than the perceived differences which made speaking of them in the same breath almost taboo back then: "Gospel and the blues are really, if you break it down, almost the same thing. It's just a question of whether you're talkin' about a woman or God. I come out of the Baptist church, and naturally whatever happened to me in that church is gonna spill over. So I think the blues and gospel music is quite synonymous to each other."

Almost all the blues Ray heard as a child, and most black gospel music, was put on the market as "race music", industry terminology for records aimed specifically at the "coloured" consumer. A decade later it was referred to as the "rhythm & blues" market, evolving eventually into "soul" music. Of course, by that time the music of Black America had become an international phenomenon, and one of the prime architects of its proliferation and acceptance was Ray Charles. But back in mid-Thirties Greenville, RC Robinson was taking in every sound around regardless of label or category. It was a catholicism of taste that he would carry with him into later life.

One afternoon in the autumn of 1935, when RC was five, and his younger brother just over four, tragedy struck. The two children were playing in the backyard of their house while their mother was indoors ironing, fooling around as kids do by a big metal bathtub that was full of rinse water. Somehow, George leaned over the rim of the tub and fell in. "At first I thought he was still playing, but it finally dawned on me that he wasn't moving, he wasn't reacting. I tried to pull him out of the water, but by that time his clothes had gotten soaked through with water and he was just too heavy for me. So I ran in and got my mom, and she raced out back and snatched him out of the tub. She shook him, and breathed into his mouth, and pumped his little stomach, but it was too late."

The effect of this experience was traumatic; a family member – and your closest friend – drowning before your eyes, and being unable to do a thing about it. The memory was branded on Ray's mind for evermore, as he was to confess 40 years later: "I can see it almost too vividly. It shines inside my head."

Worse was to follow.

A few weeks after his brother's death, Ray started crying – not the tears of grief, the youngster had shed plenty of them in the immediate aftermath of the family's loss – but thick tears of mucus that sealed his eyelids shut when he awoke. His mother would bathe his eyes every morning until he could open them, but the damage to his sight was already evident. The range of RC's vision became shorter, the images more blurred. A visit to the (white) doctor who dealt with the coloured populace in Greenville, Dr McLeod, confirmed that something was seriously wrong; he gave Retha drops and ointments, and arranged an appointment at a clinic in nearby Madison. There, after further examination, the prognosis was blunt and final; Ray remembered clearly the doctor, "his face glum, his head hanging down", announcing that the boy was definitely going blind, and there was nothing that could be done about it. The malady was, it seems, the result of an inherited condition known as congenital juvenile glaucoma.

Despite her frail physique, Retha was a strong woman mentally, and she was determined that her son would learn to cope with his impending disability as fully as possible. As his eyesight slipped away, she insisted he carry on with his day-to-day activities normally, helping him deal with the challenges his condition threw up. Then, "even though she'd only gotten to fourth grade", she taught him all she could in the basic skills of what generations of kids knew as the essential "three Rs" – reading, writing and arithmetic. "She had knowledge all her own; knowledge of human nature, plus plenty of common sense," Ray recalled.

"It didn't happen like one day I could see 100 miles and the next day I couldn't see an inch," Ray explained to Ben Fong-Torres in a 1973 interview for *Rolling Stone* magazine. "I guess I was too small to really care that much. I knew there were things I liked to watch. I used to love to look at the sun. That's a bad thing for my eyes, but I liked that. I used to love to look at the moon at night. I would go out in the backyard and stare at it. It just fascinated the hell out of me. And another thing that fascinated me that would scare most people is lightnin'. When I was a kid, I thought that was pretty. Anything like brightness, any kind of lights."

With his condition worsening, Retha insisted that the boy continued with his little household chores, and sent him on errands – often to the consternation of passers-by – around Jellyroll and the rest of Greenville, so that he could get used to what aircraft pilots call "navigating blind". But there was only so much his mother could do, and as RC's sight disappeared almost completely, she realised the next problem was going to be school.

There were no schools for the blind in Greenville, and it was out of the question for him to attend a regular local school. But Retha knew that if she didn't organise her son's education as soon as possible, he would almost certainly face a life of destitution – or worse. "One of these days, I ain't gonna be here," she kept reminding him, and then he would have to fend for himself. So she set about investigating the possibilities for six-year-old Ray's education.

With the help and advice of various folk in the white community – including Dr McLeod, Miss Lad who worked in the post office, and A.D. Reams, one of Greenville's leading businessmen – Retha was able to secure a state-funded place for RC at the Florida School for the Deaf and Blind in St Augustine. And despite the child's understandable reluctance to leave all he knew, his friends and his mother and Mary Jane – "they were my whole world" – towards the end of October 1937 little RC Robinson, just seven years old, was alone on the train from Greenville, making the 160-odd mile journey to St Augustine.

Second only to when he witnessed his brother George's death a couple of years before, this was certainly the unhappiest day in his life.

The Florida School for the Deaf and Blind in St Augustine housed 400 students in all, 90 of them in what was known as the Coloured Department on the South Campus, the white pupils residing in a separate building, the North Campus. Everything was strictly segregated – this was the South in the Thirties, where "Jim Crow" still ruled most aspects of life – and the Coloured Department was completely self-contained with its own school rooms, dining room, laundry and (exclusively black) teaching staff. Throughout his adult life, Ray Charles recalled with a mixture of incredulity, anger and humour the sheer madness of segregating blind children by colour, colour they couldn't themselves recognise: "Imagine separating kids according to colour when we couldn't even *see* each other, now ain't that a bitch!" Within the South Campus, blind and deaf kids were also separated for more practical reasons than mere bigotry born of tradition and, within those groups, boys from girls.

For the first week or so at the school, Ray related years later, he did nothing but cry. His eyes hurt increasingly whenever he looked towards the light, the last glimmer of sight quickly fading. He missed his mother, he missed Mary Jane, he missed Greenville. He felt alone, really alone, for the first time in his life.

The other kids – almost inevitably – were quick to tease him as a "crybaby", taunting that didn't stop when it was discovered he was wearing hand-me-down clothes donated by the state for the poorest pupils. But, perhaps thinking of his mother's determination that this was for his own good regardless of how unhappy she also felt about his leaving, he gradually knuckled down and simply got on with it.

Those first few weeks of settling in were productive enough for RC. Becoming familiar with the daily school routine – up at 5.30, followed by breakfast, morning chapel, classes, lunch (which they called "dinner"), practical work (assembling brooms, cane chairs and so on, at which he became particularly adept), playtime, evening supper, a study hour, and so to bed – certainly eased the pain of missing his home and family. In fact he began to enjoy many aspects of life in the institution. He looked forward to chapel, with a song accompanied by the music teacher Mrs Opal Lawrence, even if the sermon that followed from the Principal, Walter Rembert, could be tedious for a seven-year-old. And as a bright child, he enjoyed learning in class, and showed every prospect of progressing well.

The first thing he had to master was learning to read Braille, tutored by Otis Knowles, and this came surprisingly easily: "In fact, it only took 10 days or so, and within a couple of months I was able to read storybooks like *Living On John's Farm* and *The White Rabbit*. We called those primers. Didn't seem like much of a chore."

His ability with Braille was to prove essential when he began formal music lessons the following year, but for the time being his only exposure to music was the obligatory song at the morning chapel service ('America The Beautiful' was one that stayed with him into later life), Sunday services, and listening to the bigger boys and girls practising on the piano.

Then, just as he was getting "into the groove of school" as he later put it, two events were to set Ray back emotionally, albeit temporarily. The first was the Christmas vacation, or in young RC's case, the lack of one. Because his place in the school was entirely state aided, the costs of travel to and from home at vacation time were covered only for the major summer vacation at the end of the school year. Retha Robinson certainly couldn't afford to bring her son back any time, so RC's first Christmas after starting at St Augustine was spent alone at the school. All the other kids left for home, so once more he felt truly alone; for two weeks over the holiday, he was the only kid on the campus – "I cried my little eyes out."

And no sooner had the rest of the pupils come back – even the kids who teased him most were welcome company for Ray after their absence – than his right eye started giving him real trouble. It wasn't a question of being able to see – his sight had all but gone by now, and blindness was a condition he had got used to – but an actual throbbing, excruciating pain that wouldn't go away. The school doctors quickly decided he would have to have the eye removed, and he was moved to the white-only North Campus to undergo the operation. The prospect would scare most people, and for a little boy of seven it was positively terrifying, but the constant pain was becoming unbearable. So the operation went ahead, his right eye was taken out, and the last glimmer of eyesight went with it. By the time he had fully recovered, Ray's first year at St Augustine was coming to an end and the summer vacation approaching. It hadn't been an easy induction into school, and he just couldn't wait to get on that train back to his Mama, Mary Jane and all the other folk in Greenville.

The summer months through July, August and into September saw RC in his element. He was back with his family, and back with some friends – Johnny Williams, Mary Lee, Wilbur Miller and the rest – with whom he'd played before he began going blind. And of course there was the music. He stopped off at Mr Pit's as soon as he had the chance after he arrived in Jellyroll, and he was up there on that chair learning new little tricks on the piano like he'd never been away. And every Sunday there was more music, of the sanctified variety. Retha had always made sure little Ray attended church – the New Shiloh Baptist – regularly, where he was also a member of the "Sunday school" group, the Baptist Young People's Union, that sang hymns and learned stories from the Bible. He and Johnny Williams were even invited to the homes of two ladies of the church to sing gospel songs around the piano some Sunday afternoons. And music was to occupy a great deal more of RC's attention when he got back to school in September, when he commenced formal music lessons for the first time.

His principal music teacher was Mrs Opal Lawrence, wife of another of the music staff, Ernest Lawrence, and her first task was to teach the youngsters to read music notation in Braille. The discipline involved differed from that of sighted players in two ways. For pianists, it meant reading with the right hand what the left hand was to play, and vice versa, then merging the two. It also meant that, on any instrument, the musician had to memorise the parts as it was impossible to "sight read" scores while playing.

"When you study classical music as a child and you're blind, what you do is you *learn* the songs," Ray would explain. "You study them and you learn to play them. Once you learn the songs through the Braille system, then you play them. With blind kids, as opposed to sighted kids, when you study music you must read the music with your fingers. I'd read three or four bars of music with my fingers, and then play it. You can't just sit there and play as you're reading the music. You have to first learn the bars of music, practise it, and then play it and memorise it."

This process was further complicated by the fact that they were taught in the European classical tradition, with compositions by Bach, Mozart and other classical composers: "Some of them might have 200 bars," noted Ray.

Mrs Lawrence was strict about the discipline involved in learning the piano correctly; she had no time for RC indulging himself in the boogie-woogie he had learned from Wylie Pitman, or the blues and jazz to which he was increasingly drawn.

"Classical music is a great foundation for playing jazz," he told the distinguished jazz critic Whitney Balliett. "You play correctly, with the right fingering. With classical music, you play exactly what the man wrote, but in jazz, when you get rid of the melody, you put yourself in. So every time I thought my teacher wasn't listening, I played jazz.

"Of course, the teacher would catch me, and that didn't go over too well. She'd say, 'What the hell are you doing, boy; what's the matter with you; you lost your mind? Get to your lessons.' "

But from the start, RC was a good pupil, and a fast learner. Music had become a passion – indeed had been since back in Greenville when he first heard Mr Pit at the Red Wing Café, Tampa Red on the jukebox and the likes of Roy Acuff on country music radio. Classical music was a means to an end. He knew he wanted to play jazz and blues, and learning piano "the hard way" was the best route to acquiring the necessary technique.

Ray's main access to the popular sounds of the day was via the school radio, and by the time he was 9 or 10 popular music was dominated by the big bands – in the main, white big bands – of Tommy Dorsey, Glenn Miller and others. Some of the bandleaders – like Harry James and Benny Goodman – achieved the status of present-day pop stars, including a musician who vied with Goodman in popularity and captured the youngster's imagination: "That's when I took up the clarinet. I was a great fan of Artie Shaw, so I started playing a reed instrument. When I heard Artie Shaw do 'Stardust' . . . I flipped . . . and Artie's Gramercy Five was one of the first small combos which made me sit up and take notice."

Ray wasn't the only "musical" kid in the school by any means, of course. There was a hard core of "jazz cats", most prominent of whom when RC was 10 or so was "one of the big boys", Joe Lee Lawrence. Blind Joe Lee was a younger brother of Mrs Lawrence's husband Ernest, and played spectacular piano in the style of the great Art Tatum. And, as Ray was to admit years later, even though Joe Lee never *really* approached Tatum's level – who indeed ever did? – "Man, I was impressed." And, diversions on the clarinet notwithstanding, the piano was still RC's number one instrument. By and by, as he became a senior "big boy" in the school, so Ray was to assume the status of the musical main man previously enjoyed by Joe Lee.

Just rubbing shoulders with Joe Lee socially became part of an extra-curricular learning curve for the younger student. There would be unofficial jam sessions in the practice rooms when the teachers weren't around, Joe Lee, James Kendrick and other members of the musical "in-crowd" bashing out some hot rhythm & blues for the kids, who, Ray remembered, would all be "jumping, dancing and carrying on like lunatics". It wasn't long before he was providing the musical action himself with tunes like Meade Lux Lewis' boogie hit 'Honky Tonk Train Blues', often with James Kendrick on drums. He and Kendrick also entertained officially from time to time at end-of-term concerts. RC was also in the school choir, and in an informal gospel vocal group which the kids put together themselves, in addition to playing piano and sometimes singing at the Friday assemblies of the South Campus Literary Society. By the time he was 10 or 11, Ray Charles Robinson was a leading light in the school, music-wise.

When he was 12 years old, RC began writing arrangements for the school orchestra, a small outfit of between nine and a dozen players. "As a student, I was always playing music that somebody else wrote, and I got the idea in my mind that I would like to write music myself. The first time I wrote an arrangement and heard it played back to me, you can't imagine how excited I was. I mean, to write something and then have musicians play it back to you, and you hear it and you hear your ideas, your thoughts – that was the most exciting thing to me."

What players, producers and arrangers all agreed on later in his life was that Ray had a phenomenal "ear" – accentuated no doubt by his blindness, but a natural gift all the same – that enabled him, like all great composers and arrangers, to "think" for the whole orchestra, the ability to imagine in his head what a particular collection of notes played by a dozen or more instruments would sound like: "If you can read music, you can write it, and I think certainly what helped me is that I'm a piano player, so I know chords. Naturally, I can hear chords, and I could always play just about anything I could hear. It was just a question of learning how to put it down on paper. I just studied how to write for horns on my own . . . like, understanding that the saxophone is in different keys . . ." By the time he was 14 he was able to write arrangements by calling out the notes as someone wrote them down, instrument by instrument. It was a technique he continued to utilise for the rest of his life.

Horizons were expanding, both geographically and musically. Ever since that first Christmas which he was forced to spend alone away from his family, the staff at St Augustine had a collection amongst themselves to raise his fare home each year. Then, of course, there was the long summer vacation. Now totally blind, he got to know Greenville better than ever as he ventured into its streets, learning to memorise the directions and distances between this point and that, the location of crossings and intersections impressing themselves in his mind as clearly as any street map. Inspired by his mother's constant urging that he should learn to be as self-reliant as possible, regardless of his blindness, he made it his business to get around relatively unhindered by his disability. As he points out in his autobiography, the three things he never wanted to own when he was young were a dog, a cane and a guitar ("seems like every blind blues singer I'd heard about was playing the guitar").

It was during these forays to the other parts of town that RC got to know another couple who, like Mr Pit and Miz Georgia, ran a café with a jukebox stacked with the jazz and blues hits of the day. Henry and Alice Johnson took a liking to the youngster, who would also occasionally play the piano in their establishment, and when they moved 40 miles west to Tallahassee they invited RC to spend some of his summer vacations with them in the black quarter called Frenchtown.

Ray always remembered with pleasure his days staying with the Johnsons. There were the Bryants who ran a grocery store just down the street, whose daughter Lucille showed him how to operate the cash register as she served customers; there was the motorcycle riding, when the blind teenager learned to ride up and down Tallahassee's hilly roads, following the sound of a friend riding in front; but most of all, there was the music.

Henry Johnson belonged to some kind of fraternal lodge and he managed to persuade them to raise money to buy RC a clarinet. More importantly, the music-struck youngster got to sit in on piano with the student band of the Florida Agricultural and Mechanical College, which included two musicians destined to be world-famous jazz players, saxophonist Julian "Cannonball" Adderley and his trumpeter brother Nat. And, when he was 13 years old, he got his first paid gigs with a professional band, in a small combo led by a guitar player called Lawyer Smith. They would play local cafés and clubs, dances, even high school proms, all around Tallahassee; Lawyer took a liking to the blind teenage pianist – whom he also featured singing on the occasional number – and hired him for a couple of dollars a night whenever the kid was in town.

Back at school, from the age of 12 or so he had been allowed to go "off campus" on his own, exploring St Augustine as he had Greenville – in fact it was in St Augustine that RC had his very first experience of playing in front of an audience of strangers, even before his debut in Tallahassee, when the school arranged for him to perform at ladies' tea parties and social clubs, polite gatherings where he would play popular tunes more or less straight without any wild boogie breaks or jazzy solos. Payment was usually in kind, candy or fruit, or maybe a dollar or two from a collection taken at the end of the function.

And it was off campus where RC was now getting most of his musical education, via the sounds coming out of café jukeboxes and record stores around St Augustine and Greenville, and the first intoxicating taste of the smoke-filled atmosphere of the "jazz life" that the dates with Lawyer Smith's band introduced him to. Plus of course the omnipresent radio: "I can't remember a single Saturday night when I didn't listen to the *Grand Ole Opry* on the radio."

As well as the Southern "roots" music of country, gospel and blues, Ray was listening to plenty of jazz, and jazz-derived pop music. He adored Artie Shaw, and the other white big bands of Goodman, Tommy Dorsey, Gene Krupa and the rest, and their black counterparts – Jimmie Lunceford, Lucky Millinder and the "jazz aristocracy" of the Count and the Duke, Basie and Ellington. Piano players obviously loomed large in his focus of attention and, as well as the unassailable mastery of Art Tatum, musicians like Earl Hines and Teddy Wilson were also a prime source of inspiration.

Pop singers, as always, dominated the airwaves, and although he was familiar with white singers like Bing Crosby and Dick Haymes his preference was for the vocal stylists who fronted the black big bands – "Al Hibbler singing with Duke, Ella (Fitzgerald) singing with Chick Webb" – and vocal groups such as The Ink Spots.

There was one performer, however, who was to influence Ray Charles Robinson more than any other, as a pianist and singer – Nat "King" Cole. "In my early career I was a great fan, a great lover frankly, of Nat Cole, he was my idol . . . I mean I idolised the man," was how Ray put it to me when I interviewed him in 1975.

Nathaniel Adams Coles, born in 1917, had formed the King Cole Trio in 1939 with guitarist Oscar Moore and bass player Wesley Price, the latter subsequently replaced by Johnny Miller. His integration of a smooth vocal style and cool jazz piano immediately took off, the Trio's first hit, 'Straighten Up And Fly Right', making the national Top 10 chart in 1942. Young RC was equally impressed by Cole's singing and playing. Right from those first tentative gigs in Tallahassee when Lawyer Smith would give the young pianist a vocal spot, RC was on course, as he confessed years later, "to become a junior Nat Cole". The star's style brought together all the elements that appealed to Ray at the time – a jazz feel, strong melodies, a swinging rhythm section and a touch of the blues. He loved the way Cole could handle a vocal, the smoky texture of his voice bringing a blues sensibility to ballads as well as up-tempo numbers, and the fact that he was also an accomplished jazz pianist – a point often forgotten when Nat became better known for a string of hits with lush orchestral backings later in his career. But right then, when RC was in his early teens, and growing both musically and physically by the day, for him Nat Cole was already undisputed King.

Ray's professional music, however, was strictly part-time – "semi-pro" as they say in the business – by virtue of his age if nothing else. Between vacations in Greenville and Tallahassee, there was still school in St Augustine, though its contribution to his musical development – in RC's mind at least – lessened as his "off campus" activities assumed greater importance.

But a further traumatic event in a young life already scarred by tragedy was to prove the catalyst that triggered both RC's departure from school and his entry into the music life as a full-time professional. In mid-May 1945, the 14-year-old was summoned by his teacher Mr Lawrence and told bluntly that his mother had died the day before. No reason, just the bare fact that Retha Robinson had died, and would be buried a few days later; RC was to go home to Greenville right away.

The news hit him with a stunning finality, its impact worse than that of his brother George drowning or the onset of his own blindness. "That was the most devastating thing in my whole experience – bar nothing, period," Ray recalled years later, ". . . from that moment on, I was completely in another world. I couldn't eat, I couldn't sleep – I was totally out of it. There's no way to describe how I actually felt. I was truly a lost child."

2

Dues Paying

"In my early career I was a great fan, a great lover frankly, of Nat Cole, he was my idol . . . I mean I idolised the man. And I tried, I tried my best, to sound like him, and some people say I did a pretty good job."

– Ray Charles

'Drown In My Own Tears' was something Ray would sing 10 years or so later, but it would have expressed perfectly the depths of depression he found himself immersed in, plunged in darkness and unable to surface, in the days following his Mama's death. He would hardly speak, couldn't eat, and accepted no comfort offered by those around him, be it Mary Jane, Mr Pit and Miz Georgia or the Johnsons who came over from Tallahassee as soon as they heard the news of Retha's passing.

"I couldn't eat and I had to go to the hospital for about six days," he would tell writer Al Aronovitz. "They had to feed me through my veins because I never was able to cry, you know it hurt me so bad. And they kept sayin' if I could just cry I would be all right, if I could just break down and cry, but I couldn't, it was all up in my throat."

Dr McLeod ascribed Retha's death to heart failure, resulting from her choking in her sleep after eating some sweet potato that disagreed with her, but as Ray reasoned years later, it was probably brought on by the long-term sickness that had plagued the 31-year-old woman for most of her adult life. "There were no hospitals, no specialists. Who knows what happened or what the real name of her sickness was?"

Those around him became so concerned about the effect his mother's death was having on RC, his lack of communication with any of them trying to help him, that they decided to ask a lady known as Ma Beck to see him. Ma Beck – her real name was Rebecca Mae – was one of those elder maternal figures who were highly respected in country communities in those days. She was midwife, medicine woman and personal counsellor to the folk of Jellyroll, and known to everyone. She was no stranger to young RC; she'd delivered his brother George, and was a shoulder to cry on when he died – and she had tended his mother in her bouts of illness.

She reminded the boy, firmly but with feeling, of what his mother had always stressed to him – that she wasn't going to be around for ever, he was going to have to look after himself. Now that time had come. "So stop acting crazy, boy," Ray remembered her saying, ". . . you gotta carry on, RC." That was the call that RC needed, almost as if Mama was there urging him on. He braced himself even while he was still being comforted in the arms of Ma Beck, and made it to his mother's funeral with quiet dignity and a new resolve.

Just how that resolve was going to manifest itself was not immediately clear in RC's mind, but he was determined not to let his mother down. Somehow, he had to start anew. Through the summer vacation months he did the usual – pottering around Greenville, going over to Tallahassee, playing some dates with Lawyer Smith's outfit. But the more he thought about it, the less inclined he was to stay at school for much longer. He wanted to get out into the real world which he'd already got a taste for. And in RC's case, that "real" world meant the world of music. Meanwhile his "other" mother, Mary Jane, worried about the boy's future now Retha was gone and, perhaps sensing he was getting restless, told him about some people she knew in Jacksonville, the Thompsons, who would be willing to take him in.

So when the September term commenced at St Augustine, it wasn't long before RC Robinson quit, less than two weeks after his 15th birthday. There was a disciplinary matter with a member of staff that triggered his departure, but it seems it was what he wanted, an excuse to follow his instinct. He reflected in later life how the school had served him well, but now he had to move on: "I made up my mind to move to the biggest city in Florida – Jacksonville – and see what was cooking."

Fred and Lena Mae Thompson made RC more than welcome from the moment he arrived. They lived near downtown Jacksonville at 752 West Church Street in the coloured district, La Villa, sharing the house with Lena Mae's sister Louise. It was through Louise, as a friend of Mary Jane, that the Thompsons had got to hear about young Ray Charles Robinson in the first place. With no children themselves, they "adopted" the teenager as if he was their own. They were even willing to clothe and feed him, and wouldn't take anything for his upkeep, but RC was determined to "pay his way". He told them from the start that he hoped to make enough money to keep himself – and pay his share of the rent – by playing music professionally.

As was his way, RC soon got his bearings around the city after a couple of introductory walks with Fred, one of which took him to the local branch of the American Federation of Musicians which was based in the union hall just a block away from West Church Street. Fred knew this was where the youngster would make the right musical connections if he was going to get any work, and RC knew it too. Pretty soon he became a frequent visitor to the hall, playing the piano there whenever he got the chance, listening to the other guys practising, and in his small way making his presence felt. That way he found an "in" into the local music scene, a bona fide union card, and fee-paying gigs.

As a member of Local 632, RC started picking up casual work with various outfits, purely ad hoc dates where a band needed a "dep" pianist for the night or with a scratch pick-up band put together for a particular date – or sometimes occupying the solo piano stool in a café or jazz joint. All low profile, low money, but invaluable experience.

RC was, at that point, in a jazz or pop musicians' career where playing live is the best form of practice. There was nothing like being "thrown in at the deep end" among musicians who might never have met before, blowing (and that didn't just refer to horn players) their way through jazz standards and the pop tunes of the day, ad-libbing furiously with the kind of "hot" solos the crowd wanted to hear. But this kind of almost instinctive playing was not for rank amateurs; it was crafted via a solid knowledge of chord sequences and the necessary technique to improvise around them spontaneously, often at break-neck speeds. It was an art nurtured in the musical hot-house of the casual gig circuit and after-hours jam sessions, the latter being a particularly fierce training ground where newcomers were shown their place in no-holds-barred "cutting contests". Despite the camaraderie musicians displayed for each other in the professional context, getting each other gigs and so on, they were deeply competitive; as Ray recalled, "Man, it was a wild-assed horse race."

Very soon, the teenage newcomer became a regular face on the Jacksonville scene when he wasn't working himself, hanging out at jazz spots like Manuel's Tap Room and the hottest joint in town, the Two Spot. He played the occasional date as a dep pianist at the Tap Room with the Alvin Dowling band, and eventually got to play at the Two Spot with the resident big band led by Henry Washington. "Sitting in" as a guest player at first, then doing paid dates for four dollars a night, this was RC's first experience of working in a fully fledged 17-piece big band.

All this time, whether playing solo dates, dep gigs or the increasingly regular spots with the Washington band, RC was perfecting a little act which seemed to go down well wherever he performed, based very consciously on the styles of his idol Nat Cole and to a lesser degree the Los Angeles based pianist-singer Charles Brown.

Texas-born Brown was another Cole-influenced stylist with more of a leaning to blues, a university-educated singer whose sophisticated-sounding West Coast approach was often referred to as "nightclub blues". As pianist and vocalist with Johnny Moore's Three Blazers he broke through nationally in 1946 with a big hit on the Aladdin label 'Driftin' Blues', and at the end of 1947 scored again with 'Merry Christmas Baby', thereafter a regular seasonal hit for years to come. He would leave the group in 1948 to go solo, making number four on the R&B charts in 1949 with 'Get Yourself Another Fool' and topping the chart twice over the next three years with 'Trouble Blues' and 'Black Night'.

Ray admitted his style was in open imitation of the two singers in those early days, particularly Cole. "I tried, I tried my best, to sound like him, and some people say I did a pretty good job," he told the author. "I ate, slept, and drank everything Nat "King" Cole. I wanted to be like him because he played the piano and sang and put all those tasty little things behind his singing . . . I practised day and night to sound like Nat Cole. In the days when I was coming up, I had a *lot* of feeling for the songs of Nat Cole because he did what *I* wanted to do, and that was to play and sing at the same time."

RC's favourite dates were playing with Henry Washington, whether as just one part of the instrumental ensemble or upfront doing his own spot. But, even though he would end up with a similar size outfit of his own one day, at that time big bands were generally on the way out. In the economic climate of the post-war years, most of the jazz orchestras – who had all but disbanded in any case when their members were drafted into military service – re-formed as smaller, financially viable units. The big-name outfits like Tommy Dorsey, Billy Eckstine and Count Basie were the exceptions that proved the rule, and even the Ellington band only survived during the Forties because the Duke subsidised it with his record and songwriting royalties.

19

At the most popular end, the small groups were often fronted by a new "honking" breed of saxophone player, men like Arnett Cobb, Red Prysock and Big Jay McNeely who'd cut their teeth in the big bands before fronting what were starting to be called "rhythm & blues" outfits, the forerunners of rock'n'roll. Stagecraft was almost as important as musicianship in these self-styled jump bands, where the wailing horn men would work the audience to a frenzy, often ending up on their backs screeching up-tempo blues for all they were worth.

In terms of hit records, two names typified small-band jazz in the pop charts, Earl Bostic and Louis Jordan. Bostic was a powerful-sounding alto sax player with a phenomenal technique whose records were jukebox favourites across America through the late Forties and early Fifties. Jordan, being a vocalist as well as alto player, had the edge in the popularity stakes; good-humoured songs like 'Is You Is Or Is You Ain't My Baby', 'Choo Choo Ch'boogie' and 'Caldonia' made him and his Tympany Five one of *the* big names in the latter half of the decade.

David Newman, a mainstay of the small band that Ray would form a few years later, pointed out that Jordan came from a wholeheartedly jazz background. "Actually Louis Jordan had played with people like Chick Webb. He was a very accomplished musician, but he was never strictly a blues man, he went into the rhythm & blues, in many ways he started it when he had that combo."

"I was a real fan of Louis Jordan, that's all I can tell you," Ray explained on an *Omnibus* documentary for BBC television in 1986. "He did 'Let The Good Times Roll', I liked that, and 'Going To Move To The Outskirts Of Town' . . . I was a real fan of Louis. I like people whose music did something for me. Some of the good stuff that Louis Jordan did was just with him playing alto and a guy playing trumpet – then later on he added a tenor saxophone player – but the early stuff, just him and the trumpet player and a rhythm section, they were just so unique. Everything blended, everything matched. I can really understand when people talk about painting, how all the colours just sort of come together like they're supposed to – the same thing is true in sound too. I was crazy about his music."

And Jacksonville, like many places in the country no doubt, had its own Louis Jordan – in the person of Tiny York. Vocalist and tenor saxophonist York fronted his own five-piece, specialising in Jordan covers, almost what today might be called a tribute band though not carbon copyists by any means. And when he offered the "Nat Cole" kid a place in the band, to have his own spot on a tour of mid-Florida centred on Orlando, 16-year-old RC jumped at the chance.

Tiny's plans for getting regular work in Orlando were short-lived however. A few dates led to nothing more, and some of the important anticipated gigs fell through; almost as soon as they'd started the trek, the band was broke. Tiny put it to them straight – and for that they never blamed him for their misfortune – they could stick with it and return to Jacksonville, or split right away. RC chose the latter course. "Orlando was a chance to cut loose even more. I was still in Florida, still in my home state . . . but this was a new adventure. I wanted to see what living completely alone was like."

And to start with at least, living alone was pretty grim, a period Ray would remember as the hardest in his life. He rented a $3-a-week room in a boarding house, the landlady allowing him credit till he got some work. He ate meagrely – "I had a lot of days when I ate sardines and dried beans and bread to survive" – but survive he did. He hung around the Orlando clubs trying to pick up gigs, but the town was full of players in the same situation; the war was just over, musicians who'd been drafted were returning home, and work was thin on the ground. For a young cat new to the scene, to say the competition was fierce would be an understatement: "Work was very sparse. I might work a couple of nights and then no more for two weeks or three weeks – whenever something came along. Hit and miss, really, that's what it was."

The local club scene was dominated by two nightspots, the Sunshine Club and South Street Casino, the latter run by Acie Price. Price also led a small combo, and put together line-ups for gigs around the area. After RC had been around a couple of months, Acie threw some gigs his way, usually in small-deal joints out of town where the musicians got paid $4 a night – if they were lucky. They would work from 9 pm till one in the morning, and often the venues were "fish fries" where eating and drinking took precedence over the music on offer. "In one corner they might have been frying fish and selling beer and soda and stuff like that," said Ray. "The people were out there on the dance floor dancing, and the band was stuck back in the corner somewhere. We were usually in the back, so if any trouble broke out, we would make sure there was a window to climb out."

Work didn't always guarantee money, of course. Ray got ripped off from time to time like most other players, but despite his disability, no more so than his fellow musicians. It would have been too easy for cash "in the hand" payments to fall short when counted out to a blind man, but RC soon devised a fail-safe method – he insisted, where possible, in being paid in single dollar bills.

Acie Price's main competition on the Orlando club scene was the Sunshine Club, where the resident 15-piece big band was led by a charismatic tenor player Joe Anderson who, Ray recalled, "always recognised and appreciated musicianship". In the spring months of 1947 Anderson started to book him for dates at the club, and when RC mentioned he had written some arrangements for his high school band back in St Augustine, Joe invited him to do the same for his outfit. For the most part, Joe used what are known as "stock" arrangements, books of pre-written charts you bought over the counter just like any book. Only the classier bands could usually afford to have original charts written for them, but Joe struck lucky as the youngster was happy to do them free. RC, likewise, knew it was an opportunity worth more than money – he was writing full arrangements for a professional band of musicians for the first time.

Things were looking up at last for RC. He had started playing alto sax – an instrument he had toyed with at school but never developed, always preferring the clarinet. He was also doing some writing for a small jazz combo he occasionally gigged with, led by trumpeter Sammy Glover, and around the same time composed his first song, a number called 'Confession Blues'. Two years later it would be a minor hit as the B-side of his first record release.

With all the impetuousness of youth, as soon as the teenager started making a couple of dollars to spare here and there – and burning with even more ambition than ever to make something of himself as a musician – he went out and bought himself a record player: "I figured that was all the nourishment I needed."

In his autobiography Ray recalled the first records he bought, all on 78rpm singles of course (long-playing albums were in their infancy, and beyond the reach of his modest finances). There was Norman Granz's *Jazz At The Philharmonic* series, which presented a fusion of "old school" swing players like Benny Carter and Roy Eldridge with bebop modernists such as Dizzy Gillespie and Charlie Parker; he collected vocal discs from Nat Cole to Sarah Vaughan, Ella Fitzgerald and Billie Holiday; there were saxophone giants Lester Young and Dexter Gordon, trumpet ace Fats Navarro . . . the list goes on.

One incident, however, was to cloud the otherwise sunny aspect of mid-1947 for Ray Charles Robinson. It affected him badly at the time but, he was to realise later, was of long-term benefit.

The big-name bandleader Lucky Millinder had hit town, on tour with his 16-piece orchestra, playing the Sunshine Club. Now this was a big deal for the Orlando venue; they didn't come any bigger than Millinder, not on the Sunshine's budget anyway, and his band was rated by all the musicians and fans in the area as one of the best in the business. He even had a star vocalist, Sister Rosetta Tharpe, who was enjoying a hit with 'That's All' at the time.

With his growing reputation as a performer in his own right and more than competent sideman in various outfits, plus his burgeoning talent as an arranger, RC was garnering respect as something of a local prodigy on the Orlando scene. So when word got round that Millinder was auditioning for a new pianist, it didn't take much for his fellow musicians to persuade him he would be in with a good chance.

After the confident youngster had played a few numbers, Millinder gave him a four-word answer that was as painfully honest as it was abrupt: "Ain't good enough, kid." RC was shattered; he went back to his boarding house room and cried. "I just wasn't prepared for out-and-out cold rejection." What seemed an all-out condemnation of his talents, he later realised, was merely a judgement that at that moment in time he wasn't good enough for the job in hand, not that he wasn't *any* good. For the "self-assured little motherfucker" as Ray described his attitude in retrospect, it was a put-down that made him even more determined to succeed.

As autumn approached, the gigs started to get scarce again. Refusing to let local circumstances get in the way of his increasingly focussed ambition, RC decided it was time for another move. Somebody suggested Tampa, 60 miles or so southwest of Orlando on the western coast of Florida, and it seemed like a good idea. By the time his 17th birthday came round, RC Robinson was gigging with two quite different bands in Tampa, a black rhythm & blues combo and a white country group, but the town was to prove a springboard to new horizons in more ways than one.

RC's first place of residence in Tampa was a flophouse. But though money was short, he didn't have to stay there long. As with his previous sojourns in new towns, almost the first thing he did after arriving was to get himself acquainted with the geography, and essential to that was finding out where the major music places were. In the case of Tampa, the biggest and most prestigious club in the black part of town that flourished on and around Central Avenue was the Blue Room Bar & Grill. And it was there that he soon met with guitarist Gossie McKee, an amiable character who was playing the upstairs lounge with the Manzy Harris band, and who remembered seeing Ray at the Two Spot when he'd been passing through Jacksonville on tour.

Through Gossie the youngster managed to rent a room in the South Emery Street house of two sisters, Fredericka – "Freddie" – and Lydia Simmons; the elder sister, Freddie, was a schoolteacher (and a girlfriend of Gossie's) who also gave music lessons, but most important of all to their new house guest was that she let him play the piano that occupied pride of place in their living room. This was the first time in RC's life that he was living in a house with a piano, and he made the most of it.

Very soon the young blind kid began to make his presence felt in Tampa, and found himself a gig with Charlie Brantley's Honeydrippers, a local seven-piece "Louis Jordan" outfit. Brantley's take on Jordan was 100 per cent – "He almost *became* Louis" was how Ray put it – and all he wanted RC for was to play piano, not as a vocalist per se. But Ray was happy to be working, and to oblige with whatever the bandleader required: "In Charlie Brantley's band I wasn't even the vocalist. Of course, they let me sing one or two songs before the show was over, but Charlie had his own singer, Clarence Jolly. Otherwise, I was just his piano player, and I was happy to do that because I needed the money. If he needed me to sing, I'd sing; if he wanted me to play the piano, that's what I did; if he wanted me to write an arrangement, I'd write an arrangement. Whatever it took to make a dollar."

Soon after the Honeydrippers dates started, RC also got a gig that in retrospect could be seen as a portent of things to come, when he was hired by the Florida Playboys, a white country band. The Playboys were looking for a pianist, and one of the band, whose day job was in Tampa's major music store, remembered the teenager who would come in the shop and fool around with the instruments. RC subsequently auditioned for the band, and was in: "They offered me the job and I grabbed it. I was a Playboy."

The outfit had a real country music line-up, with two fiddles, a steel guitar, regular guitar, bass, drums and piano and played whites-only venues around Tampa, honky-tonk bars and the like. RC was no stranger to the repertoire – he'd grown up with all the country classics via the *Grand Ole Opry* every week – and played it with the same natural feel that he had for the blues. He even got his own feature spot singing 'Waiting All For You', and learned to yodel as well, but again was in the band primarily as a piano man.

Country music of course, particularly in those days of strict segregation in the South, was considered white peoples' music – some even called it the white man's blues – so for a down-home group like the Playboys to hire a black pianist would have seemed a sure-fire recipe for trouble. Ray had two views on why he was accepted, often by raucous audiences that more liberal Northern folk would have labelled "redneck". He played country music with as much feel and expertise as the rest of the band but, more crucially, being blind meant he wasn't the notional "threat" that black men represented to the local bigots – a threat that he defined frankly in his autobiography as "white men worrying 'bout black cats fucking with their women".

It was around this time that RC got involved with his first serious girl-friend. He'd had relationships already, but all pretty casual affairs. Via a mutual friend named Marian he met 16-year-old Louise Mitchell, and very soon the two were teenage lovers. Infatuated with each other as teenage lovers often are, they spent all the time they could together, to the increasing consternation of Louise's parents, and when the couple announced they planned to move in together, her folks put their foot down. What future would their daughter have with a blind piano player?

As the parental pressure increased, the young pair made the classic response to such circumstances – they decided to elope. RC's jobs with both Charlie Brantley and the Florida Playboys had come to an end, but he'd managed to save some money for the first time in his life, and he and Louise took off for Miami. They rented a room, and within a couple of days RC even got some gigs at a club, O'Dells. Three or four idyllic weeks followed, RC playing at night, the two making love most of the day. But the Mitchells back in Tampa weren't giving up that easily, and after several emotional phone calls the couple agreed to return home on condition that they could live together. This they did, renting a room for themselves for $3 a week.

Now he was seemingly settled in Tampa for the foreseeable future, RC needed a regular gig again, one that would pay the rent and more. As luck would have it, the perfect opportunity fell into his lap. Manzy Harris, having left his gig at the Blue Room, was looking for a Nat "King" Cole stylist, and knew just where to turn. Drummer Harris had been offered a residency at a new whites-only club called the Skyhaven, on condition that he could put together a Cole-type group, and with his ex-Blue Room guitarist Gossie McKee and bass player Otto McQueen, he just needed RC's near-perfect take on Nat Cole to complete the combo. The Manzy Harris Quartet played the residency at the Skyhaven through the winter months of 1947–48, with RC Robinson as its front man. They played a varied selection of blues, novelty songs and standards, with RC's Nat Cole numbers the crowd-pleasing high spot of every set.

So despite his broadening material and constant self-education musically (just playing with the Florida Playboys had introduced him to different techniques and brought a whole new raft of songs into his potential repertoire), Ray's vision of how he might "make it" up the professional ladder was even more centred on his "Nat Cole" act. That was the way to go, the angle to exploit, for the moment at least. "I *wanted* to sound like Nat Cole," he would admit. "That was my purpose . . ." But where he might make that next step up was an unanswered question, though it was becoming increasingly clear it would be outside the confines of Tampa or indeed the state of Florida.

Thinking about his life up to this point, half a year or so off 18, RC realised he'd travelled no further than the perimeters of Florida. Yet there were musicians passing through in touring bands from all over the country, guys with stories of people and places a thousand, two thousand miles away. He heard them talking about New York, Chicago, Los Angeles – the big cities that boasted hundreds of clubs, where most hit records were made and the main promoters were based.

He also heard, from his partner Gossie McKee, of places in the North where folk didn't care that much about what colour your skin was. Gossie had toured right across the country with a review called "Harlem in Havana", and even had a girlfriend patiently awaiting his return someday up in Canada. Gossie was getting itchy feet, and now RC was too, but there was no way Manzie or Otto had any ambition to travel further than the Tampa city limits, being older than the two teenagers and settled with families. "Eventually, I got tired of Florida . . . I got the feeling one day – just an impulse – and I said to myself, 'I'm going to leave here because I'm not going anywhere, I'm not doing anything.'"

Eventually, he and Gossie decided to make a move, despite RC's reluctance to leave Louise. But neither wanted to go to the biggest cities, where they thought they might just get swallowed up as two more anonymous musicians among hundreds. They needed to move somewhere well away from Florida and the South, somewhere where there was likely to be some action but small enough for newcomers to make their mark. "I just couldn't imagine myself goin' to New York or Chicago or even Los Angeles. They sounded so big, man. I guess I always felt that I was pretty good, but I wasn't so sure of myself to want to jump out into a big city like New York. I was too scared for that. So what I wanted to do was pick a town that was far away from Florida, but not huge," Ray told *Rolling Stone* magazine in 1973.

So one night at his house, RC got Gossie to go and find a map of the United States and open it out on the table, and select a reasonable sized city as far away as possible from Florida. His friend soon homed in on Seattle on the north-eastern seaboard in the state of Washington not far from the Canadian border. So that was it; they would go to Seattle.

It took a bit more persuasion on Gossie's part to convince RC that even though he didn't want to leave Louise, he had to make the move. Eventually, in March 1948 Gossie went ahead, taking his friend's collection of records with him as "insurance" that RC would follow him, which he did in a week or so, after an emotional farewell, during which he promised to send for Louise as soon as he started making some money.

Musicians talk about "dues paying", when a musician earns his stripes by the tough apprenticeship of just gigging – often not knowing when the next job will come along, travelling in all weathers to play dates for peanuts, playing unsocial hours to uninterested audiences. RC Robinson had certainly paid his dues over the previous couple of years since his mother had died, and was determined that the only way to go was up – up north to Seattle, and up to the next step on that ladder to success.

3

Swingtime in Seattle

"The gods were smiling on us when he came to Seattle, we all knew that there was something special about him. We called him R.C. He was sophisticated."

– Ernestine Anderson, *Seattle Times*

Five days and nights in the coloured section at the back of a bus didn't sound *too* bad to RC, anxious to get as far away from Florida as possible once he'd made the break, but by the time they got to Seattle he was wrecked. The $500 he had tucked away from his savings was for survival in the big city, not for spending on the way, so he lived on snacks and candy for the journey, even taking a Travellers Aid hand-out for a zero-star hotel in Chicago when the bus stopped for the night. "When the bus finally rolls into Seattle I'm a mess. Tired groggy, lost . . ." was how he remembered hitting the vast West Coast port.

He soon hooked up with Gossie McKee, who'd been busy getting to know the feel of the local music scene since he'd arrived from Tampa, and had a hotel room in the centre of the coloured district on Jackson Street. He'd even found them a gig! The Black & Tan club was just off Jackson, and Gossie had been offered some spots there as long as he could find a pianist to make up a duo. He told them he was waiting for his piano-playing buddy to arrive from Florida, so that same evening the pair turned up at the Black & Tan and played a guest spot while the house band took a break.

The crowd loved it, but more importantly they were approached by the proprietor of the more prestigious Elks Club who offered them a regular weekend booking at his grand-looking Jackson Street nightspot. Hardly 24 hours in town, and RC Robinson's confidence was back – he knew he was about to make his mark in the big city.

The engagement at the Elks Club was a huge success, and by the

summer of 1948 RC was in a position to send for his girl Louise as promised, and rent a house for them both at 1809 24th Avenue. Unlike most
freelance musicians of his age – he wasn't yet 18 – RC was already settled,
independent, with a house and partner, "grown up for his years" as the
saying goes. It was a characteristic that certainly impressed other young
musicians hustling for gigs around Seattle, guys like 15-year-old trumpeter
Quincy Jones, whose family had just moved to the city from Chicago.

Quincy was to strike up a friendship with Ray that lasted a lifetime.
Recalling his first impressions of the kid from Florida in an interview for
the American Academy of Achievement in 2000, he said: "Ray showed
up, and he was around 16 years old [sic], and he was like God . . . He had
an apartment, he had a record player, he had a girlfriend, two or three suits.
When I first met him, he would invite me over to his place. I couldn't
believe it. He was fixing his record player. He would shock himself
because there were glass tubes in the back of the record player then, and
the radio. And I used to just sit around and say, 'I can't believe you're 16.
You've got all this stuff going.' Because he was like he was 30 then. He
was like a brilliant old dude."

In his autobiography, Jones recalled their first meeting, a coming
together of kindred souls which was apparent from the start: "He was a
thin dude, brown-skinned, and he played his ass off. He played piano and
sang like Nat "King" Cole and Charles Brown, and also played bebop alto
sax like Charlie Parker. He had a little Bud Powell in his piano playing
too. I sat through a set and afterward introduced myself. He said his name
was Ray Charles and it was love at first instinct for both of us."

Writing in the same book, Ray gave his own recollection of their first
meeting: "This 14-year-old [sic] cat comes up to me talking about music,
about jazz, about Dizzy Gillespie and Charlie Parker. He said, 'I'm Quincy
Jones and I play trumpet and I want to write music,'" stressing how they
immediately bonded: "When you're blind you become a soul reader.
Everything a person says is a soul note. It comes straight out of their
soul, so you read a person immediately. Quincy had a loving style about
him . . . We hit it off right away."

Very soon the older teenager was teaching the other the rudiments of
writing and arranging. "Quincy and I became very good friends because I
could write music and he wanted to learn how to write. He would come
over to my house in the morning, wake me up, and sit at the piano while I
would show him how to do little things. That's how we became very close."

Quincy had tried writing some basic charts for Bumps Blackwell, a local vibraphone player he was gigging with occasionally, but couldn't get it right until RC showed him how. "He knew how to arrange and everything. He taught me how to arrange in Braille, and the notes. He taught me what the notes were, because he understood. He said, 'A dotted eighth, a sixteenth, that's a quarter note and so forth,' and I'd just struggle with it and just ploughed through it. I didn't understand key signatures in front." From those seemingly bizarre lessons conducted via Braille notation with a teacher less than three years his senior, Quincy's writing skills developed apace, a fact he always acknowledged during a hugely successful career as a composer and arranger.

Another good friendship Ray made in Seattle was with the jazz singer Ernestine Anderson, who performed with him occasionally at local clubs. When the *Seattle Times* ran Ray Charles' obituary, she recalled how he made an immediate impression on the local scene: "The gods were smiling on us when he came to Seattle, we all knew that there was something special about him. We called him R.C. He was sophisticated. He had it all together, so much so we all thought he was older than us. It was years later I found out I was older than him! He and Quincy, they treated me like I was their little sister. They protected me. Ray used to have his cheques sent to my address for safety's sake. He'd hop out of a cab, come up the walk, go up the stairs and knock on our door. 'Are you sure he's blind?' my father said."

After three or four months at the Elks Club, RC and Gossie were offered an even more attractive residency at a fancier nightspot called the Rocking Chair, on condition they found themselves a bass player – the club manager said he needed a trio. The pair were becoming well known to the local musical fraternity by now, and the way they had been wowing the crowds at the Elks confirmed a growing reputation, so it didn't take them long to find a recruit. Milt Garrett was considered one of the best bass players around, and at 24 he'd certainly been around – a lot more than the two out-of-towners who were now offering him a job. He had something of a reputation – not just as a good musician, but a doubtful character in some other ways, who'd served time in jail for rape and assault, and was a known heroin user – but the two took him on, purely on the strength of his musical prowess.

So, Milt Garrett's dubious credentials notwithstanding, the trio was booked into the Rocking Chair at $45 a night. "It was a nice easy sound," Ray recalled. "We worked at the club, the Rocking Chair, and we would play these Nat Cole things and then sing the blues – we're *always* gonna sing the blues. . . ."

Things were certainly starting to take off, and with a three-piece line-up they sounded even more akin to the Nat Cole trio. They called themselves the McSon Trio, the name coming from the "Mc" in McKee and the "son" in Robinson, and started appearing in lots of venues in and around Seattle, places like The Black & Tan, the 908 and the Washington Social Club, while still holding down their regular nights at the Rocking Chair. They even started regular spots on a local radio station, KRSC, and their own short TV series which, someone told Ray later, was probably the first programme of its kind featuring black performers.

Possibly instigated by the impending TV spots, or just a growing consciousness of the Trio's image – they'd acquired matching suits and had some publicity photos taken by this time – Ray started wearing dark glasses regularly. Gossie and others pointed out to him that his sightless eyes were not particularly attractive to the public, so he bought a pair of sunglasses, just normal "shades" rather than the wrap-around style that would later become his trademark.

It was while playing at the Rocking Chair that Ray Charles Robinson got his first really big break in the music business. Upstairs at the club was a private room where gambling took place, and one night a character came downstairs into the club room where the Trio was playing. During the break he introduced himself as Jack Lauderdale, head of a Los Angeles record company called Down Beat; he liked what he'd heard, he said, so would they be interested in making a record?

"Man, I was so glad, I didn't ask him how much money I was gonna get. I didn't *care*. I would have done it for nothin'," Ray recalled. "There was nothing about any advance or money up front. All the man said to me was that he was gonna record me, and we'd have a hit. I didn't even ask about the terms."

Lauderdale was as good as his word. He told them they could cut a couple of sides the very next day, there in a studio in Seattle. When they got to the studio, the eager youngsters were told it was a strictly one-take situation, no room for mistakes, what was cut – straight onto 16-inch transcription discs – was cut, and that would be it.

They decided to record a cool-sounding ballad very much in the Nat Cole style which had actually been written back in the Deaf and Blind school by RC's older school friend and mentor Joe Lee Lawrence (though credited to R.C. Robinson on the subsequent disc), 'I Love You, I Love

You (I Will Never Let You Go)'. Listening to it now, it still sounds almost as much like Cole as it does Ray Charles. With Milt Garrett's loping bass, Ray's crisp nightclub-oriented piano and Gossie McKee's light, laid-back guitar it's small wonder that their take on the hugely popular Nat Cole trio had audiences enthralled.

The other song they chose was the first RC had ever written, a couple of years earlier in Orlando, 'Confession Blues'. Still smokey-voiced cool, this was RC in Charles Brown mode – Cole stylist with a down-home edge – with just a four-bar guitar break followed by eight on piano reminding us that these sophisticated-sounding musicians were blues players at heart.

That session, in November 1948, represented Ray's commercial debut on disc when it was released as a 78rpm single in February 1949, but wasn't the first time he had made a recording. Back in Tampa a year earlier, when he and Gossie were still half of the Manzy Harris Quartet and riding high at the Skyhaven Club, RC had bought a wire recorder. Now museum pieces, the somewhat primitive wire recorders enjoyed a brief vogue in the late Forties before tape machines took over as the preferred format for home recording.

Jamming with friends, he would let the machine run as they played semi-improvised blues, the recorded spools of which he subsequently lost. According to Ray years later, one (if not more) of these titles – 'I Found My Baby There' – would crop up on obscure labels from time to time. "Someone must have found it in Tampa collecting dust," he said. "I never got any money from it. And I never even bothered to find out who had gotten hold of it." The track, and a couple more that sound suspiciously like they were recorded under similar circumstances if not on the same occasion, still crop up on CD collections. The sound is overloaded with echo, the result of technical shortcomings rather than deliberate effect, the drums all but buried in the crude recording, guitar and blues-drenched piano almost competing to be heard. But Ray's young voice comes through with a wailing, almost sanctified quality that was to resonate throughout his music in years to come.

The Down Beat single, a fulfilled ambition in itself for RC, had the group billed erroneously on the label as the Maxin Trio, but there was another name-check which would be of more interest historically: piano and vocal were credited to "Ray Charles". Jack Lauderdale had raised the issue of RC's name when he recorded the Trio in Seattle; R.C. Robinson sounded too formal, Ray Charles Robinson too long-winded, Charles Robinson was frankly boring, and Ray Robinson would be confused with the current boxing champ "Sugar" Ray Robinson – the only option left was Ray Charles, and that seemed to sound just right. So, almost by default, RC Robinson had become Ray Charles.

As might be expected, the record did well in Seattle, and the Trio's standing in the local music scene – and that of its front man Ray Charles – was elevated accordingly. Likewise when the B-side 'Confession Blues' made the national Race Records chart in *Billboard* magazine, climbing to number five and remaining in the lists for three months, Ray knew his name – along with that of the Trio – could be found in trade magazines, record shops and on jukeboxes all over the United States.

The next time the Trio stepped into the small Seattle recording studio, in June 1949, things had a more professional feel. For their part, the three were oozing with a confidence born of seeing a record with their name on it in the stores for the first time. Jack Lauderdale meanwhile signed them formally to the label, in the kind of deal – that guaranteed virtually nothing for the musicians – that had become almost *de rigueur* across the record industry where yet-to-make-it artists were involved (and a good many established names too).

Whatever, RC – or Ray he was now being addressed more and more – accepted the situation as another stepping stone. "All I knew was that I wanted to make a record; this was a big thing to me at that time. Jack was the first person I signed with, and I have to give him credit. I don't know what he heard, but he must have heard something." Jack Lauderdale clearly *had* heard something, though he couldn't put his finger on it any more accurately than Ray could tell where his career was bound. But there was a quality coming through, a texture and attitude in the young singer's voice and piano playing that went beyond any mere Nat Cole imitation. In any case, Cole was riding high and Lauderdale was no fool: why would he throw good money at a second-hand version?

The Cole angle went down well with audiences of course, so Ray was not likely to jettison the inevitable "Nat" spot in the Trio's set, not for the moment at least. And he *did* sound like his hero, and was happy to sound like his hero, on a variety of material, not just the Cole hits. But as his confidence grew and his technique matured – not just as a singer, but as a pianist and arranger – gradually the myriad influences that he'd absorbed since childhood were beginning to surface in his music.

There had always been the bedrock of boogie and jazz, since the days he sat at the knee of Wiley Pitman as a three-year-old, but now there were daring flourishes of bebop licks thrown into piano choruses, and there were even occasional hints – no more than that – of his ultimate piano hero Art Tatum, whose virtuosity he could aspire to but never equal. And the nuance of his vocals started to echo older, earthier voices he'd grown up with, country bluesmen like Sleepy John Estes and Charley Patton, and the fire-and-brimstone preachers of Sunday morning church.

But for the job in hand the Maxin Trio recorded a straightforward cross-section of the ballads and blues that characterised their live act, half a dozen or so numbers over two days. No new releases materialised however, and they began to think that Lauderdale had had second thoughts about his new signing, until in October he sent them airline tickets to Los Angeles – for just two people, Ray and Gossie. Assuring the justifiably anxious Milt that he still had a job with them when they got back to Seattle and their regular gigs, the two flew down to Southern California to make some more records – this time they would be going out on the Swingtime label, after the jazz magazine *Down Beat* had forced a name change by threatening legal action.

At these recordings it was Gossie's turn to begin to feel sidelined, when they set up in the LA studio in mid-November and Lauderdale brought in a second guitarist, Tiny Webb, for the session. It was becoming apparent that he had plans for front man Ray Charles over and above any that might involve the rest of his group. And Ray seemed happy to go along with it, no questions asked.

The session went well with six numbers in the can, two of which were released on the Swingtime label almost immediately – 'How Long Blues' and 'Blues Before Sunrise', written and recorded by blues singer-pianist Leroy Carr in the late Twenties and early Thirties respectively. On the originals, Carr and his guitar partner Scrapper Blackwell strip the blues to its bare necessities, Carr's warm voice and precise phrasing unequivocal in its direct simplicity; an example Ray Charles, just turned 19, was beginning to emulate with apparent ease.

Things ran far less smoothly, however, on the return to Seattle. Tensions began to run high between Ray and his two colleagues, both the latter feeling they were being eased out of the picture as the spotlight focussed more and more on the increasingly charismatic front man – both on stage and off. And the rising tensions were usually exacerbated by drug use, both on the part of Milt Garrett *and* Ray, who had been injecting heroin for a year or so.

It's pretty certain that even without Garrett's presence, Ray would have fallen into the habit in any case. The stuff was all around on the Seattle music scene and, like any other 18-year-old, he was curious. A regular junkie being in his group just made the process easier, the dope more accessible. Not everybody got hooked of course, Gossie McKee for one. It was something you got into, or you didn't – and life turned out a lot sweeter for those that didn't.

For an ambitious kid – not yet possessed with 100 per cent self-confidence, though getting cockier by the day – more than eager to get as much into the music scene as possible, it also seemed like another "in" on the road to success. Nobody forced it on him, as he would stress years later, reflecting on the habit that was to haunt him for 16 years: "Dope was something musicians did among themselves – privately – and they had to like you to include you in . . . nobody was stuffing it down your throat or up your nose."

Inevitably, both Ray's drug use and his highly stimulated ambition was impacting on his home life with Louise. The couple had had their share of ups and downs, the lowest point being when Louise – pregnant with the baby they both wanted – miscarried. Added to which Louise's folks never gave up trying to persuade her to return to Tampa. And now Jack Lauderdale was making overtures to Ray to split from Seattle (and the Trio) and move down to LA permanently. The rows got worse, and after one domestic fight Louise rang her mother who, as usual, urged her to come home. Getting Ray on the phone, she repeated the demand, to which he replied that if she liked to send a ticket, he'd get her daughter on a bus to Florida right away – but no way, he stressed, was *he* going to be the one that sent her home. To their surprise, Mrs Mitchell called his bluff, and a ticket arrived a few days later.

Not even remembering quite what the fight had been about, the stunned couple decided it was probably for the best. Ray's burning ambition would give them no rest, and drug-fuelled mood-turns made living with him difficult to say the least. "As much as we wept . . . she still left," he recalled. "And I let her."*

In the immediate aftermath of their parting, the split affected Ray perhaps

---

* Unbeknown to either at the time, Louise was pregnant again, and Ray would subsequently support their daughter Evelyn as and when he was able, in later life meeting up and keeping contact with her and her mother. Louise would die of a stroke in November 1995, Ray sending a taped message to be played at her funeral.

more radically than he had anticipated. Now he was alone again, and the Maxin Trio was falling apart – which was more his fault than the others', as he was the first to admit. He gave up the house he'd shared with Louise and moved into a third-rate hotel. Uncharacteristically maudlin as he brooded over his fate for weeks on end, when in May of 1950 he got the call he was beginning to think might never come. Jack Lauderdale rang to repeat his invitation, asking his despondent recording artist to come to Los Angeles where he would organise a session with a full band. That was all Ray needed; he was on a train to LA the very next day.

In 1950 Los Angeles was probably the most glamorous place on earth. It was the centre of the movie industry, where the newly restored Hollywood sign spelled out the location in 45-foot-high letters. The low-level whitewashed buildings and streamlined freeways criss-crossing the metropolis were straight from the pulp novels of Raymond Chandler, the palm-lined boulevards stretching west to the Pacific in Santa Monica, avenues of dreams. And, along with New York City, it was one of the twin centres of the music industry.

The Big Apple had the history of course. Harlem had been the home of Ellington at the Cotton Club in the Thirties, and bebop was nurtured along 52nd Street in the Forties, but 1950 heralded the birth of the cool, the new West Coast jazz coming out of LA. And big city rhythm & blues might have been burgeoning in Chicago, Memphis and NYC, but this was where Charles Brown operated – and to Ray, that meant something. Likewise, for all the record and publishing companies huddled around Tin Pan Alley in Manhattan, here was Nat King Cole's label Capitol Records, near the corner of Hollywood and Vine.

As far as Ray was concerned, it was something of a star-studded line-up that Lauderdale had booked for the session at Universal Recording Studio towards the end of May. Among the eight-piece band the horn section included ex-Lionel Hampton alto man Marshall Royal (who would begin a 20-year tenure with The Count Basie Band the following year) and tenor player Jack McVea, who'd hit both the R&B and pop charts in 1947 with a Louis Jordan-style novelty number 'Open The Door Richard'. In fact it was McVea, 18 months earlier, who'd recommended to Jack Lauderdale that he check out the amazing pianist he'd heard in Seattle, after he'd played a club date there with the McSon Trio in support.

McVea, a "honkin'"-style sax player, took the break on the upbeat 'I'll Do Anything For You', but it was the other jump number 'Th' Ego Song' that Lauderdale and producer Lloyd Glenn picked for an immediate release – with Ray still very much in Charles Brown territory vocally but flexing his musical muscles in the liberating setting of a full band – as a flip side to one of the two blues they'd recorded, 'Late In The Evening'.

As well as producing from time to time, Lloyd Glenn was a well-respected pianist in California and one of the artists on Lauderdale's books. The Swingtime (formerly Down Beat) roster also included blues singers Jimmy Witherspoon and Lowell Fulson, Fulson being the label's biggest name and in that spring of 1950 enjoying a huge hit with his single 'Every-day I Have The Blues'.

So Ray was elated to be in such prestigious-sounding company, and spent the next few weeks getting to know LA and its music scene. He played various clubs across the city, both in the coloured area that radiated out around Central Avenue and, north of there, the smarter "white" parts of town stretching across the showbiz mecca of Beverly Hills and Holly-wood and southeast to the Downtown area which was the city's commercial hub. When he wasn't playing at nights he would be hanging out, getting his face – and name – around, being introduced to people. By and large he took everybody as they came, acted cool enough not to appear *too* impressed, whoever they were. He had a hit record on Swingtime, he was going to *be* somebody, he didn't want anyone to think he was just another new kid on the block.

But cool kid or not, the one occasion on which Ray Charles was completely phased was when he met his all-time hero Art Tatum. It was at the Club Alabam, and, as Ray would retell the story years down the line, a hush fell over the room when the piano colossus walked in. The two were duly introduced, and Ray found himself literally speechless. He clammed up, and could hardly stutter out a greeting, let alone tell the maestro how he'd collected all his records, and admired his playing. "I was in such awe, I didn't know what to say. What do you say to God?"

Things were moving fast. To capitalise on Lowell Fulson's chart success with 'Everyday I Have The Blues', Jack Lauderdale decided that the bluesman needed to tour, promoting his latest offering on Swingtime, 'Blue Shadows'. What better idea than to put his new rising star in Fulson's band, where he could plug his own single in a feature spot every night? They played some warm-up dates along the California coast – Lloyd Glenn occupying the piano stool when Ray wasn't available – before setting out on the road proper at the end of June, 1950.

4

A Whole Lot of Rhythm & Blues

"I decided what I'm gonna do, I'm gonna do something exactly like me, and this is the only way I will know if I can make it on my own merits, on my own sound, or not. And I had to know that, I had to know it."

– Ray Charles

Lowell Fulson was one of those artists who personified the link between the old country blues and its post-war big city successor rhythm & blues. Born in 1921 in Tulsa, Oklahoma of a Cherokee Indian father and a mother who sang and played guitar, he grew up with music and, having learned guitar as a youngster, by the late Thirties was touring the Southwest with the country blues singer Alger "Texas" Alexander. During the war, while on Navy service in Oakland, California, he met record producer Bob Geddins, who put him on various small record labels including Big Town, Gilt Edge and Down Beat.

His big electric guitar style, typical of the "West Coast Sound" being pioneered then by bluesmen like Clarence "Gatemouth" Brown and T-Bone Walker, initially scored only locally, then late in 1948 he reached number six in the R&B charts with 'Three O'Clock Blues' on Down Beat. Its follow-up on Swingtime 'Everyday I Have The Blues' did even better, so he was a hot ticket as far as audiences were concerned when Jack Lauderdale put together the touring band, with the label's newest name, Ray Charles, on piano.

Right from the start, for Ray the trip was an education. It was one thing gigging around local clubs, a one-nighter here, a residency there, never moving much further than the environs of the city he was based in, be it Orlando, Tampa, Seattle or LA. Now they were headed out across the vast expanses of the Southwest, through New Mexico and Texas, Arizona and Oklahoma, travelling as far east as New Orleans, Louisiana by September.

"Lowell had a station wagon and a Roadmaster Buick, and we drove for days and days and days on end," he recalled.

The dates were mostly small dance halls and clubs, all on the "coloured" circuit of venues that saw few white faces in their audiences. And, on the road, colour meant a lot more than just who came to your gig. Even when he was fronting his own outfit a couple of years later, Ray and his musicians were subject to the "Jim Crow" apparatus of the segregated South. "In those days we put up with 'the usual things'. I didn't go into the Hilton Hotel, I didn't go into the Sheraton, I had to stay in rooming houses. I had to make sure I stopped at the right gas station, where they had restrooms for coloured, and if I was hungry I couldn't stop at just any restaurant to eat, so if it was a long distance between places and I saw a restaurant, I had to go around to the back door and let them hand me out sandwiches."

In his autobiography, Ray told how during appearances in Texas guitar man T-Bone Walker and Kansas City blues shouter Joe Turner were among artists added to the bill, with the Fulson band backing them. T-Bone was an architect of the guitar style that characterised Lowell's playing, and a great favourite with Ray as well, so backing him on piano was a real buzz. Likewise, the expansive voice of Big Joe Turner had been a formative sound from Ray's earliest days in Florida; with hit sides accompanied by boogie-woogie pianist Pete Johnson he'd rightfully earned the title "Boss of the Blues". Perhaps an even bigger thrill – though not the heart-stopping trauma that shaking hands with Art Tatum elicited – was when the city-to-city path of their next tour itinerary crossed that of Ray's vocal hero Charles Brown. It happened during the following summer in Alabama, the two ending up jamming together on an old upright piano.

But this first trek with Lowell Fulson was just a taster of things to come, and when the two vehicles – Lowell in the Buick, the rest of the band and their instruments following in the station wagon – headed back to LA at the end of October 1950, the next thing Jack Lauderdale had lined up for Ray was another session at Universal Recording.

Ray's "Nat Cole" act was still a big crowd-pleaser in his feature spot, especially in contrast to the down-home blues of Fulson's material, so this time in the studio Lauderdale, to Ray's delight, had booked the guitarist and bass player from the original Nat Cole trio, Oscar Moore and Johnny Miller.

If the sides recorded on November 24, 1950 had been after the 7-inch 45rpm disc took off as a popular format – which wasn't to happen for five or six years yet, even though it had been introduced in 1949 – an Extended Play release of all four would have perfectly summed up Ray Charles' music at that time.

There's a straight, no-frills ballad, 'All To Myself', which wasn't going to set the world on fire, pure supper-club material, Ray the cool serenader with a backing of muted bass and guitar, and celeste instead of piano. The nearest we get to carbon-copy Nat Cole is on an old standard dating from 1909 which had made the charts in 1947 in a version by screen comic Danny Kaye, 'I Wonder Who's Kissing Her Now'; but even Ray's piano break is instantly forgettable. Listening to these tracks, which have appeared in dozens of compilations of Ray Charles' early material over the years, it's the other two numbers which for the first time revealed aspects of a developing individual style.

'Lonely Boy' is pure Charles Brown blues, as uncanny a replica of the Los Angeles singer as 'I Wonder Who's Kissing Her Now' is of Ray's other chosen model. But just listen to the piano. "Blue" notes – the flattened thirds and sevenths that imbue even the most basic blues and jazz with a unique melancholy – dominate the harmonic mix under and in-between Ray's vocal lines. The instrumental break, which Ray brings in with a grandiose full-fisted flourish worthy of the boogie-woogie masters of old, gives way after eight bars to a final four from Moore's guitar, accompanied by a yell of encouragement from someone in the background.

Just as 'Lonely Boy' provides us with a first aural glimpse of an emerging instrumental style, the same can be said of 'Baby Let Me Hold Your Hand' with regard to Ray's singing. Described by Michael Lydon in his 1998 biography *Ray Charles Man And Music* as "Cole plus Brown plus a quality uniquely Charles", the voicing has a harder edge than is evident on Ray's previous Swingtime sides.

But, more tellingly, there's a moan, an intonation that isn't precise enough yet to identify, that's coming from somewhere way back a generation before. Little RC Robinson would have heard it all around in Thirties Florida, from the scratchy 78s on Mr Pit's jukebox to the call-and-response sermons uttered by fiery preacher men from Baptist pulpits.

Following its release in January 1951, 'Baby Let Me Hold Your Hand' went on to sell far more copies than Ray's previous modest success 'Confession Blues', but more significantly it marked a point in his evolution when Ray consciously decided that he should be developing his "own" voice. Even though there was a hint of something new in his vocal on 'Baby', to most of the record buyers who edged it into the *Billboard* R&B Top 10 – and his live audiences – he still sounded amazingly like Charles Brown and, more particularly, Nat Cole. He began to realise it was time to do something about it.

"One morning I just woke up and I began to think as I lay in bed, I remembered the things that people were saying to me: 'Oh, you sound just like Nat King Cole,' 'You sound *just* like Nat Cole,' 'You sound *so* much like Nat Cole' – and I began to think to myself, 'Wow, nobody, not one time, said Ray Charles, not once.' Sure I was doin' what I wanted to do, I *wanted* to sound like Nat Cole, that was my purpose . . . but I began to realise that I'm losing *me*, and I started to think, 'Well, now for heavens sake, am I good or am I not, I cannot live off of Nat Cole for ever. If I'm going to be accepted, if I am good, let me find out whether the public will accept me for *my* sound.' Nobody told me, nobody influenced me, nobody said a word to me, it was just something . . . you know how sometimes you're lying in your bed, and your thoughts go through your brain . . . and I decided. I said, 'Well, what I'm gonna do, I'm gonna do something exactly like *me*, and this is the only way I will know if I can make it on my own merits, on my own sound, or not.' And I had to know that, I had to know it."

Way across the continent in his office in New York's Manhattan, one person who could hear more than mere imitation in the single was Ahmet Ertegun. Ertegun was the founder and proprietor, with his partner Herb Abramson, of Atlantic Records, which was starting to become one of the most influential rhythm & blues labels in the country.

"I heard 'Baby Let Me Hold Your Hand' and the B-side ['Lonely Boy'] and I was very impressed," said Ertegun. "He had a real under-standing, even on those first records I heard, of the sound of that time, which included Nat Cole and so on . . . but to me he didn't sound like he was imitating anybody, 'cos he had his own personal style. 'Baby Let Me Hold Your Hand' and the B-side had nothing to do with Nat Cole. He sang like Cole in his personal appearances, songs like 'Straighten Up And Fly Right', but his style was closer to Charles Brown than Nat Cole. But it also had intimations of many others . . . Blind Willie Johnson, Big Bill Broonzy, very early Muddy Waters." But it was going to be a full year before Ertegun's interest was to materialise into anything further than that.

Prior to the single's release, Lauderdale reasoned, that he needed to have time to promote it, so just days after the recording session at the end of November 1950, the Fulson band was back on the road, plugging Lowell's current release 'Lonesome Christmas' and Ray's imminent New Year offering.

By the end of the year, when the band swung into Houston, Texas, Ray had settled down to the regime of touring. He enjoyed the camaraderie of the other musicians, had his own spot every night, and could sense his star was in the ascendant. He was also arranging for Fulson, tight jump-blues charts for the small band with its guitar and horn section line-up. Ray particularly liked writing for the horns, which comprised trumpeters Fleming Askew and Billy Brooks, alto player Earl Brown, and a future hard-bop tenor star, 16-year-old Stanley Turrentine, who joined the outfit when they arrived in his native Pittsburgh and Ray decided they needed a second saxophone.

Compared to their previous trek this seemed like major league stuff. Jack Lauderdale had fixed them up with a professional road manager, and not long into the tour they even acquired a proper 30-seat band bus, just like all the big-name outfits on the road. A bus, naturally, needed a driver, and via Howard Lewis, a Texas-based booking operator who controlled most of the Southwest gig circuit, they hired Jeff Brown – a name that would be closely linked to that of Ray Charles in the years to come. Ray, of course, was still just another member of the band backing Lowell Fulson – an already established blues name – for the majority of the time they were on stage. When 'Baby Let Me Hold Your Hand' was released in the opening weeks of 1951, it was a minor, but nevertheless crucial, hit. It raised Ray's profile, not only in the charts of *Billboard* magazine, but on jukeboxes and radio stations across the country.

Lowell Fulson himself, meanwhile, had followed up his hit 'Everyday I Have The Blues' with 'Blue Shadows', topping the R&B charts in the process. And it was this success probably more than anything else that led to the Fulson band, with rising star Ray Charles as a client in his own right, being signed by the giant New York agency Shaw Artists. Since the mid-Forties Billy Shaw had represented some of the cream of Black American music, including Charlie Parker, Dizzy Gillespie and, in the R&B field, Charles Brown. For Ray Charles, it was a relationship that was to last for the next 15 years or so.

The tour zigzagged all over the country, from the deep South of Louisiana and Alabama to the northern industrial landscapes of Pennsylvania and Ohio. And it was in Ohio that Ray met his first wife, Eileen, introduced by trumpeter Billy Brooks who was going out with her friend Artelia. Eileen Williams was a pretty beautician from Columbus who Ray took to immediately, and the feeling was reciprocal. When the band played a Cleveland date in July, Ray asked her to go with him and the band to Atlanta, Billy extending the same invitation to his girlfriend.

No sooner had they hit the Georgia state capital than Billy and Artelia married, which, in Ray's words, "got me to thinking . . . Eileen was a really lovely chick and we had a very smooth relationship." So, just a week later, they got married too, on July 31, 1951.

It wasn't unusual for various girlfriends to travel in the band bus – and there was plenty of room in a 30-seater – and on the way to Atlanta Eileen got into the groove of life on the road. But now they were married, the couple wanted something permanent in the way of a home base, and Eileen didn't want to sever her ties with Columbus and her lucrative beautician business. So during a short break from touring, they found a place in Columbus, a self-contained apartment in the upstairs part of a large house on East Lang Street.

Marriage and the responsibilities it implied may have seemed a restrictive commitment for an itinerant musician like Ray, but it also signalled an increasing independence on his part from the day-to-day arrangements of the rest of the band. And it was a signal made even more conspicuous when he bought a car.

"Does that sound strange to you? A blind cat buying a car?" Ray posed the question in his autobiography, reasoning that with the independence of his own vehicle all he needed to know was the address and time of a gig, so he could turn up, work, and then split to do whatever he pleased: "This way I called the shots." He purchased a second-hand Oldsmobile, and hired a driver, Al Curry; Ray Charles was ready to hit the road.

The car was a Rocket 98, near-relative of the legendary Rocket 88, which, incidentally, gave its name to what is widely reckoned to be the first rock'n'roll record.[*] The Fifties were well and truly under way, and for Ray Charles, rhythm & blues generally and the music industry at large, there were big changes on the horizon.

Ray's new-found independence, and his increasingly pivotal role in the musical policy of the Fulson package, didn't sit easily with either the

---

[*] 'Rocket 88' by Jackie Brenston & His Delta Cats (a *nom de disque* for Ike Turner's Rhythm Kings) hit number one in the R&B charts in June 1951.

band's road manager, Wilbur J. Brassfield, or Lowell, the titular leader of the outfit. Ray enjoyed writing arrangements for a sizeable band – it had now grown to a 10-piece with five saxes in the line-up – and exerted a bandleader's discipline when it came to rehearsing, sidelining Fulson's musical authority in the process. But the latter appreciated that it meant a slicker show, and a slicker show meant more gigs for better money. Years later, the bluesman was still keen to point out who was really in charge, as he stressed in a 1976 interview with Stephen Rosen for *Guitar Player* magazine when asked about the famous names who'd passed through his ranks: "Yeah, I worked with all those people . . . no, that's wrong, they worked with me. In fact, I gave Ray Charles his first bottle of champagne when he made his 19th birthday."

Brassfield, who'd previously worked as road manager for Louis Jordan, had been hired by Jack Lauderdale early in the tour, and looked after all the non-musical aspects of the band's day-to-day organisation. It was Brassfield who had convinced Lauderdale that the band needed a bus, and it was he who would liaise regularly with the Shaw agency as dates were confirmed on the tour itinerary, taking care of all the essential details: venue, times, hotels, and – most importantly – money. Touring bands were usually paid half in cash and half via the agency, the cash element being used for on-the-road wages, hotels, gasoline and so on, and it was the road manager's job to administer these ongoing finances.

From Brassfield's point of view, the singer/pianist who was becoming a mini star of the outfit in his own right was also becoming a growing irritation. As he took on more musical responsibility with writing arrangements etc., and seeing his own popularity growing as a result of 'Baby Let Me Hold Your Hand', Ray began to ask for more money. Though loath to acknowledge his pianist's increasing influence on the musical profile of the band, Fulson agreed to each demand, with Brassfield – equally reluctantly – acquiescing. The road manager also begrudged Ray's self-sufficiency as far as transport was concerned; when they weren't actually playing a gig he might be in Columbus with his wife, with old friends in Florida . . . anywhere that time allowed. As far as Ray was concerned, keeping his distance in this way satisfied an independent go-it-alone instinct that would shape much of his career in years to come.

Meanwhile Jack Lauderdale, whose stake in the tour would only manifest itself in terms of records sold, realised it was getting on for a year since they had recorded 'Baby Let Me Hold Your Hand'. When the tour wound up back in Los Angeles at the end of October, he booked studio time for Ray and the full touring band.

On the four originals recorded in one afternoon, we can start to hear the real Ray Charles emerging for the first time. He's not crooning *à la* Cole any more, and these aren't mere hints – a moan here, an inflection there – of the low-down blues of his heritage. Now he's shouting the blues, screaming them sometimes, within tight riffs and staccato punctuations from the horns which emphasise even more a vocal energy that was hitherto – on record at least – an unknown quantity.

'Kissa Me Baby (All Night Long)' is a light-hearted up-tempo blues, with four-bar vocal breaks before a repeated eight-bar chorus – but on the ride out, the horns have it, big riffing R&B with Ray yelling them along over the second 12. The intro to 'Misery In My Heart' is reminiscent of the great Chicago pianist Jimmy Yancey, before an impassioned vocal answered by the trumpet-led horns and the band singing a "bye bye baby" background riff. In 'The Snow Is Falling' Ray takes another slow 12-bar, enriching it with blues-drenched piano chords echoed by the horns. 'Hey Now' is another rocking blues, like 'Kissa Me' each verse brought in with vocal breaks, with an arrangement that pre-empted Ray's classic 'I Got News For You' by a decade, and a couple of lines of lyrics including "You even cry so loud, you give the blues to your neighbour next door" that would appear later on 'A Fool For You'.

Just as he'd done the previous year, Lauderdale decided to release the next Ray Charles single – with 'Kissa Me Baby' as the top side – right after the Christmas/New Year holiday, in January 1952. But things weren't going too well for the West Coast label – little "indies" like Swingtime needed either big hits, or lucrative lease deals to one of the major labels for their material, just to keep their heads above the financial water. In Ray Charles, despite his underlying faith in the singer's talents, Jack had seen neither. So when 'Kissa Me Baby' didn't make the impression they'd hoped for, he decided maybe it was time to cut his losses.

Conversely Billy Shaw, head of Shaw Artists, knew that to keep on drawing the crowds his artists had to have records in the market place, so when he heard Lauderdale was looking to let Ray go, he put the word around some of the bigger indies including Chess in Chicago, King in Cincinnati and Atlantic in New York City.

Atlantic head Ahmet Ertegun and his partner Herb Abramson leapt at the chance. Ertegun had been excited about Ray Charles since 'Baby Let Me

Hold Your Hand' a year before. Now was his chance to follow through.

Ertegun recalled how he was a willing listener to Shaw's lobbying: "The records that I loved so much that he'd made on Swingtime were not hits, were not big enough hits for the Shaw agency to be able to book him as a star performer. It was Billy Shaw, who was my friend, who arranged for Swingtime to sell us his contract . . . [he] said, 'I know you're gonna make records that hit because of the way you have with Joe Turner and so on' . . . Finally he said to me, 'Look, why don't you record him? I would be able to book him if you made some good records.' I said, 'I guarantee we'll make great records with him – how do I get him?' He said, 'You buy his contract. Lauderdale is ready to sell. He wants $2,500.' I said, 'Done deal.'"

Historically seen as a New York parallel to Sun Records in Memphis and Chess in Chicago, the third contender in the formative triumvirate of indie labels that turned R&B into rock'n'roll, back in 1952 Atlantic Records was a pioneering jazz and rhythm & blues label that was already making its presence felt on the music scene. Formed in 1947 by Ertegun and Abramson, it evolved largely as the inspiration of Ahmet Ertegun and his brother Nesuhi, jazz-fan sons of the Turkish Ambassador in Washington.

From the outset the Ertegun brothers were as enthusiastic about blues and boogie as they were about jazz per se. Today, Ahmet sees this as being a crucial factor in moulding the character of the label. "When I was a jazz fan as a kid, we not only collected Louis Armstrong and Duke Ellington, but we also collected Bessie Smith and all the other blues singers, and we collected all the great boogie-woogie players and so forth," he said. "I think, for example, that Jimmy Yancey is a jazz musician, whereas some people think that's more like blues, blues meaning rhythm & blues, and rhythm & blues smells of rock'n'roll, and jazz purists turn away. . . ."

Although he didn't start working for the label until late 1954, Nesuhi played a key role with his brother in its genesis, initially promoting live jazz and blues as amateur enthusiasts, as he explained to me in an interview in 1976: "We made concert promotions in Washington, jazz and blues singers, because nobody else was doing it. I had Leadbelly, Joe Turner in the early Forties, but also a lot of jazz names, Lester Young, Mez Mezzrow, Zutty Singleton. We got more into blues after a while. And when we said jazz, we were kinda purists . . . same with blues. So we kinda became experts in that. We gave a lot of concerts . . . but it was always a hobby. Then I had a jazz record shop in California. I was behind the counter eight hours a day, only blues and jazz records, we didn't carry the popular records of the day, again it was an extremely purist kind of shop. And I taught at UCLA on American music, which included jazz, blues, work songs, ragtime, gospel, all of that. I did that for four years before I moved to New York and started to work for Atlantic which was in 1955, end of '54. Ahmet was really the founder of Atlantic and I came in some years later."

When he did come in, Nesuhi – who died in 1989 – was to play a crucial production role, including ground-breaking album projects involving Ray Charles. But in the label's earliest days, it was Ahmet who laid the foundations in the late Forties and early Fifties that put it at the cutting edge of rhythm & blues.

"There were labels who weren't too active in those fields, I'm talking about Columbia and RCA and so on, and then there were a few small independents – Aladdin, Specialty, Modern, Savoy. Now when Atlantic started it had very little money, there was no real financial backing, we weren't rich at all in those days."

When Ertegun and Abramson (who had already run the National label from 1945–47) launched Atlantic, it was with $10,000 backing from the Ertegun family dentist Dr Vahdi Sabit, a fund that was used up almost immediately.

"But Ahmet was eyeing up good musicians all the time, and they could see that he knew a lot about the blues. We used to listen to records for hours and hours, for years, so people used to come to us and say, 'Who's this guitar player?' – we were really experts. And Ahmet had spent a lot of time in the Howard Theater in Washington, DC where a lot of the big black acts played – the black big bands and singers. Both of us used to hang out backstage at the Howard Theater, and that's how we got to know Louis Armstrong and Ellington, Jimmie Lunceford and whoever – and lot of singers – so when you get to know some, through them you get to meet others.

"So the only way he was able to sign artists was by becoming friendly with them, 'cos he sure couldn't give them more money, or even as much, as most of the other companies because he didn't have it in those days. So it was due to personal contact and through friendship – because we had become very friendly with them through our concerts promotions and so on – we always tried to feature people we liked more than the ones that were famous or very popular. It was really through a personal relationship."

Ahmet's "personal touch" extended to some artists he'd never met before. "For instance, one night he was in Washington," continued

Nesuhi. "This would be in the late Forties, '49 or so, he went to a club and there was an unknown girl singing, it was Ruth Brown. Immediately he said, 'Look, I've just started a company called Atlantic and I'd like to record you.' She'd never received a recording offer before, she was very young, she said, 'Fine, great,' and they made a deal right there and then, in a small club in Washington. Anyway, she was involved in a bad car accident on her way to New York to record, and Ahmet took care of her, made sure she was OK before she eventually recorded in New York, and she became very big."

Subsequently a record by Ruth Brown, 'So Long', was the second big R&B hit enjoyed by the label, following closely on Stick McGhee's 'Drinkin' Wine Spo-Dee-O-Dee', both marking the label's commercial breakthrough in 1949.

By the time Ray Charles was contracted to the company in February 1952 (a willing signatory, though he played no direct part in their deal with Lauderdale), the name Atlantic, with R&B hits from Al Hibbler, Joe Morris, The Cardinals, The Clovers, Big Joe Turner plus a number one with 'Teardrops From My Eyes' for Ruth Brown, represented a growing influence in Black American popular music. So Ray certainly didn't have a problem with the move: "Originally, I didn't know anything about it. By the time I found out, Atlantic had already bought the rights from Jack. Naturally, buying my contract didn't mean anything if I didn't agree to go along, but Atlantic had the contract from Jack and, of course, it was all right with me. I didn't see anything wrong with it."

The very fact that Billy Shaw was considering Ray Charles' future as an individual artist was a further indication that his days playing with Lowell Fulson were numbered, but for the moment the tour continued. The Shaw agency had started booking the package into bigger theatre venues, including – to Ray's delight – the famed Apollo Theater in Harlem. It meant a visit to New York City, where his new label and agency was based, and his debut at the most prestigious venue on the black music circuit.

The Apollo, still to be found on 125th Street, had been a landmark venue for many years, proving itself a launch pad for talent from the Thirties with jazz, swing and blues names like Bessie Smith, Count Basie, Louis Armstrong and Ella Fitzgerald all appearing there. Its notoriously discerning audience came into their own on the legendary Wednesday Amateur Nights. It was assumed that if you scored there, you could make it just about anywhere, and notable Amateur Night debuts included those of Billy Eckstine, Sarah Vaughan and Billie Holiday. Outside of Wednesday nights, many other successful careers got a kick-start by appearing at the theatre. The Fulson band – and Ray – were received well enough, during a week-long stint over the first week in March that was headlined by pioneer doo-wop group The Orioles. On the display bill, Lowell Fulson and His Band was described as "featuring Ray Charles, Blind Pianist".

The New York dates gave Ray his first chance to visit his new agency personally. He got on right away with Billy's son Milt, who booked the jazz acts, and Billy's wife Lee, who mothered him from the start: "I've never known a sweeter or kinder woman. She was like a mother to me, and I can't tell you how I adored that lady," Ray would recall. His first encounter with Billy himself, however, was a little more daunting, getting a no-nonsense warning on the lines that if the agency didn't come through, then he didn't need the agency, but if *he* didn't perform for the agency, *they* didn't need him. It was a straight statement of where they stood with each other, from one of the toughest-sounding dealers in the business, and it made the intended impression.

Also during the week Ray met with Herb Abramson and Ahmet Ertegun for the first time. Their new signing was staying in Harlem just a block from the Apollo at the Braddock Hotel on 126th Street and Eighth Avenue, and the record men went up there to say hello and welcome him to the label.

At the end of the Apollo stint the band moved on to Cleveland, Ohio, followed by the Regal in Chicago, which was where Ray finally said goodbye to Lowell Fulson. The resentments that had been building over the months finally came to a head when Ray contested the fact that Fulson and road manager Brassfield had been paying him less than the fee that Shaw Artists were booking him out for. Brassfield for his part had been urging the bandleader to sack his pianist because of his heroin habit, but until now Fulson had resisted. But now it was Ray who broke the awkward stalemate that had existed for some time, and simply quit when Lowell said no to his latest demand for more money.

He moved back to Columbus and his wife Eileen, but things hadn't been running smoothly on that front either. His absence didn't help, and every time he got the chance to go home – just once or twice every few months – he found she was developing an increasingly serious drink problem. Ray had a thing about women drinking, he simply didn't like it, although he admitted it was hypocritical on his part: "If I find a woman doing a lot of drinking, I don't complain . . . I just split."

And split he did, from a marriage that had lasted barely a year, though it would be another year or so before they actually divorced.

So now Ray was truly independent once again, but this time with a sense of purpose buoyed up by a place on a major agency's books, and a contract with Atlantic Records under his belt.

The next touring jobs, both short-lived, were with Atlantic artists, but more by coincidence than design. The powerful Texas booker Howard Lewis put Ray on a series of dates across the Southwest with one of his all-time heroes Joe Turner, then through the summer he toured with trumpeter Joe Morris' band. The Morris gig was similar to the Lowell Fulson job, Ray playing piano with the band and featuring in his own spot, and writing some arrangements. Morris had enjoyed a number one in the R&B chart with 'Anytime, Anyplace, Anywhere' back in 1950, and was still getting plenty of work off the back of it. Ahmet Ertegun recalled that the Morris band at that time included jazz luminaries Cecil Payne on baritone sax, Johnny Griffin on tenor and Philly Joe Jones on drums, with Ray on piano – "And that was some band!"

Whatever, for Ray Charles it was just a gig, nothing permanent, from here on in he was his own man. He began to realise that while one-nighters with this outfit or that, or on his own when the occasion arose, were the bread and butter of his existence, the next stage of his career was almost certainly to be decided in his first recording sessions for Atlantic Records.

"I got with Atlantic Records because they heard the version of 'Kissa Me Baby' that I did on the old Swingtime label, the first label I was on. That was strictly me, not trying to imitate anybody. I was still a little scared because I could get work sounding like Nat Cole or I could get work sounding like Charles Brown. I could get jobs, and I wanted to make some money, but there came a point once I was with Atlantic, I just said to myself, 'Hey, if I'm gonna make it in this world and be accepted, I had better be accepted the way I sound,' so I dropped all the imitations and stuff. Completely."

5

Messin' Around

"I thought he was the best singer I'd heard of all the singers I was hearing in those days. He seemed to have so many of the great attributes of Black American music, he contained in his art so many different facets of Black American music."

– Ahmet Ertegun

Ahmet Ertegun reasoned that the tried and tested formula that characterised the label's already successful output was as good a launch pad as any for their new signing. "So we thought, well, to start with we'll make a couple of hits with him in the Atlantic mould, and we used the musicians and the arrangers and the studios that we used where we had created the so-called Atlantic sound." But the results of that first session on September 11, 1952, though adequate, did not produce the "couple of hits" that Ertegun had hoped for.

The "sound" that had evolved at Atlantic in the short time since their debut hit with Stick McGhee in 1949 was the result of the four-handed collaboration of partners Ertegun and Abramson, who acted as both producers and A&R (artist & repertoire) men, seeking out new talent and supervising recording sessions, plus ex-bandleader Jesse Stone and – most crucially – engineer Tom Dowd.

Already hitting 50 when Ray Charles signed with Atlantic, Stone had worked as an arranger for some legendary jazz names including Jimmie Lunceford and Chick Webb, before joining the company as staff arranger on its formation in 1947. The only black American in the fledgling organisation, he was partly responsible for guiding Ahmet Ertegun from an original jazz orientation in company policy to the more adventurous rhythm & blues approach which was to pay off almost immediately. It was Stone who accompanied Ertegun and Abramson on "field trips", seeking out new sounds – and talent – in blues bars and juke joints down south. In the Atlantic studio set-up Stone wrote arrangements, hired the backing musicians and generally looked after the music – including contributing some original songs of his own.

Twenty-one-year-old Dowd was already something of a name on the New York recording scene as a freelance engineer when Atlantic first used him on their earliest releases. "He was working for Atlantic before I got there. He was a freelancer at that time, so he worked as an independent contractor. Soon after I arrived, which was in 1953, he got closer and closer to the operation, and then he came on board and was part of the staff," Atlantic producer Jerry Wexler told me, still amused by Dowd's previous history in nuclear fission. "He had had experience with the Manhattan Project, because he had studied physics at Columbia, and was actually working on the genesis of the atom bomb!"

Dowd had virtually taught himself recording skills on "straight" music sessions with conventional pop singers, polka-bands and the like, but experienced a sudden influx of jazz and R&B artists in the face of a threatened Musicians' Union studio ban due to start in January 1948. "Just prior to the ban, the last month of 1947, I think every studio in New York City was recording for 24 hours a day, working with whoever walked in the door," he said. "I did one or two gospel and jazz dates for Atlantic as an engineer, and then I think the first record I made for them that was a success was either 'Teardrops From My Eyes' by Ruth Brown, or 'Drinkin' Wine Spo-Dee-O-Dee' by Stick McGhee & His Buddies."

The new customers – not just Atlantic but all the jazz, blues and gospel outfits – required a broader recording approach than Dowd's previous clientele. Very soon he was creating a sound, crisp in the upper range but rich in bass tonalities, that was tailor-made for the kind of acts Ertegun, Abramson and Stone were recruiting to their new label.

By the time Ray Charles first walked into the studio above Patsy's Restaurant at 234 West 56th Street, Tom Dowd – although he wasn't to join the label full-time for another four years – had established himself as the technical architect of an already recognisable Atlantic "sound". It was a sound that he moulded in synthesis with the musicians themselves, with a sensitivity he thanked Ray for as much as anyone: "Two musicians made me super-sensitive to the art of recording. They were both pianists and they were both blind. Until I worked with George Shearing and Ray Charles, I was walking round with cotton in my ears. They offered me whole new insights into the communication between artist and control room. They operated on a higher plane than anything I had previously imagined."

Jerry Wexler, who joined the label as a producer and partner in 1953, recalled in his autobiography how Dowd achieved amazing results on what by later standards was decidedly primitive equipment: "It was up to him to find a true mix of timbres, bass, treble, and mid-range; to load as much volume as possible without distortion. Tom pushed those pots [volume controls] like a painter sorting colours. He turned microphone placement into an art. Most of all, in those days of mono, he was responsible for catching the right mix on the fly. There was no 'We'll fix it in the mix'. Single tracking was get-it-or-gone."

The tiny studio doubled as company office when there was no recording taking place, with Herb's wife Miriam Abramson looking after the books. Jerry Wexler described the scene: "It was the top floor of a very old building. The bottom floor was occupied by a restaurant, Patsy's Restaurant, which is there to this day, an Italian restaurant. It had a rickety staircase, and the slowest elevator in the East, and when you got to the top floor we had a few rooms. The largest room became Ahmet's and my office which we shared, we had desks which were patty-cornered to each other. When a record session came along, we moved the desks over to one wall, put one desk upon the other – and thereby encountering vertebral angst for decades – and Tom Dowd would set out the folding chairs, the camp chairs, and set up the mikes, so that's where we recorded."

Miriam, however, found the constant furniture-shifting less disconcerting than she did the presence of Ray, with whom she never felt comfortable: "He had a drug problem, and we had a tiny loo. Really, it was just like a cupboard and it had a loo in it. And during a session he would go in and you could hear him hitting his head against the wall. It was quite weird . . ."

For that first session, the studio was crowded by the time the band set up. Jesse Stone had booked, as usual, some of the best players around, with future Modern Jazz Quartet Atlantic star Connie Kay on drums, Lloyd Trotman on bass, and a horn section that included Jesse Drakes on trumpet, Sam "The Man" Taylor on tenor sax and Dave McRae on baritone.

Two of the numbers (both self-penned) were still loosely in the Brown-Cole mould, even though Ray had been conscious of the need to establish his own style over the past few months. But what that style was to

53

be still proved elusive, and while 'Midnight Hour' and 'Roll With My Baby' certainly weren't crude impersonations, to the casual listener the resemblance is very apparent. 'Midnight', the "Brown" track of the two, has its moments – a 32-bar blues with long, languid horn lines that led into a soulful piano break that lets you know it's Ray, no mistake.

The other two tracks recorded that day were of a different order – there was definitely something cooking here. From its opening wailing trumpet, 'The Sun's Gonna Shine Again' (another original composition) is an altogether earthier affair; Ray is whooping rather than crooning, shouting rather than schmoozing, over insistent riffing from the horns. And 'Jumpin' In The Morning' – a Sam Sweet composition which Jesse Stone brought to the session – is, like the title suggests, a tight jump-band shoutin' blues in Kansas City mode, with Ray's boogie left hand carrying the horns until he breaks out with some powerful blues-bop piano, and what can only be described as a (pre) rock'n'roll ride out.

Astonishingly, in retrospect at least, Abramson and Ertegun decided to release 'Midnight Hour' and 'Roll With My Baby' as Ray's debut on Atlantic, the two least "original" takes of the session. At the time it probably made sense; they were the tracks with some commercial "identity", albeit a surrogate one. Whatever, the single – Atlantic #976 – sank without trace soon after its October release, as did the follow-up in early 1953, featuring the other two tracks from the session.

Clearly the potential they all saw in Ray Charles was yet to be realised, but Atlantic, unlike many labels, was willing to give it time – a factor Ray would appreciate, looking back years later, putting it down in part to the fact that Ertegun, Abramson and the others at the company were actually hip to the music: "I was a youngster, but they felt I was talented. There was no pressure on me that the first record be a hit. They just kept saying, 'Hey man, you just come on in and keep recording the music.' That was their attitude, which is something you don't find today. I mean, you go into a company and you make a couple of records and if it don't hit you're out, finished. Another thing about the people at Atlantic, they can tap their feet to the music, they can snap their fingers on the two and four beat. Which is something else you hardly don't see today."

After the first Atlantic no-go sales-wise, Ray headed back down south; he had a living to make. He played some club gigs in New Orleans, followed by a series of one-nighters across Texas and the South West arranged by the "territory" booker Howard Lewis. There were dates with Joe Turner, blues harmonica man Little Walter, even one with his ex-colleague Lowell Fulson and Atlantic R&B chart-toppers The Clovers, but mostly he was the headliner in modest venues where he'd play with local musicians who'd been arranged by the promoter beforehand.

In New York meanwhile, Ahmet Ertegun pondered what to do next with Ray Charles, amid a burgeoning list of successes for other Atlantic artists including two R&B number ones, by The Clovers and Ruth Brown. Jesse Stone recalled that Ray was "very temperamental and hard to get along with, it was hard to persuade him to do the rock type things. But finally . . . he came into the studio and said, 'Okay, I'm not saying anything, you guys tell me what to do and I'll do it." Rather than pre-booking a studio band, with Ray coming in "cold" to a selection of songs and set of arrangements, Ahmet decided to run some rehearsal sessions first – just Ray, himself and Jesse Stone without the session men, Tom Dowd taping anything interesting that they might want to refer back to.

The ensuing "jam", in which Ray and Ahmet began by bouncing around lots of boogie and blues riffs, was to become the stuff of legend, largely because of segments of Dowd's tape that circulated years later. The interpretation that some latter-day listeners put on the stop-start studio snippets was of Ahmet Ertegun literally introducing Ray to styles he'd never heard before, weaning him off Cole and Brown and on to boogie and blues.

Nothing of course was further from the truth, although even Ahmet's brother Nesuhi would endorse that view to some degree in retrospect: "Ahmet was trying to get him a little more into deeper blues . . . I would never say Ahmet was coaching Ray Charles, but would say, 'Listen to Cow Cow Davenport, listen to Tampa Red,' all kinds of blues singers Ray didn't know . . . He was only young, he was from the West Coast [sic], so he hadn't been exposed fully. He knew gospel, and he knew church music and so on, all the changes, but when he heard the great blues singers of the past . . . I think both Ahmet and Jerry [Wexler] spent a lot of time with him and taught him songs, played him records and discussed that sort of thing."

This perception seems to have centred on Ahmet playing a song he'd written, 'Mess Around', which he'd based on a riff by the boogie-woogie pioneer Charles Edward "Cow Cow" Davenport. Ray confessed never to have heard of the piano man, but on hearing Ahmet's snatch of the riff joined in with a perfect copy of the Davenport original.

"When I wrote that song 'Mess Around', I based it on a riff from Cow Cow Davenport, and when I asked him if he knew Cow Cow Davenport . . . he'd said he never heard of that, but when I started to play it, he said, 'Yeah, I know that,' and he started to play it, because he had an unconscious memory . . . somebody played that, and as a child he must have heard all that music. And you know he had an incredible memory, but he didn't particularly know who Cow Cow Davenport was, or who Pinetop Smith was, but if you started to play a little bit or sing a little bit then he would just go into it, and there it was, he was doing it."

Similarly, when on the crude taping Ahmet could be heard singing the number – albeit tunelessly – it was misconstrued as him teaching Ray how to perform the song: "Because of a studio tape that was floating around, a lot of fuss has been made about my singing this song to Ray so he could memorise it and get the off-beat. We were running through it, that's all."

Nevertheless, it's reasonable to assume that with his extensive knowledge and appreciation of blues – as a passionate fan and then equally enthusiastic professional – Ertegun introduced Ray to much of the *detail* of music that the latter had always understood instinctively, putting names and titles to recordings that had been unspecified but omnipresent in his consciousness since childhood.

At the actual recording session a week later, on May 17, 1953, the rhythm section was the same as the previous November with Trotman and Kay on bass and drums respectively, but with the addition of the Cuban percussionist Candido Camero (soon to become famous simply as Candido) on conga drums. Jesse Stone also booked a three-sax horn section comprising Dave McRae, Freddie Mitchell and Pinkie Williams, plus the celebrated session guitarist Mickey "Guitar" Baker.

The six tracks laid down that Sunday reveal a far more expansive Ray than on the earlier Atlantic sides, with an on-mike confidence with Jesse Stone's arrangements and the general dynamics that clearly benefited from the preliminary "rehearsal".

The world-weary humour of Memphis Curtis' 'It Should've Been Me' recalls the hip humour of the best of Louis Jordan, a streetwise monologue echoed by the pleading chorus line ". . . It should've been me with that real fine chick . . .", while 'Heartbreaker' is a horn-driven jump blues written by Ahmet Ertegun under the *nom de disque* he'd use many times, Nugetre (Ertegun backwards).

'Sinner's Prayer' is an atmospheric blues confirming the down-home roots of Ray, guitarist Baker and composer Lowell Fulson, who co-wrote it with Lloyd Glenn. 'Losing Hand' by Charles Calhoun is a similarly stark statement, Ray's plaintive voice tinged with echo as piano and guitar respond in kind, and 'Funny But I Still Love You' (Ray's only composition in the set) is a blues ballad where the influence of Charles Brown can still be sensed.

But it's Ahmet's other song, the aforementioned 'Mess Around' that's the stand-out of the session. From a boogie intro that Cow Cow Davenport would have found hard to emulate, Ray is shouting and whooping over the tight horns while his piano carries all before it, breaking into a 12-bar solo matched by a honking tenor chorus that Ray urges on "Now you got it boy . . .", and a ride-out that adds up to two minutes 34 seconds of rockin' blues heaven.

When Atlantic released a two-volume anthology *The Ray Charles Story* in 1962, his early recordings for the label were summed up on the back sleeve of Volume One: "His first two Atlantic sessions were with studio musicians, arrangements by Jesse Stone, songs supplied by various songwriters. The resulting sides were good journeyman R&B, but Ray was still under wraps. Nevertheless, 'Losing Hand' is still a blues masterpiece, and the conversation between Ray's piano and Mickey Baker's guitar is now and always after-hours balm in excelsis.

"On balance: because Ray didn't write the songs and only lightly influenced the arrangements, and because the band was a for-hire studio cadre, the records are only important because Ray sang and played the only way he knew how – beautifully. And because Ahmet Ertegun wrote him a stomp that is part of the literature today – 'Mess Around'."

The liner notes were written by Jerry Wexler, Vice President of Atlantic Records, a role he had assumed in June 1953 after having been taken on as a partner when Herb Abramson was drafted into the Army. In fact the Ray Charles session in May was one of the first he would attend in a career that would figure hugely in the history of rhythm & blues, rock'n'roll and soul music.

Born in New York City in 1917, Jerry Wexler met the Ertegun brothers and Herb Abramson via a mutual interest in jazz. "We were all record collectors at the time," he said. "That was a little enclave of people in New York who knew each other, and hung out, and exchanged records, went out to hear the music live – in Harlem or 52nd Street, the famous 52nd Street, or Greenwich Village – and we'd congregate, we'd gather, at each other's houses, and we would engage in a rite which is forgotten, that is *communal listening* to records. We'd sit around and listen to a 78 of Louis Armstrong's Hot Five or an early Sidney Bechet, or a Jelly Roll Morton . . . this was the basis of our interest, antiquarian jazz, starting with New Orleans and then going on up from every period, and every change until the current time. We collected, and *feasted on* that whole music. That was our qualification to make records, because we were neither engineers nor songwriters."

As a would-be journalist and aspiring "serious" writer, after a series of rejections by the big New York papers in the late Forties, Wexler found a job as a cub reporter at *Billboard* magazine. He quickly rose through the ranks, doing interviews and record reviews and generally making himself known around the music industry. One claim to fame while at that august journal was having changed the name of the "Race Record" chart to "Rhythm & Blues".

From his home in Florida, he explained to me how it came about: "I worked under the legendary music editor Paul Ackerman, and we had a good staff, Hal Wedner, Bill Simon, Tony Wilson – these names probably don't mean a lot – but it became apparent that the 'race record' designation was becoming pejorative, because of whatever rising sensitivity in the inner city, and so on. The same thing sort of happened with hillbilly when it changed to country & western. We used to close the book on a Friday at *Billboard* and come back on a Tuesday, and we had a little Friday editorial meeting and Paul said, 'We gotta change the name. On Tuesday let's get together with some suggestions.' It was as simple as that, I came in with some ideas, I thought, 'Rhythm & blues, that sounds good.' That fitted, so it was simple, nothing arcane . . ."

But he wasn't particularly happy with the change, not initially at least. "It was really against my wishes," he would tell journalist Bill Holland. "I figured it's in the purview of people being described to describe themselves. You know, it has been a big thing, [using terms] from 'coloured' to 'Negro' to 'black' to 'African-American'. And back then, the word 'race', used as an adjective, always had a great deal of esteem attached to it. Because, back in the day, when you called a man a 'race man', that was a man who lived, exuded and swore by his essential Negritude. Back in Harlem, they would say, 'That man is a race man to the bricks' – meaning from the top of his head to the ground. So 'race records' was okay with me. However, I wasn't the one who made the decision."

And Jerry Wexler wasn't alone in being doubtful about the rhythm &

blues tag. The R&B producer and songwriter Henry Glover, for instance – who penned a future Ray Charles hit 'Drown In My Own Tears' back in 1951 – felt it was a "tongue-in-cheek, trade name given to Negro music to keep from saying 'race'," and, in retrospect, that " 'soul' was an expression of black resentment toward that designation."

Fellow jazz fanatics Herb Abramson and Ahmet Ertegun offered Wexler a job with their newly formed record company, which he initially turned down, saying he'd only consider joining them as a partner. So when Uncle Sam called up Herb for what would be a two-year tenure of duty, they made Wexler an offer they hoped this time he couldn't refuse – for a $2,000 investment in the company, he would be made a 13 per cent owner and full partner. He didn't refuse.

Right after the May 17 session Ray travelled down to his hometown of Greenville, Florida, to attend the funeral of his "second" mother, Mary Jane. News of her death had come through while they were recording, but Ray had half expected it for some time. She'd been ill for months – in fact he'd been covering her medical bills – so all there was left to do was to pay one last tribute to a part of his past that was now gone forever.

And while Atlantic were putting out his next single – 'Mess Around' backed by 'Funny But I Still Love You' released in June – Ray was back in New Orleans. The Crescent City, historically the cradle of jazz and by the early Fifties the hub of a thriving rhythm & blues scene, was a comfortable spot for Ray. He felt at ease there, the hot humid summers and mild winters making for a more leisurely tempo of life that allowed him to sit back and reflect a little, while at the same time involving himself in the local scene.

"There were good sounds in New Orleans back then . . . and I sat in with as many of the cats as I could," he said. "The blues were brewing down there, and the stew was plenty nasty. I was experimenting with my own voice and doing fewer and fewer imitations." His piano style developed too; having gradually moved away from the light-fingered sound of West Coast jazz to a bluesier approach, he was now taking on board the more rhythmic, percussive elements of New Orleans players like Professor Longhair (Roy Byrd), Fats Domino and Huey "Piano" Smith. He was in no hurry to leave the "Big Easy" (as the old French city was also known), and ensconced himself in Foster's Hotel, just a couple of blocks from the Dew Drop Inn, *the* prime venue on the local black music circuit.

Jerry Wexler, meanwhile, had been cutting his teeth in the Atlantic studio control booth with Ahmet, and in August the two decided it was time for a recording trip out of town – Wexler's first. They had a session booked in New Orleans at Cosimo Matassa's famed J&M Studios (aka Cosmo's) with vocalist Tommy Ridgley backed by the Edgar Blanchard Band, a line-up of horns, bass and drums, with Blanchard on guitar; when they hit town, they asked Ray to come in on piano.

After the Ridgley takes the two New Yorkers suggested Ray try a couple of sides. He'd gone to the session unprepared for anything other than playing back-up, so just rolled out a couple of low-down blues. There is nothing remarkable about either number, both are slow-tempo "cryin'" blues with Ray's voice hard-edged over the mournful sax harmonies. 'I Wonder Who' was an original, while the other, 'Feelin' Sad' (released in September, with 'Heartbreaker' from the previous session as the flip side) was written by Eddie Lee Jones, known professionally as Guitar Slim.

Mississippi-born Slim was one of a new breed of wild men of the blues. As well as wearing outlandish zoot suits in garish colours (which he would often match with bizarrely dyed hair), his stage act involved him prowling around the audience, and sometimes even the street outside, his solid-bodied electric guitar still connected via anything up to 350 feet of cable. He played loud, very loud, and his use of feedback and electronic distortion was way ahead of its time. An unlikely catalyst in the next stage of Ray Charles' artistic development, yet that's what he turned out to be when Ray was booked to work on a session with him late in October 1953.

The two very different musicians weren't strangers. Slim was managed by the proprietor of the Dew Drop Inn, Frank Painia, who had given Ray some work backing the singer/guitarist at the club. By the time the recording session at Cosmo's was fixed, they'd got to know and respect each other, Ray – now more anxious than ever to break away from any residual "imitations" – being impressed by the other man's flamboyant singing that reminded him a little of the hell-fire preachers he'd heard as a child.

Although Ray was just booked as pianist, as soon as the recording got under way (with Cosmo Matassa supervising production) he assumed control of the backing musicians, all time-served session players who were used to the discipline of charts and arrangements rather than Slim's less than organised approach. Four sides were cut in a session that lasted till

dawn, including 'The Things I Used To Do' that went on to be a huge
hit, as Jerry Wexler would recall: "Without portfolio, Ray had sketched
out a head arrangement for Slim's 'The Things I Used To Do', playing
piano at the date and directing things from the keyboard. This record was
to sell a million copies for the Specialty label. Nobody knew it then, but
this was a big breakthrough for Ray – he had, in effect, written his first
commercial hit arrangement."

Ray, too, only saw any significance in retrospect, at the time the session
seemed no big deal: "I wound up producing the tunes and writing the
charts off the top of my head . . . Maybe 'producing' is too big a word.
What happened was really this: we got in the studio and I took over.
Wasn't anything I had planned. It evolved naturally. We needed some
riffs, we needed some ideas, and everyone was pleased to let me lead the
way."

Ray's lengthy sojourn in New Orleans was marked by another milestone
in his musical development. Right after the Guitar Slim session he put
together a seven-piece band, the first of that size he'd organised himself, to
work on a regular basis, and set out in November on a series of dates
through the Deep South of Louisiana, Alabama and Mississippi. The
line-up consisted of Wallace Davenport and Freddie Mitchell on trumpets, Joe Tillman on tenor sax, O'Neil Geraldo on alto and Warren Bell
on baritone, plus Lloyd Lambert on bass and drummer Oscar Moore –
some of the Crescent City's finest.

At the beginning of December Ahmet and Jerry were due back in New
Orleans to record Joe Turner, one of the label's biggest names at the time,
laying down 'Midnight Cannonball'. Ray told them he had some numbers
he'd like to record while they were in town, which he'd arranged with the
pick-up band. Cosmo's was unavailable all week, so they settled to record
in the studios of a local radio station, WDSU.

This wasn't as unusual as it sounds today, and Ahmet, Jerry and Ray
were to make several crucial recordings in what Ahmet remembered as
being far-from-ideal environments: "Well some of them were in terrible
circumstances, like when it got to be the top of the hour, say nine
o'clock, and you'd stop because they'd have to give the call letters of the
radio station. But you know something, it was difficult but it was a lot
of fun."

Fun, maybe, but according to Jerry Wexler also fraught with frustration:
"There'd be some old duffer who knew nothing about records and we'd

say, 'Okay, be ready in two bars, saxophone coming up,' and a minute later he'd turn round and say, 'What, sonny? What'd you say about a saxophone?' As Nesuhi Ertegun explained, it was a solution born out of necessity: "I think Ahmet did two or three sessions like that . . . when he didn't have time to come to where you were, you'd go to the radio station, and it was not the best equipment. But Ray's band and Ray, you know he went beyond all that, he was able to transcend all those problems, and just give his message."

But what impressed the two Atlantic men most on December 4 was that Ray arrived with four original songs and ready-made arrangements he'd already worked on with the band, they had to do virtually nothing but operate the tape equipment. Not only that, but for the first time a uniquely Ray Charles sound was emerging.

Three of the numbers, 'Ray's Blues', 'Nobody Cares' and 'Mr. Charles Blues' are straight 12-bar songs, but these are fresh, very modern sounding takes on the form; the band is precise and authoritative, like they've played together forever, and Ray's voice exudes a new confidence, almost as if vocally he feels he's found himself at last. And the fourth title, 'Don't You Know', is something else again, the exclamatory four bar breaks –

> *Say have you heard baby,*
> *Ray Charles is in town,*
> *Let's mess around till the midnight hour,*
> *See what he's puttin' down*

used as a springboard for some memorable riffing and the first hints of those soulful vocal acrobatics, the sanctified–sounding shouts, screams and whimpers which would characterise Ray's style in the months and years to come.

Jerry Wexler recalled how the number, and the whole session, was a foretaste of things to come. "While the side didn't sell big, it contained a jazz-funk riff that was immediately adopted by the hippest players of the day, from Horace Silver to Cannonball Adderley. Even Miles Davis took note.

"This was a landmark session in the growth pattern because it had Ray Charles originals, Ray Charles arrangements, a Ray Charles band. It was a non-A&R oriented date. Ahmet and I had nothing to do with the preparation, and all we could do at the session was see to it that the radio technician didn't erase the good takes during the playbacks."

From there on, Wexler and Ertegun were 100 per cent sure that the label's faith in Ray Charles was completely justified. Where his burgeoning musical evolution would take him – and them – they couldn't imagine, but they knew the only direction was up, as Wexler would recall. "Having witnessed an act of creation like that, in the New Orleans sessions, you could only have good feelings about what was going to happen next with this guy; Ray was so full of changes, such a protean type, you could never truly anticipate his next move."

As always, up to now at least, Ray left it to the record men to ruminate on what to release next. Atlantic chose the novelty 'It Should've Been Me' from his May 1953 session for his next single, backed with 'A Sinner's Prayer' from the same studio date; it wasn't a bad choice – it would go on to be the first record by Ray Charles to break out nationally. Meanwhile he was back on the road, seeing in 1954 in Houston, Texas.

Following a New Year dance date with R&B stars T-Bone Walker and Amos Milburn, he was invited to a Houston radio station, WCOH, to be interviewed on the *King Bee Show*. During the on-air chat, Ray mentioned that one of his favourite gospel groups, Cecil Shaw and the Cecil Shaw Singers, happened to hail from the city. No sooner was his spot on the show over than a call came to the station for Ray – it was one of the Cecil Shaw singers, Della Howard, thanking him for the plug and asking if he'd like to meet Cecil Shaw. Ray jumped at the chance. The two met at the Crystal Hotel, and a couple of days later the gospel singer introduced Ray to his attractive lady vocalist who'd engineered the meeting.

The two hit it off immediately. Ray was fascinated by the quiet, reserved woman who didn't smoke or drink. "I called her B 'cause her middle name was Beatrice. And I liked her right away," he would recall. An intense relationship developed through the early months of 1954, a courtship which Ray kept up via phone calls and typewritten letters when he was on the road. He even rented a small apartment in Houston just to be near her, but – perhaps thinking about Della's close-knit family and remembering the pressure he had got from Louise's parents back in Tampa – he was anxious to get her away and into a place of their own.

After months of trying to persuade her to move north to Dallas, Ray finally got his way when Della became pregnant later in the year. They moved into a motel, the Green Acres, while they looked for a permanent place to live, which they eventually found at the beginning of April, Della being eight months pregnant by that time. They got married on April 5, 1955, immediately moving into their new home at 2642 Eugene Street in

South Dallas. At the end of May, while Ray was on the road, by sheer coincidence playing Houston, Della Beatrice Robinson gave birth to a baby boy, whom they named Ray Charles Robinson Jr.

But between meeting his future wife and becoming a father (for the second time) less than 18 months later, equally significant changes would occur in Ray's professional life. By the spring of 1955, Ray Charles would have his own band on the road, and a major hit in the national R&B charts.

As the one-nighters continued through the early months of 1954, one thing was becoming increasingly apparent, particularly after the New Orleans recordings in December '53 when Ray arrived in the studio with a ready-assembled band which he'd rehearsed and written charts for beforehand — he needed a band of his own. Ray was convinced that should be the next step, as were Jerry and Ahmet at Atlantic, but the people who had to be persuaded were the Shaw agency and bookers like Howard Lewis. They would have to finance it in the first instance, and sell Ray for fees to cover the whole ensemble. To attract that kind of money, you needed bigger-selling records than Ray Charles had yet managed.

But things were looking up. Not only did Guitar Slim's 'The Things I Used To Do', with Ray as producer, hit number one in the R&B chart, 'It Should've Been Me' started to make an impression nationally as well. As winter turned to spring, Ray became increasingly frustrated with having to rely on pick-up bands of varying reliability, especially when 'It Should've Been Me' crept into the Top 10 R&B listings. On the phone to New York he lobbied Billy Shaw to the point of becoming a nuisance, and when that didn't prove effective started on Howard Lewis, main source of the lucrative work in Texas and the South-west.

What seemed to have turned the tide in Ray's favour as far as the two hard-nosed businessmen were concerned was when Shaw offered Lewis a couple of weeks of Ruth Brown dates for July, provided they could organise a backing band. The solution was staring them in the face – not to mention pleading down the telephone line most days – let Ray put a band together. It wouldn't be just a pick-up band, but the Brown gigs would be a useful test run – if it didn't work out, Ray could forget any more ideas of leading his own outfit for the immediate future.

With the New Orleans pick-up band he'd used for his last recording session as a notional template, Ray set about finding the right musicians.

He wanted the same four horn line-up (which became five when he played alto) including two trumpets. With the rhythm section and himself on piano, he very soon had the beginnings of what he would describe as "a bitch – one of the tightest little bands around".

Howard Lewis, and more specifically his son John, also organised transport for the embryonic outfit, a sedan and a station wagon, complete with road manager to drive Ray and whoever else took the sedan, and generally look after day-to-day business. The job was offered to Jeff Brown, who John Lewis and Ray knew well from when he'd driven the Lowell Fulson band bus, and who was to become a permanent fixture as Ray's de facto manager for the next 10 years.

In plenty of time for the Ruth Brown dates, Ray had recruited his first ensemble which included Renald Richard and Charles "Clanky" Whitely on trumpets, A.D. Norris on tenor sax and Jimmy Bell on bass. It wasn't a line-up that would stay together for very long, but it represented the first manifestation of the Ray Charles small band which would become a legend in the annals of rhythm & blues.

When the mini-tour with Brown was finished the band headed north for some dates in Cleveland, then across country to the West Coast and Los Angeles. And it was in LA that Ray would bring on board a musician who would be forever identified with the Ray Charles sound of the Fifties and early Sixties, sax player David "Fathead" Newman.

Born in Texas in 1933, Newman grew up in Dallas, where he began to play music while at Lincoln High (it was there he acquired the nickname "Fathead" after a music teacher called him that when he fumbled an exercise). After school he soon found himself on the local gigging circuit, in 1950 joining alto player Buster Smith's band. Smith's pedigree was formidable; he'd played with the legendary Kansas City names in their formative years through the late Twenties and Thirties – Walter Page, Benny Moten, Count Basie – and was even an early influence on Charlie Parker when the pioneer of bebop was still in KC. So playing with Smith, who Newman called his "hometown mentor", was no small deal.

During the early Fifties Newman hit the road with pianist Lloyd Glenn's band, then made his record debut in 1952 playing alto behind Zuzu Bollin on 'Why Don't You Eat Where You Slept Last Night'. Also on the session was another future Ray Charles sideman from Dallas, Leroy Cooper, who'd join Newman again on Lowell Fulson's 1954 classic, 'Reconsider Baby'.

It was while he was still with the Smith band that Fathead first got to know Ray Charles, when their paths crossed while Ray was touring with Lowell Fulson in 1952. "It was somewhere in Texas, Oklahoma and Arkansas, that sort of area . . ." he would recall. The two hit it off right away and, when he wasn't working, Dallas-based Fathead would often hook up with Ray as he worked the South-west, driving his car sometimes and sitting in on gigs here and there. As well as a mutual involvement in drugs – both were regularly mainlining heroin – the two had a more positive, musical bond in their basic passion for jazz.

"Because we're roughly the same age, we came up on the same sounds," Newman told David Ritz in 2003. "Our first love was big bands. We'd been raised on Buddy Johnson and Tiny Bradshaw. But we'd also been radicalised by bebop. Bird [Charlie Parker] turned our world upside down . . . so we learned to do it all." But, as he explained to me, bebop didn't often pay the rent: "Yeah, we both had that, but it was the blues we were surrounded by, and that was what the people wanted to hear, that was what was popular. In order to earn money you had to play the music folks wanted . . . it was almost a must, you couldn't very well earn a living playing bebop or jazz." Long after his tenure with the band was over, Newman would always remind people of the jazz backbone of the Ray Charles band: "Ray made his mark as a rhythm & blues man, but the fact is we played just as much gospel and an awful lot of real jazz."

Fathead was principally an alto player, but Ray was looking for a baritone in the line-up so Newman was hired in that capacity. Now with his four-strong horn section, Ray was writing the arrangements exactly as he heard them in his head.

"He was an excellent arranger," Newman told me, "and he liked arranging for five horns which consisted of three saxophones and two trumpets, that was what we had and that's what he liked to arrange for. We had two saxophones, we had tenor and baritone, and Ray played the alto part so that made three reeds and two trumpets. He would do these arrangements, and what was funny he never wrote the arrangements in Braille, he just dictated the arrangement out to someone and they'd take down exactly what he said right . . . 'cos he had everything in his head, and he had perfect pitch. I don't think I ever remember seeing him write any arrangement, it just came straight from his head, and dictated to someone who did the notation. And because he had perfect pitch, he didn't have to be around a piano or anything."

Through the autumn of 1954 the band worked its way back eastwards, across into the Midwest and back down into the southern states. On the road, while the rest of the guys were relaxing, Ray would dictate charts to trumpeter Renald Richard who'd write them down, tricky arrangements that required spot-on musicianship and faultless discipline in the ranks. But military precision wasn't the name of the game – they had to be able to improvise too. As well as Ray taking solos on piano and alto, trumpets and saxes would all get to flex their musical muscles in tightly defined breaks written into the numbers, particularly on the "jazz" opening to their show before Ray did any vocals.

In this way the "sound" evolved outside the confines of the recording studio, each number being rehearsed, then tried and tested every night in front of a live – and demanding – audience. Likewise with Ray's composing and singing: new songs would be crafted on the road, while his voice came into its own with material – and an instrumental environment – that reflected more and more his blues and gospel roots.

Ahmet Ertegun recalls how this process became the catalyst for Ray's outburst of creativity, confirming the company's faith in him after nearly three years with Atlantic Records: "We'd had just a minor success with the records we made . . . but they were successful enough for Ray Charles to be able to put a band together and go out on the road as the headliner, and the minute he started to do that was when he came into his great flowering.

"He was then able to compose and write and to perform songs that he rehearsed with his band on the road, and when we came in to record they were not only ready, they were eager to put down the terrific things they'd put together on the road. So it was an entirely new experience for me, because instead of having struggled writing songs and trying to get them to perform them . . . the experience changed to recording things that Ray had perfected on the road and had already passed the test of public acceptance."

To put a more precise point on it, the moment it came home to Ahmet and Jerry Wexler that they didn't need to suggest songs to Ray as they usually did with their artists, that from here on his potential would be unlocked by simply letting him do his own thing, was on November 17, 1954.

The band had some dates at the Royal Peacock club in Atlanta and Ray was keen to let the Atlantic men hear some new items he'd written and got into shape gig by gig, songs he was sure would be good for their next session in the recording studio. Not just that, he wanted them to hear his new band, *his* band, for the first time. He rang them, suggesting they come down right away, which they did without hesitation. What they heard was to change their lives forever.

"We got with him in the afternoon at the Peacock nightclub, where he had his band set to play for us," says Ahmet. "Except for Ray and the band, the place was empty, and as soon as we walked in Ray counted off and they hit into 'I Got A Woman', and that was it."

6

Hallelujah

"When I started to sing like myself – as opposed to imitating Nat Cole, which I had done for a while – when I started singing like Ray Charles, it had this spiritual and churchy, this religious or gospel sound. It had this holiness and preachy tone to it. It was very controversial. I got a lot of criticism for it."

– Ray Charles

Wexler and Ertegun were totally knocked out by all the new numbers that Ray and the band hit them with that afternoon. They needed to go into a studio right away, but the best they could find in Atlanta was, again, a radio station, courtesy of an enterprising local DJ, Zenas Sears.

Sears had started in radio in Atlanta before the Second World War, at which time he occasionally got to work with black gospel groups. Then, when he was sent to India in the armed forces, he found himself broadcasting to the troops who were 85 per cent black, this way discovering what he called the "subculture" of blues and rhythm & blues. Back in civilian life and in his old job, he was determined to give this music more exposure, knowing there was an audience for it in the black community and probably in the white one as well.

Against the grain of the station he worked for, and radio generally at that time, he broke the mould as a white DJ playing black music on a white station: "When I came back here and got my job back there was not a black artist on record in any radio station, and the only black people who would come were the delivery and a guy who'd come in and sweep up. So I started a show, six in the morning; I didn't think the manager would mind – he never got up till 10, got hung over about 11, started drinkin' again about two (well earlier but he was on the way by two o'clock) – and he *didn't* mind. As a matter of fact it was fairly successful, and I got into it, then I got fired when the owner of the station discovered what we were doing."

He then moved to WGST, a commercial station which was part of the endowment of Georgia Tech, and did the same thing there on a night-time show. He was still at WGST when he heard from the Atlantic guys – whom he knew from their previous forays into Georgia – that they needed some studio time, which he arranged for the very next day.

"Ray was here, and the studio was about it in Atlanta. WGST wasn't a huge radio station but they had a big studio, fairly large. But nothing compared to now . . . very basic equipment and good taping, and engineers. And we would go off the air at one o'clock to one-thirty depending on how many commercials I had – this was at night – and record after that. We didn't charge an exorbitant amount . . . we didn't charge anything for the use of the studio, the engineers made a buck and that was it . . . we did it because it was available. It was reasonably good, though nothing compared with today."

As Ray had discovered in New Orleans, radio stations didn't offer ideal studio conditions, and this one was no different: "Just a little bitty studio, I think it was WGST or somethin', and they weren't equipped for recording. But we went in there and we struggled and we managed it," was how he recalled the session in *Rolling Stone*. But despite what Jerry described as "much confusion" when they couldn't play anything back in the control room because someone was reading the news, ". . . it had now happened. Ray was fully fledged, ready for fame."

Sears recalled how recording was also interrupted while he read commercials. "They'd rehearse while I was on the air . . . wham, wham, then hush up because I've got to do some commercials – they were all live – and if we had a newscast of course they'd have to quit, or it would have all filtered through. Most of the time it didn't matter too much during the commercials, but there was one time when I got really annoyed. It was a session when they were really whamming away and the last part of my programme was religious music, gospel, and I was trying to do something very delicate and somebody opened the door and that whole thing came right in . . . a real wild instrumental."

Ray built up a relationship with Sears and the local Atlanta scene which manifested itself in a number of ways. "He did some very nice things in the community, being blind and having suffered with blindness and a good deal of pain. We had a winter where it was suddenly very cold, and at that time the heating for most people was on an open gas heater or a fireplace or something. There were a lot of flash fires all through Georgia, and there was a hospital here that specialised in burns for children – it was Harris

Hospital or something like that – and there were about a hundred kids there as a result of all those flash fires. We asked Ray to come over with us, two of us one time, and talk to the kids, and explain to them how they could get along, and to play the piano, which he did. And he went back there a good bit, even though it was an emotional problem for him to work with those kids."

The tracks recorded at the Atlanta radio station speak for themselves. The nearest thing to a conventional blues is the 12-bar 'Black Jack', where Ray bemoans his luck at the card table with a harder edge to his voice than previously, accentuated by crisp echo and a sparse accompaniment. 'Greenbacks' is a humorous jump number on the same laid-back lines of 'It Should've Been Me', breaking for a baritone solo from Fathead Newman.

It's the other two tapings, however, that signpost the radical direction in which Ray Charles' music was moving. 'Come Back Baby' is an eight-bar blues with recognisably strong gospel musical connotations in both its churchy harmonies and the 3/4 "waltz" time signature, while 'I Got A Woman' confirms his mixing of the secular and the sacred in a way that was to confound – and upset – many listeners in mid-Fifties America.

'I Got A Woman', co-written by Ray and Renald Richard, is constructed as an archetypal gospel tune – the critic Nat Hentoff would describe it as "a secularisation of the gospel song 'My Jesus Is All The World To Me'," while others saw it as a straight rewrite of 'I Got A Saviour (Way Across Jordan)' – an up-tempo 16-bar progression that "lifts" the listener with each four-bar change, confirming the optimism of Ray's lyrics just as joyfully as the church equivalent would celebrate the glory of the Lord, heaven's salvation or whatever. But it raised the hackles of many in the black community, including the musical fraternity – and a honking rhythm & blues tenor sax break didn't help matters.

Ray was always adamant that not only was the gospel-blues crossover of 'I Got A Woman' a perfectly natural development for him, but the song represented the first time his music made an impression on the white market as well: "I was just being myself. You got a choice in this world, you either gonna be yourself, or you ain't. We did 'I Got A Woman', and of course it created a lot of static from a lot of people. But then, on the other hand, it was a hit. It was a hit in the black community and the white community.

"I didn't think of it being gospel influenced until somebody pointed it out. You say to yourself, 'I think I'm going to write something, and here's the way I want it to go.' And that's exactly the way it came about. I didn't realise that people were going to say, 'Oh, that's very gospelly,'" Ray would explain. "I was raised in the church and was around blues and would hear all these musicians on the jukeboxes and then I would go to revival meetings on Sunday morning. So I would get both sides of music. A lot of people at the time thought it was sacrilegious, but all I was doing was singing the way I felt.

"But that was *me*. That's where I'm coming from, that's why some people say I started the so-called gospel rock, or whatever . . . that was truly me. 'I Got A Woman' was the song that caused the white populace to pay me some attention. You see before then I had made records that were big records in the R&B field, for instance we had done songs like 'It Should Have Been Me', like 'Mess Around', we had done songs like 'Baby Let Me Hold Your Hand' . . . These were all songs that were all big, but they were not big in both fields. In those days they were strictly rhythm & blues or race music as we called it."

It also had its detractors among white "bible belt" fundamentalists in the South, where it was on a list – along with The Drifters' 'Honey Love', 'Work With Me Annie' by The Midnighters, and Lowell Fulson's classic 'Everyday I Have The Blues' – of 30 "objectionable" discs to be banned by radio stations between 1951 and 1955.

The punching tenor break on 'I Got A Woman' was taken by Don Wilkerson, who'd replaced A.D. Norris not long before the band hit Atlanta, indicative of the state of flux among the personnel at this point. The trumpets on the recording were Joe Bridgewater and Clanky Whitely, the latter leaving not long after. The drummer, Glenn Brooks, would also soon depart – he stayed on in Atlanta, his place taken by Bill Peeples, while the bass player on the session, Jimmy Bell, also exited before the end of the year.

As usual, while Atlantic made up their mind on what to release first from the recent session, the band continued its workaday trek of one-nighters and short residencies. There wasn't much doubt as far as Ahmet and Jerry were concerned – 'I Got A Woman' was the outstanding track among four strong contenders – despite some initial hesitation on account of the song's gospel style, as Zenas Sears would recall, remembering his own ill-advice which the New Yorkers thankfully never paid too much heed to: "They took a long time putting it out because they were a little worried about that gospel feeling that went with it. I thought it was not a good idea – of course I told Sam Cooke he should never go into the pop field, he was number one in gospel with a nice steady income, I spent an hour trying to talk him out of making a pop record!"

The record eventually appeared in record stores early in January 1955, backed with 'Come Back Baby'. The flip side looked like it might be the one to take off initially when it scored heavily in Atlanta after some heavy plugging from R&B DJ "Jockey Jack" on WERD, but by the end of the month it was 'I Got A Woman' that was climbing the national R&B Top 20 chart, hitting number two early in March. Indicative of the record's popularity was the release of an "answer record" (a regular follow-up to hits in the Fifties) by singer Geneva Valliere, 'You Said You Had A Woman', on the Cash label in Los Angeles. Suddenly, Ray Charles was a bona fide record star, selling to both black and white record buyers.

That same year other black rhythm & blues records by performers like Fats Domino and Little Richard impacted on predominantly white mainstream pop, producing – via the pioneering DJ Alan Freed, former country swing yodeller Bill Haley and a still-obscure Elvis Presley – a new teen-oriented music called rock'n'roll. On January 10, 1956, almost exactly a year after 'I Got A Woman' was released, Presley would cover the song in his first session for RCA records, at which he also recorded 'Heartbreak Hotel'.

The next session for Atlantic was another radio station set-up, this time in Miami. The band had been so busy on the road that Ray hardly found time to marry Della Bea, soon to have their son, early in April. But, as his bride must have realised, this was going to be the pattern of their married life. Jerry and Ahmet flew down to Florida for the recording, which was to take place in the small hours of the morning of April 23 after Ray and the band had finished playing a date with Faye Adams at the Palm in front of 10,000 people.

On the four numbers they laid down, the band's sound – Ray's sound to be exact – comes over as even more confident and focussed, than the tracks from the previous Atlantic session. There were two straight-ahead blues – the instrumental 'A Bit Of Soul', where the piano echoes the playing of the great blues pianist Jimmy Yancey before what sounds like an overdubbed alto solo from Ray, and 'Hard Times' on which his voice lays bare levels of emotion he'd hitherto only hinted at, the horns coming in with long-note church-tinged harmonies for the final two choruses. But it's the other two songs, 'This Little Girl Of Mine' and 'A Fool For You' that confirm the gospel influence as representing the radical central thrust of Ray Charles' musical development.

'This Little Girl Of Mine' is an infectious up-tempo shouter with a Latin feel to the rhythm, based closely on the gospel song 'This Little Light Of Mine', while on 'A Fool For You' Ray's performance represents the *delivery* as much as the structure of church music. The 6/8 double waltz-time with the piano straight from a revival meeting, horns expansive and preaching, Ray's voice singin' sanctified – this is truly spiritual music, but the confessional lyrics concern very earthly matters rather than any heavenly devotion. When he screams at the end of the final verse "Oh lord, I'm a fool for you" it could be the voice of a holy-rolling preacher, except he's calling the name of the Almighty to beseech the woman who doesn't return his love.

"It's very understandable to be able to relate the blues and gospel because they both are looking for the love, hope and faith in God . . . and of course, you're looking for the love, hope, faith and durability of your woman," Ray explained to writer Steve Turner in 1982. "If I use the word 'God' in a song it's strictly used in some kind of phrase to describe something like 'God, you're beautiful'. But never in terms of singing about God."

"Ray Charles has got the blues but he's cryin' sanctified. He's mixin' the blues with the spirituals. I know that's wrong. He should be singin' in a church," blues singer Big Bill Broonzy was to famously protest, and Clara Ward, the celebrated gospel singer, was adamant in her misgivings about his appropriation of 'This Little Light Of Mine' which was one of her best-known records. Blues and gospel were part of the same Black American culture, but to mix them was simply taboo. Yet when Ray *did* mix them, the potent result appealed to black audiences across the nation, and in doing so introduced a new music to that culture, a music that didn't have a name yet. When it did eventually acquire a label, its roots in religion were clearly acknowledged: it was known as soul music.

In his much-acclaimed account of black American music in the latter half of the 20th century, *The Death Of Rhythm & Blues*, Nelson George describes how, in linking the spiritual and the sexual, "Charles made pleasure [physical satisfaction] and joy [divine enlightenment] seem the same thing. By doing so he brought the realities of the Saturday-night sinner and Sunday-morning worshipper – so often one and the same – into a raucous harmony."

Quizzed in innumerable interviews as to the gospel roots of his music,

Ray clearly didn't see it as an issue: "It's like saying my music sounds like a lot of the old blues. If you say my music sounds like a lot of the old gospel songs, yeah, well, you're right. But, so what?" He sang gospel-style in the same spirit that he sang blues – and later country – as part of his natural musical make-up: "I personally feel that it was not a question of mixing gospel with the blues. It was a question of singin' the only way I knew how to sing. This was not a thing where I was tryin' to take the church music and make the blues out of it or vice versa. All I was tryin' to do was sing the only way I knew how, period."

Ray nevertheless stressed that in his view gospel as such *was* distinctly separate from the blues. "Church music is church music and blues is the blues. Some people want to connect up the two, and I guess in a way they are connected in some sense because they were both used for communicative purposes. They say the 'reels' or the blues is devil's music, and [that is] one of the reasons even today why, since I play jazz music, I won't record a religious album. Because in my teachings, I was brought up that you don't serve two gods. If you're gonna play the blues, then play the blues. If you're gonna do religious music, then do religious music . . . It may be antiquated, I don't know, but I still feel the same way today."

Fathead Newman recalled the fuss about Ray's "gospel" R&B soon dying down: "There was a bit of controversy over that, but it didn't last very long. People came to realise it was just what he was doing with his music, that was the direction the music was going in."

In his sleeve notes for *Ray Charles At Newport* in 1958, Kenneth Karpe even drew on the unlikely pen of George Bernard Shaw in reference to the argument – "Among the pious I am a scoffer: among the musical I am religious."

And where Ray led, eventually most followed. Chris Barber, the veteran British jazz musician, was a pioneer in promoting American blues singers in the UK when they toured with his band during the Fifties. He recalled how even Broonzy was to change his tune: "Outside the church the movement was beginning to spring up that said, 'This is just part of our experience, part of our music.' For instance, when Big Bill Broonzy first came here in 1950–51, he was booked to appear with the gospel singer Mahalia Jackson. She refused, and he agreed with her – you don't mix blues and religious music – yet by 1956 he was touring with us and accepted that he could throw in gospel numbers in the middle of his act."

And the tables were completely turned, as gospel expert Tony Heilbut would point out, when sacred singer James Cleveland "also cut Ray

Charles' 'Hallelujah I Love Her So' in 1959, an early acknowledgement by (a) gospel singer(s) that two could play at the same game."

It was Ray's blending of blues and gospel musical forms, Barber felt, that set him apart from any previous manifestations of gospel in the secular pop field. "The thing about Ray Charles is that there were so few singers, either when they were singing the original gospel music or gospel-influenced pop music, who had the gospel feel *and* the blues feel, in fact you could count them on the fingers of one hand. In gospel there are major chords, different harmonies, the whole thing is different. Later there were younger ones who came along who, having heard Ray and Aretha [Franklin], assume that is what you do and do have both. But up to that point Ray was the first, without any shadow of a doubt, to have both.

"If you listen to a lot of gospel groups from the Twenties and Thirties, they almost sound like barber-shop quartets, there's no blues in it at all, it's almost akin to traditional jazz in its harmonic concept. Blues chord sequences might exist in it, but it isn't done in a bluesy way. This resulted in the Mills Brothers in popular music. And you had the beginnings of the more soulful gospel music in the Thirties which came out in pop music as The Ink Spots, then you had the next line which came out as The Platters. These are all gospel styles simply transferred into popular music, with very little reference to the blues."

Barber also mentioned Professor Alex Bradford, known as the "Singing Rage of the Gospel Age" (who claimed his 'Can't Trust Nobody' was the origin of 'I Got A Woman') who was another who pioneered the extension of sacred songs to secular contexts, but from a gospel starting point: "Alex Bradford always says Ray Charles learned it all from him. You can hear all the religious part of Ray's style in Alex Bradford." As well as writing more gospel "standards" than any other performer in his time, Bradford also wrote for various friends in the rhythm & blues field, telling Tony Heilbut: "Ray Charles told me I was his ideal as a gospel singer, and if I ever wanted to send him a song, all I'd have to do is announce my name and he'd give it first preference."

When the band moved on from Florida, Ray began to put into place the final piece of the jigsaw that would complete the sound he was looking for – and which would make his music seem even more steeped in the rhythms and textures of the church. He'd gradually convinced himself that what a lot of the new numbers needed was the backing of some other voices, preferably a permanent vocal group, and he knew just where he might make the first step in that direction.

Mary Ann Fisher was a beautiful-looking blues singer who had sat in with the band a couple of weeks before they'd hit Miami, when they played a gig at the Army base in Fort Knox, Kentucky. On the strength of one song, Duke Ellington's 'I Got It Bad, And That Ain't Good', Ray had offered her a job with the band with her own feature spot, telling her they'd be back in the area in a few weeks' time and she could start then if she wanted to join them. Which, when they returned to Fort Knox, she did without hesitation.

Just as Ray had done a spot within Lowell Fulson's show, now Mary Ann was featured in *his* act, with a selection of blues, what Ray described as "sentimental and torch songs", supper-club smoochers like 'Black Coffee' (which Ray would record as an instrumental on 1956's *The Great Ray Charles*) and a Charles original 'What Kind Of Man Are You?' which she recorded sensationally backed by the fledgling Raelettes two years later. And when Ray teamed her with Don Wilkerson and Fathead Newman as a vocal trio, it was the embryo of the backing group he now knew he wanted. "He wanted to have some background singers, and he didn't have any background singers, so *we* were actually the first Raelettes!" Newman would recall. But it was clear in Ray's head that it would be an all-female group when it happened: "I wanted more . . . I wanted to hear several female voices behind me – a strong feminine sound to enhance my vocals."

Ray and Mary Ann's relationship soon developed into something more than merely professional, although on-the-road romances – or at least sexual liaisons – were nothing new to him. Ray Charles was a consummate womaniser, and any domestic arrangements concerning girlfriends, wives or even parenthood, were filed away as a quite separate element from his day-to-day agenda. Be it women, drink or drugs, what went on when he was working – and he was working most of the time – wasn't mentioned on the home front, by tacit and mutual consent. His 15-year marriage to Della probably only lasted as long as it did because this was the case.

Conversely, as he saw it, he generally fulfilled his family responsibilities to the best of his ability, given the nature of his working lifestyle. This was certainly true after Ray Charles Robinson Jr arrived on May 25, 1955, although typically, after a brief trip to Dallas to hold his new-born son for the first time – "He was so small I was scared I'd hurt him . . . he felt like the most delicate creature I had ever touched" – Ray was back on the road.

Atlantic released 'A Fool For You' and 'This Little Girl Of Mine' at the beginning of June, and the single soon followed 'I Got A Woman' to number two in the R&B chart. As the band continued their still predominantly southern schedules of one-nighters, a crucial alteration in personnel occurred; after an argument with Ray concerning drugs, Don Wilkerson left the band, Fathead moving onto tenor sax with Emmott "Jay" Dennis stepping in on baritone. From here on Fathead Newman was to leave an indelible mark on the sound of the Ray Charles band of the Fifties. But an even more memorable change in the line-up would manifest itself for the first time at the next recording session, when Ray's ambition for an all-girl group to provide backing vocals materialised at last. Significantly, the inspiration was firmly rooted in the church, as he would tell David Ritz: "People like James Cleveland and Albertina Walker and the Davis Sisters. I loved their background sounds, the way the girls echoed and built up the lead vocal. Loved the contrast."

In October, Atlantic put out a single taken from the 'I Got A Woman' Atlanta session, coupling 'Greenbacks' and 'Blackjack' in what would be another appearance by Ray Charles in the R&B Top Five, and by the end of November Ray was ready to record again. This time it was in the company's own studio in New York City, and as usual Jesse Stone was in charge of booking any session musicians. When Ray suggested they add some female voices as extra backing, Stone brought in a vocal trio that he'd helped to put together the year before, and who'd recently made number nine in the R&B chart with their Atlantic single 'In Paradise'. They'd also done backing vocals on the label for LaVern Baker, Ivory Joe Hunter, Joe Turner and Chuck Willis, whose 'It's Too Late' with the trio Ray particularly liked. Called The Cookies, they comprised Marjorie "Margie" Hendricks, Ethel McRae and Dorothy Jones.

Of the four tracks laid down on November 30, three – 'What Would I Do Without You', 'Mary Ann' and 'Hallelujah I Love Her So' – were written by Ray. 'Mary Ann' is a sexy tribute to his on-the-road paramour, its funky Latin percussion passages – which Atlantic sax star King Curtis used as an instrumental tune called 'Chilli' some years later – breaking into straight mid-tempo R&B from time to time. 'What Would I Do Without You' features a tenor solo by Don Wilkerson who was brought in specially for the session, and is an early example of Ray merging a country feel with gospel. 'Hallelujah', is Ray Charles in joyful mood, again his sanctified-sounding celebration being not about any saviour in heaven but his "baby" who lives next door:

> *Every morning 'fore the sun comes up*
> *She brings me coffee in my favourite cup*
> *That's how I know, yes I know,*
> *Hallelujah I just love her so*

'Hallelujah', as well as making the R&B best-sellers and marking another crossover into the young white market, was destined to be one of *the* classic anthems in the Ray Charles songbook.

The fourth track, 'Drown In My Own Tears' was written by Henry Glover, and originally a big seller in 1952 for Sonny Thompson with a vocal by Lulu Reed. In Ray's hands it became an emotionally charged lament backed by what can only be described as ecclesiastical horns, and played in the waltz-inflected time signature that has more in common with the prayer meeting than the dance hall.

Then, drenched in echo, on the last chorus we hear for the first time the full erotic power of Ray with a vocal group – what Jerry Wexler would describe in his autobiography as "the 'amen corner' that became an institution in pop music" and explain to me in more detail. "In the Baptist church, the black churches, there would be one group of particularly devout and responsive congregants who would gather together and would do the 'amens' and the call and response, and their 'amen corner' became sort of a metaphor for particularly fervent believers."

In Ray's hands it became a secular baptism in sound that while clearly appealing to the senses was to herald a new music of the soul.

7

The Right Time

"After Ray had a series of hits, a lot of musicians began to talk about him. They weren't all rhythm & blues musicians . . . one of the first people to tell me he liked Ray Charles was Miles Davis."

– Nesuhi Ertegun

It was another six months before Ray teamed up with The Cookies again, and two years before they evolved into his regular backing group which eventually became known as The Raelettes. In the meantime, it was life on the road as usual. And usual meant the almost exclusively black rhythm & blues circuit. It was the trek of clubs, ballrooms and theatres where, although Ray Charles was now more often than not top of the bill, he still had sometimes to look out for being short-changed on cash, booking the right (coloured) hotel, even sitting in the right end of the diner or choosing the non-white bathroom on a road stop. But "looking out" was not an option for Ray; he had the ears, but for his eyes he depended on the reliable loyalty and support of Jeff Brown.

Ray's relationship with Jeff Brown had come a long way since the Dallas taxi driver was hired to drive the Lowell Fulson band bus five years earlier. Right away they'd established a rapport, Jeff looking after the blind piano player when he needed a little help finding this, or the directions to that. It was Jeff who made sure road manager Wilbur Brassfield observed the single-dollar-bill policy when paying Ray, and Jeff who would spring to his defence when the other musicians' taunts and teasing got too much.

It was Jeff Brown who Ray, on leaving the Fulson outfit, promised to hire as manager just as soon as he got his own band together. Which of course he did, and by 1956 Brown was not just his boss' eyes, but all-round Mr Fix-it. It was Jeff who liaised with promoters, fixed recording dates with Atlantic, kept the show on the road, ensured Ray's strict

Ray Charles Robinson: a studio publicity shot from the late Fifties. *(Michael Ochs Archive/Redferns)*

Ray's old boss, rhythm and blues star Lowell Fulson. *(Michael Ochs Archive/Redferns)*

Charles Brown, along with Nat "King" Cole one of Ray's early idols and stylistic role models. *(Michael Ochs Archive/Redferns)*

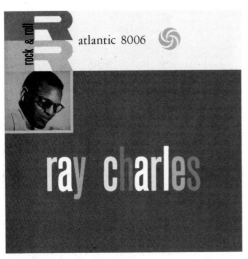

rock & roll
atlantic 8006

ray charles

Ray's first album - sub-titled *Rock & Roll* – released in 1957.

'What Kind Of Man Are You' – Mary Ann Fisher in the mid-Fifties. *(Michael Ochs Archive/Redferns)*

Atlantic supremos (left to right) Jerry Wexler, Ahmet Ertegun and Miriam Abramson, with stars of the label's R&B roster in the background. *(Hulton Archive/Getty Images)*

'Soul' singing before it had a name – Ray Charles in the mid-Fifties. *(Michael Ochs Archive/Redferns)*

Ray at the Newport Jazz Festival, July 1958. *(Hulton Archive/Redferns)*

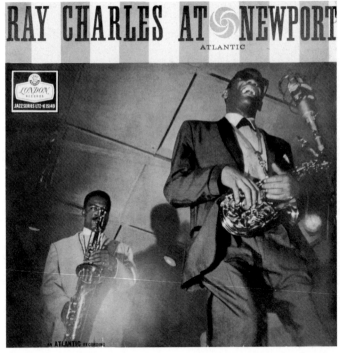

The iconic cover of the Newport live album, with a photograph by Lee Friedlander.

Soul brother – jazz vibraphone star Milt Jackson.
(Mosaic Images/Corbis)

Ray's lifelong friend Quincy Jones, already a musical
force in the Fifties. *(Christian Him/Jazz Index)*

The man who helped create the Atlantic sound – and launch Ray Charles – producer Jerry Wexler. *(Michael Ochs Archives/Redferns)*

Atlantic founders, the Ertegun brothers Ahmet (left) and Nesuhi. *(William Gottlieb/Redferns)*

Ray in full flight at a late-Fifties club date with the small band. *(Paul Hoeffler/Redferns)*

Ray running through charts and at the piano, at a studio recording session. *(Michael Ochs Archive/Redferns)*

Tenor sax maestro of the Ray Charles band, and many of his classic recordings, David "Fathead" Newman. *(Mosaic Images/Corbis)*

Ray signs to ABC-Paramount; here with label president Sam Clarke in December 1959.
(Michael Ochs Archives/Redferns)

Spin-off album from the 'What'd I Say' single, released in Britain on the London label in 1960.

The press greet Ray and The Raelettes at D'Orley Airport, Paris, 1961. *(Mephisto/Rex Features)*

demarcation between domestic family and on-the-road "friends" was always observed, and calmed down the all-too-frequent arguments that flared up among the musicians – the latter usually involving drugs.

Ray had been injecting heroin regularly since his earliest days in Seattle when, as an eager-for-experience youngster, he literally pestered fellow user musicians till they gave him a taste, as he later described in *Rolling Stone* magazine: "I was about maybe 17, 18 years old . . . I wanted to be among the big fellas, like cats in the band . . . and I wanted to be a part, so I begged and pleaded until somebody said, 'Okay, man, goddamn it, come on . . .'" Although not all the musicians on the scene were junkies, there were drugs around in abundance, and once someone acquired a liking for the "hit", it was all too easy to develop a habit: "Once I started, I saw no reason to stop. In those days, it didn't even cost that much."

Sometimes within the music fraternity, and especially in the close-knit society of a touring band, alliances would develop along the lines of users and non-users, junkies and (as they saw it) straights. The whole essentially private – but shared – ritual of shooting up created a bond between the users and at the same time alienated outsiders. It was just this alienation that had led to Gossie McKee's disaffection with the McSon Trio where Ray and Milt Garrett were both on heroin, and conversely the bond that drew Ray and Fathead Newman together long before the sax player was recruited into the band.

Business-wise a heroin habit could prove a liability, even if the user had it seemingly under control – a junkie was simply considered unreliable. A major argument Wilbur Brassfield used when lobbying for Ray to be sacked from the Fulson band was that his drug use was causing problems. Likewise when Ray was trying to convince the Shaw agency and booker Howard Lewis that he should have his own band, both had their reservations on account of his habit – could he hold a band together?

Many would ask why these same business concerns should not find it in their interest to help get an artist like Ray off drugs, but there has always been very much a laissez-faire attitude in the music industry to the issue. If it didn't drastically interfere with live appearances or record "product", it was the musicians' problem, not theirs. Plus the fact that dope-taking in the music business was not restricted to the performers. Ray's closest contact in the Shaw agency for instance, Billy Shaw's son Milt, had been a heroin user since first starting in the business as a teenager in the late Forties.

It was a dispute over drugs that led to Donald Wilkerson leaving the band in mid–1955, and again on a particularly violent occasion when bass player Whiskey Sheffield smashed his instrument to pieces. And as always it was Jeff Brown who had to straighten things out, calm people down, massage bruised egos and placate nervous promoters. No such diplomacy could prevent near-disaster, however, when the band was busted for dope just a couple of weeks before the 'Hallelujah' recording session.

They were playing Philadephia, the Town Hall Ballroom, and Ray, Fathead, Roosevelt "Whiskey" Sheffield and Jay Dennis were ensconced behind locked doors in the band room, shooting up dope, when the police burst in. The drug squad had been tipped off by the promoter, and immediately arrested the four, plus drummer Bill Peeples who was in possession of some marijuana. Just for good measure the cops took in the rest of the outfit too – except for Jeff Brown – including Mary Ann, holding them in the police station cells until the magistrate's hearing the next morning.

Although it was clear which musicians had been using narcotics at the time of the raid, the magistrate decided they should all be held on $2,000 bail pending trial. Ray claimed he didn't know what he was injecting, he thought it was probably an anti-flu shot, and Jeff bailed him out. The two made for New York, where a lawyer negotiated a deal with the Philly police in which Ray paid $6,000 for all charges to be dropped. It was a classic shake-down, the hand-out ensuring there would be no further recourse to the process of law, and after a week inside, the rest of the band were released, travelling to Dallas where they were to wait for Jeff and Ray.

This was why Ray had done the 'Hallelujah' session with a studio line-up hired by Jesse Stone, that included ex-band members Don Wilkerson and trumpeter Joe Bridgewater. Plus of course Raelettes-to-be, The Cookies.

The first release from that session, right at the start of 1956, was 'Drown In My Own Tears' backed with 'Mary Ann', which by the end of March had put Ray's name once again in the R&B best-sellers nationwide. The next time he and the band were in the studio, during May, the sound Ray had been aiming for with a fully integrated vocal group backing would be realised, and the results were sensational.

The session was in the New York studios, and The Cookies featured heavily on all three tracks recorded that day. 'You Better Leave My Woman Alone' (an adaptation of the gospel song 'You Better Leave That Liar Alone') is an up-tempo call-and-response number with the three girls establishing the chorus line, allowing Ray greater freedom to improvise than he'd hitherto enjoyed on record, especially on the ride-out before the closing reprise of the vocal riff. With an instrumental opening that's a pre-cursor to the intro of 'Busted' recorded some seven years later, the other Charles original 'I Want To Know' is a loping 12-bar blues, The Cookies repeating the title phrase under Ray's vocal.

But it's the Doc Pomus song 'Lonely Avenue' that sends most shivers down the spine, a doomy mid-tempo blues in which the only let-up from the bleak lyric is Fathead's authoritative tenor break. At the time of its release it was described as a "black 'Heartbreak Hotel'" in some quarters, and not without justification. Where Elvis Presley tells us he's *found a new place to dwell . . . down at the end of lonely street, at Heartbreak Hotel*, conclud-ing *I get so lonely I could die*, Ray describes how *I live on a lonely avenue, Little girl, since you said you're through* with The Cookies joining him to reinforce his message at the end of each verse

> *I could die, I could die, I could die*
> *I could cry, I could cry, I could cry*
> *I live on a Lonely Avenue*

Elvis' first national hit was still riding high in the *Billboard* pop charts, having just slipped off the number one spot after eight weeks in pole position. It would be hard to think that someone didn't have this in mind when the Pomus song – which has a not dissimilar structure to the chart-topper – was chosen for the session. But as was often the case in songwriting in the Fifties – and indeed since – there would be more than one "inspiration" suggested for the song. In his 1971 book *The Gospel Sound*, Tony Heilbut points to strong similarities between 'Lonely Avenue' and 'How Jesus Died' by The Pilgrim Travellers' Jess Whitaker.

Presley was in the vanguard of the rock'n'roll revolution taking place in pop music, a revolution driven by a new, younger audience for music that was still not far removed from its rhythm & blues roots. And when RCA Records followed 'Heartbreak Hotel' with Elvis' debut album *Elvis Presley*, which shot to number one on the LP chart and stayed there for the next 10 weeks, there on the third track of side one was 'I Got A Woman', recorded at the same session as the hit single. In fact Elvis had laid down a version of the song when he was still with Sun Records in February 1955, just two months after Ray's release, though it never appeared on disc.

In the meantime Atlantic released 'Hallelujah I Love Her So' and 'What Would I Do Without You', the single marking another entry in the R&B

Top 10 with sales that were increasingly shared between black and white record buyers. This racial mix in the market for rhythm & blues was an accelerating trend as radio jocks around the country followed the lead of pioneers like Cleveland's Alan Freed (by now broadcasting out of New York City) and Zenas "Daddy" Sears in Atlanta, playing the music of Fats Domino and Joe Turner, The Clovers, Ruth Brown and Ray Charles as a natural part of the new rock'n'roll agenda.

The single's climb up the R&B list was followed in the same direction in September '56 by 'Lonely Avenue' backed with 'Leave My Woman Alone'. Then, between the ever-rigorous touring, came three days of recording sessions in New York with the band, on November 20, 26 and 27. On the third date they cut four R&B sides, but what went before was of more significance in many ways – it was the first opportunity the band had been given, jazz players to a man, to record some 100 per cent jazz instrumentals, something they probably yearned to do given that every night they played a jazz set before Ray and Mary Ann performed any vocals.

The jazz sessions were produced by Ahmet Ertegun's brother Nesuhi, and were a follow-on from some instrumental tracks he'd cut with Ray seven months earlier. Nesuhi, who had come into the company in a full-time active way in 1954, had joined specifically to develop the label's jazz catalogue, and by April 1956 had signed a number of jazz luminaries including Shorty Rogers, Lennie Tristano and The Modern Jazz Quartet. Nesuhi was keen to record Ray in a strictly jazz context, and was aware of the buzz he was creating among that fraternity, often musicians who rarely took much notice of rhythm & blues players: "After Ray had a series of hits, a lot of musicians began to talk about him. They weren't all rhythm & blues musicians . . . one of the first people to tell me he liked Ray Charles was Miles Davis who said, 'You've got a fantastic man there, you know, you should do something more with him. He's great in what he's doing, but he can do more than that.'"

The April session had been with just a trio – Ray plus the great Oscar Pettiford on bass and Joe Harris on drums. Ray Charles' marriage of blues and gospel with modern bebop style piano is at its most apparent when stripped to this basic instrumentation, a synthesis the sleeve note by Gary Kramer describes as "a stimulating blending of the essences of jazz without attempting an antiquarian restoration". The trio recorded four items: a self-penned blues 'Dawn Ray', two standards – 'Black Coffee' and George

Gershwin's 'The Man I Love' – and a version of the jaunty pop song 'Music, Music, Music' which inspired Leonard Feather to comment, "With the right improvisatory approach and an adequate harmonic basis you can take almost any tune and make it swing."

The band that laid down the rest of the jazz tracks in November consisted of Newman and Dennis on saxes, Joe Bridgewater (who was back in the fold regularly) and John Hunt on trumpets, Roosevelt Sheffield on bass and drummer Peeples. At least six of the tracks featured arrangements by Quincy Jones, and over the two sessions the material ranged from laid-back blues to a clutch of standards that included Fats Waller's 'Ain't Misbehavin'' with a full-on solo from Fathead, 'My Melancholy Baby' and 'I Surrender Dear', plus a working of Charlie Shavers' 'Undecided' charted by Quincy and Ernie Wilkins that exuded the swinging confidence of an Ellington small group. And a soulful instrumental version of 'A Fool For You' entitled 'Sweet Sixteen Bars', with just Ray and the rhythm section, which laid bare how near the surface the church was in his piano playing, a point he explained in the sleeve notes to the subsequent album *The Great Ray Charles*: "All music is related. Gospel music background is important to a jazz musician, for it draws out feeling. What you speak of as *soul* in jazz is *soul* in gospel music. The important thing in jazz is to feel your music, but to *really* feel it and believe it . . ."

This mention of *soul* in jazz was evidence of a developing attitude among black musicians in America which very soon became a fashionable style. It's highly significant that Ray was using the phrase as early as 1957, when the album was released, as he was always considered one of the, if not *the*, original influences in what became the "soul jazz" movement.

There had been a tendency for hip black musicians of the bebop era to shun reminders of the poverty and hardship of the rural South where most had their roots, and that included the down-home sounds of country blues and fiery gospel meetings. But with the emerging civil rights movement a new pride in Afro-American ethnic culture developed, a pride that was to very soon manifest itself in music. Ahmet Ertegun, for one, felt that Ray Charles and others played a key role in bringing this about: "In the Thirties and Forties, not a jazz player would play blues changes. And if they did, they'd try to hide it. They must have felt that blues were retrogression. It was only with the advent of people like Ray Charles, who was not only a great blues singer and player, but a great jazz musician, that black performers came to realise that blues was their heritage."

The author and academic Gerald Early would go as far as to describe it as a conscious move by players to "ethnicise" jazz: "Black musicians were saying, 'We're going to invent a musical style and form that white people can't copy . . . it's going to be so ethnicised that they really can't copy it without absolutely looking like a minstrel show.' "

Writing in the Black American magazine *Ebony*, Lerone Bennett Jr described how . . . "New York musicians began in the late Fifties to reassess the Negro folk idiom – the cries, chants, shouts, work songs and pulsating rhythmic vitality of gospel singers and shouting choirs." He spoke of "one of the most astounding about-faces in jazz history" as conservatory-trained musicians "turned from the academy and faced the store-front church."

Certainly around the mid-Fifties hard boppers like Art Blakey and Cannonball Adderley (who Ray had sat in with in the student band of the Florida Agricultural and Mechanical College in Tallahassee when he was 13 years old) had started employing the terms "funk" and "soul" to describe their gospel-driven, call-and-response style instrumentals, and Ray was a major source of inspiration: alto sax player Jackie McLean described "soul" as being "rooted in what Ray Charles sings, blues and gospel music." As writer Roy Carr recalled: "Horace Silver, Art Blakey and Cannonball Adderley were the first to admit that all those classic small band sides Ray Charles cut for Atlantic Records . . . determined the sanctified stance of their own ground-breaking quintets."

So it was doubly significant that the most outstanding take in an out-standing couple of days in the studio was a number by one of the above-mentioned architects of "soul" jazz, Horace Silver. 'Doodlin'' is as cool as it gets in terms of light, swinging blues, with sublimely understated saxes and muted trumpets prefacing solos by Joe Bridgewater and Fathead. When *The Great Ray Charles* was released in August 1957, this was the track that had the biggest impact on those jazz musicians who hadn't already cottoned on to Ray's music.

By the end of the decade, "soul" was the most commercially successful end of the jazz spectrum, reflected in hugely popular albums by the likes of Adderley, Blakey, Silver, Lee Morgan, Bobby Timmons, Hank Mobley and organ star Jimmy Smith; albums whose very titles – *The Sermon, Home Cookin', Soul Stirrin', Them Dirty Blues* – made it absolutely clear where they were coming from. The development of the style was a perfectly natural one given the background of the musicians concerned, but Ray's synthesis of gospel, blues and jazz ahead of any of them was certainly influential, as Horace Silver would obliquely acknowledge.

"There was no conscious movement, just certain individuals happened to be doing a similar thing. It doesn't relate to bebop as such, it was sort of a natural thing with me . . . I've always liked gospel, always liked the blues, it kind of naturally crept into my music, something I subconsciously incorporated into my writing and into my playing. It's evident that Ray Charles had his roots in gospel and blues, so he was onto a funky thing because I suppose he must have grown up in that environment like most black people do, but then some are more influenced by it than others.

"Ray was into rhythm & blues, while Art Blakey and myself, we were into jazz, but some of that rhythm & blues and gospel infiltrated itself into our music – some of our music, not all of it. Ray Charles is a great musician, and his basic roots are rhythm & blues and gospel. Now he loves jazz too, but he has infiltrated a little jazz into his style of writing and playing and singing, but his basic roots are R&B and gospel. My basic roots are jazz, and *I've* infiltrated a little of the gospel and the blues. So it's the reverse with both of us."

On the sleeve of the 1961 Atlantic compilation LP *The Genius Sings The Blues*, pianist Billy Taylor wrote of Ray ". . . he should be credited along with Horace Silver and the other 'soul brothers' with leading the modern jazz musicians back to another of the many sources of jazz inspiration still present in its original form."

The day after the second batch of jazz recordings, the band was back in the studio to lay down four R&B numbers, the up-tempo 'Get On The Right Track', an atmospherically sorrowful 'It's All Right', and the two strongest items 'Ain't That Love' and 'Rockhouse'.

'Rockhouse' was a solid two-parter instrumental with Ray's boogie-style walking bass figure underpinning a piano riff deftly punctuated by the horns. Bill Doggett's 'Honky Tonk' was a current double-sided instrumental that had been in the pop charts since August, reaching number two, and it seems hardly coincidental that Ray and the Atlantic team should contemplate a similar release. However, 'Rockhouse, Parts 1 and 2' wasn't to appear as a single until two years later.

With a tambourine intro straight out of a church meeting, 'Ain't That Love' was a hand-clapping excursion into sanctified territory with The Cookies offering a call-and-response answer to Ray's exclamatory vocal lines, and, backed by the angelic harmonies of the girls, one of Fathead's finest R&B breaks committed to tape. Jerry, Ahmet and Ray agreed it was a must for the next single release, in January 1957.

Ray and the band's touring schedule through 1956 and 1957 reminds one of the montage of place names beloved of Hollywood show-biz biopics, while the list of stars with whom they shared bills up and down the country reads like a who's who of mid-Fifties rhythm & blues. Muddy Waters, Chuck Willis, The Flamingos, J.B. Lenoir, B.B. King, The Moonglows, Mickey & Sylvia – all and many more co-starred live with Ray Charles between June '56 and January '57. He was getting major exposure on the gigging circuit, which endeared him to the predom-inantly (though by no means exclusively) black audiences, but his records still didn't quite make it out of the R&B charts into the mainstream pop field. By May, with another single coming on the market – 'It's All Right' and 'Get On The Right Track' from the November session – it was deemed time to get back in the studio.

The four tracks laid down on May 28 again confirmed various aspects of Ray Charles' ever-developing repertoire during this period. 'That's Enough' is a powerful exchange between Ray and The Cookies based on a gospel song of the same title by Dorothy Love Coates, the smooth voices of the girls' answering in potent contrast to Ray's harder-edged bidding. And once again, Fathead Newman's solo break positively crackles with energy. The ladies of the ensemble are a similarly intrinsic part of the dynamic on 'Talkin' 'Bout You' – a 16-bar chanter similar in structure to 'I Got A Woman', based on 'Talkin' 'Bout Jesus' – their completely inte-grated role in the overall arrangements now confirming, track after track, that they are an essential part of what is quickly evolving as the classic Ray Charles sound.

The cheekily titled 'Swanee River Rock (Talkin' 'Bout That River)' represented a new departure for Ray. It was one thing reworking standards from the great American songwriters of the 20th century, as jazz singers of every calibre had always done, but something else entirely to take an overtly sentimental song from the pre-phonograph days of the 19th century and give it his gospel-blues treatment. Yet that's exactly what he did with Stephen Foster's 'Old Folks At Home' (more popularly referred to as 'Swanee River'). The nearest precedent in the rhythm & blues field had come a year before when Fats Domino charted with 'My Blue Heaven', but that previously anodyne ditty was from 1927, the Foster song dated back to 1851. It was an early signal that Ray's choice of material would recognise few boundaries.

And if the participation of a female vocal group in Ray's music needed further confirmation, the answer came in the most sensational track from the session, a Ray Charles original on which Ray didn't sing a note. Over his churchy waltz-time piano he leaves it to Mary Ann Fisher and The Cookies to voice 'What Kind Of Man Are You?', one of the most emotionally charged recordings of that or any other era. When Mary Ann pleads

> *I, I, I just can't satisfy*
> *Oh yeah, no matter how I try*
> *Yeah, yeah, why do you tell me lies?*

her soaring pitch-perfect delivery straight out of Sunday choir but expressing more sensual desires than are ever uttered in church, we're listening to as concise a musical definition of "soul" as anything Ray would sing himself. Whether the lyrics – *I'm always left alone, How long can this go on* etc – referred specifically to his relationship with Mary Ann at that stage is a matter of conjecture.

Atlantic had decided to shelve the jazz album, which would be made up of a selection of the trio tracks from April '56 and the band sides recorded the following November, until after the release of his first vocal long-player. Called simply *Ray Charles*, this was a collection of tracks that had all appeared on singles, the earliest being 'Mess Around' from four years previously. It was the sixth in an opportunistically titled series called "Rock & Roll" in which the company packaged their top R&B artists with an eye on the broader pop record market.

The album liner notes by Guy Remark indicated how the market for Ray Charles as a live performer was indeed broadening by the middle of 1957: "Anyone who has followed him on one of his trans-continental one-nighter treks that Ray continually makes, and had seen the thousand that greet him everywhere . . . knows that it is no exaggeration to say that Ray Charles has already become a legendary figure." Flamboyant PR-speak maybe, but a clue to how Ray's burgeoning popularity was still best measured in terms of his concert performances rather than record sales – a situation that a disappointing reaction to his debut LP did nothing to alleviate. His singles were regularly making the R&B charts, the one-nighters were now almost inevitably sell-outs, but he had still to crack the lucrative mass record market represented by the pop charts. It was a situation which would finally start to change when 'Swanee River Rock' entered *Billboard*'s Top 100 late in the year.

The jazz album, *The Great Ray Charles*, was released in late August 1957, featuring just one of the earlier trio tracks – 'Black Coffee' – and seven with members of the band. The other three tracks from April '56, along with another five items from the November band sessions, would not appear until 1961 as *The Genius After Hours*. And as that first jazz album was hitting the stores, in early September Ray was back in the New York studio to cut some more jazz sides, this time with Milt Jackson, the virtuoso vibraphone player from Atlantic's biggest jazz outfit The Modern Jazz Quartet.

Studio engineer Tom Dowd remembered Ray raving about Jackson's playing some months earlier, and Nesuhi Ertegun, as jazz supremo on the label, put the idea to Milt of the two making an album together. "In those days I did all the recordings of The Modern Jazz Quartet, so of course I saw Milt Jackson maybe three times a week. I must have cut 25 albums with the MJQ which I produced myself, so I suggested to Milt – who strangely in those days was a bigger name than Ray Charles, especially on an album cover, Ray was a singles R&B artist and jazz and rhythm & blues were still separate then – 'How about making an album with Ray Charles?' and he said, 'God, I would love it . . . I love the way he plays,' and then I talked to Ray and he said, 'Yeah, he's one of my favourite musicians.'"

Nesuhi booked some stellar names to accompany the pair in a line-up that featured Basie tenor sax man Billy Mitchell, guitarist Skeeter Best, Oscar Pettiford on bass, and the MJQ's drummer Connie Kay. But the icing on the cake as far as instrumentation was concerned was the unusual instance of Milt Jackson playing both piano and guitar at various points, and Ray Charles laying down some incisive solos on alto sax – something that was completely unexpected as far as Ertegun was concerned. "Ray came with an instrument case, so after a while I said, 'What's in there?' and he said, 'An alto sax.' I said, 'Alto? Who's gonna play it?' and he said, 'Me.' I said, 'I never knew you played alto sax,' so he said, 'I wanna try to take a chorus on the blues – I just want to see, if it's no good tell me, we won't use it' – and he does, and it was brilliant. I mean, his technique is a little rough, but he sure could play the saxophone . . . it was a surprise to all of us."

Ray's alto solos are indeed among the high points, with a primitive, edgy tone and sparse phrasing which echoes his own blues voice as much as that of any saxophone stylist. The totally relaxed recordings, Nesuhi assured me, were completely unrehearsed, with all the musicians addressing themselves to the simple challenge of just "playin' the blues" as masters of both their instruments and the genre itself. The resulting album featured particularly extensive work-outs in 'Soul Brothers', Leroy Carr's 'How Long Blues' and 'Blue Funk', all eight or nine minutes long.

In the liner notes of a 1970 all-instrumental Atlantic compilation, *The Best Of Ray Charles*, Ralph J. Gleason described the "illusion of simplicity" of 'How Long Blues'. "It sounds so easy but it is impossible to duplicate, and it is not only because of the infinite shading of phrasing and time but because of some other almost mystical quality that is the essence of jazz communication."

The title of the Jackson album couldn't have been more apt. "The words 'Soul Brothers' which we used for the title of the album were something Milt Jackson actually said in a conversation with me. He said, 'We should record together, we're soul brothers,' so it stuck in my mind, that that should be the LP title."

Ahmet Ertegun claims that it was only after the phrase appeared as the album title that it gradually became part of the language. "Nobody called anybody 'soul brother' in those days . . . I mean now 'soul brother' means a black person, but it didn't mean that then. What we meant by 'soul brother' was that they [Jackson and Charles] had a commonality of spirit." So *Soul Brothers* it was, released in mid-1958, with a track that was not included – 'Bags Of Blues' – eventually appearing with takes from an April '58 Charles/Jackson session as *Soul Meeting* in 1961.

"Ray Charles at 26 is obviously one of the most successful of the rock'n' roll performers," wrote Bill Randle on the *Soul Brothers* cover, managing to identify Ray with four musical disciplines in three simple sentences. "His band is a great blues band and his vocal style, obviously inspired by gospel influences, is a joy to hear. He is one of the very few jazzmen who have been able to be successful in more than one field of the music business."

While the band swung on its seemingly never-ending tour of one-night stands through the South and Southeast, 'Swanee River Rock' became Ray's 15th single released by Atlantic, immediately scoring in the R&B charts. More significantly however, in November 1957 it became Ray Charles' first-ever entry in the national pop charts at number 70, making it to the Top 50 in December when it reached number 42. Its popularity was confirmed when Ray's version of the song was covered on the Capitol label by rock'n'roll saxophone ace (and ex-Charles Brown sideman) Plas Johnson.

Meanwhile, through the autumn *The Great Ray Charles* had also been performing strongly both at the cash registers and on radio. Two tracks in particular caught the attention of on-air DJs, 'Doodlin'' and 'Sweet Sixteen Bars', so much so that Atlantic decided to release them as either side of an extended play (EP) 45. When 7-inch 45rpm discs took over from 10-inch 78s in the mid-Fifties, the EP became popular with record buyers where four rather than two regular songs were packaged on one disc, rather like a mini-LP. In this case it was the ideal format for two tracks that were nearly twice the length of the average single and, as the end of 1957 approached, Atlantic Records' top-selling single, EP and LP were all by Ray Charles.

At the end of November Ray achieved one of his long-time ambitions as he topped the bill at Harlem's Apollo Theater, after making his debut there back in February 1952 when he was a "feature spot" name with the Lowell Fulson band. And the increasing respect being accorded him by the jazz world was evident when he was invited to appear on an all-star bill at the prestigious Carnegie Hall, alongside Dizzy Gillespie, Thelonious Monk, John Coltrane and the first lady of jazz singing, Billie Holiday. Ray was particularly impressed by Holiday, even though her voice wasn't what it had been "she could still whip your ass just from her experience". Kenneth Lee Karpe, who presented the event, recalled the concert: "It was the first time Ray appeared before a jazz audience and since his previous recordings were geared for the rhythm & blues audience, the Carnegie patrons did not know what to expect. Ray Charles gave himself completely to that audience and they embraced him with a warmth seldom felt in any concert hall."

Reviewing the Carnegie Hall concert for the December 7 edition of the *New Yorker*, critic Whitney Balliett wrote: "The (Dizzy Gillespie) band also dished up accompaniment for Ray Charles, a blues singer and pianist, who apparently awed by his surroundings, at first offered a variety of timid and unoriginal piano solos on standard tunes, and then finally, as if in defiance, sang a raucous and moving version of 'I Want A Little Girl', which startled the audience into its first big response of the evening."

There were a few changes in the personnel of the Ray Charles band through the latter half of 1957. In the summer New Orleans trumpeter Wallace Davenport, who Ray had played with years before in the Crescent City, joined the line-up for just two months, though he would be a more permanent part of Ray's bigger orchestra some time later. Likewise baritone sax man Leroy Cooper – "Hog" as he was known on account of his size – came in around the same time, only to leave at the end of the year, then return for lengthy spells with Ray that saw him as a part of the outfit for the next decade and a half.

Cooper had crossed paths with both Fathead and Ray long before he actually joined the band's ranks. Another product of the fertile Dallas R&B circuit, he first heard of Ray Charles through sax player Stanley Turrentine who was working with Ray in the Lowell Fulson band. "Stanley Turrentine kept telling us about this fantastic piano player who was blind," said Cooper.

And Hog and Fathead had played together on numerous occasions – they were both on the 1954 Lowell Fulson date that produced the hit 'Reconsider Baby' – so it was hardly surprising that Newman offered his friend a chance to join the Charles band when Jay Dennis left in mid-1957. "Fathead Newman was playing baritone and living in Dallas – I knew him locally because I'm from Dallas – and he wanted me to play baritone so he could go to the tenor, so that's the way I went into the band," Leroy would recall. "I was on another gig, and the gig folded. So Ray Charles' manager called me the same day, and I thought somebody was pulling my leg. I said, 'I can't believe this.'"

It was all change in the rhythm section too. Two years or so on the road was enough for drummer Bill Peeples, his place being taken by Milt Turner, while bass player Whiskey Sheffield was succeeded by Edgar Willis. Willis – soon dubbed "the Peeper" because of his glasses and scholarly look – would stay a regular fixture in the Ray Charles ensemble through to the late Seventies, eventually doubling as bass player and road manager.

It was Edgar Willis who made possible an interview I conducted with Ray in 1975, as a result of first meeting him in Liverpool when the Charles band was playing there in 1964; he and some of the guys wanted to know where musicians hung out for a late-night drink – I told them I knew just the place. The Blue Angel club was famous for impromptu jam sessions, usually involving members of the then-booming local R&B scene, but none so memorable than that night when Willis and a couple of other Charles sidemen graced its stage. Sadly Edgar died in 1993.

Rather grandly cited on some Atlantic record covers by his full name of Bennie Ross Crawford, Hank Crawford as he was usually known was recommended to Ray by John Hunt and Milt Turner, both graduates of Tennessee State University which Crawford also attended. "There was a couple of my friends in the band a little bit ahead of me – Milt Turner, who was the drummer, and John Hunt, who was a trumpet player,"

Crawford would recall. "I was in school in Nashville at the time. I'm from Memphis, and I was going to Tennessee State. Those two guys were from Nashville. Ray came through Nashville to do a concert. At the time, Leroy Cooper had just took a little leave of absence, a little break. And Ray needed a baritone player. So my couple of buddies, John Hunt and Milt Turner, just mentioned my name. I went down, I think I had a little rehearsal that evening with them. I played the gig that night, which was in, I think it was about October. He called me in January for the (permanent) gig three months later. And I left school and went with him."

So Hank Crawford replaced Hog Cooper on baritone in January 1958, with Ray doubling on alto on live dates. As Cooper explained to me: "In December the band took a break, and I stayed in Dallas, and when they got ready to go back out – Ray was living in Dallas then – I stayed. I didn't like the road then, I was married and so on . . ." Cooper returned when Crawford was briefly out of the line-up ". . . I went back to the band in '59, when Hank Crawford had left, I was back to get my old job back, then when Hank came back about a month later, Ray just kept on the three of us . . ." Hank took over on alto: "He had a fancy baritone, I think it was a Conn with one of those Berg Larson mouthpieces, so I bought it" – becoming the band's musical director during his five-year tenure with Ray. He saw the Ray Charles Orchestra evolve from a small band to a large big-band ensemble, but it was playing in the smaller unit that he found most satisfying: "That little small band, it was just something else, we used to go on and do an hour before Ray. We had the bandstand hot for him when he came up there! We would play Ray's stuff, and it was a hell of a little jazz band too. We'd play the blues, man, we'd play jazz. All of the musicians were qualified – Marcus Belgrave [who joined later in '58] and people like that. We were all jazz musicians that played the blues."

It was around the time that Hank Crawford started with the band that Ray finally recruited The Cookies as part of the on-the-road ensemble rather than just using them for recording dates. He'd broached the subject back in early December when he was in New York playing the Apollo, and two of the girls – Ethel McRae (who would subsequently be billed as Darlene McRae) and Margie Hendricks – were up for it, but Dorothy Jones didn't want to leave New York. Through Hendricks Ray found another singer to replace Jones, Pat Mosely Lyles, and once Ray had obtained permission from her mother for the 16-year-old to join, Pat

Lyles was a Cookie. But not for long – within a year or so The Cookies would be re-named The Raelettes.

With The Cookies part of the touring outfit, Ray's predilection for a variety of female company was stimulated afresh. He'd never been, or ever pretended to be, monogamous in his relationships. Since his days in Seattle with Louise, his "official" partners, up to and including his wife Della, were under no illusion that when away from the domestic home (which was most of the time) Ray had other women. Most of these affairs were casual – sexual dalliances with club employees, girls from the agency office, the inevitable "band chicks" (who would have been dubbed "groupies" a decade later) – with just a few longer standing. The latter included his on-the-road liaison with Mary Ann Fisher, but this too was now coming to an end, a demise hastened by the presence of the three new female faces in the line-up. Ray was particularly taken with raunchy-voiced Margie Hendricks, and before long she had taken Mary Ann's place as "Mrs Charles" within the ensemble.

The real Mrs Charles in the meantime was pregnant with their second child, and as the band headed to New York for another recording session at the end of February 1958 plans were being made for the family home to move from Dallas to Los Angeles. Between tour dates Ray had found time to seek a suitable house with the help of Milt Shaw, and by the time their new son David was born in April the Robinsons had moved to 3910 Hepburn Avenue in an affluent part of the black LA enclave of South Central.

The female voices which listeners were by now familiar with on Ray Charles' records added a whole new texture and dynamic to the live performances. Up till then backing vocals were occasionally handled by a couple of members of the band, or just as often simply not written in as part of an on-stage arrangement, while Mary Ann Fisher performed her feature spot as a separate part of the act – which she continued to do when the girls arrived, resisting any suggestion that she become an integrated member of The Cookies. But the added presence of the trio on numbers like 'Drown In My Own Tears', 'Ain't That Love' and 'Talkin' 'Bout You' established once and for all the pure experience of a Ray Charles performance as the nearest audiences would get to the fiery intensity of a hot-gospel meeting outside of the church.

It was arguably this recreation of the actual religious event of a church service in the secular arena that upset traditionalists in the black community most, more than Ray's appropriation of various sacred songs and chord structures. As Gary Kramer suggested in the liner notes to *The Great Ray Charles*, citing the critic Marshall Stearns, it was the emotional dynamic of the "call-and-response" of a church meeting that gave gospel its unique flavour, to be subsequently reflected in jazz: "The way tension is built up and given climactic release is a technique learned from the gospel singer. Most important of all is the sense of theatre that has been passed on to jazz from Negro religious music."

Now Ray Charles was evoking that sense of theatre in the context of rhythm & blues, the final touch in his creation of a music for which there was as yet no accurate category. It wasn't blues, it wasn't even strictly rhythm & blues – but with its churchy harmonies, Ray's moaning and wailing on vocals that have been described as bouncing "between the bedroom and the blessed", and what writer Peter Guralnick would call "a kind of lascivious church choir" in the provocative form of The Cookies/Raelettes, it sounded to many as plain blasphemy. "I got a lot of criticism from the churches, and from musicians too," Ray told Robert Palmer in an interview for *Rolling Stone*, ". . . then when they saw it was working, everybody started doing it."

"Ray is symbolically something," said the legendary jazz critic Ralph Gleason. "I mean not just in the way he does religious songs with secular lyrics, not just in the way he talks about 'soul' and sings it, but in the way that, no matter where he goes, the crowd rushes up to touch him, the laying on of the hands as if he is giving miracles. And I suppose that, symbolically, there is something religious to him. Maybe it's because he has so successfully transgressed all the bounds of white society and survived. Maybe it's because there's a trinity to him – his narcotics, his blindness – and the fact that he's a Negro. That's his crucifixion."

There were certainly other performers emerging in the late Fifties who also forged a link between the worlds of church music and rhythm & blues. Sam Cooke came out of an actual gospel group, The Soul Stirrers, to grace the R&B and pop charts with his rich sweet-sounding voice on 'You Send Me' in 1957. His change of direction also caused concern in the gospel community, but mainly on the grounds that they had lost a unique and popular voice to the secular field.

Several gospel performers had hit records in their own right, like the Five Blind Boys Of Mississippi whose 'Our Father' was one of the few gospel records to make it into the *Billboard* R&B chart. Their demonstrative lead singer was Archie Brownlee, of whom gospel authority Tony Heilbut wrote: "He would demolish huge auditoriums with the bluesiest version of 'The Lord's Prayer' . . . he would interrupt his songs with an unresolved falsetto shriek that conjured up images of witchcraft and bedlam." In another context, it could have been referring to a performance by Ray Charles.

Years later, Ray would acknowledge the similarity between church congregations "falling out, filled with the spirit" and his own ecstatic audiences. "Churches can be very warm, but I've seen people 'fall out' at concerts too. Music can do a hell of a thing to people. If I want to I can whip the crowd up to a frenzy and make them almost go crazy with music. Just with music. If you ever get two or three people clapping, the next thing you've got the whole place clapping . . . You get people going in a direction, you get a groove going, and as people themselves get happy it generates an electricity that builds up."

And Atlantic Records' vocal group The Drifters all had a background in sanctified singing, their lead singer Clyde McPhatter first singing professionally with a gospel group at the age of 14. Biographer Bill Millar even went as far as to declare: "Groups like The Drifters were instrumental in breaking the barriers which divided gospel from the blues and popular music. They virtually destroyed the distinction between the sacred and the profane, and created the means by which Aretha Franklin and Ray Charles could become the most popular singers in the world."

James Brown on the other hand, like Ray Charles, would appropriate aspects of church music for his own musical ends, though in his case it was his personal delivery that was borrowed from gospel rather than the structure and arrangements of the songs themselves. Brown – whose band The Famous Flames evolved from a group called The Gospel Starlighters – was heavily influenced by such legendary "hot gospel" shouters as The Sensational Nightingales' Rev. Julius Cheeks and The Dixie Hummingbirds' Ira Tucker. Tucker in particular was famous for what was known as "hard singing", where the preacher would exhort the congregation with shouts and moans, often running up and down the church aisle and collapsing in ecstasy.

But although Brown's first R&B hit came in 1956 with 'Please Please Please', his crowd-stirring act which he would similarly climax by "collapsing" before being helped off stage, only really came into its own in the late Fifties and into the early Sixties. An incident when the future "Godfather of Soul" did actually upstage Ray Charles with his extravagant showmanship took place during a package show at Newark, New Jersey, sometime in 1957. The bill was headed by Ray and Little Richard, and

Brown, determined to excel himself in the face of such competition, pulled out all the stops. The concert was held in an enormous dance hall, where the stage, far above the dance floor with the audience standing below, was joined to a balcony at the back of the hall (where the rest of the fans were seated) by two narrow support beams. As his act climaxed with 'Please Please Please', Brown suddenly leapt on to one of the beams, "tightroping" across the vast space, still shouting and moaning, before collapsing into the crowd on the balcony. In terms of church-inspired theatre, it was an act that even Ray and the flamboyant Richard Penniman would have found hard to follow.

It was 1960 before James Brown broke through into the pop charts with 'Think', going on to be black America's "Soul Brother No 1" through the middle of the decade, a title that would have fitted Ray Charles perfectly some years previously.

The Cookies hadn't been on the road with Ray very long before they were all in the studio again, cutting more tracks in New York on February 20 and 28 which would further endorse his growing status as the most important figure on the black American music scene. From the church organ opening chords of 'Yes Indeed!', the Sy Oliver song provides a perfect setting for Ray and The Cookies' call-and-response style. The number dated back to the early Forties when on first publication it was described as a "jive spiritual", and subsequently covered by scores of artists including Bing Crosby, Tommy Dorsey and Frank Sinatra. Although credited solely to Oliver, Ray clearly applied some poetic licence to the lyrics which included some contemporary references:

> *You'll get a feelin' down in your soul*
> *Every time you hear that good ol' rock'n'roll*
> *I know you'll say oh, oh, oh yes indeed!*

'I Had A Dream' is a rolling blues employing a boogie-style "walking bass" figure led by the baritone sax which audiences would hear again to even greater effect in 'The Right Time' a few months later. 'You Be My Baby' on the other hand is perfect, joyous jump music. Ray shouts the first six lines of each verse, punctuated by the horns, before the girls affirm the message over a boisterous backing. There's a Latin touch to the conga-driven percussion parts that would characterise many more tracks in subsequent recording sessions, and the overall impact, including the blistering sax break, is pure, classic Ray Charles.

The number was co-written by Ray and the up-and-coming songwriting team of Doc Pomus and Mort Shuman. Pomus had already contributed 'Lonely Avenue' to the Ray Charles canon, and the pair would come second only to Leiber and Stoller as R&B tunesmiths in the Sixties, writing hits for Elvis Presley and Atlantic vocal group The Drifters among many others.

Talking to Liverpool broadcaster and writer Spencer Leigh in 1986, Doc Pomus would recall when he first heard Ray Charles, back in Ray's earliest days at Atlantic while Herb Abramson was still a head of the company: "Herb Abramson who was the President of Atlantic Records, woke me up from my room at the Broadway Central Hotel in the middle of the night and told me that I had to hear this sensational singer and piano-player, Ray Charles. He took me to Atlantic's studios and played me this amazing tape. Here was a guy who could sing ballads like Charles Brown or Nat King Cole and he was a great piano player. He was sensational, and I wrote 'Lonely Avenue' and 'You Be My Baby' for him."

As with 'Swanee River Rock', Ray delved into the pre-pop past when he chose the old Scottish folk tune 'My Bonnie Lies Over The Ocean' to get the Charles treatment as 'My Bonnie'. "I'd hear songs from back when I was a baby. Silly stuff like 'My Bonnie' or 'Swanee River'. Suddenly I'd say, 'Hey, I think I can fix these songs where they can fit me.'" Once again, conga drums add an extra rich layer to the rhythm section, carrying along a relaxed and churchy voicing of the ballad that concludes in thoroughly sanctified "amen" style.

There's an even sexier "amen" from The Cookies at the end of 'Tell All The World About You', an up-tempo tune straight from a revival meeting, with Ray screaming in exultation over the girls' chant:

> *I wanna walk about it, talk about it,*
> *Tell all the world about you*

Meanwhile the conga drum seemed to be quickly becoming an integral part of the Ray Charles sound.

It was a sound that was by now one of Atlantic Records' trademark properties. In the late Fifties, if you thought Atlantic you thought Modern Jazz Quartet, you thought Charles Mingus, you thought The Coasters and Ruth Brown. And increasingly, in America at least, you thought Ray Charles. That sound was crafted and honed to perfection by the same individuals who had been at the control desk on all of Ray's work throughout his six years on the label, namely producers Jerry Wexler and Ahmet

Ertegun (and Nesuhi in the case of the jazz sessions) and engineer Tom Dowd.

But even Dowd sensed the challenge of a project earmarked for July 1958, despite the ease with which he'd learned to work with Ray and the band over the years. "Although Ray would always be talking to Ahmet or Jerry about his recording plans, usually the day before he was due in the studio, he'd call me up and say something like, 'Hey, partner, I'm in town and I've got a hot new song' . . . and he'd tell me pretty much what he had in mind that he wanted to do so that when the band got into the studio I'd be ready for it. We just put up a few microphones and he'd listen – he'd tell me to record it, and we would, and then I'd play it back to him and he'd say, 'I didn't want that much there,' and I'd alter it for him and he'd say, 'That's just the way I see it.'"

The project in prospect was to record a live album of Ray's forthcoming appearance at the fifth annual Newport Jazz Festival on July 5, 1958, and the precedent already set for a concert recording at the Rhode Island event was daunting to say the least. The previous year's festival had closed with a roaring set from the Count Basie band which was subsequently released on disc as *Count Basie At Newport*, the album hailed as a landmark in live jazz recordings. And also in 1957, *Ellington At Newport*, which marked the Duke's celebrated "comeback" appearance the year before following a hiatus in the band's fortunes, had climbed to number 14 in the *Billboard* charts.

Then there was the matter of jazz snobbery. There was still a huge cultural divide between jazz and R&B, among critics and many fans if not so much with the musicians themselves, and Newport founder and supremo George Wein was reportedly cautious when he agreed to introducing a "Blues Night" at the 1958 event. The line-up consisted of Atlantic R&B veteran Joe Turner, rock'n'roll star Chuck Berry, blues shouter Big Maybelle and Ray Charles topping the bill. When photographer Bert Stern shot his celebrated documentary film of that year's festival, *Jazz On A Summer's Day*, both Maybelle and Berry from the blues show ended up on the big screen. But the liner notes to the movie's 2002 DVD release, talking about Chuck Berry's performance, reveal the schism that existed in attitudes to these two closely related branches of black American music. A schism that Ray Charles' performance went some way towards reconciling.

"Berry was as far from jazz as the Moon is from the Earth. Still, despite promoter George Wein's apparent misgivings (Wein is reported to have disapproved of Berry's onstage antics, the duck walk and hip gyrations in particular) he went down well with most of the audience. But Berry's act was as rebellious in its nature as the sexually charged blues of some decades before. He was the fly in the ointment and, for all his current success, one of the least accomplished musicians on that year's billing."

There was certainly no shortage of musical accomplishment where the Ray Charles band was concerned, whose sound *The New York Times'* John S. Wilson had described as "music that sticks to the ribs, music of charms and depths that wears unusually well". Recent recruits Marcus Batisto Belgrave and Lee Zedric ("Rick") Harper (Atlantic ran their full names on the LP credits) made up the two-man trumpet section, plus another new face Richie Goldberg on drums.

This was a jazz festival, so it was with quiet confidence that Ray decided to do what they did every other night and begin the performance with an all-instrumental jazz set, kicking off with a frantic big-band-in-a-small-band arrangement of an original, 'Hot Rod'. The solos came thick and fast – in the words of Fats Waller the joint was jumping – with Ray making his debut on the Newport stage with an alto sax solo, a surprise to many in the crowd. And despite later reviews in the jazz press that claimed the band met with a muted response, the evidence of the live recording suggests otherwise – they were greeted enthusiastically from the start by the majority of the audience.

The rest of the jazz selections went down equally well. Hank Crawford had recently written 'Sherry', heralding his musical directorship of the band, while the liltingly funky 'Blues Waltz' was an early example of the soon-to-be-fashionable "soul jazz" mode. And the Latin-tinged oldie 'In A Little Spanish Town' came in with a descending chord run that we'd hear later on 'Hit The Road Jack', punctuated throughout with "Hey, ooh-ahs" from the band that pre-dated Ray's biggest instrumental hit 'One Mint Julep' from 1961. But it was when Ray went into his vocal set that he really set things alight, with performances that sound just as fresh today as they did nearly half a century ago.

The hand-clapping intro to 'Talkin' 'Bout You' brings in The Cookies in full call-and-response flight that concludes with an extended ride-out not possible on the single. The girls, incidentally, were credited as The Raelettes (spelled Raylettes*) when the album appeared in the October, so we can

---

* This spelling (and the pronunciation) gave rise to an inter-band joke: "To be a Raylette you have to let Ray."

conclude that it was around this time that the name change was made.

Ray introduces 'A Fool For You' as ". . . something that we're sure that each and everybody can understand, and that's the blues . . . *everybody* can understand the blues," before the sanctified piano and hymn-book horns underscore a seven-minute version that has the crowd roaring in appreciation as he builds to an ecstatic climax.

But it's 'The Right Time' – recorded earlier that year by its composer Nappy Brown – that comes over as the high point of the set, The Raelettes continuously chanting "night and day" over a walking bass baritone sax riff as Margie Hendricks' screams her plea –

> *Tease me, squeeze me, please me, oh don't leave me*
> *Oh baby, take my hand, I don't need no other man*
> *Because the night time is the right time to be with the one you love*

– with an emotional intensity rivalling similar remonstrations from Ray that rips the place apart.

A slow blues-shouting intro brings in what was the up-tempo finale to the show, a stretched-out version of 'I Got A Woman' with Ray improvising a whoopin' and hollerin' fade-out over a single repeated riff – and like the preacherman he is, having the congregation firmly in the palm of his hand.

The other great achievement of the evening was Tom Dowd's success in delivering a recording suitable for album release, in the face of constraints imposed by Columbia Records, which as festival sponsors were recording various other acts. "For us to presume to record Ray Charles we had to go with the way they set up their mikes on stage. When we had a band on, they weren't about to change mikes and techniques or let me engineer. So I was in a position where I'd say that I wanted to run two mikes on two spare positions and put them on these two tracks, and tell the engineer to work as best he could with the band on the other two tracks."

In this way, working with another company's engineer and not being able to do the "hand on" job himself, Dowd somehow got the results he'd hoped for. "I'd isolate the vocals and the audience on mikes that I'd run in by hand, then babysit the engineer while he was doing it, and hopefully get back to where we could convert the tape into something that we could listen to every minute of and determine whether I should use the extra voice kick that I had, or whether I should do a little stunt here and there."

The impact of *Ray Charles At Newport* was instant and profound, not least with sections of the jazz fraternity where it exerted a seminal influence on the emerging "roots" movement with its emphasis on blues and gospel in a distinctly jazz context. On a broader front, it awoke an interest among jazz fans in rhythm & blues, and vice versa, helping bridge the gap between the two genres that logically shouldn't have been there in the first place.

Also on the jazz front, Ray and the band appeared at the Cavalcade of Jazz held in Los Angeles in that same month of July, while *Soul Brothers*, released in June, was already scoring well for Atlantic across the country. In the singles marketplace, 'My Bonnie' and 'You Be My Baby' were released in August, and in September an additional member was added to the line-up of the Cookies/Raelettes in the diminutive form of Gwen Berry.

Around the same time that *At Newport* was released, Atlantic put out a compilation of tracks from various sessions, all but one previously released on singles. The new track was 'Heartbreaker', an up-tempo blues with a new sound added to the rhythm section, that of a conga drum. The track would eventually surface as a single in 1960, as the flip side to the string-accompanied 'Just For A Thrill'. Entitled *Yes Indeed!*, with two singles released at the end of November the album ensured that Ray had plenty of new product in the shops for 1958 Christmas shoppers. The singles were the two-sided instrumental, 'Rockhouse', recorded a couple of years earlier, and 'Tell All The World About You' coupled with a studio version of the *At Newport* track 'The Right Time'.

It was at the end of October that the band had gone into the studio, and although Ray and Margie's duet number lacked some of the on-stage frisson of the live version it still stands up as an emotionally potent performance between two voices who as well as working in the same band were often sleeping in the same bed.

For the other tracks laid down in New York, Ray indulged his new-found penchant for the Afro-Cuban sound of the conga drum, with star name Mongo Santamaria being brought in to do the honours.* An old Louis Jordan number, 'Early In The Morning', has everything in the mix – Raelettes, piano, conga drums, strident brass, archetypal Fathead – a

---

* Mongo, who'd earlier played with Ray on 'Swanee River Rock', would have a Top 10 hit in 1963 with Herbie Hancock's 'Watermelon Man', a Latin-flavoured spin-off of the soul jazz movement.

roller coaster of a number that's 167 seconds of rhythm & blues perfection.

In addition to the conga drums, 'Tell Me How Do You Feel' features another innovation in that Ray is playing a Hammond organ – soon to be considered the epitome of soul funk in the hands of men like Jimmy Smith and Jack McDuff. Ray's singing, and that of The Raelettes answering with "I want to know" after every line, gets more than its usual share of echo, but it all makes for another classic, albeit a relatively seldom-heard one.

Just a week later, on November 5, 1958, Ray was back in the Atlantic studio, but this time in a backing capacity when he played piano on an instrumental album highlighting the tenor and alto sax playing of David Newman. Hank Crawford was present on baritone, as was trumpeter Marcus Belgrave and the Ray Charles rhythm section of Edgar Willis and Milt Turner. The title *Fathead/Ray Charles Presents David Newman* was obviously aimed at taking advantage of Ray's burgeoning popularity with jazz as well as R&B fans, but beyond his prominent namecheck on the album cover and liner notes, Newman's boss took very much a back seat.

In fact Hank Crawford, now the Charles band's MD, performed a similar role for most of this session, writing the arrangements for all but two of the eight tracks, and contributing three original compositions. But from the opening alto statement of Ray's 'Hard Times' it's clear that this is Fathead's album, despite his modest claim that the selection of material "was to find some swinging numbers, not too far out, that everybody could understand and enjoy, and still show off the best qualities of each member of the band."

Hank Crawford's 'Weird Beard' and 'Sweet Eyes' capture the feel of the "Blue Note" hard-bop sound being pioneered on that other esteemed label of the day, while his technically challenging 'Bill For Bennie' is tricky bebop personified, all concerned blowing up a storm. Newman's only original, the eponymously titled 'Fathead', is a strident soul-blues with his tenor playing very much to the fore.

Ray's bouncy intro to the standard 'Willow Weep For Me' soon settles into a languid ballad led by Fathead's superlative alto playing, and the other standard, 'Mean To Me', once again has the leader on alto – and just listen to Hank's baritone solo. The set closes with the well-known Latin-bop number written by Cuban percussionist Chano Pozo, 'Tin Tin Deo'.

Atlantic albums, and particularly their jazz albums, were noted for their intelligent, often copious liner notes. In his piece on the back of *Fathead*, Gary Kramer concluded with a thought on the future of jazz at the end of the Fifties:

> An album like this is well timed. Jazz critics keep telling us that "modern jazz is worked out". André Hodeir concluded his recent book, *Jazz: Its Evolution And Essence*, with a pessimistic forecast about the future of jazz. Again, the most recent *Metronome Yearbook* reported as an identifying mark of the year, "the real dearth of vitality and lack of direction of which some were now accusing jazz". And so on. Young musicians like Newman confute the Cassandras. Jazz's next chapter is going to be as exciting and as rich musically as any in its past, so long as it continues to bring up waves of new musicians with the talent, technical skill and creative ardor of David "Fathead" Newman.

Talking with David Newman, I asked him whether the album was Atlantic's idea, or Ray's. "It was Ray's idea. I was really indebted to him because he introduced me, and that was my first recording on Atlantic records, and from that point on I had a contract recording for Atlantic." It was an association that would continue through four decades and many fine albums, long after Fathead had left the Ray Charles band.

The album, along with the instrumentals on the Newport set, further established the jazz credentials of the Ray Charles band, although by the time of its release in August 1959 Ray had already been named "New Star" in the annual awards of the strictly jazz *Down Beat* magazine, and also awarded the 1958 Grand Prix du Disque by the French Academy of Recorded Music as a jazz singer for his debut album *Hallelujah I Love Her So*. As Newman would reflect many years later, "Always, above all, he was a jazz player, and he loved jazz players. As a matter of fact, all his band were really jazz players. They weren't really R&B players, or blues players. They were really jazz musicians."

But Ray Charles' musical instincts and ambitions went far beyond the parameters of the jazz world with its artificial boundaries defined as much by fans and critics as the musicians themselves. His music had breached the gap between blues and gospel, and between R&B and jazz, a fact not lost on an English musician quoted in *Melody Maker* on his return from the United States in 1958: "The one new name that I heard everywhere was that of Ray Charles. He had developed careers simultaneously as a blues singer idolised by the rock'n'roll set – and as a jazz pianist and saxophonist at ease at the Newport Jazz Festival. And he uses the same band as a background for both activities."

Now Ray Charles was about to take his music onto a whole new level of popular acclaim with a creative vision that recognised no boundaries, save those between what he considered good music and bad. And the key to that next stage of Ray's musical odyssey came about in December 1958, in the unlikely circumstance of a one-nighter gig at a dance hall near Pittsburgh, Pennsylvania.

8

What'd I Say

"They were poor imitations, mine included, but it was pretty fantastic to get everyone caught up in the force of a song like that."

– Steve Winwood

'What'd I Say' represented all those musical references that Ray Charles had been utilising and making his own over the previous 10 years, coming together by the end of the decade in a single, definitive statement of what soul is all about, and one that remains impossible to challenge to this day. From the sensual reverb of the electric piano intro on Part I of the double-sided single, to the orgasmic exchanges with The Raelettes on Part II, the revelation, the pure impact – nothing had prepared anyone for this.

The nearest studio re-creation of the "sanctified" atmosphere of a Ray Charles stage show at the time, the six-minute celebration of sensual pleasure – described by writer Peter Guralnick as "a kind of secular evoca-tion of an actual church service, complete with moans, groans, and a con-gregation talking in tongues" – had evolved out of some musical messin' around by Ray and the band at a live performance in Brownsville, near Pittsburgh.

It was one of Ray's last old-fashioned dance gigs as his increasing popu-larity meant more fancy nightclubs, concerts and festival appearances. At such "meal dances", where food was served between sets, the band might play up to four hours including a half-hour break, and on this particular night they'd played two-and-a-half hours solid from 9.00 till 11.30, taken a break till midnight then played through till 1 am, by which time they'd run out of material. As Ray recalled in a 1986 TV documentary: "In those days we played meal dances in dance halls, and the dance would start at nine o'clock, then go to one o'clock. So we were playing one night and we had about 15 more minutes to do, and I couldn't think of nothin' else to play, so I just told the guys, 'Hey, you guys just get a groove goin' when I tell you to come in, and I told the girls, 'Whatever I say, repeat after me,' and we started to do it . . ."

Ray started fooling around with a little piano riff, throwing in ad lib vocals as the band joined in. Suddenly the atmosphere was electric, the crowd reaction ecstatic – "the people started dancing and were just goin' crazy over it". The next night he repeated the exercise, refining the band riffs, tightening up the essentially improvised vocals; then the next night, and the next. Suddenly, out of nowhere, they had a show-stopping number on their hands.

"So we tried just playing it in a few other towns, just the same thing to see what would happen, and someone asked me, 'Do you have a record of that?' and I had to say, 'No, there ain't no record.'" Ray decided to call Jerry Wexler, telling him he was coming to New York to record a new number.

It would be the middle of February before Ray and the rest finally made it to a studio to cut some more music. In the meantime the band bus – a customised Chevrolet limo that carried 12 with room to spare for the instruments and PA – and Ray's Cadillac (with Jeff Brown at the wheel, and now Margie, not Mary Ann, at Ray's side) rolled on through Christmas and New Year into 1959.

Ray's almost simultaneous single releases – 'Rockhouse' and then 'The Right Time' – had both scored in the R&B charts as the holiday season got under way, with 'Rockhouse' making the lower reaches of the pop Hot 100 too. Things couldn't have seemed better for all concerned, but by the middle of January Mary Ann Fisher had finally had enough.

Ray was more and more interested in Marjorie Hendricks, not just as a lover but as a singer as well, so Mary Ann called it a day. Now the vocal line-up was the four-piece Raelettes *with* Margie Hendricks, not *plus* as had been the case with Mary Ann. And Ray and Margie's affair would take on an even more serious aspect when a month or so into the year she became pregnant. His wife Della and their two sons, meanwhile, led an increasingly isolated existence in the all-taken-care-of luxury of their Los Angeles home.

When the band did get to New York, one of the numbers they cut on February 18 was another duet with Ray and Margie, a raunchy follow-up to 'The Right Time' called 'Tell The Truth'. It wouldn't be released (in its studio version at least) till the July of the following year, and at the time of recording was totally eclipsed by the on-the-road jamming number Ray had rung Jerry about, 'What'd I Say'.

The song, as Ahmet Ertegun recognised, was an affirmation of Ray's roots. "If you analyse it, there's a very strong family connection to 'Pinetops Boogie Woogie' – 'see the girl with the diamond ring', 'see the girl with the red dress on' – it's a similar thing." The overall sound, however, was pointing in one direction only – and that was forward.

Although Ray had been playing the Wurlitzer electric piano on the road since 1956 in venues where the house piano often proved unreliable, it was still only occasionally evident in his recorded output. And it was still very much ahead of its time, making the whole sound of 'What'd I Say' both back-to-the-roots and state-of-the-art R&B at the same time, as Ray would reflect: "Before then, everyone was laughing at me for playing electric piano. After 'What'd I Say', those same cats were running out scrambling to buy electric pianos of their own." And recording-wise too, the Atlantic sound in the hands of Ertegun, Wexler and Dowd was ahead of the game technically.

Just a year earlier Tom Dowd had bought one of the first Ampex eight-track recorders, allowing him to "compose" the balance of the instruments in the new context of stereo sound – a facility that immediately grabbed Ray's ear and got him interested in the actual recording process in a hands-on way for the first time.

But, as Nesuhi Ertegun would recall, what made the Atlantic sound unique at that time was eight-track recording in such a tiny studio as the one on 56th Street.

"In those days Atlantic had a studio that was only as big as this [medium-sized] room, but with very, very good equipment. An eight-track recorder – there were two in existence – Les Paul had one, in his garage, and Tom Dowd ordered a special one from Ampex. Most people, if they had a two-track recorder thought they were far out already – eight-track, nobody had ever seen one. So 'What'd I Say' was cut in a tiny studio, but on an eight-track recorder, and that's why the quality's so good – the sound today is still unbelievable."

Tom Dowd's biggest problem was in the actual content – both in the material itself and the length of the recording. Although there was nothing directly salacious in the lyrics, Atlantic were well aware of the narrow-minded attitudes such sexual connotations could offend – Ahmet and Jerry had once even risked arrest when they released Clyde McPhatter's 'Money

Honey' after it was banned in Georgia. "I actually mixed three different versions . . . one way for a single, another way for people on all-night radio stations, and another way still for an album. So the record varied in length from four minutes, 15 seconds to five and a half or six minutes, with all kinds of lyric deletions so that we could get it on the air. Because we knew it was going to be a hit record, no question."

And because they knew it had huge hit potential, the length of 'What'd I Say', however they cut it, was the other problem. They didn't want to relegate it to an album release, so the only answer was to make it a double-sided single, a commercial risk in itself. Luckily, the way the song had developed in live performance had produced a "natural" break, where after reaching a climax with the band the song comes to a premature end, only to start up again with the "Uhhhh" and "Ohhhh" call-and-response exchanges between Ray and the girls that build to an even more highly charged finale.

Once they'd heard Tom's final edit, Ahmet and Jerry knew this could be the big one. Their decision to release it in June, a time of year when danceable records tended to take off with teenage record buyers, was a tacit acknowledgement that Ray Charles' potential extended to the sharp end of the commercial pop market. As the Fifties gave way to the Sixties, the influence of young people on popular music – not just as consumers but creators – was stronger than ever. And as 'What'd I Say' made its way up the pop charts, hitting the Top 30 by the end of July, peaking at number six in August and going on to sell over a million, it became Atlantic Records biggest-seller to date.

Not everyone liked it of course. As anticipated, the near-the-knuckle sexual simulations were shocking to many – not least older, more con-servative sections of the black community. "It was banned by several radio stations. They said it was suggestive," Ray recalled in his autobiography. "Well, I agreed. I'm not one to interpret my own songs, but if you can't figure out 'What I Say', then something's wrong. Either that, or you're not accustomed to the sweet sound of love."

Later, Ray would add: "It pissed me off because the ban was lifted when white singers sang my song. What were the stations saying – that black sex is dirty and white sex is clean? It was crazy, but I didn't care. More they played it, more royalties for me.

"When I sing 'Baby, shake that thing', and 'It makes me feel so good' I figured it would fit most people, even the ones that say it shouldn't be played on the air. The people in this country, there's only two things they do, and that's kiss and hug – according to all the songs that are written here. Now, you don't have to say a word in the flesh, but I don't feel there's anything wrong with implying somethin' natural."

Incidentally, Ray always referred to the song as 'What I Say', as he had written it, but the record company managed to title it as 'What'd I Say'.

There were also those in black America who still felt uncomfortable about the appropriation of gospel music by the mass (predominantly white) market, albeit via a black hero like Charles. As author Martha Bayles puts it in her controversial critique of late-20th century pop music *Hole In Our Soul*: "Not only was sanctified music moving out of church, it was moving out of the neighbourhood."

But by and large the impact of this evocation of carnality, this "dialogue between himself and his backing singers that began in church and ended up in the bedroom" as critic Tony Russell would describe it, was to resonate with a far wider public than anything Ray Charles had previously released.

"Most rock'n'roll historians, with their characteristic bias toward youth rebellion, claim that the last two years of the Fifties were a musically fallow period. But that claim only works if you're willing to ignore Ray Charles' brilliant work," wrote Nelson George in *The Death Of Rhythm & Blues*. It's a view supported by the facts, when 'What'd I Say' became not just a huge seller in its home market but an instant favourite with Ray's already growing fanbase in mainland Europe – particularly France – and young record buyers in England.

And among the music-struck youngsters who were immediately touched by 'What'd I Say' were the embryonic Beatles. "I knew right then and there I wanted to be involved in that kind of music," Paul McCartney said about first hearing the record, and George Harrison would recall years later the first all-night party he ever went to, a Liverpool "art student" affair sometime in 1959: "The great thing about the party (and I'm sure John and Paul would agree) was that somebody had a copy of 'What'd I Say' by Ray Charles, a 45rpm with Part Two on the B-side. That record was played all night, probably 8 or 10 hours non-stop. It was one of the best records I ever heard."

By the end of the following year The Beatles were serving a fierce apprenticeship in the all-night clubs of Hamburg, where 'What'd I Say' was a guaranteed crowd-pleaser (and as effective a time-filler as it had been at its birth pangs in Pennsylvania). As Paul McCartney would recall: "That was one of our really big numbers. It became like trying to get into the *Guinness Book Of Records* – who could make it last the longest. It is the perfect song; it has the greatest opening riff ever. And if you had a Wurlitzer (which we didn't) you could keep that riff going for hours. Then it went 'Tell your MAMA, tell your PAW. Gonna take you back to ArkanSAW. See the girl with the red dress on . . .' We could string that out. Then the chorus: 'Tell me, what'd I say?' and you could keep that going for hours. Then it had the killer 'Oh Yeah' – audience participation."

John Lennon even went so far as to claim that the song marked the start of guitar-riff records: "As far as I know, that was the first electric piano on record that I ever heard. None of us had electric pianos so we did it on guitar to try and get that low sound . . . 'What'd I Say' started a whole new ball game which is still going now."

Similarly, in his chronicle *Rolling With The Stones*, Bill Wyman describes the first time Mick Jagger "sat in" with the Alexis Korner group at their legendary Thursday night residency at London's Marquee Club, the future Stones vocalist and a female singer nervously attempting a version of 'What'd I Say'. And the lead singer with the Sixties R&B group The Animals, Eric Burdon, claims to this day that the initial reason the keyboard job with the Newcastle band went to Alan Price was because . . . "He was the only guy I knew who could play the Ray Charles lick on 'What'd I Say' properly." Burdon thought the lyrics of the song were ironic: "He had one girl dancing erotic dances in front of him, and of course he couldn't see her . . ." but was most impressed by the role of The Raelettes, ". . . every time I listen to the music I get the impression they were actually having sex."

Likewise Steve Winwood, in the mid-Sixties lead singer with The Spencer Davis Group, admits: " 'What'd I Say' was hugely influential, but they were poor imitations, mine included – but it was pretty fantastic to get everyone caught up in the force of a song like that."

Aside from its impact on the up-and-coming blues and rock musicians in the UK, many of them future superstars, 'What'd I Say' enjoyed a far-ranging popularity in America, as soul singer and rock historian Billy Vera would colourfully describe as ". . . appealing to everyone from frat-house beer heads, who improvised pornographic lyrics to its verses, to tuxedoed high society types twisting the night away alongside sailors and hookers at New York's trendy Peppermint Lounge."

Brian Wilson of The Beach Boys remembered the song's impact on the group: "I loved (Ray) so much that back in 1963, after The Beach Boys got going, we used to do a live version of 'What'd I Say'. We did it because we wanted to turn people on to Ray Charles."

In pop terms, its place in time was also crucial. Coming in 1959, when rock'n'roll seemed to have run its course and the charts were dominated by the likes of Frankie Avalon, Bobby Vee and an increasingly watered-down Elvis, 'What'd I Say' was a breath of fresh air. Or, more accurately, a fiery, potent outburst of sex'n'rhythm'n'blues. To anyone with ears to hear, things would never be the same again.

On record the song was covered by a number of artists over the next four or five years. In Britain these ranged from Cliff Richard to John Mayall's seminal blues band The Bluesbreakers with Eric Clapton, while in the States it was most famously tackled by Elvis as a flip side to 1964's 'Viva Las Vegas', and Eddie Cochran, who also recorded 'Hallelujah I Love Her So' in 1959. Jerry Lee Lewis' cover was the most successful, charting in both countries with a hot-blooded pumping piano version in 1961. Dozens of other names recorded the song, among them artists as diverse as Bill Haley, Nancy Sinatra, Sammy Davis Jr and Johnny Cash.

These were not the first performers to cover Ray Charles songs of course. Since the time Elvis Presley had included 'I Got A Woman' on his 1956 debut album, songs that Ray had written – or had "made his own" – had cropped up in the work of various singers who enjoyed regular main-stream pop chart success. In fact "Woman' had been covered by Jo Stafford as 'I Got A Sweetie' in February 1955, just a couple of months after Ray's release. The Everly Brothers covered 'This Little Girl Of Mine' at the end of 1957, Harry Belafonte's 1958 *Belafonte Sings The Blues* included five numbers associated with Ray, and Peggy Lee featured 'Hallelujah I Love *Him* So', 'I Got A *Man*' and 'Yes Indeed!' in her regular stage act. And there were many more.

Rock'n'roll legend Buddy Holly – who would die five months before 'What'd I Say' was released – was particularly influenced by Ray Charles in his formative years as a budding musician in Lubbock Texas. "He liked Ray Charles a lot," his mother Ella Holley would tell biographer John Goldrosen. "He had one record by Ray Charles, 'My Bonnie' . . . he'd play that and sing it, and I'd join in and sing with the girls' chorus part on it." Later on in his short career, Holly had plans to make an album of Ray Charles' material, and even hoped to involve Ray in the project, as his widow Maria Elena would recall: "When we were in California . . . we managed to find out where Ray Charles lived, and we went over to his house, but he was out on tour. Buddy was hoping to talk with Charles and see if he'd be willing to work with him on this – help with arrangements, and maybe play on it. Buddy really loved Charles' style, and he wanted to meet him and talk with him about it."

'What'd I Say', however, was significant in that it fired the imagination of a whole new generation of young musicians and fans – particularly in Great Britain, where it was the first Ray Charles record that many heard. And what an introduction! The Decca company, which released Atlantic material in the UK market on their London label, only started delving into Ray's back catalogue in the wake of the single's success, each release eagerly snapped up by his converts and guaranteeing him cult status as the new decade began.

9

Genius

"We finished more than an hour ahead of time, and nobody would leave the studio . . . all those musicians saying, 'Play that thing once more,' and we didn't play it once but over and over again."

– Nesuhi Ertegun

Before 'What'd I Say' was released, Ray had gone back into the studio with a project more ambitious than anything he'd attempted previously, under the auspices of his "jazz" producer, Nesuhi Ertegun: "We were trying to widen the appeal of Ray Charles, because his talent was limitless, so we got the idea for the album where we decided to do one side with strings and one side with a full jazz big band. Strings arranged by Ralph Burns and the jazz orchestra by Quincy Jones.

"My first idea was to do it all with a big jazz band, but Ray insisted on strings, it was really more his desire than mine to use strings, so I said if he wants it that much we'll get them – he'd never recorded with strings before. I got the best string players in New York and the man I thought was the best arranger, Ralph Burns. Ray didn't know him, but I introduced them and they got on extremely well as soon as they saw each other. And Ralph could see this was a fantastic musician – people are always impressed because they think an R&B musician is illiterate, uneducated, but Ray Charles, he's a complete musician."

According to Jerry Wexler, Ray was already familiar with Burns' work: "The whole idea for the album was Ray Charles'. Of course we engaged the musicians but he indicated the ones he wanted. And he said to me before that session, 'Who does the strings on your Chris Connor records?' I said, 'That's Ralph Burns' – of course Ralph had worked for Woody Herman too – and so that's how we hired Ralph Burns to do the string parts for the ballad side."

On May 6 a large orchestra plus session singers conducted by Harry Lookofsky backed Ray on half a dozen standards, including 'Just For A Thrill', 'Am I Blue' and a sensational version of 'Come Rain Or Come Shine', all arranged by Burns. The six numbers would constitute side two of *The Genius Of Ray Charles*, side one of which featured a big band session recorded six weeks later, on June 23.

But this was no ordinary big band, the 23-piece ensemble featuring a large chunk of the Count Basie band plus three players borrowed from Duke Ellington, and some of Ray's own outfit too. The result was staggering, five songs ranging from the vintage 'Alexander's Ragtime Band' to Percy Mayfield's contemporary blues 'Two Years Of Torture' sung like they'd never been sung before. Plus perhaps what forever after became the definitive version, certainly the most powerful, of the R&B classic 'Let The Good Times Roll'.

As well as Ray's obvious ebullience, which comes over on every track, highlights include a blistering solo by Ellington tenor man Paul Gonsalves on the Mayfield song, and breaks by Fathead and Marcus Belgrave in which the Charles men rise to the occasion of being in such illustrious musical company. "It was wonderful blowing with those guys," David Newman would recall.

The session wasn't without its dramas, as Nesuhi would describe in detail: "The session with the strings had gone very smoothly with Ralph Burns, everything was well rehearsed – the string players don't make mistakes, you put the notes and they play them, Ray sang and played his piano . . . no problems. So we had rehearsals, picked the tunes, picked the keys . . . a real rehearsal, unlike the ones with Milt Jackson, this was really carefully prepared because we had a big band. And I hired the entire Count Basie band, minus Basie, the full band, some of the Ellington band, the Ray Charles band with Fathead, Hank Crawford and so on, and The Raelettes, so we had all these people in the studio there . . . it's almost like a legend now.

"The band were going to do two sessions, in other words record across a whole afternoon, and try to cut six sides in one go, because they all had to travel . . . the Basie band, the Ellington band, it was hard to get everybody in town. So we were going to do it on a Sunday afternoon. Basie was working at the Waldorf-Astoria, so we had to be finished by nine o'clock so they could do their gig at night."

So Nesuhi knew he would be running to a tight schedule when, on the Sunday morning, disaster loomed. "About nine o'clock in the morning, Quincy (who was supposed to be doing all the arrangements) called me at my house, and he said, 'Man we gotta cancel, we've gotta postpone the session . . . I'm not ready, I haven't done the arrangements, I couldn't finish.' I asked him what he had that was finished, he said, 'One arrangement . . . I've finished one' (I think it was 'Let The Good Times Roll') – so I said, 'Quincy, I'm gonna call some arrangers, and they're gonna write from 9 am, and if we get five different people, maybe they'll do it.' And that's the way that album was put together. I had eight copyists in the studio, writing up the parts, because we had to have parts ready for all those musicians.

"Anyway, it was both a nightmare and a miracle because it worked. And we finished ahead of time, which is unbelievable. Al Cohn did an arrangement, Ernie Wilkins did one, Al Cohn, Johnny Acea – they were all my friends, so I called them: 'Man, I know it's Sunday but please. . . .' And they said, 'For Ray Charles, we'll do anything,' so everyone worked together."

Ralph Burns, who contributed a chart for the jazz session as well as arranging the strings, was sitting by the piano when Ray called Nesuhi over and said, "The third trumpet has a wrong note in the fifth bar" – Nesuhi replied that he didn't hear it – "So I said to Ralph, 'This isn't possible, I didn't hear it.' So we decided to get each trumpet to play their part and with the third, sure enough, the wrong note was there."

This kind of consummate professionalism, combined with Ray's remarkable ear, was to impress the most hard-nosed jazz pros at the session, to some of whom "rhythm & blues" was an almost derogatory term: "Until that moment those musicians had never seen Ray Charles. Some had heard of him, but they were kind of saying, 'What's all this production for, for a rhythm & blues artist?' They didn't know at all that he was an arranger, he could write music, he knew music inside out more than any of those people. But when he heard a mistake, and had to find the right note, and started to make all the corrections in the arrangements, it shook up everybody, they all woke up and there was a new spirit in the studio.

"From then on it was smooth sailing, and we finished more than an hour ahead of time, and nobody would leave the studio . . . all those musicians saying, 'Play that thing once more,' and we didn't play it once but over and over again. Usually when you're working with those guys in New York who are recording all the time, they split the moment you say the session's over, vooom . . . out the door. But they stayed there, and it was really one of the greatest days of my life."

"We did that first side in a double session," noted Quincy Jones in Nat

Hentoff's liner notes. "We finished ahead of time, but the musicians had become so emotionally involved, they wouldn't leave the studio. The Basie guys, for example, were due at the Waldorf, but they just sat there with the others – finger poppin' and listening to the takes over and over again. After 45 minutes, Ray said to me, 'You know, I don't think anyone's left yet.'"

Jerry Wexler remembered the sense of achievement when the album was completed: "This was the biggest thing that we had ever attempted, and there was a lot of money on the line, the expense of this recording, and we were really nervous about it. But it came off very well, no problems."

And Nesuhi Ertegun realised immediately that what had been finalised that day, along with the earlier string session, represented another leap forward for the artist who was by now the hottest property on Atlantic's books. "I think that did a lot to really widen his appeal to the public. It was a very important album both for Atlantic and for me personally, and for Ray Charles because he hit a new kind of audience."

The "new kind of audience" *The Genius . . .* appealed to was as far removed from Ray's home constituency of black R&B fans as were the English kids captivated by 'What'd I Say'. It was the urbane, predominantly white, adult record buyer who enjoyed Sinatra and Sarah Vaughan, Tony Bennett and Basie. With all the trappings of a big band, strings and vocal chorus, Ray Charles – without compromising one iota of his musical commitment – had staked his claim to a place in the lucrative "quality" album market.

In that sense the album could be seen in retrospect as a template for much of Ray's music in years to come, a view with which Wexler would concur, with characteristic reservation: "For the ballads he did later on, I would certainly say so, and also for the country and western things. But I don't know if you can legitimately say that this was the antecedent, Ray may have had these ideas all along . . ."

Before the second *Genius* session, WAOK in Atlanta was responsible for one of the seminal live recordings of Ray's career. The occasion was the radio station's fifth anniversary, and promoter Zenas Sears had hired a local baseball park, Herndon Stadium, for a two-day event involving a 12-strong line-up of acts including top R&B names Ruth Brown, Roy Hamilton, The Drifters, Huey Smith and The Clowns, Jimmy Reed and B.B. King – plus Ray and his band.

"Zenas Sears had originally been a disc jockey in New Jersey who I knew very well," Jerry Wexler recalled, "and he moved out to Atlanta, and started doing rhythm & blues concerts back in those days that really were big, in the sense that he had many acts on the bill: Fats Domino, Jackie Wilson, La Vern Baker, The Drifters, they'd have six or seven acts. They could actually fill a ballpark with customers. So what Zenas Sears would do, with one mike he would record whatever concert was in progress, and then he would use excerpts from that for promos for the next one."

When the first night on May 28 didn't draw the crowds expected because of rainy weather, Sears decided he needed to do just that to rescue the second concert: "It was a promotional thing and we kept the price down. The first day it was raining, so we figured we've gotta tape and get some stuff on the air real quick, to see if we can get a crowd there the next night or we'll lose our shirt. So we taped."

As the 9,000-plus crowd roared in greeting when Ray walked on, the tape started rolling on a portable recording machine connected to a solitary microphone suspended over 100 feet from the stage: "It was a good crowd, and they were fairly close for an outdoors thing . . ." The results were sensational, and Sears was so excited he contacted his friend Wexler in New York. "I realised the tape was good, so I called Jerry and said, 'I'll send you the tape, it sounds pretty good.'"

Wexler was amazed: "He sent me a few minutes of the tape that he had done. It was remarkable on one mike, so I called him and I said, 'How much do you have on this?' and he said, 'Well, a couple of hours,' he sent them up and that was the great record of Ray Charles live."

So successful was the recording, which included the first live recording of 'What'd I Say', two riveting contributions from Margie Hendricks (a rerun of her 'Right Time' performance at Newport '58 and 'Tell The Truth') and Ray's spine-tingling six minute delivery of 'Drown In My Own Tears', that Atlantic released it as *Ray Charles In Person* the following year. With the Newport album it was to be the only concert recording of the Ray Charles small band of the late Fifties, and a dramatic evocation of the sheer emotion generated in his live performances at the time.

"We didn't want nothin' for it," Zenas remembered when I spoke to him in his WAOK office in the Seventies. "'Put a penny on the LP for the engineer,' but that was all. I didn't even let them pay me for the liner notes. But as far as I'm concerned it's 'Drown In My Own Tears', I think it's one of his great selections and one of his great performances that night."

In his 1994 autobiography *Rhythm And The Blues: A Life In American Music*, Jerry Wexler recalled the album's impact: "*Ray Charles In Person* became a classic, overshadowing his live concert at the 1958 Newport Jazz Festival, which was excellent nonetheless, and especially significant in demonstrating to the jazz community – and to the elitist jazz critics – Ray's ability to sing in several directions at once."

Just three days after the big band sessions for *Genius*, on June 26, Ray and the rest of the outfit were back in the studios to record a new single. What came out of the session were two tracks that were both landmarks for very different reasons. Starting with a haunting electric piano intro, 'I Believe To My Soul' is a mournful lament of looming infidelity –

> *Last night you were dreaming and I heard you say*
> *"Oh, Johnny" when you know my name is Ray*

in which the backing vocals answer Ray's admonishments with an "*I believe, Yes I believe*" through every chorus. But what's remarkable is that the falsetto voices making up the four-part harmony are all Ray himself, overdubbed one by one when The Raelettes simply couldn't get it together. Frustrated when one, then another of the girls fluffed it on every take, Ray sent them home and told Jerry and Tom Dowd he'd handle it.

"Then he sat down with earphones," Jerry Wexler recalled, "and proceeded to dub in each of the four girl's parts, one at a time, in his own falsetto. He didn't even listen to the harmony, just the master track. When he finished, it was perfectly tight four-part harmony, it was amazing, it sounded just like a sensational girls' group." The result was a seamless testament to Ray Charles' increasing mastery of the recording process, something he would be more closely involved in during years to come.

The other track, 'I'm Movin' On', which was to be the B-side to 'I Believe . . .' was even more significant. It was the first country song Ray would record, a rolling Hank Snow travellin' number for which Ray wanted Chet Atkins for the session but the Nashville guitarist couldn't make it. Nevertheless, it was a radical step in a direction Ray would explore more thoroughly a couple of years later.

After a "train-whistle" opening from the horns, complete with steam locomotive sound effects – all of which were inexplicably edited from most subsequent pressings of the track – Ray and the girls roll along that ol' rail-road line, a hybrid mix of rhythm & blues, whining steel guitar and Ray's trademark whoops and screams on the single-riff ride-out. But in the context of his increasingly eclectic approach to material, this was seen at the time as just another case of Ray appropriating an unlikely song and making it rhythm & blues. Further down the line a lot more eyebrows would be raised when he took country music as a whole, and made it Ray Charles.

Meanwhile, Atlantic released 'What'd I Say' as the planned double-sided single, which despite the various radio bans and other opposition made its inexorable progress up the best-selling pop charts through the summer of 1959.

In the wake of its success they put out an album entitled *What'd I Say* in September, while the single was still riding high. The LP was a compilation of previously released items that had all appeared on singles going as far back as 1952's 'Roll With My Baby'. But it was a powerful collection, showcasing some of Ray's greatest rhythm & blues tracks including 'You Be My Baby', 'Tell Me How Do You Feel' and 'What Kind Of Man Are You?' It made a particularly strong impression on the British market where many of the numbers had not been heard before, introducing fans who'd been hooked by the 'What'd I Say' single to a splendid cross-section of Ray's back catalogue. And the album's sensational cover, with a close-up of Ray at the microphone, piano keys reflected in his wrap-around shades, was as memorable as the music therein.

The picture was taken by Lee Friedlander, at the time "house photographer" at Atlantic and the man responsible for all of Ray's sleeve photography on the label. He worked with most of the great names recording for the company at the time, including Charles Mingus, John Coltrane, Ornette Coleman and Joe Turner, and with designers Marvin Israel (who worked on the majority of Ray's Atlantic albums) and Loring Eutemy, he helped elevate sleeve design to often iconic status.

Following hard on the heels of *What'd I Say*, just a month later at the beginning of November Atlantic released Ray's next single, with 'I'm Movin' On' now the top side, which edged its way into the Top 40 by December. At the same time *The Genius Of Ray Charles* appeared, the strings-and-big-band epic quickly climbing to number 17.

The "Genius" tag was the invention of Jerry Wexler and, although Ray preferred other nicknames he'd begun to acquire – churchy titles like The High Priest and Brother Ray – it stuck. "We called it *The Genius Of Ray Charles*," Wexler explained to me. "I had wanted to use that appellation maybe a year before, but Ahmet and Nesuhi thought it would be a bit egregious, a bit of hyperbole. I said, 'I don't think so, I think it will work'.

So anyhow when this record came along it was agreed, okay we'll call it *The Genius Of Ray Charles*. There's a myth around the American music business that it was Frank Sinatra who dubbed him the Genius, but that is not the case. I'm sure Frank Sinatra called him a genius, but that was not the genesis of the rubric." Sinatra did indeed say, "Ray Charles is the only genius in our business," but that actually first appeared in a 1966 article in *Life* magazine. In retrospect, Ahmet Ertegun felt that as well as working commercially, the term was perfectly appropriate when applied to Ray: "In my mind he is one of the true geniuses of our time. And by genius I mean an innovator, an artist with his own singular vision, an incredible vocalist, a great pianist, a remarkable composer and arranger. We called him 'the genius' not as a marketing ploy, but because that's what we thought he was – a veritable genius."

Ray himself was more self-effacing whenever the issue was raised. "I don't kid myself," he would tell *Esquire* magazine in 2003. "I know I'm not a genius. A genius is somebody like Art Tatum or Charlie Parker. I don't come close to those guys. I just happen to be a guy that can do a lot of little things and do 'em well."

As the Fifties came to an end, Ray Charles' achievements were unique in record industry terms, however you chose to describe him. Having brought black rhythm & blues out of the ghetto into the popular arena, he was at the sharp end of what was starting to be known as soul music. With entries in the pop charts he also had a foothold in the teenage singles market, he had a huge following among the influential jazz audience, and with his last long-player addressed the "adult" album-oriented mainstream. He'd even covered a country and western song for his most recent single. He was at that time Atlantic Records' greatest single asset, and artistically their most exciting prospect, with the Sixties getting nearer by the week.

10

One Mint Julep

"We lost Ray Charles and Bobby Darin the same year, and my partners and I thought, 'Well, it could be the end of Atlantic Records,' and the following year was the biggest year we'd had."

– Ahmet Ertegun

When Ray Charles left Atlantic late in 1959, the shock waves that ran through the label can only be imagined.

His contract had been up for renewal in October, but when he didn't re-sign right away nobody gave it much thought at first. He was on the road, the paperwork could wait till he was next in New York City. But the bombshell dropped when he *did* eventually come to see them. He told them quite bluntly that another company had made him an offer he could hardly refuse, though if Ahmet and Jerry could match it, he would stay.

With the impetus of everything going on around him, the last thing Ray would have thought about was leaving the label that had cultivated his talent and allowed it to develop as his instincts dictated. Ahmet, Nesuhi, Jerry and Tom Dowd were like family, he simply wouldn't have been where he was without them. To Ray as much as the company, the notion that he would leave Atlantic was unthinkable. That was until the idea was nurtured by Milt Shaw that he should seek a better offer elsewhere.

When the Shaw Agency's founder and boss Billy Shaw died in 1956, the business had been taken over by his son Milt, Ray's occasional drug buddy and closest confidant in the agency. Now, with his star riding high, Milt and Shaw employee Larry Myers were convinced that Ray could do even better on a label with more financial clout that would market his music specifically towards the mainstream consumer. Why be limited by recording for what was still basically a jazz and R&B label?

Ray and Milton Shaw also shared a camaraderie focussed around their mutual heroin habits, there was a "junky trust" between them – Milton helping Ray score dope via members of the entourage and so on – that Ahmet Ertegun always felt contributed to Ray going along with the idea. "Ray Charles had a man who led him around, he also bought his dope . . . Billy Shaw, who was originally part of Ray's agency had died, and his son took over the management of his booking agency, and I think that the son manoeuvred this whole thing."

Whatever, by mid-October Myers and Shaw had engineered a meeting with Sam Clark and Larry Newton of the up-and-coming ABC-Paramount label which, although only set up four years before, had the financial backing of the powerful American Broadcasting Company. Already thrashed out with the two Shaw men, the deal Clark and Newton put in front of Ray and Jeff Brown was, by record industry standards, staggering.

Treating Ray as producer rather than artist, they offered him an un-precedented 75 per cent of sales receipts after the company had recouped its recording, distribution and marketing costs, out of which the Shaw agency would receive 10 per cent for negotiating the deal. Also part of the three-year contract was a guarantee against royalties of $50,000 per year, whether they sold enough records or not.

Of course, with Jerry Wexler at the helm Ray had been increasingly involved in producing his music, so little would change on that front except to give him even more flexibility in the studio. And the icing was applied more than liberally on the financial cake when the company agreed to Ray's caveat that after five years he would own all master tapes to his material, thus allowing *him* rather than ABC-Paramount to market them in the long term. Another first in the normally exploitative world of artist-label relationships.

The first Atlantic heard of the proposal was when Ray sat down with them and spelled it out, assuring them if they could offer the equivalent he wouldn't make a move. Of course, Ray wasn't naïve. He knew the chances of Atlantic being able to match the deal were minimal, while recognising at the same time that the ABC offer was made with their own interests at heart – to get a foothold in the R&B market, to have some big-selling records and raise the profile of the company into the bargain – however generous it sounded. "ABC at the time was offering me the kind of a contract that, believe me, in those days, in 1959, was unheard of . . ." he told *Rolling Stone* in 1973. "So what they were basically after was the name, and to stimulate other names . . . so I was like a pawn."

Ahmet and Jerry were stunned, they couldn't have anticipated this in a million years. They told Ray that while they wished only the best for him, they simply couldn't come anywhere near the ABC deal. It was as simple as that.

Through November, as *The Genius . . .* and 'I'm Movin' On' climbed their respective charts and the *What'd I Say* album continued to make its mark, Atlantic heard nothing from Ray to suggest that he'd finally signed with ABC; the first they knew about it was when they heard it through a third party, confirmed when *Billboard* ran the story in their issue of December 7.

To this day, Ahmet Ertegun suspects that Ray might not have actually signed until after the deal was announced: "It was a shock to us, and it was a shock to him . . . because he didn't know about it. At the time it happened, he was not aware of it . . . because he called me after that time, he called me from New Orleans and said he was coming to New York to record the following week, and I told him that he'd been signed up to another company. I don't know for sure what happened . . . what I do know is that we did lose him. Afterwards, when there were explanations of how it happened, even though I knew it wasn't so, I never said anything 'cos it didn't matter, the fact is that we lost him."

But signed contract or not, it's clear from his own statements at the time – and over the years since – that Ray had made up his mind to go with ABC from the moment Atlantic said they couldn't match the offer. Later in life, as he did in a long in-depth interview with writer Whitney Balliett originally published in the *New Yorker* in 1970, he would pass comment on the episode rather more blandly than the tensions created at the time justified: "There was no bad feelings. It was just an honest business arrangement."

Once the deal was done, Atlantic had to face it as a *fait accompli*, though none would deny it was a huge shock to the company system, as Nesuhi Ertegun recalled: "His contract had run out, and I think the management decision was made . . . there are always these business decisions. But frankly I was extremely sorry when he left Atlantic, I mean really sorry, that was a blow to us, and it's no use pretending that it wasn't . . . because we thought we'd been right by him, and thought he should have stayed with us, but it was out of our control."

Miriam Abramson, by then Miriam Bienstock after divorcing Herb Abramson and remarrying but still an integral part of the company, was less philosophical about Ray's departure, even years later bitterly commenting:

"We felt betrayed, it was a terrible thing . . . It's an amazing thing that blind people are not as benign as they are portrayed in literature. They're supposed to have this second sight, and they're always supposed to be so God-like. But they're not: because they don't have sight, they're very, very suspicious, and they're not always the most pleasant people to work with, in my experience."

On a purely financial level, Ahmet recognised it could have heralded the demise of the label, but – with the considerable asset of their Ray Charles catalogue of course – the opposite was the case. "At the time – the why, and how, and so forth – after all that happens, who cares? We lost Ray Charles and Bobby Darin the same year, and my partners and I thought, 'Well, it could be the end of Atlantic Records,' and the following year was the biggest year we'd had . . ."

During the last three months of 1959 there were other changes on the horizon.

Margie Hendricks took leave from The Raelettes to have her baby, moving back in with her sister Lula in Harlem, to be replaced temporarily by Raelette Pat Lyles' mother Mae Mosely Lyles. It was the formidable Mae – who made it known she also sang – who Ray had sought permission from for her daughter to go on the road as a Cookie back in January 1958. Now there was a mother-and-daughter presence in the line-up, and while Margie recuperated after the birth of a son, Charles Wayne, Mae Mosely took her place in more ways than one. Although Margie would stay with the group for another four-and-a-half years, when she returned a couple of months after the birth Mae had usurped her in Ray's affections, and would remain his mistress till the end of 1964, just a little longer than Margie would remain a Raelette.

A new face also appeared in the trumpet section: Phillip Guilbeau, a young player from Louisiana who would quickly become one of the most respected musicians ever to be a permanent part of a Ray Charles line-up. And, increasing the size of the band from seven to eight, Ray brought baritone saxophonist Leroy Cooper back into the fold, the same "Hog" Cooper who'd left the band at the end of 1957. In fact Cooper was instrumental in arranging for Guilbeau to audition for the job: "We interviewed Guilbeau in Washington DC, at the Howard Theater, he was a member of the house band, and we went in there to catch them – Edgar Willis and myself."

With Hog back, Hank Crawford was moved from baritone to alto. The

Ray Charles small band, as their leader began his recording relationship with ABC-Paramount, was as musically strong a unit as any that had graced his Atlantic sides through the latter half of the Fifties. But it wasn't going to stay a small band for very much longer. Spurred both by the current success of *The Genius Of Ray Charles* and his new-found financial security under the ABC deal, Ray began thinking seriously about his long-cherished ambition to take a permanent big band on the road.

Meantime, Ray's new label was eager to get some product, to use a music industry term, out of their new investment. Ray had returned to his Los Angeles home to spend the Christmas holiday with Della and the boys, and ABC flew the house A&R man Sid Feller from New York to meet him there.

Feller had played trumpet with small groups in his home city of New York before being drafted into the US Army during World War II, after which he toured for several years with the Carmen Cavallero band. In 1951 he became one of the Musical Directors at the then new Capitol Records, where he worked as producer, arranger and conductor with Jackie Gleason, Peggy Lee, Dean Martin, Mel Tormé, Nancy Wilson et al., before joining ABC when it was founded in 1955, being a major player in the label's growth through the late Fifties. Although his previous recording work was on material that would today be filed under "easy listening", he and Ray found they had a lot in common – they'd both paid their dues as gigging musicians on the road – and got along together right away. So immediately after Christmas the band were recording again, this time in the Capitol Studios in LA.

The session marked the return of Margie Hendricks after her maternity leave, and on 'My Baby (I Love Her, Yes I Do)', trading verses with Ray in a full-on blues as the other Raelettes announce every line with "My baby . . .", she served notice that she was back with a vengeance. 'Who You Gonna Love' was another laid-back offering, while 'Them That Got' was a sardonic down-on-his-luck 32-bar blues that has the small band sounding like a much bigger outfit, Ray bemoaning his penury and ending with a spoken fade-out:

> *I need a hamburger – in fact a hot dog wouldn't be too bad*
> *I would just be grateful if I could get my hands on most anything . . .*

The three tracks, fine though they were, constituted workaday Ray, and certainly nothing that blew a fanfare for his new label. His regular fans, who like most record buyers didn't read the trade press, wouldn't even have known he'd left Atlantic until they looked at the label on his next release. A single was put out in January 1960 anyway (though the strongest track 'Them That Got' didn't appear on either side), and more or less disappeared without trace sales-wise.

What ABC wanted was a record that appealed to Ray's existing following and staked a claim in the broader market place too, something that told the world that with his new label there was a new Ray Charles. After his debut release's abject failure to set the singles chart alight – and at a time when Atlantic were making a mark there with 'Let The Good Times Roll' from the *Genius* LP – the next move was to concentrate on Ray's first album for his new record company.

Although an element in ABC's pursuit of Ray Charles was to strengthen their position in the R&B market – their only star name in that category was Lloyd Price who'd had three big hits in 1959 – Sid Feller for one wasn't at all taken aback when Ray announced he wanted to do an album of popular songs – no originals – with strings and big band. Nevertheless there were, inevitably, a few raised eyebrows. The company didn't want Ray to alienate his established following by appearing to "sell out" to a more middle-of-the-road approach, which was a very real possibility – Nat "King" Cole, Billie Holiday, even the great Charlie Parker had all suffered criticism from purists when they opted for an orchestral backing or "pop" material.

Ray had, of course, adopted a similar instrumental approach already on *The Genius Of Ray Charles*, though having the Basie band on side one balanced things out as far as most jazz-inclined listeners were concerned. But during the short time they'd known each other, Ray and Sid Feller had established a strong rapport, and the A&R man gave Ray's plan an enthusiastic nod of approval. Feller, like Jerry Wexler before him, realised from the start that, in Wexler's words, "You don't 'produce' Ray Charles, you get out of his way and let him do his thing."

What Ray had in mind was nothing short of a "concept album", years before the term was coined: a selection of mostly well-known songs connected by a single theme, American place names. He drafted Ralph Burns, who'd worked on the *Genius* sessions, to do the arrangements, and provided him with demo tapes of the songs he'd chosen. Sid booked the studio for two sessions at the end of March 1960, at the first of which Burns brought in an orchestra of 35 and a 20-strong male and female chorus, and for the second just the big band.

The songs – and Ray's take on them – varied from the roaring Basie-tinged treatments of familiar stalwarts 'Alabamy Bound', 'Basin Street Blues' and 'Chattanooga Choo Choo' to the sublime balladeering of 'Moonlight In Vermont' and 'Moon Over Miami'. There's the gospel-inspired 'Carry Me Back To Old Virginny', with just the rhythm section and Raelettes, a spirited 'California Here I Come', almost-kitsch arrangement (until Ray comes in) of strings and chorus on 'Blue Hawaii', and light-hearted versions of two oldies associated with crooner Bing Crosby, 'Mississippi Mud' and 'Deep In The Heart Of Texas'.

'New York's My Home', written by Gordon Jenkins in 1956, is a lesser-known item that has Ray, prompted by a Raelette naming alternative places, extolling the virtues of the Big Apple:

> *(What about Hollywood?)*
> *Well Hollywood's got movie stars, and movie tzars, and cocktail bars*
> *and shiny cars,*
> *And a wonderful climate they say . . .*
> *But it hasn't got the handy subway train,*
> *You can't still find a taxi when it rains,*
> *That's why New York's my home, keep your California,*
> *New York's my home sweet home*

With its witty lyric and an evocative slowed-down blues ending, it's an amusing one-off that illustrates just how broad-ranging Ray's choice of material – significantly none of it his own – was becoming. In his autobiography, Ray recalled how a lot of people were surprised to see he was doing 'Alabamy Bound', to which he replied, "That's nothin', I'm also singing 'Mississippi Mud'."

The juxtaposition of ballads and up-beat numbers, strings alternating with the brass-dominated big band, was the final formula that clinched it when the album was put together for release. And ABC, taking full advantage of the "genius" tag that Atlantic had come up with for Ray's previous album that was still showing in the charts, titled the collection *The Genius Hits The Road*.

But the track that eclipsed all others, and indeed outsold the album itself many times over, was what would immediately become *the* definitive version of an old Hoagy Carmichael number (with lyrics by Stuart Gorrell) from 1932, 'Georgia On My Mind'. Ray's bitter-sweet delivery and blues-drenched piano, set against swirling strings and an almost formal-sounding vocal chorus, became an emotion-grabbing *tour de force* in the Ray Charles repertoire, sharing with 'What'd I Say' the status of un-official signature tune. And the song – which in most people's minds thereafter meant Ray's version of the song – was to become the *official* anthem of his home state of Georgia in 1979, nearly 50 years after he was born there.

'Georgia' had always been a familiar song to Ray. He remembered how, back in the Fifties, it started to get to a driver he had at the time – possibly Jeff Brown – when he kept singing it over and over. "We're riding in the car, and I would be singing this song 'Georgia' all the time, and I don't know if the man got sick of me singing it, but he said, 'If you like that song so much, why don't you go on and record it – you're always singing it all the time.' So I said, 'Well, I haven't thought about recording it, I just like the song,' and he said, 'But you're *always* singing it.' So I thought, maybe he's trying to tell me something . . ."

Ray once said of the song: "Other writers can say things I can't say myself," and that first album for ABC marked a demarcation point where the majority of Ray's recordings would feature songs by other writers rather than originals. Released in August 1960, 'Georgia' topped the American pop charts in November, winning Grammy awards for Best Male Vocal and Best Pop Single Performance. It also became Ray Charles' first entry in the British pop charts at the end of the year. And *The Genius Hits The Road* became Ray's first album to make the *Billboard* Top 10 LPs, hitting the number nine spot after entering the chart in October 1960.

But before 'Georgia' was released, ABC put out a single in May, 'Sticks And Stones', which Ray and the band had recorded the previous month. Returning to his small-band rhythm & blues formula, with conga drum and electric piano to the fore and chorus answers from The Raelettes, it repeated the feel of 'What'd I Say', telling any doubters that Brother Ray hadn't lost the faith.

And this was certainly confirmed on the flip side, a straight down-the-line piece of classic blues. Written by "Big" Maceo Merryweather, 'Worried Life Blues' has been one of the most covered of all blues songs, before and after Ray recorded it. Despite a corny spoken intro by Sid Feller, urging, "If you have the blues, why don't you go ahead and sing 'em," it's a rela-tively unknown gem – with a one-verse alto solo from Hank Crawford that's 12 bars of simple perfection. The single was no million-seller, it just made the Top 40 while climbing to number two in the R&B listings (where it vied for position with 'Just For A Thrill' from *The Genius Of Ray*

Charles). Ray, and ABC-Paramount, was going to have to wait till the autumn, and 'Georgia On My Mind', to see any post-Atlantic action in the upper reaches of the pop charts.

Meanwhile – and in many ways a portent of things to come for both Ray and popular music generally – the album chart was where the action was starting to concentrate. Atlantic's *Genius* had shown strongly since February, and would remain in the list for the next nine months, *In Person* joined it there in September, and *The Genius Hits The Road* started its three-month run in October.

As the rival record companies battled it out in the best-seller lists, the Genius was, as usual, hitting the road, with as hectic a one-nighter schedule as he'd ever known, albeit for better money and more comfortable working conditions. He even acquired a personal valet, Roy "Duke" Wade, to look after his immediate needs, arranging his dressing rooms, leading him on stage and so on; Jeff Brown as personal manager now had too many organisational things to cope with to devote the minute-by-minute attention to Ray that had been his duty in the past. In the summer the band began travelling in a flashy new Flexibus, while Ray also bought himself a five-seater airplane, a Cessna 310, in which he would fly to gigs, piloted by Air Force veteran Tom McGarrity. This was touring superstar class, a long way from the Greyhound to Seattle or the Lowell Fulson bandwagon.

A battle far removed from the struggles for *Billboard* supremacy took place in the normally genteel environs of Newport, Rhode Island, when the annual jazz festival exploded in headline-grabbing riots. The line-up at the 1960 event was as star-studded as usual, the big names including Cannonball Adderley, Dave Brubeck, Dizzy Gillespie, Gerry Mulligan and Louis Armstrong – and Ray Charles, who was to close the Saturday concert on July 2. Even an "alternative" festival in Newport ("Newport Rebels"), masterminded by jazzmen Charles Mingus and Max Roach to protest what they felt was a pandering to commercialism favouring a handful of artists on the part of Festival organiser George Wein, didn't stop all the concerts being completely sold out.

On the Saturday, however, over 10,000 beer-inflamed college kids, unable to get tickets for the sell-out performances, clashed with police as they tried to storm the gates and gain entrance. What started with about 300 disgruntled fans rushing the cops escalated as bottles were thrown and windows smashed, tear gas and cracked heads ensuing as a near-state of martial law was declared in the town. By midnight three companies of the

National Guard were patrolling the streets. Inside the park, meanwhile, Ray was working the crowd up to a non-violent frenzy with 'What'd I Say', but as George Wein started to panic he calmed things down with some slow ballads. Even Ray's charismatic performance couldn't help things outside the gates however, and the next day the city council of the staid Victorian resort ordered the rest of the Festival to be called off. Only that afternoon's blues concert headlined (and famously recorded) by Muddy Waters was allowed to go on, the remaining two days of events cancelled.

After a well-deserved month's break from touring, Ray was back in the studios again in August – in Los Angeles this time – making his second album for ABC-Paramount. Ray had decided it was to be another collection with a theme, this time songs about girls. Repeating the *Genius Hits The Road* formula, it would feature another mix of big band and string backings, all orchestrated and conducted by the top jazz arranger Marty Paich with Sid Feller once again producing.

The treatments ranged from the upbeat 'Hardhearted Hannah' and 'Sweet Georgia Brown' to the romantic 'Stella By Starlight' and 'Nancy With The Laughing Face' with some numbers, like the old vaudeville favourite 'Margie' written in 1921, that would have been considered strictly corny in any other hands. But the stand-out track is undoubtedly 'Ruby', with the smooth strings, muted piano and polished choral backing creating a distinguished-sounding setting for Ray's melancholic vocal. It followed 'Georgia On My Mind' into the Top 30 singles chart at the beginning of December.

Titled *Dedicated To You* and released the following January, the album, without a quality classic like 'Georgia', the hip humour of 'New York's My Home' or the raunchy swing of 'Alabamy Bound', seemed to confirm the suspicions of those who feared Ray was giving in to some "easy listening" lobby at ABC. But in fact the choices of songs, and treatments thereof, were all of Ray's making, and any suspicions would be allayed completely just a month later with the album that would follow, the masterpiece *Genius + Soul = Jazz*.

As 'Georgia On My Mind' finally hit number one in the US pop chart on November 14, while climbing the sales lists in France, Great Britain and elsewhere, Ray Charles was able to bask in the spotlight as a bona fide pop star of the first order, at the same time enjoying the respect of the more "serious" jazz public; he'd graced the front cover of the "jazz bible" *Down Beat* magazine back in July, and plugged 'Georgia' on Hugh Hefner's TV show *Playboy's Penthouse*, his first television appearance since the McSon Trio's local Seattle series 12 years earlier.

Making over three quarters of a million dollars in 1960 from his record sales on ABC alone, Ray was able to look after those around him without worrying how the next bill would be paid. For Della – who was pregnant again – it meant financial security despite her husband's absence for long periods and the inevitable infidelities that accompanied it. For Margie Hendricks, it meant the welfare of her one-year-old son Charles Wayne was taken care of, and for her successor in Ray's affections, Mae Mosely (who herself became pregnant at the end of the year) it meant a new apartment on Manhattan's smart Upper West Side. For the boys in the band it still meant the $175 a week they'd been on for the past year or so.

For Ray's next album, despite it being very much a jazz project, only one member of his touring outfit would take part in the session, his new trumpet protégé Phillip Guilbeau. Sid Feller had booked a New Jersey studio during the last week in December for an ambitious couple of sessions that would feature arrangements by Quincy Jones and Ralph Burns – the core of the Atlantic *Genius* team once again.

With Sid Feller taking a back seat, the album was produced by Creed Taylor, who was heading up ABC's new jazz label Impulse! With its slogan "The New Wave Of Jazz Is On Impulse!", the label soon established itself at the cutting edge in the early Sixties, responsible for seminal releases by John Coltrane, Charles Mingus, Oliver Nelson and others. To say the brief for the Ray Charles project was ambitious would be an understatement: Taylor had booked for the first session no less than the entire Count Basie band minus its leader. With Guilbeau added to the trumpet section and Ray on Hammond organ throughout, the 17-piece ensemble was matched in power on the second day by an 18-piece comprising a hand-picked cross section of the best studio players around.

The Basie band at that time was one of his classic post-war line-ups, including Clark Terry and Joe Newman leading the trumpets, the two Franks – Foster and Wess – on tenor and alto sax respectively, Urbie Green, Al Grey and Henry Coker making up an all-star trombone team and a rhythm section that featured Basie veteran Freddie Greene on guitar and drummer Sonny Payne. The second outfit included Clark Terry and Urbie Green from the Basie band, Earl Warren on alto, the great Roy Haynes on drums, and once again Guilbeau on trumpet with Ray Charles on organ. The results were simply sensational.

On the first day five roaring instrumentals were taped revealing, in the words of Dick Katz's liner notes, "the Basie band in all its glory". They included a timely Jones-arranged version of the then current Bobby Timmons favourite 'Moanin'', a couple of Charles originals, and a power-house run-through of the old Gershwin standby 'Strike Up The Band', played like you'd never heard it before. And despite the august company he was keeping in the brass section, Guilbeau handles all the trumpet solos with aplomb.

But the undisputed highlight was the only vocal recorded at that session, 'I Got News For You'. Written by Ray Alfred, the lyric has Ray Charles admonishing his duplicitous wife/girlfriend, with some coolly sardonic observations:

> *You said before we met*
> *That your life was awful tame*
> *Well, I took you to a nightclub*
> *And the whole band knew your name.*

. . . and things don't get any better for him as the song progresses

> *You wore a diamond watch,*
> *Claimed it was from Uncle Joe.*
> *When I looked at the inscription*
> *It said, 'Love from Daddy-O'.*

The *tour de force* of the session, Ray's organ leads throughout, with a spine-tingling solo that's matched by blistering Burns charts from the rest of the band, and his screams and shouts as he repeats the concluding lines

> *Somehow your story don't ring true*
> *Oh, I've got news for you.*

The second session delivered three more instrumentals along with the only other vocal item to appear on the album. Another Ray original – 'Let's Go' – features Basie tenor man Frank Foster before another Guilbeau solo, while the old Twenties standard 'Birth Of The Blues' highlights more of Ray's organ style. And with its Latin feel (perfect for the cha-cha dance craze raging at the time), shouted interjections from the band and Ray's understated "just a little bit of soul now" after the first time round, 'One Mint Julep' was immediately to become as much an instrumental signature of the Ray Charles band as were 'What'd I Say' and 'Georgia' vocal ones.

Describing the vocal of the set, 'I'm Gonna Move To The Outskirts Of Town' – a simply stunning version of a number originated by blues singer/guitarist William "Casey Bill" Weldon in the Thirties – Dick Katz's sleeve note is worth quoting in full: "This is my favourite in the album. Not since the classic Jimmy Rushing–Count Basie version have I enjoyed this timeless blues so much. Take note of the beautiful Clark Terry trumpet introduction. Charles' moving vocal is complemented by a fine trumpet obbligato by Phillip Guilbeau. Arrangement is by Quincy Jones."

When the album appeared in February 1961, with 'One Mint Julep' and 'Let's Go' on either side of a simultaneously released single, it set the seal on Ray's acceptance by the American jazz cognoscenti. More significantly, it validated the support of legions of young people in Europe, particularly in France and Great Britain, where by this time he had achieved the status of a cult hero.

11

Cult Hero

"I never thought about my glasses being hip. When I started out, I could never even afford glasses."

– Ray Charles

There had been talk of Ray Charles doing some dates in France over the previous few months, and things were beginning to fall into place via fevered negotiations between the Shaw people and French agent Henri Goldgran. Eventually Ray and the band's first visit to Europe would be at the annual International Jazz Festival in Juan-les-Pains, near Antibes on the Côte d'Azur. But between the February release of *Genius + Soul* and Antibes there was a lot to keep Ray's attention focussed far nearer to home than the sunny beaches of the French Riviera.

February 1961 saw Ray make his debut on coast-to-coast network television, an inauspicious few minutes on the *Kraft Music Hall* fronted by singer Perry Como which did little to spread the message of what a Ray Charles live performance was all about. But in March, he got involved in a much bigger message when he refused to play to a segregated audience in his home state of Georgia.

Since he'd first gone on the road, Ray – like all black performers – had quickly got used to the idea of playing to segregated audiences. These weren't always whites-only events, but often for mixed crowds where the whites occupied the best seats at the front and the blacks the balcony or whatever, the latter even having to enter by a separate entrance in many instances. Like all aspects of "Jim Crow" it was *de rigueur* in the South, and still common practice in many places in the North, in the Fifties and early Sixties. But without that work, bands and singers simply couldn't survive, especially someone like Ray whose core following for many years had been almost exclusively drawn from the (largely Southern) black community.

But, to paraphrase a British politician talking about Africa at the time, there was a wind of change blowing across the land. When Ray was contacted by civil rights-supporting students before playing a segregated date – blacks upstairs, whites downstairs – at a small college in Augusta, Georgia, he decided enough was enough. He pulled out of the March gig at short notice and, despite a fine for breach of contract, from that day on refused to play any more such concerts. "I told the promoter that I didn't mind segregation, except that he had it backwards. After all, I was black and it only made sense to have the black folk close to me. Let him sue. I wasn't going to play. And I didn't. And he sued. And I lost."

Suddenly Brother Ray found himself at the forefront of the struggle, albeit strictly on his own terms: "It had nothing to do with Martin Luther King, although I was definitely into him when he came out. My attitude was: my people made me, and I cannot deal with the fact that they cannot sit anywhere they want to sit. I just cannot deal with that.

"I figured if I was going to pick up my cross and follow someone, it could only be Martin," Ray would say, but he decided early on that his contribution would be in the form of support – mainly financial – rather than any physical involvement in the front line. "First, I wouldn't have known when to duck when they started throwing broken bottles at my head. And I told that to Martin personally."

As he would stress to Max Jones in *Melody Maker* a couple of years later, "It means a lot to me, for what I am. I'm not a politician; I can only say the way I feel. And that is, I'd like to see the country become what it should be." And a few months later, Ray's decision not to play any more segregated dates would lead directly to the first-ever integrated concert to be held in Memphis, Tennessee.

Looking at an old picture he'd taken of Ray Charles holding a saxophone, veteran photographer of the Memphis music scene Ernest Withers described to journalist Andria Lisle pre-integration concerts in the city: "This was from an appearance at the City Auditorium – a blacks-only show. Nothing at that time was integrated, Memphis was a separate town. White people used to come on Beale Street to the Palace Theater on a special night for white attendance at the Midnight Ramble. At a given time, the black theatre switched to whites only. They didn't put signs up – it was just understood – 'no black people'. And the same thing would happen for black people at the City Auditorium."

Just how toughly "Jim Crow" could be applied in Memphis, even when the barriers were starting to come down, was vividly recalled by writer

Stanley Booth in his book *Rhythm Oil* – the occasion being an appearance by Ray shortly before he took his stand in Augusta. "My first experience on Beale Street was being thrown out of a Ray Charles concert at the Hippodrome for sharing a table with some black classmates from the newly integrated Memphis State University. There were tables for blacks and tables for whites, but no mixing allowed. 'What you mean, pattin' these nigger girls on the ass?' a cop asked me. 'I haven't patted anybody on the ass yet, sweetheart,' I said, finding myself seconds later face to face with the gravel in the alley."

The Hippodrome was run by a local black club owner, Andrew "Sunbeam" Mitchell, who among other establishments had owned Mitchell's Hotel, catering mainly for musicians, which he made available for meetings and rallies during the civil rights struggle. It was Mitchell who had booked Ray and the band into the City Auditorium, not long after the local authorities had given promoters the choice between a segregated or integrated event. Up till that point promoters, white and black, had opted for segregation for the sake of a peaceful life, but prompted by Ray's refusal to play any more segregated dates Mitchell stood his ground and the gig went ahead with a totally mixed audience – and no trouble.

Taking the very public position that he had on the whole race issue could only enhance Ray's reputation even further with his youthful followers at home and, increasingly, abroad, a staunchly liberal constituency in the increasingly progressive atmosphere of the early Sixties.

Just a couple of weeks after making his stand in Augusta, Ray embarked on his first "official" national tour, organised as an integrated 20-venue series of dates rather than individual one-nighters. Put together by LA promoter Hal Zeiger, who was organising more and more of Ray's appearances in the more prestigious venues that were becoming the norm, it meant another ambition realised – not the nationwide trek itself, but the opportunity for Ray to assemble an on-the-road big band for the first time.

Modelled on the great ensembles he'd admired since his youth, Ray set about creating his 17-piece outfit, which, using his ready-made small group as a nucleus, didn't take long: "It took no more than three or four days to select the cats I wanted." As well as his existing sidemen, the "augmented orchestra", as it was billed, featured a four-piece trombone section, two more saxes (including returnee Don Wilkerson) and two more trumpets (with another old face, Marcus Belgrave), plus a guitarist –

Sonny Forrest who'd previously been with the Atlantic vocal group The Coasters. As well as playing alto sax, Hank Crawford was Musical Director in charge of most of the charts, a department in which Quincy Jones also helped out, having disbanded his own big band with a pile of arrangements going spare. "Quincy Jones, he and Ray were great friends," Fathead Newman explained, ". . . and Quincy gave Ray Charles his book, his repertoire, which he'd had when *he* was using a big band, so that was how Ray got started with a big band, he had all these Quincy Jones arrangements. He did a few arrangements on his own, but he didn't do too many big band arrangements, he did a few, maybe five or six, but both the bands (the big outfit and core small band) started out with Quincy's repertoire."

For Leroy Cooper the expansion to a big band was an improvement as far as he was concerned: "I enjoyed it immensely because I was on the bottom, you know on the baritone, and I enjoyed playing with the big band. We had Quincy's book, as Quincy didn't need it any more. Plus all the guys in the band were writing, anybody could contribute numbers to the band. Because we were always playing before he came on. So, we had some good numbers, and some bad . . ."

So after rehearsals the company commenced their 20-city tour, which was to have its grand finale in New York's Carnegie Hall on the last day of April.

Part-way into the tour, Hal Zeigler decided that what the show needed to give it a bit more pazzazz, a bit more class, was an MC to introduce the band, introduce Ray and generally hold things together. So it was that Joe Adams came on board, doing announcements, adjusting the lighting for various songs, generally giving the whole performance some showbiz polish. He'd worked the Broadway stage as an actor – he knew about these things. He'd also been a successful radio announcer and DJ, which was how he and Ray had briefly met back in LA in 1950, when the young singer got an on-air mention from the presenter on KOWL.

As soon as he joined the Ray Charles entourage Adams made his mark as a smooth-talking hands-on operator who got things done. Ray was impressed, and before long Adams would replace Jeff Brown as both his close confidant and personal manager – a position he would retain until the final year of the singer's life.

As the instrumental single 'One Mint Julep' found its way into the Top 20 pop listings, and hit number one in the R&B chart, the tour finished at Carnegie Hall. Although at this stage something of a speculative experiment, the big band presentation would set the pattern for most of Ray's touring work for the rest of his career. If he, Shaw and Zeigler had felt it *hadn't* worked, he would have reverted (albeit reluctantly) to the tried and trusted small band format. As it was, despite some muted reviews, they were confident it had.

Meanwhile Ray's family life – to be more accurate, "families" in the plural – was getting complicated. Margie Hendricks was now completely sidelined in favour of her "maternity leave" replacement Mae Mosely in Ray's personal life, although she was still a Raelette *and* the mother of his child. Mae Mosely, who was more and more taking on the role of an alternative east coast "wife", had a baby due in August. And Della had given birth to their third son, Robert.

So, the tour over, Ray was able to spend some time in Los Angeles, at home with his official family. Work was never far away, of course. As well as some nightclub dates in the black district of South Central, arranger Marty Paich had been hired again for Ray's next album, to be recorded in the city. The plan this time was for a set of duets with a singer who had been a featured guest vocalist on the recent tour, 31-year-old Betty Carter.

Recording since the late Forties with such jazz names as Lionel Hampton, Ray Bryant and the pioneer of bop-singing "vocalese" King Pleasure, Carter had earned herself the nickname of "The Bebop Girl" and was becoming well known for her off-beat interpretations of classic tunes and adventurous scat-singing. She was signed to ABC-Paramount for her 1960 album *The Modern Sound Of Betty Carter*, and was initially recommended to Ray by no less an authority than Miles Davis. Ray first heard her with the Lionel Hampton band, as a result of which she appeared on a number of packages with the Charles show before the 1961 national tour.

The two sessions, which took place on June 13 and 14, featured a string orchestra and the Jack Halloran Singers on five tracks, with a big band line-up for the other seven. It was still in the early days of "left or right" stereo recording, as producer Sid Feller's now-quaint liner notes reveal when he describes the studio set-up for the band tracks: "Instead of the usual five-saxophone section, Ray used the regular front line of his own small band (alto, tenor and baritone saxes and two trumpets), these five playing on the left track of the tape; the conventional eight brass (four trumpets, four trombones) were recorded on the right track. This was augmented by the rhythm section, with Ray himself on piano . . . The effect is rather startling, almost in the manner of a 'challenge' of a small combo against the force of full, powerful brass."

The "ping-pong" effect that this would suggest was lost, however, in the overall magic of the vocals. Classic love songs like 'We'll Be Together Again' and 'For All We Know' are set against such up-beat swingers as 'You And I' and Rodgers & Hammerstein's 'People Will Say We're In Love', plus light-hearted standards 'Side By Side' and 'It Takes Two To Tango', literally written for the duet treatment. But the most successful in this last category was the A-side of the single culled from the album, 'Baby, It's Cold Outside', a humorous give-and-take exchange written in the late Forties by Frank Loesser but immortalised in this version. Indeed, at a 1997 White House ceremony where President Clinton presented Betty Carter with a National Medal of Arts, the President commented, "Hearing her sing 'Baby, It's Cold Outside' makes you want to curl up in front of the fire, even in summertime."

While the recording was being made, word got around Hollywood about the sessions with the result that the studio was usually full of well-wishers, fans and assorted hangers-on from the cinema and music world, including, according to Feller, some very high-profile movie stars. The Ray Charles/Betty Carter recording dates had become something of an "open house", with little room left in the control room for Sid and his engineer. At one stage, when things got a little too much, the producer had to announce to the gathered "audience" that this wasn't a concert, and could they please clear the control room after the next take.

As what he called "a commercial afterthought", Feller reminded the assembled throng that the album was due for imminent release, and they could do no better than go out and buy it, secure in the knowledge that they could tell their friends, "I was there!"

Vocalist Little Jimmie Scott, whose path had crossed that of Ray's several times as an on-the-road entertainer, and who recorded for Ray's Tangerine label later in the Sixties, remembered the impression the album made on him in a 2001 article in *Mojo* magazine: "It's a real education to young musicians and vocalists coming along. If they're listening well and have any thought about the technology of music, they could really get something out of this. Betty has to sing in her high range for most of it. It's like her high horn. If you listen to just the musical line rather than the vocal expression, on some things her voice sounds like a piccolo or something. But you see every note was in place, she was there, she could deal with it. She had a unique way of reaching for high tones but clearly projecting.

My favourite track is 'For All We Know'. That was good, I found a lot in that one. If you just want to groove a little, 'It Takes Two To Tango' is nice. The best version of 'Baby, It's Cold Outside' I've ever heard. This is a real hip album. Musicians would have really dug it."

After a two week run at New York's Apollo Theater, the small band was in the studio again for a short session that produced four of Ray's most memorable tracks, including one of his biggest hits. Three of the songs were written by the great Percy Mayfield, a pioneer of urban rhythm & blues. Among Mayfield's best-known compositions was 'Please Send Me Someone To Love' which he recorded in 1950, but his career as a live performer was compromised after he was disfigured in a 1952 car smash. He had carried on writing for a living, and the three tunes cut that day represented the beginning of a fruitful relationship with Ray.

One of the Mayfield numbers laid down, 'The Danger Zone' actually bears a strong chordal similarity to 'Please Send Me Someone To Love'. Although mooted by many as a reflection on the civil rights struggle raging in the South at the time, it could equally be interpreted as addressing the nuclear annihilation threatened by the Cold War:

> *Just read your paper and you'll see*
> *Exactly what's been worrying me*

with the chilling admission

> *That's why I'm so afraid*
> *Of the progress that's being made*
> *Toward eternity*

Equally intriguing are the lyrics for the other slow number of the set, 'But On The Other Hand Baby', a stark blues in which Ray sings, against Phillip Guilbeau's muted trumpet backing, of his unfaithful woman whose love eclipses her shortcomings. From the introductory line

> *You know I'm hooked for you mama*

the song (credited to Mayfield *and* Charles) could also read as a metaphor for a love-hate relationship with heroin

> *But on the other hand baby*
> *Your lovin' eases all my pain*
> *When you put your lovin' arms around me*
> *You make old Ray forget about everything*

Written by Teddy Powell and Robert Sharp Jr, 'Unchain My Heart' is a strong mid-tempo blues with an irresistible Latin dance beat, The Raelettes echoing every line and Fathead soaring on the break. But it was an up-beat Percy Mayfield track that was to become a worldwide smash, a singalong item with a hook that everyone recognised. 'Hit The Road Jack' has it all – the small band sound, a descending bass line that takes the listeners effortlessly through each chorus, humorous husband-versus-wife lyrics and Ray sparring vocally with a foxy-sounding Margie Hendricks backed by her female cohorts. In short, it's perfect pop. Released in August with 'The Danger Zone' as its B-side, it had shot to the *Billboard* number one spot by mid-September, and at number six was also Ray's first Top 10 entry in the UK.

Before 'Hit The Road Jack' hit the shops, Ray Charles and co. made their first foray overseas, with the much-anticipated gigs at the Antibes jazz festival. With the whole entourage in tow – including an eight-months pregnant Mae Mosely – Ray spent four days in July under the full spotlight of an eager media, including all of Europe's music press and French television. This was when it really struck home to both Ray and the band how much of an international name he had become – something it was not always easy to appreciate in the culturally insular United States.

Visitors to the festival included the English jazz singer Beryl Bryden. "He just sat and played piano with the band for 20 minutes with everybody in the audience getting fidgety," she told *Melody Maker*. "Just when I thought people might start booing he stood up and started singing 'Georgia On My Mind'. There was a tremendous hush before the screaming and clapping started. It just starts building up and up. Then The Raelettes come on and wriggle their bodies, which adds to the general excitement."

Another eyewitness was future Rolling Stones manager Andrew Loog Oldham. "His performance must be seen to be believed. He has the audience in his hands from the time he opens up . . . The atmosphere is electric, and in the quieter numbers you can't hear a sound from the audience."

One British devotee who didn't make the gigs was the singer Eric Burdon, then an art student and avowed Ray Charles fanatic: "I had tickets for the festival. I hitchhiked all the way, and I got there too late. So I headed towards Paris, and I made friends with some local Parisians who told me that there was a jam going to take place in a club the next night so

I got to see him close up in a nightclub.* Not with the whole band but with just the rhythm section. I was very fortunate on that score."

Those summer dates in the South of France, however, were a mere preamble to a three-day visit to Paris which Henri Goldgran had arranged for October. When Ray arrived in the French capital after two one-nighters in Zurich and Lyon, talk of "Le Génie" was on everyone's lips as he proceeded to take the city by storm.

Like movies, food and wine, jazz had become something of a national institution in France. During the Twenties the Black American singer and dancer Josephine Baker became a French superstar with her exotic per-formance in the spectacular jazz-influenced *La Revue Nègre*. In 1929, Jean Cocteau and fellow Parisian intellectuals had even demanded that jazz should be recognised as an art form on a par with cinema and modern painting.

Having produced Europe's first jazz legend – Belgian guitarist Django Reinhardt with the Quintette du Hot Club du France – the French capital became a magnet for a colony of Black American musicians after World War II. The most famous was saxophone star Sidney Bechet followed by such luminaries as pianist Bud Powell, blues man Memphis Slim, drummer Kenny Clarke and saxophone players Don Byas and Johnny Griffin. Miles Davis famously spent some time there in 1957, playing the Left Bank clubs, striking up a relationship with the iconic French film actress/singer Juliette Greco and recording his celebrated soundtrack to Louis Malle's film *Ascenseur pour l'echafaud (Lift To The Scaffold)*.

Indeed, Parisian record shops were stacked with American discs that had never seen a release across the English Channel, including Ray Charles' pre-'What'd I Say' material and, inevitably, the city became something of a mecca for young British kids like Burdon, still living in his native Newcastle: "I was in art school, I was free to do what I wanted, I had more money in my pocket than I ever had because I used to take summer jobs . . . and I'd go to Paris to buy records, Paris and London. But to see people like Sister Rosetta Tharpe, Chet Baker, Memphis Slim . . . as well as getting to see Ray it was just wonderland, it was terrific."

Referring to a scene in the 1986 jazz film by Bertrand Tavernier *Round Midnight*, set in Fifties Paris, Burdon recalled times when he didn't have enough money to see everything the city had to offer musically: "When I

---

* Ray had decided to spend a couple of days in the capital before returning to the States.

saw that movie . . . wow, that was me! Standing in the rain, listening to the sounds in the nightclub coming out through the cellar, through the gutters 'cos I couldn't afford to get in . . ."

It was, in the words of jazz writer Mike Zwerin, "A special place and time where Existentialists, Beats and beboppers once mingled. Jean-Paul Sartre and Simone de Beauvoir were drinking tea in the Café Flore. The writer Boris Vian blew his pocket trumpet in the Tabou. The Chameleon presented Allen Eager. Allen Ginsberg, Gregory Corso and William Burroughs were guests in the so-called 'Beat Hotel'."

So it was hardly surprising that the French should take Ray Charles to their heart when his records first broke there in the late Fifties. Ray's first release in France had been awarded the Grand Prix du Disque in 1958, and in 1959 'Hallelujah I Love Her So' was a huge hit on the much-listened-to Europe One radio programme. His name and face became a familiar item in French magazines, his records welcomed with adulatory reviews, and long before he set foot on French shores he had become a national favourite. Confirmation of just how great was France's continuing love affair with Ray Charles came a couple of years later, when the French mint actually struck a special coin in his honour.

The Paris shows, which opened on Friday, October 20, were held at the vast but spartan Palais des Sports, with two more dates added to the original three due to the huge demand. Despite some poor acoustics the capacity 6,000-strong crowd were in raptures from the opening number, hanging on the band's every note as the minutes ticked by and tension built before Ray made his entrance. Nothing could have prepared the musicians – or Ray for that matter – for the reception the Paris audience afforded them.

Listening to a live recording of highlights from the Sunday night concert, the sheer electricity in the stadium is palpable, the whistles and screams on Ray's entrance barely subsiding as he launches into 'Let The Good Times Roll', and rising again as he exclaims "Tell everybody, Ray Charles is in town . . ." There's a from-the-heart 'Georgia On My Mind' with David Newman's flute a sparse backing in place of strings, but a perfect foil for a much bluesier vocal than on record in a seven-minute version that has the crowd going berserk at the end. There's more raw blues in a spine-tingling 'I Believe To My Soul' with The Raelettes at their most musically seductive, before Ray stretches out again for another extended treatment, this time 'Come Rain Or Come Shine'.

'Hallelujah' has the crowd applauding Fathead's break in the way that appreciative jazz fans do, and an improvised ride-out that's pure gospel Ray.

A short but roaring 'Alexander's Ragtime Band' answers in two-and-a-half minutes any speculation anyone might have entertained about making the big band permanent. A muted Phillip Guilbeau plays back-up on 'I'm Gonna Move To The Outskirts Of Town', the Quincy Jones chart retaining all the power of the studio cut. Ray's on organ throughout the gig, and on 'Outskirts' simply shines.

'Hit The Road Jack' is tight, the girls spot-on, the crowd clapping on the off-beat, while 'Margie' has Ray in the finger-clicking mode of the big band swinger. A full-on soul stew is the recipe for 'I Wonder', with The Raelettes' harmonies and Ray's preachin' organ straight out of church. And 'What'd I Say' takes the ecstatic crowd just where they want to go, and some more. The whole stadium joins in the call-and-response, as Ray rides it for all it's worth.

At the time France was in turmoil on account of the independence struggle taking place in Algeria, Paris rocked by terrorist bombs and the threat of a coup by Army factions opposed to any withdrawal from the colony. To a kid like Eric Burdon this was exciting stuff: "When I went back to Paris the Algerian army revolt started. They thought paratroopers were going to jump out of the sky and take over the capital. And I was so young and dumb, I thought it was great, action going on in the streets, bank robberies every day and plastic bombs going off. . . ."

As a consequence, during the days leading up to the concert the police had turned the Palais des Sports into a vast prison, housing thousands of Algerians arrested during a street demonstration. In fact a cocktail party given in Ray's honour the day before the first concert had to be moved to the Claridge Hotel where he was staying, because the stadium was still under police control, casting doubts about the venue right up to the last minute, as the UK *Melody Maker* reported. "No one knew whether the £21,000 taken for tickets for a Palais concert would have to be returned or not."

In his autobiography, Ray has his own little story to tell involving the troubles on the streets: "The Algerian War was in full blast; bombs were exploding all over town. But the Algerians sent a note to my promoter saying that there'd be no bombings on my route from the hotel to the concert hall. 'Tell Brother Ray not to worry,' they said. And I didn't." Leroy Cooper recalled how, for the band at least, it could seem rather more threatening: "It was very frightening. Like we always had to eat late at night after concerts, and we were always afraid that those people would kick the doors open and spray us with automatic weapons . . . it was quite scary."

The British music press, particularly the "musicians' bible" *Melody Maker*, had followed the build-up to Ray's Paris debut avidly, revelling in a kind of Charles-mania by proxy that (in his absence from Britain) made the French dates all the more tantalising. Their man in Paris, Henry Kahn, jostled with fellow journalists to speak to Ray as he held court in the hotel on the fashionable Champs-Élysées. "Practically every radio station in Europe had sent someone to interview him, and I heard him repeat the same stories over and over again. He did not mind – he even seemed to enjoy it."

Ray enthused to Kahn about the Paris jazz scene and the appreciative fans in Europe: "After Antibes I came to Paris for a couple of days . . . this time I hope to get around and hear some of that great French jazz I have heard about. I don't believe I earn appreciation quite so much anywhere as I do in Europe, and particularly in France. My impression is that the European has a fuller appreciation of jazz than even the American. I always feel that the audience is with me when I am singing, and this is appreciation at its best."

"In Europe," Ray would enthuse years later, "you find people who know all about our music. I'm talking about the average person. I've been to Europe and talked to people who have records of mine that I forgot I ever made! And I find that incredible."

"And in the very early Sixties . . . the heavy art school cults were Ray Charles and Chuck Berry and Bo Diddley, Muddy Waters, Charlie Mingus, and Monk, Allen Ginsberg and Jack Kerouac, Robert Johnson." So wrote Nik Cohn in 1969 in his highly personal view of rock'n'roll history, *Awopbopaloobop Alopbamboom: Pop From The Beginning*. "Art school cults" was really a shorthand for the trendiest elements of British youth culture before the advent of the beat boom spearheaded by The Beatles and Rolling Stones. This was what the kids who would be the movers and shakers of the new decade – including those same long-haired upstarts from Liverpool and London – were listening to and taking notice of, and Ray was right there at the top of the list.

Unique among these cult figures of the time – and any other you cared to mention – Ray Charles was the one who spanned the genres, appealing to often otherwise disparate sub-groups of teen culture, as Eric Burdon remembers:

What I liked best about Ray was that he crossed the lines, playing blues, rhythm & blues, gospel, country and western, jazz and rock'n' roll. Before I got to meet the guys who eventually became The Animals I was jamming around Newcastle jazz clubs, and of course the jazz heads were very resistant to allowing someone like me on stage to jam with them. But then I played Mike and Ian Carr – who were the best players in Newcastle – I played Ian Carr an album and he listened to the first track where Ray's playing alto and it caught his ear instantly. Then the next track was the one ('Yes Indeed!') where he says, 'Deep down in your soul, that good old rock'n'roll', and Ian Carr was like, 'Did he say rock'n'roll?' . . . and I think he realised for the first time that those lines could be crossed.

And as far as Burdon is concerned, this helped create the environment in which he developed as a vocalist: "From that point on I was allowed to get up on a Saturday night and do a couple of songs with a band called Mighty Joe Allen's Jazz Band, probably the best Tyneside jazz band. So I was given the opportunity of singing a couple of songs a night, then that got to be four songs, and ended up with a little 45-minute set within their session. Really that's what started me singing." And of course, Charles was a model for actual style too. "Oh yeah . . . every singer around wanted to sing like Ray Charles . . ."

Burdon's subsequent band The Animals – whose pianist Alan Price was also a big Ray Charles fan – would be at the forefront of the British R&B boom that changed pop music forever in the Sixties. And while their blues-based repertoire was drawn from a variety of sources – most famously Bob Dylan on their first two hit singles – The Animals' albums featured half a dozen or so Ray Charles numbers including 'The Right Time', 'Talkin' 'Bout You', 'Mess Around' and 'Hallelujah I Love Her So'.

When The Animals visited New York in 1964, the first thing Burdon did was head for the Apollo, and, inadvertently, Ray's old hotel nearby. "As soon as I hit New York the first place I headed for was the Apollo, and across the street was the St Theresa Hotel, where I guessed that Ray would have stayed, but I didn't know it was until I saw the movie."

Such was Burdon's fan worship, he once sought out Margie Hendricks when he was in New York. "I was so impressed with Margie Hendricks on 'The Night Time Is The Right Time' I ran into her, I found her in New York and spent the night hanging out of her window one summer's evening. When I think back, she was probably stoned by then on junk and that. There wasn't any need to introduce myself, we immediately just became mates hanging out. It was as important for me to meet her, meet the woman behind the voice, as it was to see Ray in person."

Eric Burdon and The Animals weren't the only ones who cited Ray as a major influence. As well as using 'What'd I Say' as a show-stopper in their early Hamburg days, The Beatles even covered 'My Bonnie' on a locally cut single while in the German city, long before they made their "official" records in London. And in early biographies of the group put together by The Beatles' fan club, Ray was named by John Lennon as his favourite singer.

When The Spencer Davis Group emerged from Birmingham in 1964, keyboards man and vocalist Steve Winwood was even heralded as a Ray Charles soundalike, so uncanny were his renditions of 'Georgia On My Mind', 'Drown In My Own Tears' and 'What'd I Say': "It was kind of deliberate in a way, but at the time he was the only person . . . well, okay, you could sing like Elvis or you could sing Italian opera, or you could sing folk songs, but at the time I wasn't interested in any of that at all, so Ray Charles was the only kind of singer who I could copy to learn. I used to hear some import blues records, things like Muddy Waters and Jimmy Reed, but it was just that Ray Charles seemed to take that and pull all those things that I'd been hearing, and took them out of those limits and into a music that was less bogged down by tradition."

In an early Seventies interview, talking about Ray Charles, Van Morrison would recall what attracted him to music back in Belfast a decade before he became a founder member of hit-making R&B band Them. "I'd go as far as to say that that's how I go into the business, that's how I got here, with Leadbelly and Woody Guthrie and Jelly Roll Morton and Ray Charles. That's what made me start singing."

Other bands heavily indebted to Ray were jazz-oriented rhythm & blues line-ups with the emphasis on horn sections rather than guitars, soulful outfits such as Zoot Money's Big Roll Band, (formed in 1961 and whose debut album was titled after one of the tracks *It Should Have Been Me*), and Georgie Fame & The Blue Flames – both leaders of which played Hammond organs.

As Burdon suggests, the UK music scene in the very early Sixties was rigidly pigeon-holed, with jazz fans split between traditionalists and modernists, blues more likely to be considered as a branch of folk music, and rock'n'roll despised by both camps. The popularity of Ray Charles across the board did much to break down these barriers, and the band that embodied this process more than any other was Alexis Korner's Blues Incorporated, long considered a catalyst in the evolution of British R&B.

Although, via harmonica player Cyril Davis, the group was a launchpad for the Chicago-style blues of Muddy Waters that became the trademark of The Rolling Stones and other embryo groups, the line-up of Blues Inc also included two saxes and keyboards (and at one stage an all-girl vocal group, The Velvettes) and owed a lot more to the Charles small band than is often acknowledged. And the Blues Inc saxmen – Dick Heckstall-Smith and Graham Bond – were also part of a loose jazz-and-poetry ensemble called New Departures run by poet Michael Horovitz, which was also the name of an underground literary magazine published by the same writer.

Edition number four in 1962 – a "poetry and jazz special" – was indicative of how the borders were becoming blurred on the cultural map. Among the poems by Yevtushenko, Gregory Corso and others was a feature with songs of Leroy Carr, Bessie Smith, and the entire lyrics of the Ray Charles/Percy Mayfield number 'Tell Me How Do You Feel'. Along with the jazz fraternity, blues aficionados and straightforward fans of that "good ol' rock'n'roll", even London's new literary bohemia had taken Ray on board. While in the north in Liverpool, 16-year-old poet Brian Patten tentatively photocopied his earliest works for local distribution, including a now long-lost 'Ray Charles Poem' which, Patten remembers, referred to "his fingers turning on the light in our minds".

Ray Charles – the *idea* of Ray Charles – had become a genuine icon for an influential generation of young people. Musically, his sexually charged marriage of the sacred and sensual, the sheer abandon of his vocal style like an old-time preacher possessed – "talking in tongues" as the Bible called it – was as liberating as any jazz, as confrontational to most "adult" tastes as any rock'n'roll. Visually, the saxes behind him, the black girls with their hourglass figures, the sharp suits, the wrap-around shades – most of all, the shades – this was cool personified, you simply couldn't get any hipper.

"If you thought yourself at all hip," Cohn would recall, "you automatically worshipped him. Beat poets and hipsters and jazzmen everywhere preached him as a messiah . . . In those times, he was hip status symbol number one."

The image was disseminated largely via the album covers, the intimate close-ups, the keyboard reflected in dark glasses, the onstage shot on

Newport that Eric Burdon remembered as being the first time he heard Ray Charles: "It was probably in a record store in Newcastle when the live LP at Newport came out. There's something about the photograph on the cover. I saw it for the first time in ages the other day, and it was just like a flashback, even down to the microphone that's in front of his face with a huge guard around it, little things like that, and the fabric of his suit – electric blue – things like that."

Even when Ray did what many felt was an unforgivable about-turn into country music, committed fans like Burdon stayed as fanatical as ever. "There was this ex-boxer in Belgium, Freddy his name was, who had a restaurant with a jukebox, and he was such a great music fan there was no pop music on this jukebox. He had jazz, blues, and a lot of Ray Charles stuff. I remember putting a bet on with him that the sax solo in one of Ray's cuts was Fathead Newman playing tenor sax, and he said, 'No it wasn't, it was somebody else.' I came back a year later and he said, 'You really know your stuff, kid, you won the bet, I've checked it out . . .' From that point we became really great friends, and I remember it was on his jukebox that I first heard – he had the first releases of the singles – of Ray's jump into country and western. We were in that bar one day and these US sailors came in, and they were laughing at the idea of a black man playing country and western. Our friend Freddy jumped over the bar, dragged four of them out into the street, and beat the shit out of them!"

For photographer David Redfern, who covered Ray's shows in the UK and elsewhere from the early Sixties on, Ray's was a dynamic, moving image to be captured by the still camera: "To photograph he was great because of the way he'd roll around, hands up in the air and all that stuff, throwing his head all over the place . . . he was a very good subject."

Earlier on in the Fifties, Redfern was typical of a number of many UK jazz fans who got to hear a lot of music via the radio: "At that time I probably couldn't afford to be rushing out and buying lots of records. I used to listen to the Voice of America *Jazz Hour* a lot, introduced by Willis Conover – that was quite an influence to me. In the late Fifties I was living in Brighton, and you could pick up all those Continental radio stations on medium wave. I was a bit of a radio freak, I bought a tuner which I set up myself, so I could get Voice of America very well down there at that time. *Jazz Hour* was 11 to 12 every night, and I used to listen to that a lot, and probably first heard Ray Charles then. But I was definitely into it straight away. I knew a lot about Ray Charles before I even photographed him, but I think it was mainly via the airwaves rather than me going out and buying piles of records . . ."

The cult status that Ray Charles enjoyed among this broad coalition of jazz and blues fans, rock'n'rollers and members of the avant garde "underground" was probably enhanced in some quarters when it became public knowledge that he was involved with heroin. In those more innocent – and it has to be said naïve – times, a romantic image persisted of the tortured artist finding inspiration in drink and drugs. This had particular resonance in far-away Europe regarding the case histories of American jazz musicians known for their addictions, despite the tragically early deaths of Charlie Parker, Billie Holiday and others.

When Ray was arrested on narcotics charges at a gig in Indianapolis, less than three weeks after his triumph in Paris, it was his first high-profile brush with the law, earlier encounters avoiding the blaze of publicity that his current level of fame made inevitable. The bust was also perhaps predictable, given a series of crises over the previous months of 1961 directly related to his escalating drug use.

Ray hadn't shown up for two dates in January, one in his old stomping ground of Seattle, the other Albuquerque, New Mexico. Near-riots ensued at both venues as the band played their normal first set, then filled in for Ray on the second, their leader "delayed" elsewhere.

Then, just a week before his national tour commenced at the end of March, he severed an artery and tendon in his left hand after a fall on a glass-topped table at his home in Los Angeles. The accident was precipitated by a heroin-fuelled Ray thrashing around uncontrollably in his den while high, his plight only discovered by six-year-old Ray Jr sneaking into the room to say goodnight. As he would recall to biographer Michael Lydon: "I opened the door and saw him jumping around. His shirt was covered in blood, there was blood on the wall . . ."

According to Ray in his autobiography, after cutting his hand he collapsed asleep, "bleeding like a hog", as little Ray alerted his mother. With the aid of Hank Crawford and drummer Milt Turner she took her injured husband to the family doctor, Bob Foster, who rushed him to hospital for a transfusion – he'd lost four pints of blood. With his hand sewn up, Ray was told he couldn't use it for six weeks, but he insisted the tour should go on anyway – he'd play right-handed piano. With his left hand in a cast and Foster travelling with him for most of the tour, Ray did just that – the agency telling the press he'd slipped and hurt himself while taking a bath.

At the end of June, a near-bust happened in Chicago when Ray, Duke Wade and Donald Wilkerson were apprehended during a police raid on a drug dealer's apartment where they'd gone to score. How often money changed hands over the years to placate local law enforcers is open to question, but on this occasion the three were bailed by Jeff Brown within hours, the charges against them subsequently dropped on the basis of it being an illegal search.

But the events in Indianapolis in mid-November were far more serious. Answering persistent banging on the door of his hotel room at 9 am in the morning, when the caller announced it was a Western Union telegram Ray opened it without another thought. In burst two detectives, "stomping round like they were on TV" as Ray put it, searching everywhere till they found just what they wanted – hypodermic needles and traces of heroin in the bathroom cabinet. They'd been tipped off by a dealer who had sold Ray drugs the evening before. Frisking Ray before taking him into custody, and that included pulling up his shirt sleeves to look for the scars caused by regular injections, Narcotics Bureau Sergeant Robert Keithly told reporters, "He had some of the worst tracks I've ever seen."

At the police headquarters Ray was charged with violation of narcotics laws, press reporters and photographers being allowed to talk to him while he was still in a state of shock, among them Rick Johnson, a police reporter for the *Indianapolis Times*: "He appeared very disturbed and lonely. I then identified myself to him and asked him if he cared to talk to me. Charles said, 'Yes, I want to talk to someone.' He sat down on a bench in city jail and began to cry softly and then lost all control of himself. I waited until he regained control and offered him a cigarette. The tears had rolled down both of his cheeks and could not be concealed by the dark glasses he always wears. I asked him how he got started on narcotics. 'I started using stuff when I was 16 and first started in show business,' he told me. 'Then I had to have more and more . . .'"

Sobbing to the reporters that he had a wife and kids, and had to carry on working for their sakes, and that he'd kick the habit if he had the chance, Ray cut a pathetic figure, sitting there in the full glare of the worst publicity he'd ever had.

"He didn't finish his statement and he stopped talking for several minutes. Then he said, 'I've never taken the cure, but I'd like to go to Lexington [the federal narcotics hospital] now. It might do me some good. I guess I've always wanted to go but it was easier the other way. A guy like me has to have something to keep going.' Forlornly, Charles raised his voice. 'The grind is just too much.'"

Jeff Brown meanwhile had organised a lawyer, and within a couple of hours Ray was released on a $1,250 cash bond. Next morning they had to appear at the municipal court for a preliminary hearing which was packed with reporters, TV crews and fans – news of the bust had travelled fast. He was bound over again in the sum of $1,000 to appear on trial on January 4.

The courtroom was packed as evidence from both sides was presented to the trial Judge, who at a further hearing three weeks later dismissed the charges against Ray Charles on the grounds that the police, posing as Western Union messengers, had entered his hotel room under false pretences and without a warrant, therefore rendering their search illegal. Ray realised that his celebrity status, which probably focussed the police attention in the first place, was also on this occasion his salvation: "I got out of it all right, but only because I had bread."

The immediate fallout from Ray's arrest came as soon as the story hit the news media, with an appearance on the prime-time Ed Sullivan TV show cancelled and several one-nighter live dates put in jeopardy. But in the longer term it was an early warning to Ray, and those around him, that his habit could eventually cost him his career, and even his life.

12

Can't Stop Loving You

"I don't call myself a blues singer or a jazz singer or a country singer or whatever. I just call myself a singer that sings the blues, a singer that can sing jazz, a singer that knows how to sing country music in my own way."

– Ray Charles

Such warnings didn't register easily with Ray however. For the moment he would carry on as before despite increasing difficulties, much as he did in the rest of his private life – which became no less complicated as 1961 drew to a close.

Although he made sure his son by her was looked after financially, Ray's relationship with Margie Hendricks was now strictly musical. And although there was no question of him abandoning Della and their three sons, incidents like the hand injury a few months earlier reminded his wife that it was not necessarily going to be sweetness and light whenever Ray came home to "relax".

Also, Della was no fool; she was aware of other women out there in Ray's working life, though exactly how much she knew about the details of the Mae Mosely situation is anybody's guess. What is sure is that Ray continued to treat Mae as the classic mistress, his alternative spouse on the East Coast, and when she became pregnant he assured her he would, as with Margie, see their child wanted for nothing. Mae had given birth to a baby girl, Raenee, in August, and soon after she was born doctors realised she had inherited the same congenital glaucoma that had led to Ray's loss of sight as a six-year-old. Ray immediately arranged to meet medical and full-time nursing expenses for the child.

In November a new single appeared in the record stores, 'Unchain My Heart' backed with 'But On The Other Hand Baby', both from the same session as 'Hit The Road Jack' which was ending its three-month run in the charts just as 'Unchain' entered the Top 10 in December. And not missing an opportunity, ABC put out 'Baby, It's Cold Outside', just as the post-holiday winter freeze set in during January '62. Despite being the most popular number from the Betty Carter album, with 'We'll Be Together Again' on the flip, it failed to chart.

Ray's next single release, in March 1962, didn't make the best-sellers either, although the two tracks recorded early in the year constituted two gems from the pen of Percy Mayfield. 'Hide 'Nor Hair' is a humorous up-tempo piece with the small band in its classic soul mode, Ray bemoaning the fact that his girl has run off with the doctor.*

> *I remember so well, when she slammed that door*
> *But the girl didn't make it back no more . . .*
> *I ain't seen hide 'nor hair of my baby since that day . . .*

But it was the A-side that resonated with fans at the time, a cooler-than-cool Ray talking his way through an encounter with a female in a nightclub:

> *She slowed up a little bit and turned her head and smiled,*
> *She was 34-24-38 and dressed in the latest style*

who answers his chat-up lines with a sultry-sounding "are you talkin' to me?" before revealing that she's waiting for her old man, "a policeman on the beat".

For long-time devotees of Ray Charles, the single was a confirmation that their faith in him as the personification of soul was not misplaced – though that conviction would be sorely tested when his next album was released the following month.

Shortly before the end of 1961 Ray had let it be known to Sam Clark and Larry Newton at ABC that he wanted to make his next long-player a collection of country and western songs. The record execs – not to mention A&R man Sid Feller – were taken aback, and more than a little dubious. It was one thing for Ray to cover pop ballads, vaudeville songs or whatever – and he'd cut a country number with Hank Snow's 'I'm Movin' On' back in 1959 – but an entire album of C&W material sounded like commercial (and artistic) suicide.

---

* As it happened, "Doctor Foster" was the name of Ray's family medic.

"As a matter of fact I had a tremendous amount of problems with the record company I was with at the time," Ray told me, "because they said, 'Ray, if you record these country songs you're gonna destroy your career, because people don't know you as a country singer.'" Larry Newton remembered the conversation at ABC, reflecting wryly how it gave the lie to the idea of Ray being manipulated by the record company: "All these stories you hear about Ray being led around by the nose because he's blind, they're just not true. Nobody tells Ray what to do. For instance, when he wanted to record his first country and western album, we said to him, 'Don't do it.' Even when the distributors got it, they said, 'What is this? A joke?'"

"I went to ABC and told them I wanted to do some country songs, and of course they were nice to me, but you know how sometimes people can go, 'What? What'd you mean? Are you serious or what?' – that sort of thing. But then when they realised I was serious about it, then they became serious, and they said, 'Look, you must think about it. You might lose a lot of fans, you should think about that, it's a pretty serious route.' And I said, 'Well, I feel that if I do it, I may lose some fans, but I may gain a lot more fans too.'

"I think they were just getting ready to negotiate another contract, and I had done very well for ABC, so they didn't shoot me down too much. But I think they had a genuine concern about the fan thing, because it was so different, it was completely out of line. So I did understand that, about what they were saying to me, but they went along with me and we did the album."

As David Newman wryly recalled: "The people at ABC Records weren't exactly pleased with the idea, but eventually they just sat in there in the recording booth and let him do his thing. Then of course after he did the country and western album and it became famous, they all wanted to take credit and they were all behind it."

Sid Feller was a little more sympathetic to the idea from the start, though he too didn't realise at the time that Ray had grown up with country music. In fact Feller was the first to get wind of the star's plans when Ray asked him to gather together 40 or so country numbers from the top Nashville publishers; he was to send them to California, where Ray would select from them the material for his next album. "One day he called saying he wanted to do a country and western album," recalled Feller. "My first reaction was, 'Well, what is he doing?' That lasted about eight minutes, because I realised that he knew what he was doing. When I announced it to the executives, the president and vice president, they thought he was nuts!"

But the guys at ABC should have done their homework. Interviewed for the liner notes of Atlantic's *What'd I Say* album in 1959, Ray prophetically told *Billboard*'s Ren Grevatt: "I think a lot of the hillbilly music is wonderful. When I was a kid in Greenville, Florida, I used to play piano in a hillbilly band. I like it. I think I could do a good job with the right hillbilly song today."

As Feller warmed to the concept they started working on the project, and when they went into Capitol Studios in New York for the first session on February 5, he was as enthusiastic as Ray. For the New York sessions (the second was two days later) they used Ray's now-regular big band, with charts written by Gerald Wilson and Gil Fuller, then on February 15 a strings-and-chorus recording with Marty Paich arranging was set for United Recording Studios in Hollywood. With six tracks cut at each studio, the resulting album certainly stirred up the controversy that the ABC men had predicted, but commercially was Ray Charles' biggest success to date.

With its garish red backgound and fairly crude cut-out of a photograph by Hugh Bell, the cover of the new 12-inch LP hardly evoked the atmosphere of Ray's classic Atlantic sleeves designed by Marvin Israel. And the cumbersome title – *Modern Sounds In Country And Western Music* – sounded equally unsubtle. But what lay within was something else again. Alternating strings and big band numbers track by track, the collection represented Ray Charles' take on almost every aspect of C&W, from sentimental ballads to country-flavoured rock'n'roll.

From the latter camp, the Everly Brothers' debut hit from 1957 'Bye Bye Love' kicks things off in a swinging version with the chorus sung by The Raelettes, followed by a complete contrast in a smooth 'Georgia On My Mind'-style 'You Don't Know Me'. Hank Williams' 'Half As Much' is turned into a relaxed swing number with a breathy tenor sax break by Don Wilkerson, and 'I Love You So Much It Hurts' has Ray singing a middle-of-the-road melody almost straight. And while the big band rocks its way through Eddy Arnold's 'Just A Little Lovin'', Fathead's solo ensures it's more bebop than barn dance. 'Born To Lose' is the strongest ballad contender with Ray's blues approach taking a country standard onto a new plane.

Opening Side 2 on the original vinyl release, 'Worried Mind' shows just how close country melodies can come to the blues, a point made all the stronger by Ray's piano solo. Western Swing composer Floyd Tillman co-wrote 'It Makes No Difference Now', which in the hands of Ray and the big band takes on the aspect of laid-back riffing R&B of the old school – pure understated magic. More Hank Williams with the classic ballad 'You Win Again' takes us into one of the most surprising choices for a "country" album: 'Careless Love' by "father of the blues" W.C. Handy could have cropped up on any Ray Charles session over the previous 10 years, but the mellow big band version here made it worth the wait.

Don Gibson's best-known composition 'I Can't Stop Loving You' turned out to be the hit of the album in terms of spin-off singles, the strings, big choir and Ray's voice and piano making this – like 'Georgia On My Mind' – the definitive version of the song from here on. The album closed with a swinging version of Hank Williams' 'Hey Good Lookin'' that, like most of the album, sounds more big city than down-home country.

On hearing the first playbacks the guys at ABC were converted, they sensed they had something big, very big, on their hands. Sections of the music press, and certainly legions of Ray's traditional fanbase, weren't so enthusiastic. Some went as far as to say that Ray had sold out, opting for what they perceived as the lucrative but bland middle-of-the-road market served by smooth ballad singers and Las Vegas nightclub acts.

In answer to some of the more acerbic criticism Ray's response was that he was doing what he'd always done, singing songs he wanted to sing, in the way he wanted to sing them, a point he would continue to punch home in interviews over the years. "I said, 'I'm not trying to be a country singer, I'm just recording songs.' With country music, I was still singing me, my voice was still me, I was just singing country songs. I never tried to become a Hank Snow, a Hank Williams or a Charlie Pride. I didn't want to become a country and western singer – you gotta understand there's a difference – all I did was take the country songs, and I started to record them, and fortunately they became hits."

He elaborated to me how it was all part of a natural process as far as he was concerned. "If you take 'Stardust' and you put a steel guitar and a couple of fiddles and stuff with it, if you didn't know it you would think it was a country song too. You gotta remember, it's the instrumentation that causes songs to be what they are. So I said, 'All I'm doin' is I'm taking country songs. I'm singing them my way, and I'm changing from the steel guitar, from the fiddles (that's the 'chinky, chinky' kind of fiddle) and I'm just singing them just like I'd sing anything else. That's all I did, no more.

"It was nothing that was fantastic, nothing that was very unusual, or difficult. All I did was the same as anybody today – as you can see a great many people today take country songs and they record them in a pop vein, or a country singer will take a pop song and they'll add a steel guitar to it and some fiddles and the country sound to it, and it becomes a country feeling. So really that's all I did."

Not all Ray's committed admirers were against the album of course, some appreciated that he was opening up a musical area they'd previously been only half aware of. At the time country music, and the country music "establishment", was incredibly insular. As biographer Michael Lydon put it: "You had to *be* country to sing country in 1962." And the racial aspect, unlike Ray's forays into other musical areas, had a bearing on this – as singer Gladys Knight would point out: "Ray Charles hipped a lot of the black people to country and western bands . . . we was kind of listening before, but he made it even more down-to-earth where you could dig it."

Ultimately it was down to Ray's constant eclecticism when it came to what he liked, and what he played, as he explained to Robert Gordon: "Like I've always said, all my life I've always liked different kinds of music. If you like different kinds of things, you want to do different kinds of things. If you're a sportsman you like baseball, you like a little football, you like a little basketball, you like a little hockey, you might even care for golf . . . I'm a musician. I like different kinds of music. I like classical music, I can play Beethoven, I can play Rachmaninov, I can play Chopin. Every now and then, when I do dates with symphony orchestras, I play these things – and I shock the hell out of people."

And, as Ray would always remind interviewers, country music was part of his background. "It was the rural South, and that was the basic music on radio stations to begin with, and I always liked *Grand Old Opry*. I just liked it, I don't know why I liked it, but I guess that it's the same as why you like classical music, or why you like any kind of music.

"There's something about music, that if the right person is doing it I can always find something in it. It's having something you can relate to, that you can feel and, of course in this case, I just always loved that kind of music. Why? I've no answer to that, but I grew up listening to it, like I also grew up listening to the blues – that was all over our neighbourhood. So music from all angles always impressed me. Country music might have seemed strange to some people, for me to like it, but I truly do love it."

As soon as the album hit the shops in early April it started to climb the long-player chart, reaching number one by mid-May and staying there for over three months. It would remain in the *Billboard* album Top 40 for another year. But more incredible was the success of the first single to be taken off *Modern Sounds*, a release that was genuinely triggered by "popular demand" – and the fact that a carbon-copy cover version had appeared on the market.

The track was Don Gibson's 'I Can't Stop Loving You'. As the album got more airplay, disc jockeys around the country were playing it as their track of choice, in turn creating a listener demand that then made itself known in record stores. Distributors started pestering ABC for a single, but both the company and Ray were reluctant to put out a single just yet, while the album was still fresh on the charts and climbing. Then it became known that Tab Hunter – an actor/singer who'd had a couple of minor hits and a number one with 'Young Love' in the late Fifties – had covered the song. And he'd not just covered it, he'd copied the Ray Charles version note-for-note. "We had to make an edit because Ray's version was a minute and a half longer than Tab's," Sid Feller recalled. "We did the edit that night and sent acetates to the key radio stations." That was the last anyone heard of the Hunter version.

Frantic arrangements were put in place to get the singles pressed and into the shops as soon as possible, as Larry Newton would tell journalist Al Aronovitz: "We worked 24 hours, we worked around the clock. We got the factory to work around the clock. The next day we started shipping. We shipped initial orders, in one day – they totalled 500,000 records."

Released at the end of April, the single made the Top 100 the following week, and within a month 'I Can't Stop Loving You' had topped the US chart, with *Modern Sounds In Country And Western Music* occupying the same position in the album listings, having sold over half a million copies by the first week in June.

Sid Feller later reflected: "I didn't know that a pop artist could do country songs and become a national monument. You know how unimportant it seemed? I put 'I Can't Stop Loving You' in the number five position on the B-side of the album."

And while his latest releases made their twin assault on the charts, Ray and the band completed their second national tour, which was again organised by Hal Zeiger, then set off for Europe once more for another triumphant series of dates in Paris.

The second European visit was promoted under the supervision of Norman Granz, who, as proprietor of the legendary Verve label, had launched his famous "Jazz At The Philharmonic" package showcasing Verve artists back in the late Forties. For the next decade and a half a galaxy of top jazz names toured under the "Philharmonic" banner including Dizzy Gillespie, Coleman Hawkins and many more, plus Ella Fitzgerald and Oscar Peterson whom Granz managed. By 1962 Granz was no longer in charge of Verve Records, and was resident in Switzerland, from where he conducted his operations as the most active jazz concert promoter on the continent.

This time Ray and the Orchestra were booked to appear for nine days at the magnificent Olympia in the Boulevard des Capucines, the city's most famous varieté theatre. Topping even the response he'd been accorded on his first visit to the French capital just a few months before, the Parisians welcomed him like a returning hero. And every sold-out concert was buoyed by an even wider popularity generated by the current success of the *Modern Sounds* album.

Talking to the newspaper *l'Humanité* two days after Ray's death, the former artistic director of the Olympia Jean-Michel Boris recalled the 1962 shows: "It was my fondest memory of Ray Charles. It was a revolution at the time, the most exceptional moment during my many years (at Olympia). You could fill a venue, in spite of having to have high ticket prices, with just his name. The Ray Charles that I knew at the beginning, with the full orchestra, The Raelettes . . . those first musicians who accompanied him were *formidable*. The full Ray Charles Orchestra was really an extraordinary jazz group."

Leroy Cooper has his own theory about Ray's phenomenal popularity in France: "They were crazy, in Paris, over him. I guess it was the religious, the gospel connection. We were only about the second jazz ensemble to play in the Olympia theatre in Paris, and all those gospel-spirited songs were very inspirational to the French . . ."

From Paris the tour took in the Belgian capital of Brussels before heading for West Berlin, where they appeared at the vast Sportspalast. Packaged under the "Jazz At The Philharmonic" trademark, a live recording of the concert released in 1996 reveals Ray and the big band at their peak. Atlantic-era favourites like 'I Got A Woman' and 'Hallelujah I Love Her So' are dovetailed with his ABC hits including a reflective 'Georgia On My Mind', a spot-on 'Hide 'Nor Hair' and of course 'Hit The Road Jack'. There's only one nod towards the country album, a jumping version of 'Bye Bye Love' that has The Raelettes in close harmony heaven.

Even more than the riveting performances of 'I Believe To My Soul' and 'Come Rain Or Come Shine', the real soul-stirring number of the evening is a slower-than-the-record version of 'The Danger Zone', a particularly pertinent selection in the context of the politics of the divided city at the time. The Berlin Wall had been erected just a few months earlier, and East–West tensions were high. Whether that's the reason Ray chose to play the number in Berlin we'll never know, but it must have sent shivers down more than one spine that night.

Their European trip over, the outfit returned to the States where 'I Can't Stop Loving You' had hit the number one spot in the pop, country and R&B charts, and *Modern Sound In Country And Western Music* was on its way to become ABC's first-ever million-selling album. Equally significantly 'Can't Stop' was Ray's first chart-topper in England, France and a number of other territories including Australia, New Zealand and the burgeoning (and lucrative) market in Japan. Ray Charles was suddenly the biggest name in popular music, and sell-out dates across America that summer were fulfilled with the whole circus travelling in a 44-seater aeroplane that had cost Ray half a million dollars.

At the end of July an interview piece by Gilbert King appeared in *Melody Maker*, conducted at the Charles home in Los Angeles, in which Ray revealed a keen interest in what was happening in the UK: "I know more about Britain than you think. Eartha (Kitt) told me how tough Glasgow audiences can be, but how she was crazy for them in London. I study your hit parade, but more for the writers than the singers. I think Johnny Worth takes some beating."*

Also lounging at the poolside where the interview took place was another name from the footnotes of Sixties British pop, Neil Christian, who was obviously hustling for work around LA back in '62 – and befriended, it seems, by Ray Charles. "Sometimes I wonder what I would have done in the States if I hadn't met Ray the first week I came," he told the journalist. "He knew I didn't know many people and took me around to parties and recording sessions to make me feel at home."†

As a second single from the *Modern Sounds* album – 'You Don't Know

---

* Johnny Worth was a songwriter with several UK hits to his credit in the late Fifties/early Sixties, including three number ones under the pseudonym Les Vandyke: Adam Faith's 'What Do You Want' (1959) and 'Poor Me' (1960) and Eden Kane's 'Well I Ask You' (1961).

† Christian would go on to have a minor UK hit with 'That's Nice' in 1966, but any mentions in history books are usually restricted to the fact that his backing group The Crusaders featured the young Jimmy Page in their line-up.

Me' backed with 'Careless Love' – made its way up the charts to an eventual number two peak in September, the recording studios were booked for a follow-up LP predictably titled *Modern Sounds In Country And Western Music Volume Two*. Utilising exactly the same formula as the first collection, it had big band tracks and string section numbers recorded in New York and LA respectively, with the same arrangers and producer Sid Feller.

When the album came out the only big change from the first volume was that instead of alternating big band and strings, track by track, all the the band numbers were on side one, and the strings side two. The same variety was there, with songs by country giants Hank Williams – his signature love song 'Your Cheatin' Heart' – and Don Gibson ('Don't Tell Me Your Troubles'), the upbeat 'Oh Lonesome Me' and a soulful rendition of Hank Williams' 'Take These Chains From My Heart' that became the "biggie" of the bunch in terms of its subsequent sales as a single.

But the stand-out track for R&B fans – and apart from having its origins in the country, there remained little of a C&W feel to the song – was Ray's audacious treatment of an old western "cowboy" favourite 'You Are My Sunshine'. Written in 1940 by singer Jimmie Davis, the song was a hit for the Hollywood "singing cowboy" Gene Autry and also successfully covered by Bing Crosby. An innocuous lullaby of a song, Ray's treatment rendered it almost unrecognisable. The opening "amen" chords from the brass introduce Ray in blues mode as he demolishes the pretty melody in favour of full-on soul with The Raelettes answering the chorus line; and Margie Hendricks' interjection after a swinging brass-led break tears things apart almost as powerfully as her celebrated part in 'The Right Time'.

A second country album following hard on the heels of the first seemed to confirm the worst fears of those who'd predicted that Ray was selling out to the white middle-class audiences of the mainstream. The way Ray saw it, he was bringing this new following into the Ray Charles fold by broadening, not narrowing, his choice of material and therefore his appeal. And in any case, as he'd stress a thousand times, he'd grown up with country music: "I really thought that it was somethin' about country music, even as a youngster – I couldn't figure out what it was then, but I know what it is now," he told *Rolling Stone*. "But then I don't know why I liked it. I used to just love to hear Minnie Pearl, because I thought she was so funny. I guess I was about seven, eight, and I remember Roy Acuff and Gene Austin . . . they'd make them steel guitars cry and whine, and it really attracted me. I don't know what it is."

And the record company were just happy that their gamble – or more precisely Ray's gamble, as they had initially advised against the country "experiment" – had paid off. *Volume Two* hit the shops in October, and number two in the charts soon after, with the almost simultaneously released 'You Are My Sunshine' (backed with 'Your Cheatin' Heart') making the Top 10 singles chart in December.

With the huge success of both *Modern Sounds* albums, Ray not only took country material and made it something of his own, but also created a mass market for the music in a way it had never enjoyed before. Sure, there had been country-style hits in the pop charts, and country singers like Hank Williams and Patsy Cline who became mainstream household names, but Ray popularised the genre as never before – without actually making a country record as such. And in 1963 he became the first black artist to be named among the Top 10 performers by the Country and Western Association. "Ray took country music to the world," Willie Nelson would comment, "and in some ways the rest of us country singers are riding on his coat-tails." Ray's innovations in the genre came to define modern country and western music.

As well as broadening his appeal across all areas of the popular record market, 1962 had also seen Ray Charles establish himself business-wise when he formed his own record label. The Tangerine Record Corporation was launched as a label within the ABC group at the end of February, ABC distributing and Ray acting as A&R for his new enterprise. For the time being at least, Ray himself wouldn't appear on his own label as he was still contracted to ABC-Paramount.

The name Tangerine wasn't entirely new; in 1960 Ray had set up a publishing company, Tangerine Music, to assume control of his own songs, not long after moving to ABC. Before that Atlantic had paid him 50 per cent of publishing royalties for his original songs via their Progressive Music but with Tangerine he was the publisher of his own material. Now he was getting a foothold in the record-selling end of the business too.

Perhaps, as writer Nelson George would put it, some of Ray's signings to the record label would be "as much for his own edification as for public consumption". That certainly looked the case with the first artist to be contracted to Tangerine, Louis Jordan, one of Ray's heroes of small-band rhythm & blues from the Forties. Ray also produced albums with Little Jimmy Scott and Percy Mayfield in those first few months of Tangerine's existence, but none were to make any impact on the sales charts that Ray himself dominated so comprehensively.

When it appeared, what was hoped would be a "comeback" album for Louis Jordan – *Hallelujah – Louis Jordan Is Back!* – did nothing to help the former star's lagging career. Jimmy Scott's *Falling In Love Is Wonderful* didn't even get pressed after his previous company threatened legal action claiming he was still signed to them, but Percy Mayfield's *My Jug And I* did marginally better than the Jordan collection, introducing one of his most celebrated non-Ray Charles compositions 'The River's Invitation', an R&B hit in its own right. As well as being the official "in-house" writer at Tangerine, writing material primarily for Ray's repertoire, Mayfield would release further albums on the label, including *Percy Mayfield* and *Bought Blues* at the end of the Sixties.

As Ray widened his role on the business side of things, at the same time widening his appeal with the record-buying and concert-going public, so Joe Adams started to come into his own. Since joining the entourage during Hal Zeigler's first national tour in the spring of 1961, Adams' influence had steadily increased without any formal acknowledgement as such. Jeff Brown was still officially in charge of the band on the road, and Ray's personal manager, but Adams – impressing Ray and others around him with his crisp efficiency and suave manner – had graduated from his original role of MC and stage organiser to Ray's right-hand man in all but title.

When Ray started forming companies, Adams – who'd wheeled and dealed around LA for a decade or more – was there with the kind of advice Jeff Brown simply couldn't offer. Likewise as the touring became more streamlined and the venues more sophisticated, so Jeff's hands-on approach that had worked for years on the "chitlin' circuit" of endless one-nighters wasn't always adequate to deal with grand concert venues and high-powered show-biz promoters. Joe Adams on the other hand, with his sleeked-back hair and pencil-thin moustache – "Broadway-handsome" as the journalist Whitney Balliett would describe him – came over with a stylish authority as he made suggestions, dealt with problems and, increasingly, gave the orders.

Nobody particularly warmed to Adams' increasing authority, especially the guys in the band. Whereas Jeff Brown acted as a moderating mouthpiece for the boss, enforcing discipline with a velvet glove as he laid down the law here, gave way a little there, with Joe it was the iron fist every time.

David Newman recalled how authoritarian Adams' style could be, though he was one of the musicians to be least affected because of his long-term history with Ray: "My connection was with Ray, so I didn't have to do too much with Joe. As long as I did what I was supposed to do I didn't have to worry too much about Joe . . . I didn't have to do exactly what he . . . let's say my association was with Ray Charles, and Ray and I were very close, so Joe didn't interfere too much with me, in our business, or our past or anything. But Joe became very much the taskmaster in everything, everything became highly regimented. He was fining musicians for being tardy, being a little late, or if they didn't have on the exact bit of uniform or didn't have on the right patent leather shoes."

At the end of the day Jeff was always one of the boys, something Adams – who didn't particularly like the musicians – would never be. But with a much more high-powered organisation to run, and vast amounts of money involved compared to previously, the hard-nosed approach suited Ray perfectly.

Like many a bandleader before him – Benny Goodman and Glenn Miller were just two who were described as "monsters" to work for – Ray could seem like a tyrant when dealing with his sidemen. He would even admonish them mid-tune, in front of an audience, as Leroy Cooper would recall: "He was a perfectionist, and you had to do it right. He would tell anybody, anywhere, about the way you played . . ." But in non-musical matters like punctuality, on-stage appearance and so on, it was usually left to Jeff Brown to sort things out or apply sanctions where necessary. When Joe Adams started cracking the whip, Ray had a lieutenant who could be as ruthless with musicians off the stand as he was with them on.

By the beginning of 1963, nearly two years after Joe Adams had literally jumped on the Ray Charles bandwagon mid-tour in Detroit, Jeff Brown's days with Ray were numbered. Jeff began to sense it as surely as anyone, though nothing had changed on a formal basis. There were no promotions or demotions, no talk of pay-offs, and apparently no signed agreement between the boss he'd been faithful to for nearly nine years and his new second-in-command. For the moment the status quo prevailed, officially at least.

The first few weeks of 1963 also saw Ray involved in yet another affair with a young woman, one that would eventually test the often fragile stability of his marriage to Della Bea to the limit. Having briefly met a couple of years before, while he was gigging in Dayton, Ohio, Ray was reintroduced to 20-year-old Sandra Jean Betts in December '62, which marked the beginning of a passionate though short-lived romance. Conducted largely in motels and an apartment he rented for their clandestine lovemaking, his torrid relationship with Sandra Jean took place almost entirely in the Los Angeles area, within easy distance of his Hepburn Avenue home, Della and the boys.

When Sandra Jean told Ray she was pregnant, with a baby due in October, he assured her – as he had with Louise, Margie and Mae before her – that he would look after her and the baby; and not only that, he loved her. But as the ardour of their passion cooled – Ray was on tour most of the time once spring arrived – Sandra Jean sensed he might not fulfil his obligations as wholeheartedly as he'd promised, and sought the advice of a lawyer.

The attorney knew they had a good case, and Ray was rich – he'd earned nearly $2 million in 1962 – so in August 1963 a paternity suit complaint was filed against Ray Charles, demanding over $1,000 a month for the baby's upkeep. Ray was incensed; he would have taken care of the child, but he wasn't going to give in to what he saw as legal blackmail, as he reiterated in his autobiography: "I considered those kinds of threats – 'You gonna be exposed, Ray Charles' – blackmail, and I can't be blackmailed." He dug his heels in and fought the complaint, claiming that the baby wasn't his and the expectant mother was a mere gold-digger. Taking into account Ray's work schedule through the rest of the year, the judge agreed to postpone a trial until January 13, 1964.

His old flame Louise Mitchell even tried to get in on the act. Now married and living in Tampa, Florida (to where she'd returned when she and Ray split in early 1950) she had a lawyer demanding more support for their daughter Evelyn, now 13. Her claim was dropped when Ray, perhaps uncharacteristically, responded warmly with an increased allowance and an invitation to Evelyn to visit him in Los Angeles.

In the case of Betts *v.* Robinson, the jury didn't take long to make their decision. Sandra Jean's mother testified that Ray had told her he'd look after the baby when her daughter was first pregnant, and the prosecution even brought in the three-month-old Sheila so they could see her resemblance to her father. Ray, who admitted he'd spoken to his lover's mother on the phone, was ordered to pay $400 a month support plus costs.

But far worse was the cost to his marriage. Although Della was under no illusions about her husband's womanising, he had always kept it well away from home and out of the media's gaze. Following the court case it was out in the open, along with hurtful allegations of Ray's pledging his love for Sandra Jean over and above that for his family. That was the most bitter pill for Della to swallow as she resigned herself to restoring some normality to an increasingly strained family situation.

Straight after the winter break of early 1963, during which Ray had pursued his affair with Sandra Jean Betts, the now-annual spring tour coordinated by Hal Zeigler made its way across the United States, winding up as usual in Carnegie Hall. Just prior to the trek a stand-alone single, not a spin-off from the latest album, had been released. Though only just scraping into the Top 20, 'Don't Set Me Free' was another strong contender for the R&B charts, Margie Hendricks again the perfect foil for Ray in a call-and-response exchange with the same gritty feel that had put 'You Are My Sunshine' into the Top 10. The track – and the flip side, a meaty ballad 'The Brightest Smile In Town' – was with the big band and arranged by Gerald Wilson which suggests it came from one of the New York *Volume Two* sessions.

When Ray and the crew wound up at Carnegie, the New York audiences greeted him with an assured familiarity. With his big band at a confident peak, he wowed the critics with a sharp performance which was nevertheless genuinely soulful. And for the rest of his ever-widening public, he was now the premier name in the American popular music establishment.

But unbeknown to anyone in the American music business at the time, within less than a year that same establishment was going to be shaken to its foundations, in a musical revolution as radical as the one that had (literally) rocked the status quo with the advent of rock'n'roll in the mid-Fifties. And the reason there was no hint of the seismic change to come, no early rumblings under the cultural surface, was that its epicentre was three thousand miles across the Atlantic in Great Britain, where Ray had still to make his live debut.

Since February 1963, when The Beatles had their first UK chart-topper with 'Please Please Me'*, the British music scene had been increasingly dominated by the four Liverpudlians and their Northern contemporaries. When Ray Charles finally made it to London in May, The Beatles were at number one again with 'From Me To You', and their debut LP *Please Please Me* was enjoying its sixth week at the top of the album chart. But despite the

---

* In every UK chart excepting the least important *Record Retailer* chart, hence its non-inclusion on *1*, the Beatles' compilation of number one hits.

mop tops' pre-eminence in the charts and a media gearing up for a summer of Beatlemania, the arrival of Ray Charles had been heralded as something approaching the second coming in sections of the music press.

The most jazz- and blues-oriented of the UK pop papers, *Melody Maker* in particular made the most of the visit. The May 18 issue, as well as a front page story headlined "The Genius Hits Britain", ran a double-page spread featuring a review of the first London show, a breakdown of the big band and what they played that night, and a write-up of the concert in Brussels that had kicked off Ray's European dates. In the same edition there was also a piece on "What the stars say about Ray", plus an interview with The Raelettes. Asked whether it was hard work, "unofficial spokeswoman" Darlene McRae told *MM*'s Max Jones: "No, it's not hard. The way he teaches it to us, it simplifies it. Well, none of us read music, so the background Ray wants, he plays it for each person. It's never written down. We learn it and memorise it," adding coyly, "I think he's a very, very, very nice man."

The Brussels show was at the spacious Palais des Beaux-Arts, where a 2,000 capacity crowd greeted Ray's every move and nuance with applause, shrieks and yells of "Bravo!" In his *Melody Maker* piece Patrick Doncaster – the pop music columnist for the *Daily Mirror* – described how a murmur went round as The Raelettes brought in the opening bars of 'I Can't Stop Loving You', clearly sounding very different to the record everyone was so familiar with. Doncaster quizzed Ray about it when he interviewed him the following evening: "I know we played 'I Can't Stop Loving You' in rhythm & blues style – but it would become pretty sickening if we played it the same way every night," Ray explained. "I like to be able to improvise. But the main thing is to try to improve . . ." This was in the days when pop stars were expected to reproduce their hits note-for-note, improvisation being something you left to jazz instrumentalists. Without thinking about it – "I play the way I feel," he added – once again Ray had crossed a line.

And as David Newman pointed out to me, the numbers recorded with strings and choirs simply couldn't be replicated by the touring line-up. "We didn't have the strings, we only had the big band and The Raelettes of course, so we had big band arrangements for all of that material." The jazz feel of the live shows was also enhanced by the instrumental set that always preceded Ray's appearance on stage: "Some of the big band arrangements were strictly for the purposes of doing the jazz tunes before Ray would come on the bandstand to do his vocals."

The small group "band within a band" would get an airing when Ray appeared on alto sax before sitting at the piano. "He would also start out playing with the small band, playing his arrangement with the small band before he would start singing . . . so people would have the opportunity to hear Ray play the alto. We had some wonderful arrangements for the five horns."

On Sunday, May 12, for Ray's legions of British fans a long wait came to an end, when he took the stage for two concerts at the Astoria, a cinema that doubled as a concert venue in London's Finsbury Park.* A student at the time, I'd nevertheless managed to find the money for a ticket as soon as they'd gone on sale, avoiding the bartering with touts outside the venue where prices were escalating by the minute as showtime approached.

I was with my flatmate John Murray from the same home town in North Wales; Murray was the first person I knew to own a copy of the *What'd I Say* LP, when we were still at school. We had tickets for the second show of the evening – usually a better bet at jazz concerts, when the musicians had had a chance to warm up. Getting there a good hour before the start (another jazz-fan crony at the time always reckoned it was "better to be an hour early than five minutes late" for such events) we ensconced ourselves in the pub across the road, eager to hear what the first-house crowd had to say about the show. Forty-two years later, all I can remember is they seemed to be walking on air.

The big band's opening set was lost in a blur of anticipation. It sounded good, but until that empty stool at the piano was occupied, nobody could settle. Then when Ray was led on, alto sax in hand, the place erupted, in the words of the *Melody Maker*'s Chris Roberts, like "you would have thought it was his last number". Ray kicked off with an alto solo that just added to the tension, raised even further as he sat at the piano to take the band into 'One Mint Julep'. His whispered interjection halfway through, "Just a little bit of soul now . . ." was the first we heard of his voice; the rest of the number was virtually drowned as the crowd went crazy.

Ray ran the whole gamut that night, from his brand-new hit 'Take These Chains From My Heart', fresh in the UK charts that week, to classics like 'I Got A Woman' and the inevitable 'What'd I Say'. The Raelettes were undeniably sexy, Margie Hendricks playing her vocal tit-for-tat with Ray on 'You Are My Sunshine'. And dispelling once

---

* The Astoria would become a celebrated music venue in its own right as The Rainbow in the Seventies.

again the fear that he'd gone "soft" with middle-of-the-road material, he infused the most show-biz of numbers like 'Without A Song' with pure unadulterated soul. Suspicions I've harboured over the years, that the concert might not have been as perfect as it has seemed in retrospect, were allayed once and for all with the DVD release of a live Brazilian TV show from that time. Recorded just four months after the London gig, in September 1963, Ray, the band and The Raelettes are all simply sensational.

After London, Ray's UK dates included Manchester the following Saturday. I hitchhiked north to catch that one, sitting in the pub beforehand watching The Beatles singing 'From Me To You' on the TV pop show *Thank Your Lucky Stars*. I think it was in Manchester – though it might have been the previous Sunday in London – as Ray wrung every ounce of passion out of the Leroy Carr blues 'In The Evening', that a lone voice in the audience shouted "Peace" to which Ray repeated back "Yeah, peace!" "And love . . ." came the voice again, Ray screaming, visibly moved, "Yeah . . . and love!" You could feel the silent tingle that ran through the hall.

Ray's first British tour – and those that followed over the next few years – was promoted by the Harold Davidson Organisation, who had a virtual monopoly on big American jazz names touring the country. His right-hand man was Jack Higgins (who still looks after various UK jazz names), who recalled Ray being one of the more "private" stars compared to some bandleaders he dealt with: "I was the tour director, fixed the business side of tours, booked the halls or sold them to other people, and did all the arrangements for all the tours. I didn't socialise with all of the people we brought over. But there were certain people who became personal friends, people like Duke Ellington in particular, and Basie became a great mate, you could talk with him and have fun with him. But Ray Charles wasn't like that . . ."

Didn't his blindness have a lot to do with that? "Well I think the difference there is personalities, rather than the fact that he was blind. Al Hibbler, he was blind, and he was a great person to work with . . . but there were some I couldn't really communicate with, they were all just business as far as I was concerned, and Ray Charles was one of them. The bands travelled in coaches and big cars. We usually had all the band in the bus, and the leader (and whoever travelled with him) would be in a large car with our tour manager."

Photographer David Redfern covered all Ray Charles' UK tours in the early Sixties, and many more over the following years. He remembered the first time he was made aware of Ray's remarkable ear. "When they came to London, it was through Harold Davidson. I was one of their photographers, allowed in to do everything. I remember once I was in the wings at the Hammersmith Odeon, which you could do in those days, and that band was loud, but after the set Ray claimed he could hear my shutter. I couldn't dispute that . . . so I had to use a quieter camera from then on – and I made a point of not photographing him in the quiet numbers."

Press reviews of the Ray's UK debut were almost universally favourable, with one curious exception in the Sunday *Observer*, written by the jazz critic Benny Green. It was curious because Green had written – for a fee, one presumes – the programme notes for the Charles concerts, in which he enthused: "Charles sounds like the real thing, an authentic jazz pianist whose style has grown out of a natural feeling for the jazz idiom rather than a hoarding of technique . . . his singing and playing sound authentic yet unsophisticated . . .", talking of "instant emotional appeal" and so on. In the newspaper piece, a vitriolic tirade spoke of Ray's singing being "indecipherable", his reputation "inflated", concluding: "It would come as no surprise . . . if Charles ended the last number of the evening by firing himself from a cannon through the theatre roof."

By the time the *Observer* article appeared on May 18, Ray and the show were on their way to a gig in Geneva, followed by another week of standing-room-only dates at the Olympia in Paris. The European dates had been buoyed by the success of his latest single, 'Take These Chains From My Heart', which made the Top 5 in the UK charts and elsewhere, getting to number eight in the American market. And as the outfit returned to the States at the beginning of June, another single 'No One' had arrived in the shops. Written by Doc Pomus and Mort Shuman, the loping good-time singalong had been a minor hit for Connie Francis in 1961, while the B-side 'Without Love (There Is Nothing)' had made the Top 20 for Atlantic artist Clyde McPhatter in 1957. Neither side was going to do big things for Ray, however, both hovering briefly in the *Billboard* Top 30.

Then in July came what would have been a musical bombshell for many bandleaders – Ray lost one of his major solo voices, and musical director, when Hank Crawford decided to leave the outfit. There were no arguments or bust-ups that prompted his departure, he just felt it was time to move. He'd accepted, like the rest of the guys, the changes in emphasis over the past couple of years, even when Ray got into country and western territory: "We were kind of surprised when we first heard that was gonna happen, but after we heard it, we said, 'Oh yeah. Well, hey, no problem. He'll do what he wants to do.'"

But, as Crawford would admit to Michael Lydon, he wasn't happy with the way the band was becoming more anonymous under the tacit authority of Joe Adams, who saw it purely as a vehicle to showcase Ray and nothing else. Hank and Ray had enjoyed a more soulful relationship which was reflected in the music, and he felt that was beginning to disappear. As he told writer Bill Dahl: "I spent many hours with him . . . He would dictate stuff to me, and then he would say, 'Hey, go for yourself.' I got to know him and how he wrote. I had sort of the same kind of feeling that Ray had about the music, so it was very easy for me to know where he was coming from. I was from the gospel/spiritual thing, too, so I adjusted to Ray. He gave me those liberties, which I appreciated a lot."

So bass player Edgar Willis took over as MD, and Ray and the band went into the studio to record his next album. Using the whole panoply of big band, strings, the Jack Halloran choral voices and top-name arrangers, the album was once again produced by Sid Feller who also took care of three of the arrangements. West Coast arranger Marty Paich was hired again to contribute three, while the prestigious jazz composer Benny Carter was responsible for another three and Johnny Parker one. With a title even more grandiose – and equally cumbersome – than any of Ray's previous collections, *Ingredients In A Recipe For Soul* is, nevertheless, one of his most accomplished albums.

The underlying theme this time was rather more vague than before, Ray choosing songs he felt expressed melancholy, the blues, sadness and a little hope – but not a collection of downers by any means. It was to be more an album that expresses, like it says on the tin, "soul" in the emotional rather than musical sense – though there was plenty of the latter too.

For starters we're taken straight on a humorous hard-luck trip, 'Busted' featuring the band swinging a riff in a fine Benny Carter arrangement. 'Where Can I Go?' on the other hand is a languid modern ballad in which Ray questions where he's headed in life, followed by 'Born To Be Blue', a Sid Feller chart with classy strings and woodwind parts. One of the high points of the album comes in the old standby 'That Lucky Old Sun', which despite the over-icing of strings'n'choir has what one writer described as the most anguished vocal of Ray's entire career. 'Ol' Man River', the Jerome Kern/Oscar Hammerstein classic from the 1929 musical *Show Boat*, is in similar vein, the chorus stating the theme with suitably dramatic "straight" delivery before Ray turns it into a plaintive cry from the heart.

The biggest piano outing on the album comes in a long instrumental intro to the Leroy Carr blues 'In The Evening (When The Sun Goes Down)', Ray coming in vocally with subdued horns and Phillip Guilbeau's muted trumpet echoing every line before a solo that brings us into a build-up of roaring Basie-like proportions – this is Ray singing the blues, no more, no less.

In complete contrast, 'A Stranger In Town' is pure sophisticated pop, a marvellous Mel Tormé lyric from 1954 that Ray handles with a note-by-note precision that does every word justice:

> *Just arrived on the 7.10*
> *Thought I'd see the old gang again*
> *But you know*
> *How they come and go*
> *And I'm just a stranger in town*

'Ol' Man Time' is a swinger, a mid-tempo reflection on the inevitable passing of the years. And opening with a sugary chorus on the middle eight bridge as an intro, as soon as Ray starts singing, the often-hackneyed 'Somewhere Over The Rainbow' takes on a new life – in direct contrast to the strings and voices in this Marty Paich arrangement. The tear-jerker from Rodgers and Hammerstein's *Carousel*, 'You'll Never Walk Alone', is a suitably hopeful closer as the melting strings segue into funky horn breaks and back again. Rising to the challenge, Ray plays the emotional lift of the original for all its worth. Released in August 1963, *Ingredients In A Recipe For Soul* climbed to number two, while the first single to be taken from it, 'Busted', made number four.

In the 1990 CD liner notes, Steve Hoffman informs us that there were only one or two takes made of each song, and the entire 10 were recorded in the same number of session hours over two days. "Producer Sid Feller knew what they wanted from each other and what they expected from the musicians, arrangers and recording engineers – nothing less than perfection."

Even if 'Busted' hadn't made the charts, its perceived failure would have meant less to Ray's career than it might have done a couple of years earlier. Ray Charles' success lay increasingly in long-term album sales rather than short-lived pop hits, though the record company would continue to release singles as a matter of course. And, at a time when a chart-topping single sold half a million or more, even a modest showing in the Top 100 could indicate significant sales figures. All in all, in the closing months of 1963 things were looking good for Ray Charles.

He'd purchased the site of a new family home to be built in the Baldwin Hills area, overlooking downtown Los Angeles; a smart neighbourhood that had been exclusive to well-heeled whites until a few years earlier, and was still only affordable by the very well-heeled, be they white or black. He'd also bought, encouraged and assisted in the venture by Joe Adams, another extensive property on West Washington Boulevard just south of Hollywood, on which he would build his business headquarters and recording studios.

Another single, 'That Lucky Old Sun', was released from *Ingredients*, he was due to record a new album right after the Christmas break, there were more sell-out tours earmarked for the States and Europe, and he was to make a feature film in the early summer of 1964. The only clouds on the horizon were the looming paternity trial which Ray was sure he'd get over come what may, and a nagging issue over Jeff Brown's future which was bound to come to a head sooner or later. But for the moment, everything was just fine as the golden hues of October gave way to the darker skies of November and the final weeks of the year approached.

Ray backstage at the Finsbury Park Astoria for his London debut in May 1963, with trumpeter Wallace Davenport.
(Val Wilmer)

Relaxing backstage in London, Margie Hendricks.
(Val Wilmer)

Alto sax star of the Ray Charles reed section Hank
Crawford, at the London debut. *(Val Wilmer)*

The Raelettes on the 1963 UK tour (left to right) Pat Lyles, Margie
Hendricks, Gwen Berry, Darlene McCrae. *(Val Wilmer)*

An animated Ray at the piano, to his left bass player Edgar Willis, London 1963. *(Hulton Archive/Getty Images)*

An in-action still with Ray, the big band and Raelettes, from the 1964 movie *Ballad In Blue*. *(Christian Him/Jazz Index)*

Corny or cool? Cover art for the 1965 *Country and Western Meets Rhythm and Blues* album. *(Pictorial Press)*

Ray outside the Southridge home with Della, David, Ray Jr and (front) Robert, in 1966.
(Time & Life Pictures/Getty Images)

Valet Vernon Troupe guides Ray to the piano at a 1966 recording session. *(Time & Life Pictures/Getty Images)*

Manager Joe Adams escorts Ray on to the
Martin 404 tour plane, 1966.
(Time & Life Pictures/Getty Images)

On tour in 1966, Ray engrossed in chess which he
learned to play while in re-hab the previous year.
(Time & Life Pictures/Getty Images)

At the controls: Ray in 1966, co-piloting his private aircraft. *(Time & Life Pictures/Getty Images)*

On stage at the Newport Jazz Festival 1968, with Joe Adams making the announcements.
(David Redfern/Redferns)

Under the spotlight at New York's Carnegie Hall, 1966.
(Time & Life Pictures/Getty Images)

Poster for the Ray Charles Show in July 1969.
(Hulton Archive/Getty Images)

One of Ray's favourite gigs was always Paris – here
he plays the Salle Pleyel in 1969.
(Guy Le Querrec/Magnum Photos)

A floor-level shot of Ray in 1971, with those feet the
drummer always had to watch.
(David Redfern/Redferns)

Ray guests with singer Della Reese on her 1969
TV special *Della (Photofest/Retna)*

A still from the 1973 TV special *Barbra Streisand and Other Musical Instruments*. *(Hulton Archive/Getty Images)*

The Genius meets the President – Ray and Richard Nixon, September 1972. *(Corbis)*

13

On And Off The Road

"What makes my approach special is that I do different things. I do jazz, blues, country music and so forth. I do them all, like a good utility man."

– Ray Charles

November 22, 1963, and the attention of the whole world was suddenly, shockingly focussed on events in Dallas, Texas – the same city where Ray and Della had spent their first happily married years – when President John F. Kennedy was assassinated under the midday sun. All America was plunged into an atmosphere of despondency and gloom which would only be alleviated gradually over the following months, as winter turned to spring and sorrow gave way to hope.

The national mood was mirrored perfectly by the music scene through the first half of 1964, when The Beatles – as one US journalist put it at the time – "taught America to smile again". And from their much-ballyhoo arrival in New York in early February to their total domination of the US charts over the following months, the impact of the Fab Four would be far from short-lived. They spearheaded the so-called British Invasion of pop and R&B groups, which would alter the musical landscape forever, with far-reaching consequences for "established" pop stars, be they Elvis Presley or Ray Charles.

Prior to the coming of The Beatles, Ray had paralleled the sombre aftermath of Dallas with an album of "cry" songs entitled *Sweet And Sour Tears*, recorded and released in January 1964. Again, apart from the actual theme, the link between the songs was musically tenuous; but, as Ray's previous "concept" albums had demonstrated, that in itself was proof of his mastery of a broad palette of moods and genres.

He was no chameleon however, apeing various styles. As he had with gospel music a decade earlier, he appropriated show songs, country music, vaudeville numbers or whatever, and processed them *his* way, as he would explain to Robert Gordon in 1992: "Without sounding too egotistical, I just call myself a singer. What comes to me is what I'm trying to portray. Think of me as an actor that is doing it with notes as opposed to talking. I'm supposed to be good enough to make it convincing to you as a listener. I do what I feel fits the song, and that's what comes out."

Following something of a pattern he had established with his ABC albums, Ray recorded the big band arrangements by Calvin Jackson in California and Sid Feller's string tracks, with the Gene Lowell Singers backing, in New York City.

But much of the arranging was done by Ray himself; he would tape each song, showing what he wanted to be done in terms of the harmony, rhythm and so on, and then let Feller and Jackson have the tapes. The resulting arrangements were, in this way, faithful to Ray's ideas for a particular number.

As well as capturing the mood of the time, *Sweet And Sour Tears* stands up in its own right as a polished vehicle for Ray's gritty passion. From the country-flavoured 'No One To Cry To' to the old Johnnie Ray barnstormer 'Cry' and classic weepy 'Cry Me A River', he switches between the big band and string format with ease. On 'Baby, Don't You Cry', he demonstrates his new "swingova" rhythm (which he described as "a reverse, or backward, bossa nova"), which was Ray's own modified version of the bossa nova that was sweeping the nation in the early Sixties. But *the* standout track is 'Willow Weep For Me', in which Ray suspends the rhythm entirely for a laid-back vocal intro, before launching into an interpretation *par excellence* of the standard. And the instrumental break, with the band bizarrely launching into a strident break in waltz-time, somehow just works.

Backed with the oldie 'My Heart Cries For You', a number two charter for big-voiced pop singer Guy Mitchell back in 1951, 'Baby, Don't You Cry' was the first single culled from the album. Released in February, it crept into the Top 40 in the middle of March, only to creep out again the following week. The album fared better, eventually making the Top 10 – even though it didn't hit the chart till April, by which time Ray was almost ready to start cutting a new bunch of tracks.

With another Zeigler coast-to-coast trip under their belts, Ray and the band found themselves in New York again, and early in May were in the studio once more. Along with some material left over from the mid-1963 *Ingredients* sessions, the result was a "theme" album unlike anything they'd approached before, and in complete contrast to the melancholy of *Sweet And Sour Tears* – a collection of humorous novelty songs called *Have A Smile With Me.*

Made famous by Joe Williams during his tenure with the Count Basie band, Charles Calhoun's 'Smack Dab In The Middle' kicks things off with a brassy exuberance, followed by the cod-hillbilly hoedown of 'Feudin' And Fightin''.

From there on it's a combination of novelties like 'Two Ton Tessie' ("from Tennessee"), hoary old vaudeville ditties 'I Never See Maggie Alone' from 1926 and the even older 'Ma, He's Making Eyes At Me', and the downright bizarre 'The Thing' and 'The Man With The Weird Beard'. And just to throw things completely, there's even one "straight" tune, the Don Gibson ballad 'Who Cares (For Me)'.

But throughout this succession of what would seem trite songs, the band swings with soulful gusto, there are some crackling sax solos and Ray, as always, makes the material his own. One writer compared the combination of bluesy vocals, kitsch-inclined arrangements and wacky lyrics to the surreal R&B of Screaming Jay Hawkins, and that's not a million miles off the mark. And the album's great fun.

After another single ('My Baby Don't Dig Me' and 'Something's Wrong') that did nothing chart-wise, *Have A Smile* was released in June '64, by which time Ray and the band were in the Irish capital Dublin, shooting a full-length feature film.

If the idea of Ray singing 'The Naughty Lady Of Shady Lane' on his current album sounded bizarre, the black-and-white film about Ray befriending a blind English schoolboy was even weirder. Produced by Alexander Salkind, it was directed by Paul Henreid, who was far better known as an actor with such movies as *Now Voyager* and *Casablanca* on his c.v. From the start the picture suffered from a severe lack of finance – the reason for it being shot in Dublin – and Ray would later reflect "it could have been much hipper if the folk making it hadn't run out of money."

The film opens with the first of several live song performances before moving into a school classroom for sightless children, where Ray plays call-and-response with the kids on 'Hit The Road Jack'. He strikes up a relationship with a small boy (played by Piers Bishop), and plans for the child to see a top eye specialist in Paris, at the same time giving him the confidence to face the outside world. Through the boy's attractive but smothering mother (Dawn Addams), Ray meets her musician lover, played by Tom Bell, who accepts an invitation to be Ray's arranger on a European tour which, coincidentally, includes Paris. The theme, of coming to terms with a disability like blindness in a positive rather than negative way, obviously struck a chord with Ray.

What it lacks as a piece of convincing cinema it makes up for as a vehicle for Ray, the band and The Raelettes to showcase no less than nine numbers including 'I Got A Woman', 'What'd I Say', 'Hit The Road Jack', 'Hallelujah I Love Her So' and 'Let The Good Times Roll'. With two new compositions by Ray, 'Please Forgive And Forget' and 'Light Out Of Darkness', the film was originally entitled *Light Out Of Darkness* before finally being released as *Ballad In Blue* in the UK and elsewhere, and *Blues For Lovers* in the USA. For any Ray Charles fan who can track it down it's an interesting curiosity, with Ray playing "himself" – though not with a great deal of on-screen presence – and Joe Adams (who'd acted in a number of high-profile films including 1954's *Carmen Jones* and the more recent *Manchurian Candidate* in '62) as his valet.

The last scenes to be shot were filmed in London, where Ray talked to reporters in between sequences on a dodgem car ride at Battersea Fun Fair. "It's fun for me because I don't have to act," he told *Melody Maker*'s Chris Roberts. "All I have to do is be myself. I've found it isn't all that hard to be myself. If I had to act I would turn it down completely. I am no actor, and I have the sense to realise that and remind myself of that." Turning to music, he commented on the current boom Stateside in British R&B and pop groups: "I've heard The Beatles are doing quite well!" adding, "I don't knock The Beatles like a lot of people do. Personally myself, I might not buy a Beatles record, but they have something that makes them appealing."

Filming over, some British dates including London and Liverpool were the prelude to an eventful visit to continental Europe. In Liverpool, the local music paper *Mersey Beat* ran a news item on how a city promoter, Jim Ireland, had tried to book Ray Charles earlier for the prestigious Philharmonic Hall but found the £4,000 fee prohibitive. "We'd have had to charge £2 a ticket, and nobody would pay that," he told *Mersey Beat*'s editor Bill Harry. In the event, a rival agency presented Ray at the Odeon cinema.

In Germany, Ray and the outfit played Hamburg's Star Club, where The Beatles had famously played gruelling eight-hour sets seven days a week before their worldwide success. They were booked into the club by Henry Henroid, who was working for the British promoter Don Arden at the time. Talking to Bill Harry in 1997 Henroid recalled that US servicemen from American bases all over Germany were unable to get into Ray's sold-out German debut: "When Ray Charles was to perform, they told me to look out of the window and there was a queue of black people the length of the Grosse Freiheit, going out into the Reeperbahn – what had happened was that they'd come all the way from the American bases. So I went down and spoke to them and asked if there was an officer, and there was. I took him over to Ray's hotel and said: 'We have a dilemma. We're sold out and I have downstairs a black American officer, and they're all dying to see the show. What d'you want to do?' Ray said, 'Right, we'll do a matinee.' And he did."

In Denmark, they packed the fabulous Tivoli Gardens in wonderful Copenhagen; and in Belgium, they played to a rain-soaked crowd in the village of Comblain la Tour. The annual jazz festival in the tiny village, not far from the city of Liege, was the brainchild of an American, Joe Napoli. During World War II Joe had parachuted into the area when his plane was shot down, and was taken in by the villagers who hid him from the German army. On his return to his native Brooklyn in peacetime he started managing and promoting jazz acts, and, in gratitude for his rescue during the war, in 1959 he set up the first International Jazz Festival in the village that he'd grown to love. It became a yearly event, a regular feature, along with the all-star line-ups he booked, being the almost inevitable bad weather. The weekend in early August 1964 when Ray Charles was top of the bill was no exception. Reporters spoke of the crowds greeting Ray under beating rain, one eloquently describing the view from above the sea of umbrellas as "an enormous dented tortoise"; the British jazz photographer David Redfern recalled the conditions as "a mud bath".

And, as always, there was Paris. But the week-long sell-out at the Olympia was memorable not for the hero's welcome the French afforded Ray – that was almost taken for granted by now – but because it marked the departure of Margie Hendricks. The singer's passionate affair with her boss was long-gone ancient history, but that distancing did nothing to dampen the fire of her musical contribution. Her vocal exchanges with Ray were as impassioned as ever, her position as *the* Raelette of Raelettes seemingly unchallengeable. But offstage her lifestyle was becoming more erratic, more dependent on the heroin to which she was addicted, and her temper resulting in as many flare-ups with Ray as during the volatile period when they were "together". Things finally came to a head in Paris, and Marjorie Hendricks was fired, three Raelettes finishing the tour. After her spectacular – indeed turbulent – years as a Raelette, it was a downhill path for Margie. Struggling with attempts at making it on her own, combined with an escalating heroin habit, she died of causes directly related to her drug problems in 1973.

It was a tour that was far from finished when Margie departed. After Europe Ray and the rest took in dates in Australia and the Far East, including Sydney, Singapore, Hong Kong and Tokyo. When they got back to the States in August Ray Charles could now truly be considered a star on a worldwide scale.

As more singles came and went without making any impression on the charts – there was 'No One To Cry To' and 'A Tear Fell' from *Sweet And Sour Tears* in June, and 'Smack Dab In The Middle' with 'I Wake Up Crying' in September – albums were more than ever becoming the focus of Ray's output. This fact was not lost on Sid Feller when he decided to record the opening show of the autumn tour at the Shrine Civic Auditorium in Los Angeles for an album, *Ray Charles Live In Concert*, that would be released early in 1965. It would be Ray's first live show on record (other concert recordings only being released years later) since the ground-breaking Atlantic albums from Newport and Atlanta in the late Fifties, and a litmus test of how ABC-era Ray stood up to the earlier model as a live act.

Fans of Ray Charles as the master purveyor of jazz-tinged R&B needn't have worried. From the instrumental 'Swing A Little Taste' written by Julian Priester, one of the trombone section, the set compares well with any of the in-concert recordings available before or since. With the opener we know this band means business, a roaring swinger of a number highlighted by a no-holds-barred piano solo from Ray and a hard-bop Fathead break with a more rounded, Coltrane-like tone than usual.

'I Got A Woman' is as expansive as the classic Newport take, Ray riding the two-chord outro for all it's worth. Songs like 'You Don't Know Me' and 'Margie', both from ABC "themed" albums, get a much bluesier treatment than on the studio versions, and recent R&B sides 'Hide 'Nor Hair' and 'Don't Set Me Free' come over as raunchy as the originals – the latter number featuring Hendricks' replacement Lillian Fort on a gospelly intro and Margie's line-by-line responses to Ray's vocal.

And as well as the usual 'What'd I Say' – taken at the proper tempo rather than the breakneck speed which was often the case in concert – there's a crowd-rousing six-minute version of 'Makin' Whoopee', on which Ray improvises some sardonic new lines of his own on the old Twenties favourite. Concessions to show-biz glitz are restricted to MC Joe Adams' fulsome announcements and Ray's joke finale 'Pop Goes The Weasel' (which had become a regular part of the act by then). But all in all it's evident that the big band-based shows – on a good night at least – had lost little of their power through the first half of the Sixties.

The tour that had opened with the Shrine concert was due to wind up at the end of November before the Christmas holiday break which Ray, as usual, would spend in LA with Della and the boys. But between the spectacular start to the trek and its eventual close, the darkest storm clouds yet were about to gather over Ray's future, in terms of both his career and personal life.

It was after a gig in the Canadian city of Montreal that Ray's private aircraft, the Martin that he'd purchased in 1962 and which he and the entourage now used for most of their touring in North America, landed at Logan Airport in Boston. It was in the early hours of October 31 – Ray remembered it as being "cold and wintry" – and everyone piled off the plane as quickly as possible to be driven to their hotel in the city. Once there Ray realised he'd left his stash of drugs on board the aircraft.

He immediately got his driver to take him back to the airport, where they boarded the plane and recovered the heroin and marijuana Ray had forgotten. But the to-ing and fro-ing in the middle of the night had aroused the suspicions of customs officials, and when his chauffeur led Ray back to their car they were apprehended by the two officers and subsequently searched. Ray was arrested on the spot, and as dawn broke awaited a hearing in front of a *federal* commissioner. Although he was released later that morning on condition he would appear when summoned, Ray realised this was heavy shit he was in: "These guys weren't airport cops. They were fully fledged narcos."

A preliminary hearing eventually took place in the last week of November, at which Ray was granted further bail until a trial proper could be arranged – which would be some months in the future at the earliest. But, unlike his previous brushes with local police forces, this confrontation with the Federal law could result in a sentence of anything up to 60 years in jail.

As the bust hit the headlines worldwide, the band fulfilled what dates remained of the autumn tour amid fevered speculation in the press about Ray's possible imprisonment. The knock-on effect of this was, inevitably, a down-turn in business, as bookings were cancelled and others put on hold. Ray decided the best thing in the circumstances was to forget about any live dates for the next 12 months, by which time – if he wasn't in prison – the dust should have settled.

He had plenty to get on with at his nearly completed LA business head-quarters in the meantime, so he laid off the guys in the band until further notice. But for Jeff Brown, it wasn't a temporary break from Ray's employment that he faced that December. After months of increasing frustration at the way things were moving under Joe Adams' influence, and the Boston bust being one last straw in many ways, he finally handed in his resignation.

Ray Charles was never known for his generosity, particularly where his closest working colleagues were concerned – his band and on-the-road entourage. Indeed, in a business where miserliness was commonplace, Ray was still famous for his penny-pinching when it came to paying his employees.

And despite being the most loyal – and longest serving – of those employees, Jeff Brown was no exception. He was still on the same salary Ray had paid him in the Fifties, long before his own earnings had reached superstar proportions. As far as Ray was concerned, Jeff continued to do the same job he'd always been paid for, and on that basis he saw no reason to increase his wages. For all his dedication to his boss, which literally involved keeping the show on the road on more than one occasion, Jeff didn't enjoy any bonuses or financial thank-you's for the success he'd certainly been influential in maintaining. Not officially at least, but he did receive payments from both Milt Shaw and Hal Zeigler unbeknown to Ray, in appreciation of his essential part in the money-making business. With that, and whatever he could save from his $15,000 a year salary from Ray, he decided to invest in a bowling alley based in Houston, in his home state of Texas.

At Joe Adams' instigation, Ray began to question where Jeff could get the money to plough into such a business. A lot of on-the-road money passed through his manager's hands over the years, could it all be accounted for? And what of these payments from Shaw and Zeigler? – *he*, Ray reasoned, should be paying Jeff and no one else.

Naturally, many on-tour expenses were paid cash in hand, especially in the earlier years of Jeff's tenure, so no strict accounting could ever be produced of every penny. Realising there was no point in aggressively standing his corner and risking instant dismissal by Ray – more than likely encouraged by Joe – Jeff put his head down and tried to carry on with business as usual.

But the die was cast. Ray's suspicion, once aroused, couldn't be allayed. Jeff's position became untenable as his role was gradually relegated from one of authority to ever less essential administration. He'd always picked up the pieces when Ray's drug taking got out of hand or when there was dissension in the ranks, keeping the boat on an even keel in the stormiest of circumstances. Now, with the Boston drugs crisis, he'd had enough.

On leaving Ray, Jeff Brown threw himself wholeheartedly into the Big J bowling alley in Houston, only to have that go bust a couple of years down the line. Then he returned to road managing, looking after the Stax soul duo Sam & Dave. When that came to an end, it was down to chauffeuring in New York City, where he would die of cancer in 1996.

Another bone of contention that helped precipitate Jeff's departure was Ray's new headquarters that had been growing out of the derelict site at 2107 West Washington Boulevard in Los Angeles. As the ambitious complex started to take shape in the late summer of 1964, it soon became apparent that while both Ray and Joe Adams were about to move into expansive offices, Jeff was relegated to a comparative broom cupboard. In Jeff's eyes the building was a microcosm of the Ray Charles organisation as it stood right then, with the pecking-order clearly defined by square footage.

As far as Ray was concerned, announcing the lay-off for 1965 would allow him to put the finishing touches to the new nerve centre of his business. He even got his former Atlantic engineer Tom Dowd to help set up the recording studio, in what was soon to be named the RPM Building, RPM being the initials of the businesses therein – recording, publishing and management. With Tangerine Records, Tangerine Music and Racer Personal Management all there under the umbrella of Ray Charles Enterprises, Ray was now the head of a corporate empire – with Joe Adams as his vice president.

With the new offices and the family home – which had now moved to the Baldwin Hills neighbourhood of Southridge – all in LA, Ray had severed most personal ties with the East Coast, including those with Mae Mosely from whom he'd been distancing himself for some time. She responded with a paternity plea for two-grand-a-month support for their daughter Raenee. And at the end of February, a Federal grand jury indicted Ray on two charges of possession of narcotics and two of smuggling the drugs into the country. All in all, Ray Charles had plenty to think about in the coming months through 1965.

Meanwhile, as soon as the studio at RPM was up and running, Ray was in there making his next album, again laying it on thick once again as far as the title was concerned, *Country And Western Meets Rhythm & Blues*. It was also known as *Together Again*, which was the name of the opening track, just one of four songs by country legend Buck Owens. And the collection included two new compositions by Ray, which was something of a rarity by 1965, 'Please Forgive And Forget' and 'Light Out Of Darkness', both from the movie *Ballad In Blue*.

Already given a rockabilly slant back in 1954 when it was the flipside of Elvis Presley's first ever single on Sun Records, Bill Monroe's bluegrass classic 'Blue Moon Of Kentucky' gets Ray's "swingova" treatment on the album, and it's powerful stuff; with the rhythm section, lead guitar, Raelettes and a vocal chorus all upfront in the mix, it could be called bossa nova meets the blues. There's more swingova on 'I've Got A Tiger By The Tail', and the set also includes two down-to-earth blues items, 'Next Door To The Blues' and Percy Mayfield's fine 'Watch It Baby'. Produced by Sid Feller, it's not classic Ray Charles by any means but certainly has its moments.

The next time Ray laid down an album at RPM, in October 1965, it was a very different story. Apart from the title track opener, Buck Owens' country weepie 'Crying Time', the album marked a return to the classic sound of Ray Charles R&B with lots of soulful piano, horns and Raelettes upfront and only two ballads 'Tears' and 'Don't You Think I Ought To Know' featuring strings.

For the sessions Ray booked Billy Preston, a 19-year-old keyboard player who specialised on the organ, who he'd first encountered in Los Angeles in 1964 when they were both appearing on the *Shindig* rock'n'roll TV show. A child prodigy who'd backed Mahalia Jackson in his local LA church at the age of 10, Preston's roots were firmly in sacred music. By 1962 he was backing Little Richard on a gospel tour of Europe, where he also played with Sam Cooke for whom he recorded his first rock album. Years later Preston recalled to Wayne Robins in *Creem* magazine how he'd idolised Ray as a child. "I used to go to school around the corner from Charles' house, and I used to go over there and peek at him a lot from across the street. One day I heard him playin' at his piano, and I got up all my courage to knock on his door . . . I said, 'Oh Ray Charles, I love you, I love you,' and stuff like that. Then I just ran off."

Perhaps surprisingly, the treatment on 'Crying Time' with its full-on country harmonies and even a fiddle break in the middle, is nearer to a "pure" C&W interpretation than any of the tracks on the *Modern Sounds* albums. But from there on, it's mostly the R&B basics that Ray's taking us back to.

The second track in, 'No Use Crying', a blues in 6/8 time with a plaintive if hard-edged organ sound from Billy Preston (Ray filling in on piano), takes us into 'Let's Go Get Stoned'. We're back to church confessional time, with Preston's Hammond laying on some deeply soulful chords and The Raelettes crying in response as Ray warns of the dangers of too much drinkin'. 'Let's Go Get Stoned' was written by the later-distinguished soul songwriting team of Nicholas Ashford and Valerie Simpson, and became their first Top 40 hit as composers when Ray eventually released it as a single in May 1966.

Most of the rest is impassioned renderings of the blues as only Ray knows how, including a six-minute 'Drifting Blues', Percy Mayfield's marvellous cry for racial equality 'You're In For A Big Surprise' and St Louis Jimmy's classic 'Going Down Slow'. But the months between the previous album and this one had been one of the most traumatic periods in Ray's life. Produced by Joe Adams, *Crying Time* stands as a stark monument to that time.

After the Federal indictment in February, Ray had appeared in front of the Federal District Court in Boston at the end of March, where he pleaded not guilty and the Judge granted him further bail. But the charges still hung over him like a black cloud pending a trial, and the thought of actually doing time in prison was beyond comprehension for Ray, his family and those around him.

Plea bargaining went on between the Federal prosecutors and Ray's lawyers, and it was then that the question of Ray kicking dope arose. If he could prove that he'd cleaned himself up – or was on the road to doing so – by the time the trial came to court, it would definitely work in his favour. That, and the more immediate effect a looming prison sentence was having on his family, convinced Ray he should try to end his habit.

Until then it was a habit Ray had always been comfortable with; comfortable in the sense that despite the pain involved when he needed a fix, or the hassle in scoring for one, on a plus-and-minus balance he'd always felt the high was worth the low. But now the hurt was going to reach out as it never had before to those nearest and dearest. Despite his unfaithfulness and the resultant progeny, his family of Della and the boys was his prime concern when the prospect of jail loomed ever closer.

It was an incident in May involving his 10-year-old son Ray Jr, that finally persuaded Ray to attempt a cure. He was due to record at RCA in Los Angeles, the title song for a new Steve McQueen movie *The Cincinnati Kid*, but the session coincided with a school banquet at which Ray Jr was to receive a Little League baseball award. Ray turned up at the banquet, intending to go to the recording session after the presentation had been made, but as the time dragged on he realised he'd have to leave prematurely. As he got up to go, little Ray burst into tears at his father's departure before his proud moment. Ray Sr was mortified at his son's distress, which made him think about the impact on the child if he actually went to jail. If kicking the habit was what it took to avoid *that*, he'd kick the habit. And, as with so many decisions in his life, once Ray had a determination about something, he saw it through.

Early in June Ray contacted Dr Frederick Hacker, a psychiatrist-therapist who had a smart clinic in Beverly Hills. He offered Ray the opportunity to wean himself gradually off heroin without becoming sick, but Ray refused: "That ain't my style. I don't want to be weaned. I'll just stop," he recalled telling the doctor. In other words, he was going down the road most junkies spoke of with horror – cold turkey.

Conveniently out of the way for the anonymity that a celebrity like Ray required, Hacker booked him into a psychiatric facility in south east LA where he also had a clinic, St Francis Hospital. Checking in at the end of July, Ray went straight into the first painful process of withdrawal. Nausea, vomiting, diarrhoea – that was the seemingly unending cycle for three days or more. "I was heaving up poison, the poison which was heroin. The poison my body was now naturally rejecting."

Then came calm, but only a calm before the storm. The physical addiction was one thing, the psychological storm would be the struggle to maintain his new-found "clean", to clear his mind, as well as his body, of any need. That was where Hacker and his therapy came in, talking with Ray in long sessions that explored his life, and in particular the traumas of his childhood. And when he wasn't delving into Ray's deepest psyche, the doctor taught his patient to play chess.

Ray was in the hospital through September, gradually being allowed to ease himself into his real world with visits from Della and Joe, phone communication with his office and trips out. By the time he recorded *Crying Time* in October he was all but finished with the treatment that Hacker had to offer at the St Francis, but he still needed the doctor's testimony as to his successful cure when he once again appeared before the court in Boston just a week before the end of November.

This time in Boston Ray would plead guilty to the charges, his defence stressing that he'd now undertaken a cure with complete success, with Doctor Hacker there to testify on his behalf. Hacker stressed that his patient was a man of strong character, he was convinced Ray had kicked heroin for good. The prosecution wanted their conviction, and still argued for a two-year jail sentence. In the event, the Judge leniently ruled that sentence would be waived for another year, during which time Ray would be on probation, reporting for medical examination to monitor his condition as and when the court requested.

Ray had made a new album and put a new band back on the road by the time the Feds served him notice of the health check-up at the end of April 1966. He had just finished a week in Las Vegas when the word came, he had to show up in the McLean Hospital in Belmont, Massachusetts in two days' time. The short notice was to prevent any "cleaning up" if he was back on dope, but that didn't concern Ray – and as he conceded in his autobiography, "I was being tested."

He was housed in the most grandiose structure on the McLean Hospital campus, the Upham Memorial Hall, a brick mansion larger than many hotels but built to house just nine mental patients. Now abandoned, it was known as the "Harvard Club" because, according to a *Boston Globe* journalist "at one time, each of its majestic corner suites was said to have been occupied by a graduate of Harvard College." By the Sixties Upham had become "a dumping ground for chronically ill, elderly patients – practically all of them rich – whose families had cut lifetime financial deals with the hospital. There was little incentive to 'cure' the Uphamites because their families had paid good money never to see them again."

Whatever its attitude to its regular inmates, Ray's testing was certainly thorough, three days of examinations, mental and physical, after which he was pronounced clean. That was the last of it for the moment, until his sentencing by the Boston Court that had been deferred to the end of the year.

When Ray appeared again in front of the Boston judiciary, on November 22, a courtroom drama ensued befitting a Hollywood movie. The original lenient judge, Judge George Sweeney, had died in October, his place being taken by a known hardliner, Charles Wyzanski. Despite another recommendation from Doctor Hacker, Ray feared the worst when a sealed envelope was handed to Wyzanski. It was written by Sweeney before his demise, to be opened before sentencing took place; in it, he asked his decision in Ray's case to be put on record.

As quoted later in the *Los Angeles Times*, the letter stated: "I know this case is no longer in my jurisdiction. But I have to tell you — just as a fellow human being — that society would be better off with Ray Charles free, serving as a good example of a guy who kicked drugs, rather than being put away in prison." If Ray was proved clean, Sweeney urged a two-year probation and $10,000 fine. In the event, the other judge extended the probation to four years with a five-year suspended sentence. But it meant that, after paying the fine, Ray – thanks largely to the late Judge Sweeney – was finally free to get on with his career. And, thanks to Hacker, free of the scourge of heroin for the rest of his life.

14

Soul Brothers And Sisters

"It was simply the continuation and evolution of rhythm & blues. There were a lot of country elements in it, because of its location in Memphis and Muscle Shoals, but the basis was rhythm & blues, developing rhythm & blues."

– Jerry Wexler

"Quality Records For Family Enjoyment" was how ABC-Paramount described their range of albums catalogued on the inner sleeve of their LPs, and Ray's next collection seemed to aim at that broad across-the-market appeal. Recorded early in 1966, just as *Crying Time* was released and its title single became his first Top 10 hit in over two years, *Ray's Moods* was a stylistic mixed-bag, but no bland affair musically.

Along with a couple of fairly predictable country outings, including Don Gibson's 'A Born Loser', there's soulful Raelette-driven R&B that kicks things off 'What-Cha Doing In There (I Wanna Know)', and some solid blues including an atmospheric 'You Don't Understand'. There's even a novelty number 'Granny Wasn't Grinning That Day' that starts with what sounds like an early rap, and the cornball 'By The Light Of The Silvery Moon' on which Ray scats some lines, just for good measure.

But the two high points come in 'Chitlins With Candied Yams', a powerful instrumental concentrating on Ray's piano and organ, and a sensational version of 'Sentimental Journey'. The latter's a full-on sanctified treatment of the old pop standard made famous by Doris Day, featuring Ray, The Raelettes, plus a male voice intoning the bass vocals in doo-wop-gospel style.

For Ray, after the cathartic nature of *Crying Time* which had immediately followed his confinement at St Francis Hospital, this was a chance to tell the world that things were back to normal. But it was a rapidly changing world with which much of Ray's music seemed increasingly out of step; ironically so, given that Ray was one of the instigators of much of that change, as the primary voice of what had now come to be known as soul music.

"I don't think you could tag a certain year as the date that soul music appeared, because it didn't happen that way. It evolved over a period of time. Even today, you could ask five different people what it was and how it got started and get five different answers . . . Originally, soul music had a strong element of the church, of spiritual music. It had a gospel music feeling, and then it incorporated the sound of blues music. That's soul's make-up: the fusion of gospel and blues, all mixed up together. It's the crossover of those forms of music that makes soul unique . . ." So reflected Ray Charles on soul music, the very nature of which he had helped define: "But the feeling that comes through in the music – that's the essence of soul – the word itself tells you that."

A look at the *Billboard* pop charts for the early months of 1966 makes interesting reading. There, among the Anglo-pop of The Beatles, Kinks and Herman's Hermits – and its American counterparts in The Lovin' Spoonful, Paul Revere & The Raiders and Mamas & The Papas – were the new faces of black music. In fact Stevie Wonder, The Marvellettes, The Miracles, The Supremes, Wilson Pickett, Fontella Bass, Percy Sledge and others had so successfully infiltrated the mainstream market by the mid-Sixties that *Billboard* suspended its R&B chart through 1964, when for the first time whites and blacks were buying the same records.

The twin centres of this new music of Black America, in many ways representing opposite sides of the same coin, were Detroit and Memphis, respective homes of the Motown and Stax record labels. By '66 they represented quite different styles of music of course; just a look at the signs outside the company offices said it all – Motown called itself "Hitsville USA", the slogan above Stax read "Soulsville USA". In other words, Motown was pop, Stax was the real thing. But both had their common roots in the fusion of gospel and R&B first forged by Ray Charles more than 10 years earlier.

The smooth black pop of the Motown sound was pioneered by owner/producer Berry Gordy on his Tamla-Motown label early in the Sixties. Gordy – who admitted to being particularly influenced by 'What'd I Say' and 'I Got A Woman' – had worked in the late Fifties with Jackie Wilson, whose energetic hits like 'Lonely Teardrops' and 'Reet Petite' never really reflected the sexual mayhem let loose in his wild stage act. But Gordy's main musical architect in his Motown enterprise was Smokey Robinson. With his group The Miracles, the teenage Robinson was once "rescued" by Ray, who stepped in when the then-inexperienced group arrived at an Apollo date without the arrangements the house band expected: "He said, 'Okay, you horn players do this here; you in the rhythm section, hit it when I nod.' By the time he was finished we had an arrangement."

Smokey's vocal style was clearly influenced by that other great soul pioneer Sam Cooke, whose sweet delivery made for perfect pop but often belied the passion of his gospel roots. As writer Gerri Hishey would point out: "What Ray Charles was able to do, which even a great gospel voice like Sam Cooke never quite achieved in his rather tame pop work, was to transfer the gospel fire to the Top 10 with its heat undiminished." In December 1964, Ray had sung 'The Angels Keep Watch Over Me' at Cooke's funeral after the singer was shot dead in a $3-a-night motel room.

By the mid-Sixties Motown had become the biggest black-run record company in America, with hits in every part of the world. Its stellar roster had vocal groups like The Marvellettes, The Supremes (who as schoolgirl group The Primettes sang 'The Right Time') and Martha & The Vandellas, all of whom were indebted more than a little to the template provided by The Raelettes. Motown's solo singers included Marvin Gaye and Stevie Wonder – who as 11-year-old "Little" Stevie Wonder had sat in with Ray at a Detroit gig in 1961, and whose 1962 debut album was called *Tribute To Uncle Ray*. Gaye's style, too, owed much to that of Ray Charles, as he would freely admit: "Everyone at Motown idolised Ray. He had both the commercial success and raw feeling we were all looking for. He was the man."

The musical imprint of Ray Charles was even more obvious in the case of so-called "southern soul". As Nelson George wrote in his 1985 account of the rise and fall of Motown *Where Did Our Love Go?*: "Charles established soul as singers' music, where open, piano-based backing and percussive horn charts provided space for a generation of vocalists – Wilson Pickett, Otis Redding, Carla Thomas and Aretha Franklin were among the best – to unleash searing, passionate performances."

Ray's influence could already be easily recognised in the work of many Southern R&B artists of course. New Orleans stars Chris Kenner (who had a *Billboard* pop number two with 'I Like It Like That' in 1961) and Alvin Robinson (he hit with Kenner's 'Something You Got' in '64), for instance, both testified to his legacy – as did other Crescent City luminaries like Allen Toussaint, Jerry Byrne, Lee Dorsey and Ernie K. Doe. Soul commentator Billy Vera even went as far as to describe Jessie Hill's 1960 two-parter 'Ooh Poo Pah Doo' as a "sideways 'What'd I Say'"; in the words of R&B historian John Broven, the Top 30 single "sold to a public whose appetite for these crude call-and-response sounds had been whetted by the success of Ray Charles 'What'd I Say' a few months earlier."

But the Stax label in Memphis became the catalyst for Southern Soul with a capital "S" from its inception in the early Sixties. Founded by a white man, Jim Stewart, from the start – like Atlantic with which it would be closely associated – Stax was a mixed-race enterprise. And musically the core element was similarly multi-ethnic, several years before the colour barriers had come down formally across the city.

The Mar-Kays, a teenage group that included guitarist Steve Cropper, bass player Donald "Duck" Dunn and a two-sax and trumpet horn section clearly indebted to the Ray Charles small bands, were an early example of a white outfit playing black R&B, something that was commonplace by the mid-Sixties. Their one and only US Top 40 hit, the down-home 'Last Night' in 1961, was one of the pioneer crossover R&B hits that was hugely popular in both black and white markets when it reached number three in the pop charts.

As the basis of the house band at Stax Records, under the titular leadership of pianist Booker T. Jones, the house rhythm section at Stax became Booker T. & The MGs (standing for Memphis Group) with Cropper, Dunn and drummer Al Jackson. The multiracial quartet enjoyed a huge instrumental smash in their own right in 1962 with the funky 'Green Onions'. At the same time the Mar-Kays three-piece horn section evolved into the Memphis Horns, who likewise provided the distinctive Stax feel to dozens of hits. Between them, with assorted studio visitors and line-up permutations, the two outfits were the backbone of a sound whose relationship to the frontline vocalists was a direct descendant of the Charles small bands of the Fifties, as referred to by Nelson George.

The other crucial centre of Southern Soul was Muscle Shoals in Alabama, where Tom Stafford and producer Rick Hall built the celebrated Fame studio and established Stax's only rival in the South with the Muscle Shoals "sound". One of the first names to emerge from there was Arthur Alexander who hit big in 1962 with 'You Better Move On'. Alexander's style was country-tinged soul, the mix that typified Muscle Shoals and its black and white personnel, described by Gerri Hirshey as "part church and part hills".

One graduate of the early Muscle Shoals recording scene was vocalist and producer Dan Penn, who became a leading light in Memphis with American Sound Studios later in the Sixties, producing the Box Tops' seminal 1967 hit 'The Letter'. Penn, who was reputed to sing more black than Elvis ever did, recalled to Robert Gordon his formative influences: "When I first heard Presley I was as enthralled as anybody, Sun was knock-out. But it didn't last all that long, because as soon as he started making those slick movies and those funny little teenybopper records, well I slid away real fast and I never did go back. Here comes Ray Charles and then I don't have to worry about it no more because I know which way I'm going."

Soon there was a healthy cross-fertilisation between the two centres, with Wilson Pickett, Aretha Franklin and Don Covay among many artists who'd come up with the Stax/Atlantic soul sound – Atlantic had distrib-uted Stax from early on – making many of their finest sides in Muscle Shoals. Eventually all Atlantic's soul material was recorded down South, with Jerry Wexler at the helm – continuing a musical process he'd pioneered with Ray Charles a decade and a half earlier.

Hits like Sam & Dave's 'Soul Man', Eddie Floyd's 'Knock On Wood', Otis Redding's monumental 'I've Been Loving You Too Long', Wilson Pickett's anthemic 'In The Midnight Hour' and Aretha Franklin's sublime 'I Never Loved A Man (The Way I Love You)' were a modern manifesta-tion of Ray Charles' church-inspired vocal and instrumental revolution. Memphis-born Aretha, with her own musical roots singing in her father's baptist church in Detroit, was fulsome in her acknowledgement of Ray's influence, on her own style and soul music generally. "The voice of a life-time" was how she described him after his death. "He was a fabulous man, full of humour and wit, a giant of an artist, and of course, he introduced the world to secular soul singing." Jerry Wexler would sum up the Ray-Aretha connection in his autobiography: "Clearly Aretha was continuing what Ray Charles had begun – the secularisation of gospel, turning church rhythms, church patterns, and especially church feelings into personalised love songs. Like Ray, Aretha was a hands-on performer, a two-fisted pianist plugged into the main circuit of Holy Ghost power."

"In each case they brought something new to the table," Jerry Wexler said of soul singers in the *San Jose Mercury News* in 1994, adding that all of Ray's varied output over the years came down to soul music in the end. Ray Charles, he said, "had this blasphemous idea of taking gospel songs and putting the devil's words to them. He can take a gem from Tin Pan Alley or cut to the country, but he brings the same root to it, which is Black American music."

And just as the demise of *Billboard*'s R&B chart was triggered by soul music's incursion into the pop mainstream, so the music of Memphis and Muscle Shoals was making itself felt worldwide. And, as with Motown earlier in the decade, the impact of its influence registered particularly keenly in Great Britain.

The black pop of Motortown ("Motown" being derived from Detroit's nickname as car manufacturing capital of America) had made a huge impression on English artists including The Beatles (who covered eight Motown or Motown-style songs on their first two albums) and Dusty Springfield. Likewise the sound of Southern Soul was taken up by mid-Sixties British singers including Rod Stewart, Chris Farlowe, Alex Harvey and, later in the decade, Joe Cocker. And they all, like Steve Winwood and Eric Burdon before them, acknowledged Ray Charles as the underlying source of that inspiration.

"Soul is when you take a song and make it part of you," Ray would say in the *Life* magazine feature in 1966, "a part that's so true, so real, people think it must have happened to you. I'm not satisfied unless I can make them feel what I feel.

"It's like electricity; we don't really know what it is, do we? But it's a force that can light a room. Soul is like electricity, like a spirit, a drive, a power. People can touch people, can't they?"

A now-intriguing filmed project which Ray took part in towards the end of 1965 encapsulated the varied nature of the popular music scene that he found himself in after his year off. With the same basic band that arranger Onzy Matthews had put together for *Crying Time*, Ray appeared at the Moulin Rouge theatre in Los Angeles as part of a show put together by producer Phil Spector to be filmed as a rock'n'roll movie called *The Big TNT Show*.

Released in 1966, it featured a cross-section of pop names including Spector's classic girl group The Ronettes, R&B legend Bo Diddley, folk-rock group The Byrds, folk singers Donovan and Joan Baez, British pop songstress Petula Clark, proto-hippy band The Lovin' Spoonful, and – nearest to Ray's bag – Ike & Tina Turner. Conspicuous – but clearly at ease – in such diverse company, Ray pulled all the stops out for 'What'd I Say', 'Georgia On My Mind' and 'Let The Good Times Roll'. It looked like it was good to be back.

As soon as *Ray's Moods* was in the can, and with *Crying Time* in the stores, Ray set about putting a band together to go on the road once again.

The year off would need catching up on if he was to regain his place in the public consciousness, and only positive publicity backed by strong on-the-road promotion could do that.

The publicity came largely via the album release and a March single, 'Together Again' from *Country And Western Meets Rhythm & Blues* backed with *Crying Time*'s 'You're Just About To Lose Your Clown'. After the 'Crying Time' single's good showing in the Top 10, the new single disappointed by only scraping into the Top 20 at number 19, but both garnered decent reviews which helped cultivate a feel-good "Ray Charles is back" message in the press in the opening months of 1966.

For the band, Ray almost had to start from scratch. When the last outfit had dispersed, musicians – or Raelettes for that matter – couldn't afford to stick around and wait for the call; they had to eat, so they had to work. Ray had hardly paid them over-the-top when they were working, so they never expected a retainer when he laid them off. In the event, only Leroy Cooper and Edgar Willis returned to the fold, and Raelette Gwen Berry was joined by three newcomers: Merry Clayton, Clydie King and Alexandra Brown.

After some no-nonsense rehearsals, Ray was back on the road with a big band by the end of March. And that's the way it was to be, interrupted only by his brief sojourn in the McLean Hospital at the end of April, for the next few months. Life once again consisted of the tried and trusted one-nighter circuit with the tried and trusted formula of jazz set, Joe introducing Ray, Ray singing all the hits, Ray bringing on The Raelettes, a 'What'd I Say' finale and 'Pop Goes The Weasel' as Ray is led off to wild applause. But the new members of the band had some strong credentials between them so, despite the predictable format, musical sparks soon started to fly. Reviewers noted the solid blues playing of Oklahoma guitarist Tony Mathews, and jazz fans all knew tenor sax player Curtis Amy. Notices were good in both the music magazines and the mainstream press – and the latter, as far as ABC and the concert promoters were concerned, was where it mattered.

Ashford and Simpson's 'Let's Go Get Stoned' appeared as a single in May, just missing the Top 30, followed by 'I Chose To Sing The Blues' in August and 'Please Say You're Fooling' backed with 'I Don't Need No Doctor' in October, neither of which did any better. But the name Ray Charles meant much more than pop chart ratings at this point. The positive publicity that had been building since Ray's "return" culminated in July in a glowing seven-page tribute in *Life* magazine – in which Frank Sinatra

made his famous "Ray Charles is the only genius in our business" quote –
followed in October by a glossy 17-page supplement in *Billboard*.

Despite his much-publicised drug problems, which actually resulted in a
"sympathy vote" working in his favour in a curious way, when Ray was
virtually exonerated by the Boston court in November it was as if he'd
become Mr Clean in the public eye. He *was* clean of course, he'd seen to
that during the aching weeks in St Francis Hospital, but with the heroin
behind him he'd got rid of the main impediment to his being accepted
100 per cent by the music and show business establishment.

As if to confirm that status, in January 1967 ABC-Tangerine released an
ambitious-looking "best of" double album entitled *A Man And His Soul*,
with a gatefold sleeve and 12-page insert featuring a dozen grainy
black-and-white photographs. All the ABC-era hits were there, plus his
last two singles 'I Chose To Sing The Blues' and 'I Don't Need No
Doctor' which were not greatest hits by any means, but solid Raelettes-
supported R&B all the same. The lengthy tribute written for the insert by
the jazz journalist Stanley Dance included a telling quote from Ray: "I
don't profess to be a modern jazz artist, or a rhythm & blues artist, I like to
stay away from those titles hanging on to me, you know. I would just like
to be a good entertainer, period."

And while the album was being shipped into the stores, Ray was back in
the studio, making one of the most remarkable recordings of his career.
Basically, the Joe Adams-produced *Ray Charles Invites You To Listen* was
just another collection of songs, but it was the treatment of those songs –
with his voice pitched at a previously unheard falsetto at times – that
again stamped Ray as an *interpreter* with few equals. You would certainly
have to look to the great jazz singers from Louis Armstrong through Billie
Holiday to the likes of Ella Fitzgerald even to start making a viable
comparison.

One curious aspect of the album was the sleeve notes, in which Chris
Wilson rhapsodised about the "vision" that listening to the recordings
inspired. "As he stood in the darkness of the stage door, memories came
back with the poignancy of vanished things. Twenty years had passed
since he had first seen her standing in a crowd outside that door. He
lingered now for a moment over the vision that possessed him . . ." and so
on. Very kitsch, and very strange.

The songs, mainly standards, ranged from Irving Berlin's 'How Deep Is
The Ocean' to the old stand-by 'You Made Me Love You (I Didn't Want

To Do It)', from the wartime tear-jerker 'I'll Be Seeing You' to Gershwin's 'Love Walked In'. The 10-song collection, on which Ray uses strings on all but two tracks, would be a paean to the Great American Songbook were it not for his almost tongue-in-cheek take on the Barbra Streisand show-stopper 'People' and the Lennon-McCartney ballad 'Yesterday'.

Topping the American charts as a single when it was released by The Beatles in October 1965, the original recording of 'Yesterday' – generally credited to McCartney alone – was so ingrained as the definitive version that any cover would invite inevitable comparison. But the very texture of Ray's voice when he uttered the first lines set it apart immediately, bringing a new gritty realism to the previously evocative but elegantly melancholic song. Audaciously, in view of the original's success in the US pop chart, Ray also put it out as a single later in the year, making the Top 30 and garnering praise from its composer, who was still in shock at the idea of a true idol from way back covering one of his songs.

Just prior to laying down the tracks for *Ray Charles Invites You To Listen*, Ray had been in the studio with Quincy Jones to record the theme song for an upcoming film starring Sidney Poitier and Rod Steiger, *In The Heat Of The Night*. The film was set in a steamy Mississippi town, where Poitier's black detective from the North is called in to help the redneck sheriff (Steiger) solve a local murder, despite the latter's inbred racism. Penned by Quincy (who wrote all the soundtrack music) and released in August '67, Ray's emotional vocal over strings, big band, Raelettes and churchy organ was just as atmospheric as the Oscar-winning movie.

The album *Invites You To Listen* album came out in June, to good reviews but lacklustre sales, hovering briefly in the bottom quarter of the Top 100. Ray and the band meanwhile – with Billy Preston now a name-checked part of the line-up – had been to Europe for dates in London, Paris, Vienna and a handful of other cities, returning in May for more homeland one-nighters. After six months Ray Charles was re-established in the public consciousness just as planned.

There was only one thing that bugged him about the media attention, coverage that he and the record company had been so anxious to encourage; reporters (perhaps understandably) would constantly refer to the drugs issue as though it were still a problem. To Ray it was ancient history, and he wanted it to stay that way, as he would eventually spell out in no uncertain times in the November edition of *Down Beat* magazine. The interview piece by Harvey Siders started life about six months earlier when the journalist accompanied Ray to a show on the *USS Constellation* in San

Diego harbour, before the aircraft carrier and its 3,000 complement sailed for Vietnam.

When the reporter turned his questioning to Ray's past drug addiction, and asked if he had any warnings for "the hippies of today", "the complexion of the whole interview (not to mention Charles' attitude) changed." Ray took the opportunity to state plainly that his past drug addiction had nothing to do with the subject of his music and career, stressing that nobody made him into an addict, he did it because he wanted to. On the issue of warning the "kids of today", he had this to say: "Actually it could have just the opposite effect. A kid might figure, 'They say you can't get over drug addiction, but look at Ray, *he* licked it. Hell, if he got over it, I will too when I'm ready.'"

The *Down Beat* write-up went on to list the various civic honours that had been bestowed on Ray that year, doubtless as a result of some energetic lobbying and string-pulling on Joe Adams' part. He'd been made the national chairman of a charity he supported, the Sickle Cell Disease Research Foundation – sickle cell disease being a form of anaemia particularly prevalent among black children at the time. In June, Los Angeles' first black mayor, Tom Bradley, had announced a "Ray Charles Day". And on October 12, the article concluded, Congressman Charles S. Joelson of New Jersey read into the *Congressional Record* an unprecedented tribute to Ray, declaring, "He can see more deeply than many of us who lack his sensitivity."

Sider's two-page coverage also mentioned the three-week engagement Ray had just completed at Harrah's casino nightclub in Reno, Nevada, his debut season on the Las Vegas-centred cabaret scene, and a similar upcoming stint at the swanky Copacabana room in New York City opening on November 23. The night before he was to open at the Copa, *Down Beat* revealed, Ray could be seen on nationwide television in a tribute to "the Nashville Sound" on NBC-TV's *Kraft Music Hall*, to be followed soon after by an appearance on the prestigious *Ed Sullivan Show*.

As the high rollers, big spenders and assorted celebrities thronged the Copa every night, it seemed Ray's acceptance into the bosom of middle America was complete, just a year after his final court appearance when prison was still a possibility. But while the great and the good (and not so good) wined and dined their partners in the softly lit glow of his presence, and earnest well-fed politicians of every colour and creed were glad to press the flesh with genius, the world was changing fast. There was another America, in the streets outside the fancy nightclubs and corridors of power, where a revolution was taking place, a revolution driven by the dynamic of music.

Officially dubbed *The First Annual Monterey International Pop Music Festival*, on June 16, 1967, over 200,000 young people gathered in and around the Monterey County Fairgrounds in California for a three-day celebration of "music, peace, flower-power and love", two years before Woodstock. It was the first serious coming together of the youth-driven "alternative society", united in its opposition to the Vietnam war and with music at the top of its cultural agenda.

Filmed by D.A. Pennebaker and released the following year as *Monterey Pop*, more than 30 acts, from The Who to sitar guru Ravi Shankar, represented the cutting edge of the new scene. But what was significant was how many of the participants – including Canned Heat, Eric Burdon, Jimi Hendrix, Steve Miller, Paul Butterfield and Al Kooper – all had their roots firmly in blues music. Plus two singers who emerged as undisputed show-stealers, Janis Joplin and Otis Redding, both of whom were stylistically indebted to Ray Charles.

Joplin, with her band Big Brother & The Holding Company, virtually established herself overnight after her sensational Monterey version of Big Mama Thornton's 'Ball And Chain', and although she named as a prime influence the great female blues singers like Bessie Smith there was more than an echo of classic Margie Hendricks in her performance.

And Otis Redding's passionate, preacher-like delivery of 'I've Been Loving You Too Long', backed by Booker T. & The MGs, was pure Memphis magic. The impact of his singing was always direct, he went for the emotional jugular much as Ray did in his "revivalist" shows in the Fifties. As writer Carol Cooper put it in liner notes to a 1993 compilation album: "If Redding consciously imitated anyone on his way to a personal style, the parameters are more likely to have been Ray Charles and James Brown than Penniman [Little Richard] and [Sam] Cooke, if only because Redding – like the former pair – was naturally less inclined toward what producer Jerry Wexler always termed 'the pop compromise'."

Redding's performance came as a revelation for the overwhelmingly white audience – what they were witnessing was the simple, stripped-down personification of soul. Just as the white rock music showcased at Monterey represented a new street culture running in parallel to "straight" society, so soul was the music of a newly assertive Black America. Rising to the challenge of civil rights legislation and desegregation in every quarter of the land, "black" was now "beautiful", gradually replacing "Negro" as the accepted term of reference to Afro-Americans, with James Brown, Aretha and Otis the musical voices of the ghettos. Just like, some with longer memories would recall, Ray Charles had been during those earlier years of struggle in the Fifties.

As the latter years of the Sixties approached, with music taking its place as a vibrant, creative part of young people's lives, Ray Charles may have been living and working in that other, seemingly more sophisticated America, but the warmth and passion of his musical legacy was all around. Among the singers and musicians emerging on the new wave of blues-based rock heralded at Monterey, Ray was continually cited as the "soul father".

Taj Mahal was a case in point, a purveyor of a laid-back style of urban blues dubbed in the music press "swamp blues", a genre described by Jerry Wexler in *Billboard*: "It's country funk. The Byrds put something in it, Ray Charles added a lot. It's a pound of R&B, and an ounce or three of country." Taj became a cult favourite in the eclectic atmosphere of the late Sixties and early Seventies, and still enjoys a loyal following today. In his autobiography he explained that Ray Charles was important to him early on, as a black singer starting to develop his own style: "I first heard him when he was just starting to break away from that [Nat Cole and Charles Brown] and find his own voice, just before 'What'd I Say' came out. By then, he clearly had his own voice and way to do things. That was really exciting for me, how he used the black voice and very black musical tone, and created it in such a universal way to touch everybody. That was a very important thing for me."

Another singer whose rough-edged soul voice owed much to Ray Charles was Joe Cocker. From Sheffield, England, Cocker broke through sensationally in 1968 when he made number one in the UK with a flamboyant version of 'With A Little Help From My Friends' from The Beatles' *Sgt Pepper's Lonely Hearts Club Band*. The album *With A Little Help From My Friends* went Top 40 in the States the following year, leading to a US tour and sensational appearance at the Woodstock Festival of August 1969.

Cocker's flailing arms and other on-stage gyrations were said to be partly based on Ray's movements at the piano, and he acknowledged the Charles influence constantly in interviews. Referring to his record company suggesting an inappropriate song for his next recording, he told a writer in 1979: "I said, 'Man, you've got to understand I'm part of the soul elite, right?' I said, 'I never used to sing that shit even in its heyday. I'm a

Ray Charles freak, right? All right.'" Years later, as soul enjoyed an early-Nineties revival, he commented: "I got my thing from Ray Charles and it took years before it started to evolve into my own. With this new interest in soul and blues, there's hope for me!"

Reviewing the *With A Little Help From My Friends* album in *Rolling Stone*, John Mendelssohn hailed Cocker as "perhaps (the) greasiest British bearer of the Ray Charles tradition" – Cocker's backing group were The Grease Band. "That Cocker is a Charles imitator is beyond argument," Mendelssohn continued, "at various places on his album he even receives vocal backing from former Raelettes. But Cocker has assimilated the Charles influence to the point where his feeling for what he is singing cannot really be questioned."

Although he operated in an opposite corner of the music scene from the world of rock ("rock'n'roll" had disappeared, temporarily, from the vernacular), where he was acknowledged as an influence from the past rather than the present, Ray as ever kept his ears open. Whatever was happening in contemporary music, he wanted to hear. He was interested in the ever-increasing application of electric instruments, the radical developments in studio techniques, and new inventions like the Mellotron and Moog Synthesiser.

As always he could hear that there were some good songwriters around. Any new songs that sounded like they might work he would always consider using, whether they were from established composers like Lennon & McCartney or the proverbial man in the street, as he would explain to me in 1975: "If you brought me a song tonight, and said, 'Ray, listen to this, see if you like it', if I took it home and I liked it, I'd record it. That's all there is to it, to me. I mean I would not reject you just because you are an unknown writer, nor on the other hand would I accept you because you were a well-known writer. The whole thing with me is the song has to mean something to me, and I have to be able to do something to the song."

Indeed, there were two examples of unsolicited songs from unknown writers on Ray's next album, which he recorded in the early weeks of 1968.

15

Music Is The Message

"I cannot destroy what it took years for me to build up in one song. When I record something it may not always be a smash, but I will always be honest with the public. If I record it, I record it because I really felt the song."

– Ray Charles

Ray had been preparing *A Portrait Of Ray* through the final weeks of 1967, finally coming up with a song list that included the oldies 'Am I Blue' and Jerome Kern's 'Yesterdays', a song translated from a French record that was offered to Ray by a female photographer from Paris, and Lennon & McCartney's classic 'Eleanor Rigby'. Plus another unsolicited contribution that caught Ray's ear: "I've done songs by people who were not writers per se, we did a song by a young lady who's a housewife, called 'The Bright Lights And You Girl', and a lot of people recorded it . . . Tom Jones recorded it, and so on. But the lady's not a writer as such, you know, just in her spare time. But she wrote something I liked, and I recorded it, and that's all it took."

Sid Feller contributed a couple of arrangements, Ray using Rene Hall and the distinguished jazz and film composer Oliver Nelson for the remaining 10 tracks. The French-originated 'The Sun Died' is the big production number of the mixed-bag set, with its swooping, high-pitched strings being a feature common across most of the album. 'A Sweet Young Thing Like You' is an arresting love song and the most soulful track, while Ray's up-tempo but weirdly ethereal delivery of 'Eleanor Rigby' is oddly attractive though a tad overproduced.

Released in March 1968, *A Portrait Of Ray* just missed the Top 50, peaking at number 51 as the band began another tour across America, an America that was suddenly stunned in early April when Martin Luther King was assassinated in Memphis. At Dr King's Atlanta funeral on

April 9, Ray joined the huge procession of friends, relatives, politicians, labour leaders, foreign dignitaries, entertainment and sports figures, religious leaders and thousands of plain, ordinary folk as they followed the coffin carried in a wooden farm wagon and drawn by two mules.

As the tour wound on, with dates as diverse as the Newport Jazz Festival and LA's plush Coconut Grove nightery, things weren't all well within the ranks. For some time there had been a groundswell of discontent rising among The Raelettes, concerning their $350-dollar-a-week wage from which they paid their own expenses, including room and food, and the fines system which, though authorised by Ray, they saw as the brainchild of Joe Adams.

Ray would spell out the fine system in a *Rolling Stone* interview in 1973, explaining that he would never fine someone more than twice – "After that he's fired, period" – and the money would not wind up in his pocket, but for a party for the band at the end of the year, "So they really get it back." Ray called it a dock in pay, as the union barred musicians being actually fined, but as he explained, for the man who's not getting the money, it's the same thing. But it was Joe Adams' administering of fines that seemed to be the big bugbear.

Leroy Cooper recalled that, at first, Joe was welcomed by everyone, but not for long. "We thought that he had added class to the group, but he was into his own world, and musicians just didn't get along with him too well . . ." Leroy, like Fathead, didn't seem to get as much flak from Joe as some of the newer members, possibly because he'd been with Ray a long time before Adams joined. But when he took over as MD, he had to administer Joe's discipline in matters like dress, even off stage. "He was concerned about the appearance of guys, when we were in airports and public places, not just on the stage. When I was leader he would always tell me to talk to the guys about their mode of dress, and I would feel bad, because the guys those days wanted to wear tennis shoes and blue jeans, and I would have to tell them to dress up at airports, and relax when they got to the hotel."

Talking to Whitney Balliett in the *New Yorker* magazine in 1970, Adams outlined his approach: "When I hire a man for the band, I give him an instruction sheet, so he will know how I want him to dress and behave. No drinking on duty, no narcotics, and I will not allow profanity in public. I teach them pride in their work."

John Bryant, who would play drums with the band for a year or so in the mid-Seventies, recalled his first boarding of the band plane, on which

Joe Adams enforced a tight rule about baggage weight: "Your bags could not weigh more than 40 pounds. I had just come into LA with what I had, to start up with the band, and we went out to the airport to start the next season. Joe said, 'OK, it's a 40 pound limit,' and my bag was about three or four pounds over that, and not just mine but other people's too. And he made us take clothes out, there on the tarmac, and he put them in a bag and said, 'I'll take them back to the office and they'll be there for you when you get back off the tour.' Because he was out there with us with a scales, and he *weighed* those bags.

"That's OK from the standpoint of safety, but that just shows you he was a stickler for all that. He didn't like for the band to do anything other than its job. We'd show up, play the gig, he didn't want us to mix or anything. If there was some sort of a reception, a buffet, free drinks or whatever, he didn't want us partaking in any of that, that wasn't to be for us. These were Joe Adams' rules, and so you pretty much steered clear of him, he didn't really have a close relationship with the band. As far as he was concerned, they were employees, they were the hired help. Joe was tough, he really ran it like a military thing. There were the rules of no jeans, you had to look nice, no sneakers on the plane or on the bus going to the gig. There was to be no cursing on the bus out of respect for The Raelettes, those kind of rules."

Bryant remembered an incident on the bus involving tenor player James Clay, who'd been with the band since the early Sixties. "We got on the bus one time to go to the plane, and James Clay walked up the aisle, and he was saying something like, 'Man, if this shit sucks tonight, fuck this, fuck that . . .' and the road manager, Fred Murrell who played trombone with Ray and then became road manager, he said, 'James, you know the rules, no cursing,' so James – who'd probably had a few drinks – kind of mumbled and went to the back of the bus, and deciding he didn't like that, turned around and shouted, 'Motherfucker, motherfucker, motherfucker!' And the road manager looked at him and just said, 'I'll see you Sunday night' – which of course was when the pay cheques and fines were addressed."

The Raelettes' dispute finally came to a head on the final night at the Coconut Grove, with senior member Gwen Berry – the others had only been with the band for two years – acting as spokeswoman. After a loud argument with Ray over the matter, Berry was fired, the other three girls quitting as well. Seemingly unfazed by the crisis, Ray went ahead and used some local session singers for the final date at the Grove, then quickly went about recruiting a new line-up in time for their next engagement, at a similarly flash venue in San Francisco.

This time The Raelettes were reduced to a threesome, Estelle (Stella) Yarbrough, Susaye Green and Barbara Terrault, Terrault only staying with the outfits six months or so. Texas-born Yarbrough, on the other hand, would become the longest-ever serving Raelette in the history of the group, staying with Ray for more than 33 years, until the end of his gigging career. Interviewed after a date in Montreal in 2003, she spoke of her background in the school and church choir, and her early vocal heroes: "Aretha Franklin, Ray Charles, Gladys Knight, Marvin Gaye, Al Green . . . and I have to say Tina Turner too."

At 18, Susaye Green was the baby of the trio. A graduate of the High School of Performing Arts in New York – celebrated in the *Fame* movie and TV series – she got the audition with Ray via Dee Ervin, who was one of the composers on Tangerine's books and a family friend. She soon became Ray's special Raelette, and remained in a relationship with him for some time after leaving the outfit in 1973.

Towards the end of the year Ray decided he wanted a fourth voice in The Raelettes again, but this time a lead singer who would also manage the girls, taking charge of them musically – under Ray's auspices of course – and generally, in matters of their welfare, discipline and so on. The job went to Mabel John, a tough character well used to the R&B circuit whose brother Little Willie John had a hit with the original version of 'Fever' back in the Fifties. Then, when the band reconvened in the spring of 1969, Barbara Terrault's place in The Raelettes was taken by Vernita Moss.

Over the winter of 1968–69, when the band was inactive pending its annual spring outing, Ray worked on two new albums in the RPM studios. Both released in the first half of 1969, they represented two completely contrasting aspects of his music. With its only "theme" being as a soundtrack for a romantic evening, *I'm All Yours, Baby!* suffers from a lack of variation rather than any inherent fault in the actual material. Several of the songs, including Rodgers & Hart's 'I Didn't Know What Time It Was' and the Gershwins' 'Love Is Here To Stay' are all-time classics, but Ray's versions – with fairly predictable arrangements by Sid Feller – bring nothing new to them. The most interesting tracks on a largely lacklustre collection are 'Indian Love Call' from the musical *Rose Marie* on which Ray does some decidedly odd vocalising, and the darkly atmospheric

'Gloomy Sunday', which was memorably recorded by Billie Holiday in the early Forties.

Listening to *I'm All Yours, Baby!* draws attention to Ray's choice of material, which had been a somewhat contentious issue among purists since *Modern Sounds* in 1962. The fact that his takes on classic standards didn't work wonderfully on this occasion is one thing; but we can be sure Ray *believed* he could make the songs work for him when he went into the studio, and probably made better use of many of them in live renderings over the years. Indeed, he always insisted he had to believe that a song had something for him before he'd tackle it.

"I have had one song in particular that I lost an awful lot of money on because I didn't record it," he told me in 1975. "The people asked me to record it, they gave me half the song, a big bonus to do the song, and after I worked with it for three weeks I couldn't find anything, I couldn't get no feeling in my heart for the song. I turned it down, and the man said to me . . . 'But Ray, we're paying you X amount of dollars and we're giving you half the song, the publishing and everything . . .' The man said, 'What'd you want?' and I said, 'I don't want anything! I don't want anything, I just can't handle the song.' You could say, 'Ray, I'll give you a million dollars . . .' but it means nothing. You see I cannot destroy what it took years for me to build up in one song. When I record something it may not always be a smash, but I will always be honest with the public. If I record it I record it because I really felt the song."

I asked him if he had any particular favourite composers. "No, not favourite composers, I'm sorry to disappoint you, but I don't have any favourite composers. In other words I don't like *all* of any one composer's music. I'm not a 'George Gershwin man' or whatever. I'm not saying there's anything wrong with that, don't misunderstand me, but I'm not anybody's man per se, I'm for a song that will blend to me, because I can't sing everything. I can sing things that I can feel, but if I don't feel a song, if the song don't do nothing for *me*, then I can't do nothing for the song."

He often compared the role of the singer to that of an actor. "With singing, the name of the game is to make yourself believable," he once told *Esquire* magazine. "When somebody hears you sing a song and they say, 'Oh, that must have happened to him,' that's when you know you're transmitting. It's like being a good actor. You make people feel things, emotions and whatnot. But you've got to start with yourself. You got to feel it yourself. If you don't feel it, how do you expect someone else to?

"A good actor or good actress, what's important is how they do a part on the stage, so that folks get so involved that they forget that you're just playing a part. They get mad at you, or if you're sad they'll cry, it's that kind of a thing. And it's the same thing with singing a song. I find songs that I feel I can pour myself into, and make you believe that what I'm singing about happened to me. And maybe to you too."

Ray would also use the analogy of painting to explain how he processed other people's material. "I think that in music – or in other forms of art, like writing or painting or sculpture or whatever – we get our influences from all kinds of sources. If you're interested in some other artist's work, that's not to say you're copying them. But you *can* incorporate what you see that works for you. There was no one particular painter who first put white and black together to get grey. You learn and absorb from other people's work, anything that makes you sit up and take notice you'll take on board."

And this all had a bearing on his ultimate choice of a number. "It boils down to what I like. I like lyrics, I like a song to tell a story Then, do I like the melody? If the chord structure is decent enough that you can put yourself into it, and that goes for any song. But to start with the lyrics must tell me a nice story."

In marked contrast to *I'm All Yours, Baby!* Ray's next album *Ray Charles Doing His Thing* was a welcome excursion into contemporary soul. Consisting entirely of songs written by Jimmy Lewis, who Ray had discovered singing demos for Tangerine composer Jimmy Holiday, the album features crisply written horn parts, funky guitar and some strident bass guitar. It's late-Sixties R&B at its most incisive, with songs like 'Finders Keepers, Losers Weepers', 'If It Wasn't For Bad Luck' and particularly 'The Same Thing That Can Make You Laugh (Can Make You Cry)' demonstrating that soul-wise Ray could still cut it with the best of them when he chose to.

Neither album, however, cut it when it came to sales figures, both just hovering in the lower reaches of the Top 200 long-players. Singles likewise came and went, including 'I Didn't Know What Time It Was' from *I'm All Yours* and 'We Can Make It' from *Doing His Thing*, but neither made a showing in the Top 100. Ray's last appearance in the singles Top 20 was with 'Here We Go Again' in June '67, and in the album listing it was *Crying Time* a year before that. By the end of the Sixties, Ray Charles was an undoubted attraction as part of the show-business establishment, but his records – some good, some not-so-good, a few still genuinely inspired – were simply not making a mark any longer. ABC-Paramount were not best pleased, but Ray, like the album said, continued doing his thing.

When the caravan hit Europe once again in the autumn of 1969, back at the RPM studio in Los Angeles a new recording engineer, David Braithwaite, was busily replacing the outmoded four-track desks with state-of-the-art eight-track. And as the early months of the New Year heralded the Seventies, the new equipment was utilised on another two highly contrasting albums, one jazz and one country.

With no personnel credits on the sleeve, it was hard for the listener to decide whether the band on *My Kind Of Jazz* was the on-the-road outfit or a studio ensemble put together for the sessions, though Quincy Jones' minimal sleeve notes suggest the former. Whatever, it's a fine 10-track collection of instrumentals with some sparkling solos, including a trio of vintage soul-jazz standards by the funkiest in the business – Bobby Timmons' 'This Here', 'Sidewinder' by Lee Morgan and the Horace Silver classic 'Senor Blues'.

Plus there's Ray's own 'Booty Butt', about which Quincy had this to say: "Ray got to groovin' so good on 'Booty Butt' that he couldn't resist sneakin' in a little soulful hum, and that got so good he had to go back and overdub it a few times more. And if you think Ray Charles sounds good by himself, just imagine four of him singing together. And the beat goes *on*." 'Booty Butt' turned out to be Ray's last Top 40 entry when it was released as a single with 'Sidewinder' on the flipside, in March 1971. The British poet and jazz critic Philip Larkin was more considered in his praise when reviewing the album in his regular *Daily Telegraph* column. "The most surprising record of the month," he called it, applauding its "considerable sophistication and punch". Larkin continued: "The band is sparked off by a Fender bass and plenty of souly Lat-Am percussion, and has jetting spirited trumpet and matching saxes. 'I Remember Clifford', 'Pas-Se-O-Ne Blues' and 'Sidewinder' are the most satisfying of a remarkable set."

Released in April 1970, *My Kind Of Jazz* was followed just two months later by *Love Country Style*, Ray's other studio project that spring. In a generally prosaic collection – by Ray's standards at least – two singles emerged, 'If You Were Mine' and 'Don't Change On Me', and their respective B-sides, neither of which saw any action chart-wise. Though radical no more, Ray's take on country music could still be an inspiring, nerve-tingling experience, but at other times – like this one – merely redolent of the production-line side of the contemporary Nashville that he'd helped create nearly a decade earlier.

When the band got back on the road (though "on the road" is hardly an apt description of their airborne mode of touring) taking in another coast-to-coast trek before Europe then South America, Fathead Newman was back in the ranks, having left when Ray broke up the band for the duration of 1965. "I came to New York then, and I spent several years in New York City before returning back to Dallas, and of course going back to join the Ray Charles band in the Seventies – I played '70 and '71 with the big band again."

Between the two touring seasons, on Sunday, March 7, 1971 Ray would be involved in a memorable live date that happened by chance rather than design. Jerry Wexler had rung to tell Ray that he was recording a live concert with Aretha Franklin at the Fillmore West in San Francisco, Bill Graham's pioneering venue for the West Coast rock scene. Wexler invited Ray to come along, which he did. Aretha, who'd already played the previous two nights there, was closing her 90-minute set with a call-and-response with the crowd ("everybody say 'yeah' . . .") when she segued into 'Spirit In The Dark'. After working through the song and letting it fade into what seemed the ending, she walked off stage, returning half a minute later with Ray on her arm. "I was just minding my business enjoying the show," Ray would recall. "I'm crazy for Aretha, she's my one true soul sister, and the last thing I wanted to do was sing. But when Aretha calls, you better answer."

The crowd went bananas, as Ray sat at the piano and joined the Queen of Soul in a slightly messy 'Spirit' (a song he admitted later he didn't know) then gelled together in some soulful jamming. By this time the backing band Tower Of Power had been joined on stage by the evening's previous acts – Atlantic's sax star King Curtis (it was to be his last-ever recording), the Memphis Horns and Billy Preston – and the hippie mecca positively rocked to the spirit of soul. "The Right Reverend Ray . . . the Reverend Righteous Ray!" Aretha called out as he left the stage. Released as *Aretha: Live At The Fillmore West*, the album was a huge seller, making number seven in the *Billboard* chart.

Volcanic Action Of My Soul was Ray's major studio project through the winter break of '70–71 and, released in April 1971, marked a return to the incisive interpretation of (mainly contemporary) pop music standards. Two numbers by composer Jimmy Webb and two from The Beatles' songbook marked the tone. Webb's languid 'See You Then' kicks off the set, establishing the general mood with Ray's voice delicately balanced against lush Sid Feller arrangements and subtly poignant pedal steel guitar. The other Webb number, 'Wichita Lineman', suffers nought from being one of the over-covered songs of the era.

Lennon & McCartney's 'The Long And Winding Road' (generally believed to have been written by McCartney alone) has a similarly transient feel about it, a hazy, shifting focus that Ray puts to equally effective use on George Harrison's 'Something'. The so-called "Jimmy Brown song" 'Three Bells' gets a gospel rather than country treatment, a sentimental oldie that Ray lifts above its usual maudlin self. And most evocative of all, the traditional 'Down In The Valley' positively glows, Ray's voice murmuring gently against the pastoral sounds of the countryside. This is a subtle album, full of delicate nuance on Ray's part, the "volcanic action" perhaps an inappropriate title for the baring of a soul that sounds at peace with itself.

Volcanic Action was one of Ray's finest vinyl achievements since the inception of Tangerine as his self-controlled record label (leased to ABC-Paramount who still took care of distribution and marketing) with *Crying Time* in 1966. And, for the first time in three years, it marked Ray's appearance in the Top 100 album chart, just hovering below the 50 mark when it peaked at 52.

While the album was climbing the lower reaches of the *Billboard* listings, the band was back in the saddle, touring as frantically as ever. Compared to most bands on the road, they were travelling in the lap of luxury. Leroy Cooper remembered the change that the hit records made, when Ray became a pop star for the first time: "The pay changed, and we got better transportation and so forth, and he then bought an aeroplane in the Sixties . . . wow, travelling was completely different from then." By the early Seventies, the Martin airliner had made way for an even more luxurious Viscount, a British turbojet aircraft that cost Ray nearly half a million dollars.

But travelling could still be gruelling, and the '71 trek was no exception. After traversing America yet again, they took in the round of big cities in Europe before touring Japan, ending in Tokyo just before Christmas. While the band was still in Europe Stella Yarbrough was fired (albeit temporarily), Dorothy Berry flying in as her replacement Raelette. And after Tokyo, Fathead left again, this time virtually for good: "After that I joined forces with Herbie Mann, the Family of Mann, and that association lasted a good decade."

For Ray, however, touring – along with making records – seemed part of the lifeblood that kept him going, as he would explain to Robert Gordon in 1992 when the writer asked why he stayed on the road: "I do what I do because it is part of me. That's the best way I can put it. If you've been breathing ever since you've come into the world, why do you still want to keep breathing? To keep living. And I'm saying music is a part of me, so I'm going to just keep doing it until the Good Lord pulls the curtain down on me, and that's the way that goes."

The seeming revival in Ray's fortunes in the record charts was stalled by a much-vaunted "greatest hits" package grandly entitled *A 25th Anniversary In Show Business Salute To Ray Charles*, released with the Christmas market in mind in November 1971. No less than 36 tracks across two discs spanned the Atlantic and ABC years, but one can only conclude that any Ray Charles fans who wanted that much of his back catalogue must have owned a lot of it already; whatever, the double LP never even made the Top 100.

But the hitch was temporary. His next new album, which Ray worked at meticulously, put him back in the 100 if not the very best-sellers. And more importantly, it proved to be one of the landmark achievements of his career.

As the title suggests, *A Message From The People* is a collection of songs with a message, a concept album where the theme is a political statement, from an artist not given to many political statements. Of course, Ray had famously taken a stand against segregation, and donated financially to the civil rights campaigns – "Everybody in this movement ought to have a function," he told *Rolling Stone* magazine – but had never thrown the weight of his *artistry*, the force of his creative voice, behind that or any other cause.

From the funky opener, a celebratory declaration of the Black American anthem 'Lift Every Voice And Sing', in which Ray sings of values "true to our native land", he's laying it on the line at last. The people he speaks of in the album's title are *his* people, the people of Black America, but with a message for *all* America.

But this is no crass exercise in hectoring agit-pop, protest music for protest's sake. With arrangements by Sid Feller, Quincy and Mike Post – and Ray handling production – this was Ray once more drawing on the richness of music around him and funnelling it into something uniquely his own.

There's some startling contemporary blues from Tangerine house writer Dee Ervin on 'Seems Like I Gotta Do Wrong', while in the Stevie

Wonder Top 10 hit, the gospel-inspired 'Heaven Help Us All' written by Ron Miller, Ray pleads for a modern world full of imperfection:

> *Heaven help the boy who won't reach twenty one*
> *And heaven help the man who gave that child the gun*

A solemn-sounding 'There'll Be No Peace Without All Men As One' leads into the riches-and-poverty anger of 'Hey Mister', the "mister" in this slice of soul-funk protest being a Congressman. All the way through the album we can hear how Ray has carefully laid it down piece by piece, working over weeks – rather than in one set of band or orchestra sessions as of old – splicing a tape here, adding a track there, until he achieves the result he's aiming for. No more so than in Melanie Safka's 'Look What They've Done To My Song, Ma', which for all its corn – and it's the least convincing track theme-wise – is a state-of-the-art production for its time.

The much-recorded 'Abraham, Martin And John' is dedicated to Abraham Lincoln, Martin Luther King, John F. Kennedy and Bobby Kennedy, all American victims of the assassin's bullet – and all on the side of the angels when it came to the issue of civil rights. A country-fuelled change of pace comes with John Denver's 'Take Me Home, Country Roads', balancing his message with a more upbeat, positive view of the America he clearly loves – as does the soulful 'Every Saturday Night' with some wonderful back-up vocals.

And, with its military drumbeat and brass fanfare intro, what can you say about 'America The Beautiful', except that Ray does it again – taking the most mawkish of songs, making it his own and in doing so changing its effect completely. With his characteristic "you know what I'm talkin' about" interjections over a gospel piano and organ, he raises banal patriotism – despite a standing-to-attention session choir – to a soul-drenched psalm of praise worthy of any Sunday night prayer meeting.

A year to the month after *Volcanic Action Of My Soul* was released, *A Message From The People* hit the shops, like its predecessor just missing the Top 50 chart. Another tour took in many of the states of that same United States whose natural beauty had originally inspired Katharine Bates' lyrics for 'America The Beautiful' back at the beginning of the century:

> *O beautiful for spacious skies,*
> *For amber waves of grain,*
> *For purple mountain majesties*
> *Above the fruited plain!*

214

But despite its stirring message, when it was released as a single in June backed with 'Look What They've Done To My Song, Ma', it failed to make any impression. Talking in *Rolling Stone*, Ray would explain that the song, in the context of the album, was his way of saying that he loved America, but some of the things going on there still needed changing.

A few months later, in September 1972, Ray was to meet the one man who could effect some of that necessary change – the President, Richard M. Nixon. The invitation to meet Nixon in the White House came via the President's daughter, Julie Nixon Eisenhower, who was involved in the same sickle cell charities that she knew Ray Charles supported. When he first got word of the pending meeting, Ray was apprehensive. He didn't think he was qualified to talk politics, and despite his taking a stand on issues he had no party affiliations. Although, as he was quoted as saying at the time, "I'm certainly not a Republican."

But he was assured before the event that the one thing Nixon *wouldn't* want to discuss was politics, that simply wasn't on the agenda. The President just wanted to congratulate Ray on the work he'd done for sickle cell research. Whatever, the meeting, which was scheduled for 15 minutes, lasted half an hour – they must have found *something* to talk about. So it was that Ray Charles Robinson, the kid from Greenville, Florida who'd worn hand-me-down clothes in the St Augustine School for the Deaf and Blind, got to shake hands with the President of the United States, right there in the Oval Office.

All the Presidential plaudits in the world, however, couldn't hide the fact that career-wise, the early Seventies were not a good time for Ray Charles. The best of his recent albums – *Volcanic* and *Message* – sold only modestly, and the rest performed disastrously for a man who had been the biggest name in American popular music less than 10 years before. In pop music terms of course, 10 years can be an eternity; Ray, unlike many names that graced the chart one month, only to be forgotten the next, was in it for the long haul. But even for a lifer like him, there had to be more ups than downs, if only to keep the balance sheets in the black. And the books that had to be balanced had some formidable costs in the outgoings column, including the whole RPM operation, the band on the road, and Ray's personal all-the-year-round entourage and family commitments.

There was a gradual knock-on effect of poor record sales reflected in live engagements – which were increasingly the source of bread-and-butter money now million-seller royalties weren't regularly trickling in any more. There were still the prestige gigs of course, the grand municipal galas and concert hall orchestral specials, but increasingly the date book was filled with gigs that Ray (and Joe Adams) would have turned down as simply not being good enough a couple of years earlier. If the answer lay in a sudden upturn on the record sales graph, that certainly didn't happen after Ray's next album release just four months down the line from *A Message From The People*, a disappointing collection called *Through The Eyes Of Love*.

The album has its moments of course, as do most items in Ray's output. There's a wonderful rendering of the Gershwins' bitter-sweet classic 'Someone To Watch Over Me', and a totally atmospheric six-minute 'Rainy Night In Georgia'. Written by swamp-rock singer-songwriter Tony Joe White and a Top 5 hit for Brook Benton in 1970, Ray's lush, steamy 'Rainy Night' with keyboards on maximum reverb and swirling strings overshadows all others before or since – even the "drunken" fade-out is believable.

The other ace in the hole is 'I Can Make It Thru The Days (But Oh Those Lonely Nights)', a churchy blues in 6/4 time written by Ray, Tangerine house writer Dee Ervin and Ervin's assistant, Ruth Robinson, with whom Ray would conduct an affair that would last nearly 20 years. The relationship with the would-be journalist and songwriter Robinson began in 1970 and continued in parallel with Ray's numerous other amorous liaisons. They included Susaye Green and other Raelettes, women in cities as far flung as New York and Paris, and the ever-present Della still clinging to an increasingly fragile marriage which was held together almost solely by their shared love of, and caring for, their three sons.

In a similarly disintegrating state was Ray's relationship with ABC, and the latest album's poor showing – it barely made the Top 200 – was, for company executives watching the bottom line, the last straw. It took till the end of the year for the album to get even that far, and as two singles – 'Hey Mister' backed with 'There'll Be No Peace Without All Men As One', and 'Every Saturday Night'/'Take Me Home, Country Roads', all from *Message* – did no better over the early months of 1973, ABC made it clear they wanted to be rid of what had once been their greatest asset.

In practice that meant getting rid of Ray's pride and joy, his own label Tangerine, whose distinctive logo had featured alongside that of ABC on all his releases since 1966. For Ray, of course, Tangerine had also been the vehicle for his other ambition, to own a label featuring a catalogue of artists, not just himself. But the success of Tangerine in that direction had proved less than spectacular. It was Ray's own releases – despite modest chart showings, even the recent albums had sold around a quarter of a million copies each – that kept the label in profit.

He would admit years later that running a label required the kind of attention he just couldn't give it – not while making records and touring, which he had no intention of giving up. And even though he continued to find songs that inspired him, and collaborated with fellow artists and musicians right up to the last year of his life, he would gradually concede over the years that less and less new contemporary music excited him in the way that much had in the past.

As he told Robert Gordon in 1992 when asked about any talent coming up that particularly impressed him: "I haven't heard anybody in the modern field that I would say has blown my head off. Partly that might be my own fault, because I don't get around to hear maybe as much stuff as I could, and you ain't gonna discover nobody that's going to blow your head off listening to the radio. The radio is dead. Most of what you hear on the radio and the records is very, very simple. It seems like the record companies want everybody to sound the same. And that's another thing, when I was coming up, you could have artists sang two notes and you know who they were. When Count Basie's band played two notes, you knew it was Basie's band. You don't see that, now. Maybe I saw an awful lot in my life, but what bothers me is that I don't see anything coming through to replace it."

A follow-up to *My Kind Of Jazz* appeared on Tangerine in January 1973, entitled *Jazz Number II*, and like its predecessor was released outside the ABC arrangement under just the Tangerine banner. Featuring the Charles orchestra as it stood when the album was recorded in late '72, most of the material was contributed by Ray's arrangers, including 'A Pair Of Threes' from Alf Clausen, Teddy Edwards' 'Going Home' and 'Brazilian Skies', the Jimmy Heath-penned 'Togetherness', and 'Our Suite' by Roger Neumann. It was all good, workaday big band stuff, but nothing that raised the temperature above lukewarm.

The only other album to appear solely on Tangerine was a now hard-to-find collection of tracks by The Raelettes released in 1972 and entitled *Ray Charles Presents The Raelettes, Yesterday . . . Today . . . Tomorrow*. In April 1973, one last ABC/Tangerine single – 'I Can Make It Thru The Days' from the final ABC album coupled with 'Ring Of Fire' from *Love Country Style* – marked the end of Ray Charles' link with ABC Records that had lasted 14 years.

16

Renaissance

"For me it was always a matter of just what kind of music caught my brain and made me jump up and down and say, 'Wow!'"

– Ray Charles

Ray's original champions at ABC, Sam Clark and Larry Newton, had been out of the record division for some time, but Ray turned to them for advice as to what to do next. They both agreed that Ray should find another major to sign a new label, which was to be called Crossover – perhaps in acknowledgement of the middle-of-the-road mainstream market that his music now addressed. Newton set about finding just that deal, and in October 1973 Ray – with Newton as Crossover's president – signed to the British major, Decca Records, through which Crossover material would be released on their London label.

As soon as the deal was finalised, Ray was back at the RPM studio with Sid Feller as arranger, laying down tracks for his first Crossover album, *Come Live With Me*. Divided between one side ballads, one R&B, the strongest items on Side one come first, with the opener a delicate treatment of Meredith Wilson's 'Till There Was You', followed by an equally wistful rendition of the Jaques Brel/Rod McKuen contemporary classic 'If You Go Away'. After 'It Takes So Little Time', the ballad side closes with the countrified title track, written by the Nashville husband-and-wife team Boudleaux and Felice Bryant.

Ray's own 'Somebody' opens the B-side, with some raucous shouting from The Raelettes accompanying a politically dubious side-swipe at feminism on their boss' part. The strongest R&B track is another country-tinged number from the Bryants, 'Problems, Problems', which The Everly Brothers took into the Top 5 in 1958, here rendered with some down-home harmonies, walking-bass part and picky guitar. Ray's

Tangerine associate Jimmy Lewis (who'd penned all the songs for *Ray Charles Doing His Thing* back in '69) wrote 'Where Was He', another country-flavoured selection for the ostensibly R&B side. 'Louise' is a jump-funk mover of no great consequence, while the exclamatory chorus of the gospelly closer 'Everybody Sings' is reminiscent of Leon Russell's 1969 'Delta Lady'.

Released right at the beginning of 1974, *Come Live With Me* proved a disappointing start for Crossover and Decca, being Ray's first album for over a quarter of a century not even to make the Top 200. The title-track had been rush-released as a single in October '73 before the album was completed, and that too failed to signal a breakthrough for the new label, dawdling, after a slow climb, in the lower reaches of the Top 100.

And as sure as spring followed winter, another tour followed for Ray, The Raelettes and the rest of the ensemble. The annual schedule, as far as the members of the Ray Charles Show were concerned, comprised two seasons. They would take January and February off, and then for about the last two weeks of March he would reconvene the band in Los Angeles to rehearse for a week or two before commencing their tour in April, which would go through to the end of the year. That was typically about three months off and nine months on, non-stop. It was a pattern that had evolved through most of the Sixties and would continue through the Seventies and Eighties, with the 17- or 18-piece big band, the five Raelettes, Ray's valet, a road manager, another assistant and Joe Adams of course – in total about 27 or 28 people travelling together. In addition to everyone's personal luggage, there were all the musicians' instruments and associated equipment, plus The Raelettes' gowns and eight changes of uniform for the band – and nearly a hundred shirts, so every musician could have a clean shirt every day!

And despite frequent changes of personnel over the years that had seen the departure of some of Ray's most legendary sidemen, it was a strong band that took to the road – and skies – for the 1974 trek. There were Count Basie alumni, trumpeter Johnny Coles and bass trombonist Henry Coker, some hot recent entrants including trumpet ace Tony Horovitz and Dallas trombonist Ken Tussing, alto player Clifford Solomon who'd just joined, and Ray Charles veterans Edgar Willis, Leroy Cooper, Phil Guilbeau and Texas tenor heavyweight James Clay. And it was Clay who recommended a new recruit to the band when Ray decided he needed to change drummers early on in the tour.

"My ride pulls up to the hotel in Denver, and I notice a young man standing next to his drums. He waits for a cab, ready to leave. I get out, carry my drums toward the entrance behind him. We eye each other. I walk closer, and he gives me a thin smile that telegraphs gloom, frustration and defeat. 'Good luck, man,' he says. 'I hope you come out better than I did.'" So wrote drummer John Bryant in the *Dallas Morning News* in October 2004, recalling the day he turned up to audition for Ray in July '74.

Bryant, like James Clay a native of Dallas, had met the sax man in 1973 while still a 20-year-old student at North Texas State University. He'd heard about a place in South Dallas called the Woodman's Auditorium that was famous for Sunday afternoon jam sessions, as he explained to me: "All of the Dallas black jazz musicians played there on Sunday afternoon, including Fathead, James Clay and a number of other musicians that would play with Ray. This was the neighbourhood that Ray lived in when he had a home in Dallas, and Leroy Cooper's family lived just a couple of blocks around the corner, and also just a couple of blocks from where Ray lived was the Woodman's Auditorium. It was just like a Union building, but every Sunday afternoon they would have jazz jam sessions, and everybody would show up with their brown bag and their chicken, and they'd listen to all the local jazz musicians play. That was Fathead, and James, and Red Garland and so on.

"I walked in through the kitchen into the back of the club with a friend of mine, a black bass player who took me, and I was about the only white guy in there so I just kind of hung back in the corner in the shadows, watching and listening. The band took a break and James Clay left the stage, and came straight over to me and said, 'You must be a musician.' He asked me if I wanted to sit in, so I sat in and played a set, and got to know him, and would go back again and again." So began a friendship with James Clay that would lead to Bryant getting the job with Ray Charles.

"I came home one afternoon, and one of my roommates told me I had received a call, from Ray Charles. I thought, 'Wow, this is kinda funny . . .' and he said, 'Here's the number, give him a call back.' I thought it would be a valet or an assistant or something like that, and I called the number – it was in Denver, Colorado – and Ray answered the phone. He said, 'Hold on a minute, I'm just getting out of the shower.' I was still kind of wondering whether this was true or not, whether it was a trick of some sort. And sure enough it was Ray, and he said, 'James Clay told me you're a fine drummer and wondered if you're interested in doing the gig.' I said,

'Sure', and he said, 'Well, can you be in Denver tomorrow?' and I said 'Yes!'"

Bryant got to Denver, and despite some apprehension after encountering the previous drummer on the hotel steps, passed the audition, which also constituted a rehearsal for a gig in Connecticut. "So the very next day, after one rehearsal, we got on his plane and flew to Connecticut, and started a five-night stand at an open-air festival. The thing that was kind of tough on me was that my ears got plugged up with the flying, and they didn't clear after we landed, so I couldn't hear very well. I was kind of nervous about all of that, but it went fine, and we went off from there."

Talking to John Bryant, I asked him about the famous Ray Charles left foot, which drummers would ignore at their peril: "That was the unique thing with Ray because of his blindness, and it was the connection that he had to keep the band in line, rhythmically and with *his* tempo. He knew that if he could make that drummer connect with his tempo, which he expressed through his left foot, then he could keep the rest of the band in line. That was his thinking, and so it became very important. And Ray had to know you were watching him, and he *would* speed it up or slow it down a little bit sometimes – and you never knew if it was because of the way he was feeling, or he was just trying to test you, to make sure you were paying attention." As Ray's long-term publicist Bob Abrams explained to *Ability* magazine, "You know you're getting a good show when Ray's socks fall down . . . his feet are going up over the piano. One sock falls half-mast. It's because of all the energy he expends. That's his exercise."

"Even if you're playing with another star, and the star feels it's too fast or too slow, they can just kind of give you a look," Bryant continued, "and you know what's going on. Ray couldn't give you that look, he had to express it and it had to be fast, he had to come out with it quick, and he had to give you his level of emotion, he couldn't mess around. The blindness really had a lot to do with that. Specifically, the leader, or the singer, or whoever's the star, can turn to the conductor and the conductor's going to look at the drummer, or *they're* going to look at the drummer, and give an up or a down, the tempos too fast or too slow . . . it happens pretty easily if you can look at someone. But it's another story if you can't look at that other person. That was a unique aspect of performing with Ray."

Ray was notorious for berating musicians on stage when they made a mistake, or didn't play something the way he wanted it played, and drummers – no doubt including Bryant's predecessor – were in the firing line more than most. "All it took was a few sharp words in your direction – I mean Ray could get hot fast – if it wasn't right, or the way he wanted it. It was with other musicians too, but mainly drummers . . . he had a closer relationship in the heat of the moment with the drummers than he had with anybody else. He really gave a hard time to a number of drummers, famous drummers like Mickey Roker at the Montreux Jazz Festival, and Ed Shaughnessy on *The Tonight Show*, and Paul Leim, an excellent Nashville drummer. They are just a few of the examples I know of, when Ray really came out and said things, that everyone could hear, that were embarrassing – and it was tough, it was tough on everyone."

After an incident early on when he tried something new in 'What'd I Say', only to incur Ray's immediate wrath, John quickly learned to keep his head down and play it by the book – that is, Ray's book. "I never really got it in the public arena where it was something that really embarrassed me, but I know other drummers did, and Ray just didn't care. He didn't care who heard him, he would come over to the microphone and just say things like, 'You're not following me, you're not watching me, you're not playing it right, do it this way . . .' so it would be a very pressured situation, and I learned quick that I did not want to be in that position. I was going to watch his foot, and I was going to stay with him, and I wasn't going to take it like it was a contest between him and me. He was the boss, I wanted to please him, and after I made a few choice mistakes, I figured out how to please him."

When asked whether he was difficult to work for, Ray always put up a spirited defence. "There may be some folk who may say that," he would admit, "but I think most people who work with me will tell you that as long as they do what I expect them to do – because I only expect them to do what I know they can do – there's no problem. I've heard musicians say, 'I don't think Mr Charles knows I'm in the band,' but someone else will tell him, 'You play a wrong note, and you'll soon find out that he *does* know you're in the band.' "

Ray expected the best, and gave of himself the best. And he was very much of the old school persuasion when it came to the personal discipline involved in making music to the standard he demanded. "I think the first thing you must do is be honest with yourself," he told Robert Gordon in 1992. "Do you really genuinely feel you have talent, do you have something to offer or something that you have a feeling about? And if you do, the only thing I would say is don't get the idea that you're supposed to get it done in one night or one shot or one record or one anything. Even the Good Lord didn't make the world in one day. And he could have done anything he wanted to do. What that means is practising. A lot of people don't like or enjoy doing that, but I really feel that if you're gonna be good, you gotta practice. I've never met anybody that was genuinely good that didn't practice. Practise whatever the hell you do."

Attention to Ray's timing was particularly crucial on slow numbers like 'Drown In My Own Tears', where he would play so slowly that, according to Leroy Cooper, it was impossible to count time – "if you counted, you'd always end up ahead of him." They called it Ray's "death tempo", and the musicians – drummers especially – had to watch his every nuance, every move of feet, shoulders and head.

"It's very, very important to Ray, the timing," Clifford Solomon would comment in 1986. "Every move the man makes on stage is a signal for something, he directs the band with his feet, with his head – he's keeping time."

James Clay was more adamant: "If a drummer can't understand that, he ain't worth the trouble . . . I wouldn't play drums for him for love nor money."

Trumpet giant Dizzy Gillespie described Ray counting in a number during a show they played together: "Ray plays the blues slower than anybody in the world, slow, slow, slow. He says 'one', and I walked over to where the bass player was standing, about a mile away or something, and when I got over there I heard him say 'two' . . . that was the slowest count I ever heard."

Although Ray was renowned for his tight-fistedness when it came to paying his musicians, Bryant acknowledged that by the mid-Seventies the $500-a-week deal wasn't *that* bad, compared to the other big bands often struggling to stay on the road. And you got to travel in comfort. "He had his own jet, so we would fly everywhere, which was nice – it wasn't a bus gig. A lot of those gigs, like Woody Herman and Maynard Ferguson, Buddy Rich's band, all those big bands travelled by bus and it was kinda rough going. I had been approached by Woody Herman's band to play with them while I was with Ray, but besides enjoying being with Ray and getting comfortable with the gig, although I would have loved to have played with Woody Herman, it didn't pay as well and you went everywhere on a bus, so it just wasn't as appealing."

Having said that, the guys with Ray still had to watch the pennies, and even pay their own hotel bills. "There was a per diem for it, but the rule was when you came to a new town, and you were going to be there more than one night, you had to stay in the hotel one night that you were booked in, then after that if you wanted to find a cheaper hotel you could do so. So of course there were all the stories about 'ghosting' – there'd be one guy with his name on the room, but there might be two or three other guys staying in that room, that's why they called it ghosting. We'd get to a place and say, 'Who's Casper tonight?' [after Casper the Ghost] meaning the guy who was going to share his room."

And on occasion, Ray would also display unexpected generosity, like one night in France when he summoned Bryant to his dressing room during the break after the band's opening set: "Ray was always close enough to work, he always got to hear the band's set. So I came in to his dressing room, and he said, 'John, come here, I wanna talk to you, sit right down here . . .', and it was like a booth sort of a seat, so I get in first, and then Ray gets in and sort of pushes me up against the wall. So he's leaning in to me on my right side, and my left side is pressed up against the wall. And he says, 'John, the way you played tonight, that's the way I want to hear you play every night, I loved it, it was great, and I'm going to give you a $50 raise . . .' So that's the way he would work, it was very immediate and direct with Ray, he was always listening to the music, always reacting, and whether it was good or bad, you were going to get it, right there and then."

Although, once Ray Charles took to the stage, the band assumed the role of being a showcase for his performance, he nevertheless expected it to be up to the standard of the other big name outfits. "A number of the musicians in Ray's band had played with Count Basie, with Duke Ellington or Buddy Rich – these guys would go back and forth between the big bands – but what you learnt with Ray right off the bat was that this is a show. The first priority was to do what Ray wants and to complement what Ray wants, as opposed to some of those other bands where it was about the music, and showing off the individual players."

But, as Bryant would explain, Ray was proud of having a group of accomplished jazz musicians, and would constantly test them accordingly. "He would throw in a chart, or a tempo . . . for instance his arrangement of 'Marie' was extremely up-tempo, probably as fast as 'Caledonia' by Woody Herman, or 'Woodchopper's Ball', or Count Basie's 'Jumpin' At The Woodside'. Ray wanted to compete with those bands, and think that his band was every bit as good. On the sets where we would play instrumentals before Ray would come out, he would load it down with charts that were challenging. He wanted to feel that his band was as good as Count Basie, Duke Ellington or Woody Herman.

"But, when it came down to the show, it would go to another thing, it would become, 'We're backing Ray Charles,' and when The Raelettes would come out, it would be that also. So it had a very different dynamic than the other bands."

John C. Marshall, a British guitarist who played with the Charles band in the early Eighties, recalled an incident when the band had been on the road for a couple of months. "We were in Lyon (France) with the band and doing a rehearsal for the coming performance, and Ray was immediately aware of the fact that no one was really paying attention. 'Listen guys,' Ray said, 'I got the feeling that you want to play jazz. Well let's do it!' And Ray started to play 'Giant Steps' in a really murdering tempo, then follows with 'Scrapple From The Apple', and it went on that way for more than one hour and a half. The whole band was steaming, really cookin', and at the moment that everyone was raising the roof Ray stands up and says: 'Well gentlemen, so much for the jazz, let's now do the job.'"

For The Raelettes, too, it was a slick operation run on strict lines. Ray would rehearse the girls far more thoroughly than the band, going over and over parts literally for hours until they got it just right. And in matters of their appearance and presentation, Joe Adams could be as much of a stickler for perfection as he was with the guys. But despite the discipline, the periodic grumblings over money and inevitable in-fighting, at the end of the day to be a Raelette was an achievement for a young singer. As Merry Clayton (who had quit the group when Gwen Berry was sacked in 1968) would recall years later, "To be a 17-year-old, to be going on a national tour, flying in a plane with Ray Charles, one of the greatest entertainers in the world – you couldn't have asked for anything better than that. Your gowns and your clothes had to be perfect, your make-up had to be cool, you had to be *cutified*. You had to be gorgeous, smell good, it was a privilege to be a Raelette – you had to be a little *diva*, honey!"

And, like the boys in the band, Raelettes came and went over the years. As the 1974 tour made its way across America and down into Mexico, it was without Susaye Green, who had left the previous year to join Stevie Wonder as a singer and songwriter, although she would continue her relationship with Ray to the end of the decade.

Once the tour was over, Ray was back at RPM, laying down tracks for what was to be one of his finest albums ever, bringing his music sensationally into the contemporary arena of the mid-Seventies. Aptly, the record – the second on the Crossover label – was called *Renaissance*.

One reason for the album's artistic (though not commercial) success was simply technology. Ray had at last cottoned on to the synthesiser, the box of tricks that had become a feature of much modern recording, and a favourite device of Stevie Wonder, who introduced his one-time mentor to its possibilities. Throughout *Renaissance* we can hear the electronic wonder whoosh and swirl under Ray's voice, introducing new textures and colourings to his already rich aural palette.

Like *Message From The People*, it's another collection heavy on social consciousness, with gems like Randy Newman's wry 'Sail Away' with its gospel chorus-and-organ treatment, the big R&B sound of 'We're Gonna Make It' and a brassy waltz-time 'Then We'll Be Home'. Mickey Newbury's 'Sunshine' is a slice of country pie with a soaring steel guitar in the mix, Joe Raposo's 'It Ain't Easy Being Green' (think Kermit the Frog) has some strident Memphis-style horns, while appropriately melancholy strings and woodwinds bring in Charles Aznavour's tear-jerker 'For Mama / La Mamma'.

But it's the riveting Stevie Wonder opener, 'Living For The City', that's the most memorable track. From its murmuring synth intro to The Raelettes ride-out with a double-tracked Ray, an anguished cry from the ghetto never sounded so soulful – or danceable for that matter. "Oh Lord, why hast thou forsaken me?" Ray pleads at the end of a spoken monologue telling of "the rats and the roaches" infesting the inner-city squalor. You just know he's been there.

Renaissance didn't appear until June 1975, by which time it was Ray Charles showtime across Europe. Despite some glowing reviews, it fared little better than *Come Live With Me* sales-wise, with a single of 'Living For The City' likewise bombing in the charts – though the latter would be awarded a Grammy in March 1976. While preparing *Renaissance*, Ray had also been cutting a third volume of *My Kind Of Jazz*, like its predecessor a workmanlike selection of instrumentals, highlighted by a spirited version of the Horace Silver soul-jazz classic 'Sister Sadie'. *My Kind Of Jazz Part III* came out in October, as the caravan headed for the Far East.

Before they flew out to Japan, Singapore and Australasia, John Bryant left the band. There was no bad feeling on his part, unlike the hapless drummer he'd followed into the job with Ray. He simply felt it was time to move on, and stayed in touch with his old boss: "Whenever Ray would come to Dallas I would always go and see him, and I always kept my relationship with the guys in the band, so I'd go to the concert and would hang out and see all my pals, and they'd always say, 'Hey, go see Ray, I'm sure he'd like to say hi to you.' So I'd always go to Ray's dressing room, and we would talk . . . we always had a good relationship."

So good, in fact, that during the Nineties Ray would call on him to deputise from time to time when his regular drummer had to take time off. But looking back, Bryant is sorry he hadn't hung on in there just a little longer. "I left the band before they went to Japan, which I do regret because a live album was done there, and it was the same band I played with except for me. And some cuts have been released on this new (the Ray movie) soundtrack that's just come out, I do wish that I was on it, so I'm sorry now that I jumped off quite so soon. But that's the way it goes sometimes, timing is everything."

The album *Ray Charles Live In Japan* is sensational, with one of Ray's best line-ups of the Seventies in full flight. The roaring pre-Ray instrumental set – which includes 'Metamorphosis' from *My Kind Of Jazz Part III* and a hotter-than-hot 'Blowing The Blues Away' – confirms that, on a good night, Ray's band at the time certainly fulfilled his ambition to have an outfit on a par with the other top names on the big band circuit. And things don't let up when Ray takes the stage, with Joe Adams' usual histrionic introduction kicking in to a version of 'Let The Good Times Roll' that would have any audience on the edge of their seats. The performance features the best of the old and new of the period, including a long blues stretch-out on 'Feel So Bad' in which Ray pulls out all the emotional stops, a serene 'Am I Blue', the inevitable 'Georgia On My Mind' and 'What'd I Say', and a crucial 'Living For The City'.

In a stroke of calculated opportunism, early in 1976 Ray decided to re-release a single of 'America The Beautiful' – it was the year of the country's Bicentenniel. From there on, the song – more importantly, *Ray*'s version of the song – became an emotional turn-on for US audiences, and would achieve anthemic status during moments of national catharsis over the years. And in those opening months of the year, Ray also started planning what would be one of his most ambitious recording projects yet, a handsomely boxed double album of George and Ira Gershwin's *Porgy And Bess*.

The idea had been nurtured by jazz promoter Norman Granz when Ray was touring Europe the previous year, Granz having famously recorded the work with Louis Armstrong and Ella Fitzgerald in the Fifties. "Two years ago I got the urge again," Granz would write in the lavish brochure that accompanied the album, "Ray Charles as Porgy. Not since

Armstrong did I hear any singer with the passion for these great songs as with Charles."

Talking to Michael Hobson in a 1999 newsletter of the Classic Records vinyl reissue company, Ray recalled how it came about. "Norman Granz and I were in Europe together – he used to promote our tours in Europe, and on the tours we would ride together a lot, in the same car. Just me and him. Of course he loved to bring his tapes, 'cause he loved jazz. You know that. And we were just talking and stuff, well obviously he was good friends with Ira and George Gershwin. So he said to me one day, 'Ray, you sing every goddamned thing, what about *Porgy And Bess?*' So I said, 'I think that's a great idea, the only thing is we've got to find somebody to do Bess's part.' He said, 'I'll leave that up to you, whoever you think you want to do it with, and we'll go into the studio and do it.'"

Initially Ray wanted to do the project with Gladys Knight, but at the time she was still riding high after her 1973 chart-topper 'Midnight Train To Georgia', and there was no way her record company, Buddha, would agree to Ray's insistence on owning the master tapes. Granz then suggested the British jazz vocalist Cleo Laine, whose work Ray was familiar with. "I'd heard Cleo Laine sing, and I liked her voice. Plus, I figured she could handle the music, because *Porgy And Bess* ain't that easy. You've got to have some musical ability to do it, and I knew she could. And I liked her voice, so I asked Norman to talk to her, and see if it's all right with her. And she was for it right away."

Cleo Laine was contracted to RCA Records at the time, so Granz approached them and – albeit reluctantly, one would assume – they agreed to their artist appearing despite Ray retaining the masters. Ray claimed they did it for Granz, who they happened to like. And, of course, they got a finger in the pie: the album was flagged as an RCA release in the US, in Britain coming out under the Crossover/London imprint.

As credited in the album notes, Ray and Cleo went into the RCA studios in Hollywood from April 20 to 23, with Ray also recording some instrumental tracks on July 13. According to Ray, however, the two singers recorded their individual songs quite separately, with Ray doing most of his takes in California, Cleo in New York, the two getting together just a couple of times for the duet pieces. And contrary to the credits, the sessions, subject to availability for them both, stretched across five or six months through the first half of 1976.

When they did get together, Cleo Laine rather than Ray was the one already familiar with the music of *Porgy And Bess*. She knew the lyrics, and would explain to Ray the chord structures of the pieces they sang together – which was a great advantage to Ray, to know what a duettist was going to do in this kind of shared project, as opposed to working with backing singers where he would always be the main driving force.

Written as a "folk opera" by the Gershwins in collaboration with the author of the original novel *Porgy*, DuBose Heyward, the 40-year-old work was a challenge for Ray from the start. Initially, he wasn't even sure about the arranger who Granz had assigned to the project, Frank DeVol, but was soon firmly convinced when he started hearing what DeVol had in mind.

At first Ray – and Norman Granz – felt Cleo Laine was trying too hard to be theatrical in an operatic sort of way; "dramatic" was how he put it. What they were looking for was emotion rather than drama. But as everyone relaxed into the frequently demanding music, there emerged a work of far greater strength than its muted critical reception implied at the time.

It's not clear whether it was the first track they recorded together, but on 'Summertime', after an instrumental version of the song with Ray on organ, Cleo eases herself into the vocals with a nervous edge to her voice that soon reveals a remarkable control and range. From there on, she and Ray more or less alternate solo tracks when they're not duetting, with Ray preceding several numbers with an instrumental take featuring himself and the rhythm section only.

The amazing variety of the work gives both singers plenty of chance to flex themselves. Ray's in fine form on the up-tempo 'A Woman Is A Sometime Thing', and spars with Cleo as he once did with Betty Carter on 'I Got Plenty O' Nuttin''. He wails over a down-home blues harmonica on 'Crab Man', while Cleo reciprocates with 'Here Come De Honey Man', and Ray's in full R&B mode with an electric piano-led 'There's A Boat Dat's Leavin' Soon For New York' that features some crackling solo breaks from the brass.

The outstanding duo track is undoubtedly 'It Ain't Necessarily So', with the sweeping strings of the 70-plus ensemble breaking into up-tempo changes of pace that make an overfamiliar tune a totally fresh experience. And both vocalists get to sing sanctified, accompanied by the Reverend James Cleveland Singers; Cleo on the marvellous 'Oh, Doctor Jesus', and Ray on the soulful closer 'Oh Lord, I'm On My Way', where churchy horns and a heavenly choir culminate with a truly gospel "amen" ending.

In his highly detailed – and laudatory – liner notes, the critic Benny Green writes of Ray's organ playing on 'Summertime' achieving "a reshaping of the whole conception of the song, which somehow remains respectful to what Gershwin had in mind."[*] In conclusion, he voices one tongue-in-cheek reservation about the album: "The only thing seriously wrong with it is that nobody has yet discovered a way of letting George Gershwin hear it. If only he could have heard it, I think I know what his reaction would have been."

In its smart-looking presentation box, *Porgy And Bess* probably made an ideal Christmas present for some folk when it went on sale in November 1976, but didn't sell in sufficient numbers to bring much seasonal cheer to either Crossover or Decca. Meanwhile, the other major event in Ray's life that year had been even less likely to inspire goodwill than the gloomy record sales – his wife of 21 years, Della, had finally filed for a divorce.

In a long haul of legal acrobatics and financial haggling that lasted from May through to the following April, Ray and Della's respective lawyers grappled with the complex ins and outs of the star's finances. First and foremost there was the house at Southridge, and other properties that Ray owned including their previous place on Hepburn, the RPM building and so on. Then there were the myriad business interests represented by Ray Charles Enterprises and its subsidiary companies like Tangerine Music and Crossover Records.

After months of bitter and acrimonious wrangling, in which Della's claims were rebuffed time and again by Ray's people, agreement was reached that gave Della the Southridge home, a cash payment of a third of a million dollars, a trust fund for the three boys and $4,000 a month support for her and youngest son Robert. By the end of 1977 the divorce was made final, and what had been an increasingly tenuous marriage bond was no more.

Other less traumatic changes were taking place too. Towards the end of '76 Mabel John had heard the call of the Lord and given up the life of a Raelette for one helping the needy in Los Angeles, Dorothy Berry taking over as leader. Not long after, baritone sax loyalist and latter-day bandleader Leroy Cooper said goodbye: "I left at the end of '76, and I got

---

[*] It was the same Benny Green who wrote of the "incessant barrage of rolling piano chords" from "the jazz pianist who lies half-buried under an inflated reputation" after Ray's London debut in 1963.

a job down in Disneyworld." And, after just three albums not counting the live Japanese set, Decca decided to call it a day as far as Ray Charles and Crossover was concerned. For his next album, which he had been laying down during the winter break of early 1977, Ray was going to have to find another label deal.

At this point one of the biggest ironies in Ray Charles' history would take place – his return to Atlantic Records, the label which had nurtured his talent in the first place only to have him turn his back on them at a seminal point in his career. Ahmet Ertegun and Jerry Wexler's bitterness at Ray's departure back in 1960 had mellowed over the years, and when he made it clear he was looking for a new home for his music they were definitely interested.

They felt they knew the score with Ray, and were willing to take on board both the matter of him owning his masters, and personal foibles that they were well familiar with. And Atlantic was a multi-million-dollar operation now. It had grown over the years, and was owned at this point by Warner Brothers as part of the massive WEA (Warner, Elektra, Atlantic) conglomerate. With flamboyant rock music megastars like The Rolling Stones, Led Zeppelin and Crosby, Stills & Nash on their books, Ray's occasional moods and idiosyncracies paled in comparison.

Ahmet's brother Nesuhi even had an office in London, as head of WEA's European wing, which was where I spoke to him in October 1976 when he told me that they had stayed in close touch with their former top star: "I must say that through the years we've remained friends. Six months ago they had a big testimonial dinner for Ray Charles, and Ray wanted Ahmet to be chairman. So Ahmet was chairman of this thing, over a thousand people in a California tribute to Ray Charles. Which proves that, 20 [sic] years after he left Atlantic Records, all the personal ties remain."

So, to quote a phrase Ahmet Ertegun had used a quarter of a century before when buying Ray Charles' original contract off Jack Lauderdale, it was a "done deal".

Ray delivered the tracks he had been working on through the winter as his first Crossover album for Atlantic, and, released in October 1977 as *True To Life*, it turned out to be one of his best.

Ray's glorious cover of Johnny Nash's 'I Can See Clearly Now', with its thumping Seventies bass and bold-as-brass horns, is a funkily optimistic opener that has the lot. "I can see a bright, bright sun-shiny day," he tells us, amid a heady mix of girls, guitars, conga drums and sunshine. Second up, Sid Feller arranged one of Ray's finest ballads of the era, 'The Jealous Kind', as he also did for the strident oldie 'Be My Love' in which Ray makes the Mario Lanza warhorse from 1950 all his own.

The other ballad of the pack, Lennon & McCartney's 'Let It Be' (again, a song generally believed to have been written by McCartney alone) stands up well, considering it was one of The Beatles' least satisfactory tracks in its original. 'Let It Be' and 'I Can See Clearly Now' were both arranged by Larry Mahoberack, who also handled the Gershwin classic 'How Long Has This Been Going On?' and 'Anonymous Love'. 'Anonymous', with a double-tracked Ray, a soul vocal group that doesn't sound like The Raelettes, and some conga-dominated percussion, is pure funk-driven R&B very much of the time. And 'Game Number Nine', arranged by Ray and written by Dee Ervin, is a typically Ray Charles slice of talking hokum, with its synth and electric keyboard breaks making it a funky, contemporary successor to 1962's marvellous 'At The Club'.

Two of the finest tracks on the album – though what's "best" in all this bunch is generally too close to call – were arranged by Roger Newman. 'Heavenly Music' tells of a vision of a heavenly band of musicians made up of all the greats, "playing sweet songs of love", a gospel-flavoured opus complete with a cappella hand-clapping over the electric piano break. And the biggest surprise is the Newman-arranged take on Rodgers & Hammerstein's much-beloved hit from *Oklahoma!*, 'Oh, What A Beautiful Mornin''. After the opening "There's a bright golden haze in the meadow", it's an audacious waltz-time jazz version that only Ray Charles would dare to attempt, and he succeeds magnificently.

True To Life was an auspicious start to Ray's renewed relationship with his old compadres at Atlantic. As with all his last few albums (with the exception of the Norman Granz-produced *Porgy And Bess*), Ray had produced *True To Life* himself. The only change after *Come Live With Me* was that instead of David Braithwaite he now had Bob Gratts (who like Braithwaite had cut his teeth at Motown) as the RPM house recording engineer at his elbow.

Even so, Ahmet Ertegun felt the album wasn't enough in tune with current styles production-wise. But Ray insisted he was taking on board contemporary trends in the recording process, as and when he felt fit. As with all aspects of his music, he applied any innovation to how he wanted to treat a song, rather than applying his treatment to the innovation. So a song would sound cutting-edge when Ray deemed it should – and that wasn't always, by any means.

Ahmet's feelings notwithstanding, *True To Life* did better than any of Ray's other mid-Seventies output when it was released in October '77, making the *Billboard* Top 100 amid generally favourable reviews. But after an Asian tour followed by the Christmas holiday, when Ray got back to thinking about putting together his next collection at RPM, it seems he may have taken heed of his label boss' reservations after all.

Using two of the arrangers from *True To Life*, Roger Newman and Larry Mahoberack, plus Harry Goodnight, Ray and Bob Gratts came up with an album that was 80 per cent pure disco pop. Things get off to a get-down-and-get-with-it start with 'You 20th Century Fox', penned by ex-Raelette Mabel John and another Tangerine writer Joel Webster, and its stereotypical Seventies funk all the way with a lyric full of references to the dance floor and folks who "like to party".

There's more of the same throughout, with staccato brass over a bed of funky synth ripples and chukka-chukka guitar, with some dubious lyrics including Jimmy Lewis' 'Take Off That Dress' in which Ray is pleading not for someone to disrobe but for "his" woman to put on something more modest in front of other men! There's some relief from the funk in the countryish 'We Had It All', but even Seals & Crofts' 'Riding Thumb' features those disco-lite horns.

Side two partway fulfils the promise of the title *Love & Peace* with hints of socially conscious lyrics on some of the tracks, but the message in 'No Achievement Showing' – if there is one – is buried down in the mix, Ray's voice processed almost beyond recognition. There's a rambling polemic going on in 'A Peace That We Never Before Could Enjoy', another Joel Webster and Mabel John number, but Ray's voice remains relatively restrained throughout. Likewise in 'Is There Anyone Out There?', after a straight start with just electric piano, even the incursion of horns and a choir fails to lift things.

We have to get to the final song, 'Give The Poor Man A Break' by Jimmy Lewis, to hear Ray getting really animated. After the title is chanted repeatedly on the intro fade-in, there's a dynamic here – with vocal breaks punctuated by more disco horns – that's lacking on the rest of the set. The sentiment might be banal, Ray addressing "Mr President" with "Foreign policy is all well and good, but what about the poor folks here in our neighbourhood", but at least its heart – and musical intent – is in the right place. That's something that can't be said for most of the album. Despite what he said about *True To Life*, Ahmet Ertegun was even less enthusiastic about *Love & Peace*, and when it failed to make the slightest impression after its September release, he for one was not the least bit surprised.

For Ahmet and Jerry Wexler, and indeed for veteran fans who had followed Ray's career for almost as long as they had, this period was bound to be clouded with a nostalgia for Ray Charles' glory years. Anyone harking back to when he turned Black American music on its head in the Fifties, totally changing pop music in the Sixties as a result, could only feel chastened by the patchy record output and increasingly programmatic live appearances of the late Seventies. It came as something of a welcome boost, therefore, when for the first time since 1971's 25th Anniversary double album, his entire career was addressed – and this time much more substantially than in a "greatest hits" record collection.

Since the autumn of 1976 jazz writer David Ritz had been working with Ray on his autobiography, and now, exactly two years later, it finally appeared in print.

Hailing from Dallas, Texas – a city with many Ray Charles associations over the years – Ritz was a life-long fan, and he and his subject had spent countless hours talking and taping their conversations, the journalist then arduously transcribing the tapes, Ray checking the Braille copies of those transcriptions. Eventually, after inevitable qualms on the publishers' part over the sex'n'drugs aspect of Ray's frank admissions (which both authors insisted stayed in) *Brother Ray* was published to broad critical acclaim – and healthy sales in the bookshops.

Delving deep into Ray's inner personality and oft-forgotten memories during their long sessions together, by keeping everything in the highly colloquial first person the book shone a fascinating light on the soul of the man whose life story up till then had only been briefly spelled out in press interviews and sketchy album notes. And in doing so put into (an admittedly personalised) context the sheer impact of his work on the music of the Fifties and Sixties. As with the movie biography, *Ray*, made a quarter of a century later, there were criticisms that many of the supporting characters in Ray Charles' history were reduced to two-dimensional sketches and perfunctory name-checks. But this was *Brother Ray*, the High Priest of Soul telling it like it was, strictly from *his* point of view.

For his next album Ray decided to return to the tried and trusted formula of mixing the familiar with the unknown, the old with the new, the lavish with the simple. Again with Mahoberack and Goodnight arranging, plus

James Polk and his loyal stand-by Sid Feller, Ray and Bob Gratts lined up the team for what would be his third Atlantic album of the Seventies, *Ain't It So.*

Ray really indulged his penchant for longer numbers on this collection, with just three tracks taking up the whole of Side 1, a brassy intro bringing in an up-tempo disco-beat version of 'Some Enchanted Evening' just to get things going. And if the five minutes-plus wasn't long enough for Ray – he ends Rodgers & Hammerstein's *South Pacific* standard with a soul-shouting fade-out – then 'Blues In The Night' is even more of a marathon. From the opening "My mama done told me . . ." we can sense that this is going to be one of Ray's slow, slow performances, but the extended soulful treatment never sags; there's not even an instrumental solo, just Ray's lightly accompanied voice uninterrupted throughout.

The first side closes with a light ballad with strings, 'Just Because', a song by French writer, Robert Fitoussi. On Irving Berlin's 'What'll I Do', after a conventional half-spoken prologue Ray launches into a contemporary R&B version that does for the 1924 standard what he once did similarly for 'My Bonnie Lies Over The Ocean'. The weakest track in the bunch is a slightly ponderous take on Barry Manilow's 'One Of These Days', but any impending ennui is soon alleviated by the country-soul flavoured 'Love Me Or Set Me Free' – written by Tangerine songsmiths Jimmy Lewis and Frank Johnson, and replete with Stax-style horns and some tight harmonies from The Raelettes.

A warm, relaxed cover of Mentor Williams' 1970 hit for Dobie Gray 'Drift Away', with those Memphis horns again, takes us to the down-home country anthem closer, Ray's voice resplendent over electric piano and pedal steel guitar as he pleads '(Turn Out The Light) And Love Me Tonight'. All in all, *Ain't It So* stands up as one of Ray's better outings of the period, but like most of his product in that era it sank without trace after its release in September 1979.

Outside the recording studio it was a fairly uneventful year, save for Ray's long-overdue recognition by his home state of Georgia when, on March 7, the state government made his version of 'Georgia On My Mind' the official state song. Ray performed the number at an impressive ceremony in the Capitol building in Atlanta, at which a public apology was offered to him for the state-wide performing ban that had been imposed back in '61 after he refused to play to a segregated audience.

And at the end of the year, after the now almost ritualised touring across the world, Ray rounded off the Seventies – a decade that had seen more downs than ups in his fortunes – with a cameo role in a movie that was a glorious two-hour-plus celebration of R&B and southern soul, John Landis' *The Blues Brothers*.

Written by director Landis and comedian/actor Dan Ackroyd, the comedy starred Ackroyd and John Belushi as the brothers Jake and Elwood Blues, frantically trying to raise money for their old orphanage by getting their old R&B band together one more time.

Ray had already been involved with Belushi and Ackroyd in November 1977, when he appeared on the cult TV satire show *Saturday Night Live*, which the pair hosted. As well as mugging it up in zany sketches, Ray re-formed his small band for the occasion with a line-up that included Newman, Crawford, Cooper, Belgrave and Guilbeau for a medley of hits from his earlier Atlantic era.

In *The Blues Brothers* Ray plays the blind proprietor of a music shop where Jake and Elwood are trying to buy an electric piano, which provides one of the many excuses in the film for a musical sequence – in which Ray bursts into 'Shake A Tail Feather', with everyone in the surrounding streets suddenly joining in the party in true Hollywood style.

The song is one of the highlights of the soundtrack album of the film, Ray being joined on vocals by The Blues Brothers and backed by a classic Stax-sound line-up that includes Steve Cropper on guitar and Duck Dunn on bass. Other cameos by music legends feature Thirties jazz star Cab Calloway, soul "Godfather" James Brown and soul queen Aretha Franklin; when R&B fanatics Belushi and Ackroyd planned the movie, they insisted on approaching Ray to take part, the film being a tribute to the music he helped create.

And as the Eighties began, Ray was preparing what would be his final album in the Crossover arrangement with Atlantic, another stylistically mixed bag entitled *Brother Ray Is At It Again*. Again he brought in several arrangers including Sid Feller and Mike Post, with himself once more producing.

Listening to the opening track, Eugene McDaniels' 'Compared To What', you would be forgiven for thinking that Ray was still on his disco kick. But through the emotive 'Anyway You Want To' and a compelling version of the Bruce Roberts and Carole Bayer Sager ballad 'Don't You Love Me Anymore?' – with a stunning trumpet solo by Bobby Bryant – it quickly becomes clear that he's put together a typically eclectic collection on a par with the previous *Ain't It So*.

'A Poor Man's Song' continues the class consciousness that Ray expressed in *A Message From The People* and *Love & Peace*'s 'Give The Poor Man A Break', while he brings a touch of soul to Robbie Robertson's old-timey 'Ophelia' from The Band's *Northern Light – Southern Cross* album. Finally, Ray's own 'Questions' is a reflective 12-bar blues worked up into laid-back funk with a jazzy lead guitar and subtly applied strings. In it he poses some tough questions, hence the title –

> *Why so many people suffer,*
> *When they ain't done nothing wrong*

concluding with a wry aside in the last verse

> *I didn't mean to sound too morbid,*
> *and I hope I didn't spoil your day*

As one review put it: "Nobody else could do that little chuckle like Ray, or have it mean even one tenth as much. Suffice it to say, it doesn't sound like Ray was all that sorry if his questions ruined anybody's complacent bliss."

But fine though the album was, *Brother Ray Is At It Again* did nothing to raise either Ray Charles' position in the sales charts or his profile in the media. Indeed, during 1980 many more people would become aware of Ray's presence – some undoubtedly for the first time – as a result of his few minutes in *The Blues Brothers*, than had via all his records over the previous few years.

After four albums on his old label Atlantic, Ray's recording career was at a hiatus once again, and as he and Ahmet Ertegun parted company for the second time – but on this occasion without acrimony – he decided to sit back and take stock. He celebrated his 50th birthday on September 23, 1980, and after the regular touring was over and Christmas had been and gone, for the first time in over a decade he didn't go into the new year with another album in the pipeline at RPM. Not for the first time, his career had come to a crossroads; his next move, when he eventually made it, would be focussed over a thousand and a half miles due east, in Nashville, Tennessee.

17

Country Roads

"With country music, I was still singing me, my voice was still me, I was just singing country songs. I never tried to become a Hank Snow, a Hank Williams or a Charlie Pride. I didn't want to become a country and western singer."

– Ray Charles

Veteran country star Willie Nelson is quoted as saying, "With his recording of 'I Can't Stop Loving You', Ray Charles did more for country music than any other artist." The enormous success of that single, and *Modern Sounds In Country And Western Music* from whence it came, certainly made for a huge boost in the popularity and public awareness of country *material*, but as Ray would say to *Rolling Stone* in 1973: "When I sing 'I Can't Stop Loving You', I'm not singin' it country-western. I'm singin' it like me."

With 'I Can't Stop Loving You' and *Modern Sounds* Ray Charles may have popularised the country repertoire, exposing it to a far wider audience than it had enjoyed before. But he did that by making it his own, by injecting Ray Charles – and Ray Charles' soul – into Hank Williams, Eddy Arnold and so on.

Since then, country music had come a long way, its position by the early Eighties in the American music mainstream due in no small way to the breakthrough that Ray had triggered 20 years before. The kind of old-time music that Ray had listened to as a child, when every Saturday night the *Grand Ole Opry* was beamed from Nashville, had been referred to as "white man's blues"; it was the music of white working-class folk across rural America. As Jerry Wexler reminded me, it was known as "hillbilly" music before being rechristened country and western. Now it had become a multi-million-dollar branch of the music industry, and city-slick in the process, the rhinestone-studded sound coming out of

Music City (as Nashville had been dubbed) could well be called the soul music of white Middle America.

And there was certainly a soul to country which Ray for one had always recognised. Like blues and gospel music, blues and country had a lot more in common than their musical segregation would suggest. The harmonies, the rhythm and indeed the similar relationship to church music demonstrate the common roots of country and blues, not to mention the incidence of 12- and 32-bar blues in the repertoire of Jimmie Rodgers, Bob Wills and other country trailblazers in the Thirties and Forties. As Ray put it during the last year of his life, talking about a country number on his final album *Genius Loves Company* that he'd first recorded in 1983, "Country and blues ain't just first cousins, they're blood brothers."

Perhaps subconsciously harking back to his days with The Florida Playboys, but very consciously looking forward to where he was going next musically, by the end of 1981 Ray had decided to tackle country from the inside. Rather than just playing country songs in his own fashion, he was going to play country music per se.

In between the regular round of touring work, Ray had let it be known around the music industry that he was looking to spread his wings in the direction of Nashville, and in early 1982 entered into protracted negotiations with the head of CBS Records' country division, Rick Blackburn. Six months later he'd struck a deal, and begun putting things together at RPM for his first 100 per cent country album, working on songs for which he was going to be using banjo, fiddle, pedal steel guitar – the whole panoply – with some of the best players Nashville had to offer.

Over the years Ray had established himself as a popular figure with country music audiences. He'd guested on country TV shows and even played the *Grand Ole Opry*, so there was a ready-made constituency for his music within the C&W community; and when his first "real" country album *Wish You Were Here Tonight* appeared on the Columbia label early in 1983, it didn't disappoint them. CBS trailed the album for the Christmas '82 market with a single, 'Born To Love Me', which just made the country Top 20 – not bad for yet another Ray Charles experiment which many music industry insiders had doubts about from the start.

Opening with the amusing '3/4 Time', it's clear that the album, with its steady tempos and straight harmony vocals, isn't only following country convention in its instrumentation. The title track is a real tear-jerker, the other strong ballad on the collection being the equally riveting 'Ain't Your Memory Got No Pride At All'. There are humorous numbers including 'String Bean' and 'Shakin' Your Head', and a couple of strong rockers: the powerful 'I Don't Want No Stranger Sleepin' In My Bed' and a rousing version of The Bellamy Brothers' 1976 chart-topper 'Let Your Love Flow'.

Produced by Ray with most of the arranging done by James Polk, the album – with some heavy media promotion from the CBS giant – proved a moderate success. As were the two follow-up singles, '3/4 Time' backed with 'You Feel Good All Over' released in March and 'Ain't Your Memory Got No Pride At All' and 'I Don't Want No Stranger Sleepin' In My Bed' which appeared in the August. For Ray and his new label it was a promising if not spectacular start to their relationship.

As the second single was released, between some exhausting touring which took them across America and to Europe twice, Ray managed to lay down the basic tracks for his next Columbia album. As with the debut, he would produce the songs at RPM before taking them to Nashville where various elements would be added – involving local session players – before the whole thing was mixed down to what he wanted.

On the road, meanwhile, the touring could be arduous, and this often showed on stage when the big band's performance was efficient, note-perfect – and little else. "Nowadays, Charles' performance unfolds in an atmosphere of stifling decorum and politeness, full orchestra in harness, affording no margin for error, and thus none of spontaneity," Mick Brown would write in *The Guardian* newspaper, reviewing Ray's appearance at the Capital Jazz Festival in London in 1984. And Barney Hoskyns would recall in *Mojo* magazine how Ray's vocals merely hinted at the glories of the past: "I saw Charles play in the early Eighties and found his show desperately stale and passionless. Nothing, however, could persuade me that the man who sang 'Tell The Truth' and 'I Believe To My Soul' isn't still tapped into the mother lode of soul."

His second bona fide country album, which wasn't released until July 1984, *Do I Ever Cross Your Mind* comes over as increasingly assured compared to its predecessor, confident in its utilisation of traditional elements. Ray, if anything, sounds more comfortable than first time around, in a musical environment which – though of his choosing – must have posed a challenge to get to grips with. Highlights include successful versions of Don Gibson's 'Woman Sensuous Woman', the Eddy Arnold ballad 'Then I'll Be Over You' and a Ronnie Rogers song with a theme worthy of Merle Haggard 'Workin' Man's Woman'.

Closely rivalled by Ray's cover of Bobby David's '(All I Wanna Do Is)

Lay Around And Love On You', the title track is the strongest item on the album. With some great lyrics that speak of "that melancholy jailer Father Time" by Billy Burnette, son of rockabilly veteran Dorsey Burnette, Ray would reprise the song on 2004's *Genius Loves Company* in tandem with Bonnie Raitt.

There had been nearly a three-year gap between the actual release of Ray's final Atlantic album and his first with Columbia. As if conscious of the need to "catch up" a little, he set about preparing his next country venture almost immediately after *Do I Ever Cross Your Mind* was completed in the late summer of 1983. And this time Ray decided to go the whole hog for that genuine country sound, with an album made in Nashville studios with a Nashville producer and Nashville musicians throughout. Not only that, but what proved to be an absolute classic featured some of the biggest names in country music in a series of duets, titled *Friendship*.

To sit in the producer's chair, Ray and CBS acquired the services of one of the top names in the country music capital, Billy Sherrill. As a house producer at Columbia, Sherrill had discovered Tammy Wynette, co-writing and producing her hit 'Stand By Your Man' in 1968. Going free-lance in 1980, he had also launched the careers of Tanya Tucker and Janie Fricke and worked successfully with such country luminaries as Charlie Rich, George Jones and Marty Robbins. By 1983 he was the most in-demand producer in country music.

Sherrill and Ray got together with George Jones in October for a taster track that was put out as a single the following month, making the number six position in the country charts. With Nashville supremo Chet Atkins on guitar, the humorous 'We Didn't See A Thing' (backed with 'I Wish You Were Here Tonight' from his Columbia debut LP) was a useful try-out for the album to come, which they worked on in earnest through the first half of 1984.

'Two Old Cats Like Us' with Hank Williams Jnr sets the honky tonk feel of much of the album, a two-man tribute to rockin' music of all kinds:

> *Everything*
> *from western swing*
> *to that good old rock'n'roll*

The Oak Ridge Boys accompany Ray on the up-tempo 'This Old Heart', starting with a slower-than-slow Charles intro that must have tested the most seasoned of Nashville session men to keep time. Janie Fricke is the only female voice on the collection, on the close-harmony 'Who Cares', while the jaunty 'Rock And Roll Shoes' with B.J. Thomas has Ray sounding particularly relaxed in the surroundings, a regular Nashville cat, bringing things to a funky close on an R&B-style ride-out.

The old Cole Porter song, 'Friendship', has Ricky Scaggs trading lyrical licks with Ray on this gentle country take on the wartime standard. The nearest thing to a "straight" ballad comes with Mickey Gilley and 'It Ain't Gonna Worry My Mind', and the album starts to sound in danger of sagging when this is followed by 'Little Hotel Room' with Merle Haggard, despite the latter's reputation for grittier material.

Things get back into a soulful southern groove however on the Johnny Cash track, the waltz-time 'Crazy Old Soldier', in which the mellow, wistful voice of the "Man in Black" is matched by Ray assuming an almost secondary role to a fellow giant of American music. Laid-back, certainly, but with an emotional build that belies its gentle dynamic. The atmospheric sounds of the Mexican border are evoked by Ray and Willie Nelson in 'Seven Spanish Angels', complete with acoustic guitar and choir, and marvellous lyrics by Troy Seals, who also penned the previous track and the opener 'Two Old Cats'.

The finished album, released in February 1985, spawned two singles that appeared earlier, in July and November '84 – 'Rock And Roll Shoes' (backed with 'Then I'll Be Over You' from *Do I Ever Cross Your Mind*) then 'Seven Spanish Angels' and 'Who Cares'. 'Shoes' made it to the C&W Top 20, while 'Angels' climbed to number one on the country chart by March 1985. The *Friendship* album also topped its respective C&W list. Ray's strategy, to become part of the important – and highly lucrative – country mainstream, was paying off handsomely.

Not long before the release of *Friendship*, on January 28, 1985, Ray entered a Los Angeles studio to get together with over 40 other music stars – all appearing for no fee – to take part in a unique venture. Organised by singer Harry Belafonte, the session was set up to make a record dedicated to alleviating hunger in the Third World, particularly in the famine-ravaged areas of Africa. The song was called 'We Are The World', and the collected artists billed themselves as "USA For Africa". Written by Michael Jackson and Lionel Richie, the single was produced by Ray's old pal Quincy Jones. The stellar line-up, as well as Richie and Jackson, included Stevie Wonder, Tina Turner, James Ingram, Diana Ross, Dionne Warwick, Al Jarreau, Paul Simon, Kenny Rogers, Billy Joel,

Willie Nelson, Bruce Springsteen, Kenny Loggins, Steve Perry, Daryl Hall, Huey Lewis, Cyndi Lauper, Kim Carnes and Bob Dylan.

Each featured vocalist got to sing one line as well as joining in on the ensemble choruses, and organising just that was a challenge given that the participants were only gathered together that night, with no prior preparation. "To get two artists in a room is to invite chaos," Belafonte would tell NBC TV's *Today* show on the 20th Anniversary of the session in 2005, "but here you are with dozens of the best and most powerful artists in popular culture, who had relegated their managers to a place in Siberia – and as a consequence, it was completely art on art."

Quincy remembered issuing a warning: "Check your egos at the door." "One by one as they came in, they started to see each other, and they couldn't believe it. When I think about that night, I get goose bumps." As he assigned lines in turn to each of the superstars, Quincy decided to give Ray – as an "elder statesman" of the gathered talents – a closing solo spot. The record was an instant success, hitting the *Billboard* number one spot on March 23 and staying there for four more weeks. It went on to enjoy a total of three months in the Top 40 chart, and eventually raised over $60 million for African famine relief.

Ray's general stance on socio-political issues remained ambiguous. He jumped at the chance to take part in 'We Are The World' without hesitation, even though it was rare for him to commit to any kind of professional appearance without a fee. He had "campaigned" through his music for the underclass of Black America in various "message songs", and his stance on segregation in the South was a matter of record. Yet he played in South Africa, in the face of an international artists' boycott of the apartheid regime. And he'd twice appeared at Republican Party events alongside President Ronald Reagan in the space of a year, in 1984 and '85 – but of course it was for a fee, a regular paid gig, as he was quick to point out.

The touring season started up again in the spring of 1985, interrupted only by a plane accident in October in which the trusty Viscount, now starting to show its age, skidded off the runway while landing at the tiny airport in Bloomington, Indiana. Although badly shaken, no one was seriously injured, but the incident brought to an end Ray's flying the entourage in his own aircraft. From here on, it was a case of commercial flights for long distance travel and a tour bus for shorter hops.

As the end of the year approached, Columbia brought out a collection of Christmas songs that Ray had been preparing since before the previous Yuletide. With a picture of Ray with a sleigh full of gifts on the sleeve, *The Spirit Of Christmas* features Marty Paich arrangements of some very familiar tunes. By and large the sacred numbers such as 'What Child Is This' take second place to the merry romps through 'Santa Claus Is Coming To Town', 'Rudolph The Red-Nosed Reindeer' and 'All I Want For Christmas'. Lesser-known items, 'That Spirit Of Christmas' and 'Christmas In My Heart', work well as vehicles for the classic Charles ballad treatment, while 'Winter Wonderland' gets what one reviewer described as "a soul transfusion the likes of which you won't see on many televised Christmas specials". The biggest surprise comes with 'Little Drummer Boy', an unlikely candidate for a soulful interpretation, but it works.

On January 23, 1986, the first induction dinner was held for the Rock'n' Roll Hall of Fame, which would find a permanent home in Cleveland, Ohio from 1995. The dinner, which was hosted by Quincy Jones, was held in New York City and, along with Ray, the other nine founding members honoured that evening were Chuck Berry, James Brown, Sam Cooke, Fats Domino, The Everly Brothers, Buddy Holly, Jerry Lee Lewis, Elvis Presley and Little Richard.

Once again, Ray was being honoured as a national cultural hero, after the doldrums that had beset his career through the late Seventies. Any chat show host worth his salt wanted him on their show, and Ray appeared with the biggest, Johnny Carson, on the latter's *Tonight* show. As well as goofing with Madonna, he gave Carson some down-home philosophy on coping with blindness. "Sighted people always think it fascinating what blind people can do, but it's not fascinating at all, it's very simple. People come into my studio, and they look at my console and they see all those LED lights just flashing, and they say, 'How d'you see all of them, how d'you see what they're doing' . . . and I say, 'I don't *know* what they're doin'.' The thing is, if the music that comes to my ears, if I don't hear any distortion, I know it's right. If you want to do something, you can make yourself about as independent as you want to be, but you must have the will, it doesn't make any difference whether you're blind or not. I've known some people that have all five senses, and they're pretty pathetic to me . . ."

Before the 1986 touring started, which would take Ray and the orchestra across the well-worn routes of North America and Europe, he was back in the Nashville studios with Billy Sherrill, this time to record a solo album, *From The Pages Of My Mind*, with mostly the same session musicians as on the *Friendship* collaborations. Co-produced by Sherrill and Ray, in many ways it's a more varied collection than the guest-star vehicle, and with a relaxed sincerity somewhat lacking in the previous country set. Harking back to Ray's classic country on ABC, there's a lot more use of strings, which brings out the best in his interpretive skills on such material. He's particularly emotive on 'Dixie Moon', in which he gets to the soulful heart of the song, and Bobby Whitlock's fine 'Slip Away'.

Ray also found time to collaborate on a pop single by Billy Joel, 'Baby Grand', which would make it to the Top 5 in *Billboard*'s Adult Contemporary listings. The track, which also appeared on the singer's Top 10 album *The Bridge*, was produced by a friend of Quincy Jones, Phil Ramone, who would later work with Ray on the final album of his career.

When it was released in September, *From The Pages Of My Mind* fared moderately sales-wise (with one track, 'A Little Bit Of Heaven', making number 76 in the country chart) but marked the end of what might be seen as Ray's flirtation with Nashville. His next album — and his last for Columbia — would be a back-to-basics affair concentrating on what he was best at, a broad variety of material performed with a strong R&B backbone. But another year would slip by before he finalised the project.

Meanwhile, in August, Ray got news that he was being awarded one of the most prestigious citations he would ever receive, the Kennedy Center Honors Medal, which was given for distinguished achievements in the arts. When it was presented at a White House ceremony in December, the gala concert that followed climaxed with a performance of 'America The Beautiful' by a children's choir from the St Augustine Florida Deaf and Blind School. Ray felt he couldn't have been honoured better than that.

And Ray was back in the Washington corridors of power the following April, when he spoke before Senate subcommittees for Labour, Health and Human Services and Education, urging Congress to increase funding for research into hearing loss. He told the senators, who were visibly impressed by his lobbying, "Most people take their hearing for granted. I can't. My eyes are my handicap, but my ears are my opportunity. My ears show me what my eyes can't. My ears tell me 99 per cent of what I need to know about my world."

Ray's concern in this direction had first been prompted in 1983 when he began experiencing abnormal hearing problems in his left ear. "I was hearing sounds within sounds," he would later tell *Ability* magazine, a condition which an LA specialist, Dr Jack Pulec, subsequently described as "autophany" – when a normally closed tube leading to the ear stays open, allowing sounds from inside the throat to enter the ear, therefore being heard alongside "normal" sounds. A small operation conducted by Dr Pulec seemed to do the trick, but the potential problem it raised concerned Ray to the extent that he volunteered to sit on the board of Pulec's Ear International Foundation, a Los Angeles-based non-profit organisation for the hearing impaired.

Then in 1986 he had set up, with Dr Pulec's advice and help, the Ray Charles Robinson Foundation for Hearing Disorders, through which (via personal donations and fund-raising appearances) he provided money for research in developing electronic implants and other devices to aid those – especially children – with extreme hearing difficulties. Since its creation, the Foundation, with Ray's encouragement and ongoing funding, has helped pioneer radical developments in auditory physiology and hearing implantation. Each such implant procedure costs upwards of $40,000, which the Foundation pays to have done. In June 2004, *DrumBeats Magazine* reported that of some 145-celebrity charities, the Ray Charles Robinson Foundation was rated as one of the top five most efficient non-profit organisations with zero administrative overheads.

Aside from the April meeting with the senators, 1987 unfolded much on the same pattern as recent years, although now he was in the latter half of his fifties, Ray was receiving more frequent civic accolades and other awards – not least of which was a Lifetime Achievement Award from the National Academy of Recording Arts and Sciences.

Also more frequent were the concert dates with string orchestras, which had started in the early Eighties with Sid Feller arrangements taking the place of the big band charts. These "string gigs" were often held in grand civic concert halls or arts centres, and Ray would just have to turn up with his rhythm section, Feller often acting as conductor. Sometimes the string ensemble would be a local symphony orchestra, on other dates it would be made up of musicians booked specially for the occasion via a local agent. Ex-drummer John Bryant was one such "fixer" who would hire the players for Ray when he had a string engagement in the Dallas area.

Having worked on it off and on through the year, as 1987 became 1988 Ray got the final mixes of his new album laid down. Recorded on home ground at the RPM Studios, Ray came back to his "mixed bag" formula sounding refreshed after his artistic sojourn in the country. On *Just Between Us* Ray hits all the buttons of his versatility, from the opening up-tempo R&B 'Nothing Like A Hundred Miles' to the humorous finale, the oldie 'Save The Bones For Henry Jones' which has Ray jousting with Lou Rawls and his old *Soul Brothers* partner Milt Jackson on vibes.

In between the mood ranges from the heartfelt ballad 'I Wish I'd Never Loved You At All', with Gladys Knight guesting, through the slow bluesy 'If That's What'Cha Want' to a country-flavoured 'Over The Top'. Quincy Jones features on a great working of the Gershwin standard 'Let's Call The Whole Thing Off', but the R&B high point comes on the guitar-driven blues of 'Too Hard To Love You', written by guitarist and singer/songwriter Calvin James, then known by his original name of James C. Johnson.

James recalled how Ray not only used the number, but booked him to play on the track. "The phone rang and that unmistakable voice said, 'Jim Johnson . . . this is Ray.' I thought someone was playing a joke. Then he said, 'I heard your song, 'Too Hard To Love You', and I want to record it.' Like I'd say no to Ray Charles! Then he said, 'And I want you to play guitar on it.' I said, 'Ray, I'll do it under one condition . . . that you don't be hollerin' at me.' Ray said, 'WHAT?' and I said, 'I heard about you.' Ray laughed – 'I promise I won't yell at you.' He kept that promise. We had one beautiful night and one great day in the studio together."

As well as recording the song, Ray gave Jim Johnson his start in the publishing business by agreeing to co-publish the song, rather than taking full publishing rights as he normally did when he signed writers to Tangerine Music. "We stood at the reception desk and Ray dictated the contract to his assistant, Ethel," James remembers. "When she gave it to me to sign, I just made the motions. Ray could tell I hadn't put the pen to paper. He shook his head and told me to sign it for real. His senses were so sharp." Ray also gave Johnson some forthright advice about playing his music and the music business generally – "Attack, Johnson, always attack!" "Ray was grabbing my wrist and shaking it as he said it, I'll never forget that moment."

The album finished, Ray was on the road again in May 1988, but not before two very different appearances in New York City. First there was a 100th birthday tribute concert at Carnegie Hall in honour of Irving Berlin, who many regarded as the father of American song, and about whom songwriter Jerome Kern once said: "Irving Berlin has no place in American music – he *is* American music." To celebrate the long life of the man who wrote such evergreens as 'Easter Parade', 'White Christmas', 'There's No Business Like Show Business' and 'Alexander's Ragtime Band', as well as Ray the line-up included Shirley McLaine, Tony Bennett and Marilyn Horne, the latter leading the whole ensemble in a spectacular 'God Bless America' finale with the aisles filled with uniformed Boy and Girl Scouts.

The concert, promoted by ASCAP (the American Society of Composers, Authors and Publishers) was broadcast as a three-hour special on CBS TV, with Ray performing stunning versions of the Berlin classics 'How Deep Is The Ocean' and 'What'll I Do'. Characteristically, Berlin, who led a reclusive existence in later life, refused to acknowledge the tribute and apparently didn't even watch it on television.

Next up was a project with Ray Charles, a small band involving old buddies David Newman, Phil Guilbeau and Hank Crawford, The Raelettes, an orchestra and the New York City Ballet, in choreographer Peter Martins' American Music Festival ballet *A Fool For You*. The 40-minute piece had dancers performing to a medley based on some of Ray's classic records, and was a hit with the capacity audience at the Lincoln Center. When it made a return appearance a year later, the live performance telecast, on *Live From Lincoln Center*, was viewed by over 2.7 million households.

Like so many of his albums through the Seventies and Eighties, the sheer quality of *Just Between Us* failed to impact on its sales. It was undoubtedly a difficult time for an artist like Ray. Whereas he once had a self-created niche in the market place – whether as an undisputed soul icon, or mainstream favourite with a unique interpretation of standards and country songs – now Ray's commercial identity was harder to sell. In an era when album-oriented rock ruled the airwaves and record company promotion budgets, "quality" entertainers (a broad description that took in everyone from Sinatra to Streisand) relied more and more on lucrative live work in Las Vegas supper clubs and big auditoriums – and their back catalogue of classic recordings.

It was a fact that, after four albums of which only one made any significant showing, CBS were only too aware of. They'd signed Ray primarily as a "country" artist anyway, and he had chosen to revert to his wider, more varied repertoire. So when they decided to part company in the autumn of 1988, the separation was entirely mutual.

18

My World

"You ask me what I'd like to do that I haven't done, and I say, 'Nothin'!' I haven't any mountains to climb or oceans to swim. I've been an extremely blessed individual. I'm not clamourin' for more trinkets. If I were to die tomorrow, I could say I've had a good life."

— Ray Charles

By 1989 Ray Charles was once again without a label to release his material, but as always he carried on preparing songs for his eventual next album. But curiously, Ray's next outing to hit the shops was a single that originated – and was only released – in Europe. While touring there, as had become almost a habit, Ray met with Jean-Pierre Grosz, a lifelong fan and jazz entrepreneur with whom he'd first got involved in 1978 when the Frenchman passed him some numbers by a songwriter friend – one of which, 'Just Because', Ray used on his Atlantic album *Ain't It So*.

Now Grosz was managing jazz singer Dee Dee Bridgewater, and had booked her to open Ray's show at the Paris Palais des Sports – the same vast but draughty venue where Ray had made his Paris debut in 1961. Grosz suggested Bridgewater and Ray record a duet together, Ray agreed, and not long after a single ''Til The Next Somewhere' was topping the charts in most countries across Europe. It would also signal the start of a more ambitious working relationship between Jean-Pierre and Ray in the middle years of the Nineties.

He also recorded another duet single late in 1989, released under Quincy Jones' name (on the latter's Warner subsidiary label Qwest) as "featuring Ray Charles and Chaka Khan". Catching on immediately on the disco dance scene, by the early weeks of 1990 'I'll Be Good To You' – a high-energy revival of a 1976 hit by The Brothers Johnson – had peaked at number 18 in the *Billboard* pop charts, topping the R&B chart and also scoring heavily in the UK (where it made 21) and elsewhere. The single also went on to win a Grammy for the best R&B vocal by a duo or group. But never forgetting his musical roots, while climbing the charts on a disco kick in November he was named chairman of the Washington-based Rhythm & Blues Foundation.

And as the new decade approached, Ray got the label deal he was looking for, this time struck with Mo Ostin, President of Warner Brothers Records which was now part of the massive Warner-Elektra-Atlantic group, WEA. He was still working on songs he'd been readying for the best part of the last year; they would constitute his debut on Warner Brothers, when the time came.

But at the beginning of 1990, Ray's profile was raised to a far greater degree than any of his recent record releases had managed to achieve via a series of TV commercials for Pepsi cola in which he was teamed with football star Joe Montana of the San Francisco 49ers. In one of the ads a blindfolded Montana takes "the Pepsi Challenge", trying to tell a Coke from a Pepsi. In front of Montana sit *two* Diet Cokes, but he's not fooled. Then, as he pulls away the blindfold, he, and we, see Ray Charles sipping a Diet Pepsi. The jokey ads immediately connected with the cultural heartland of Middle America – sports fans – that same constituency that probably remembered Ray's country output more than anything else he'd ever done.

Commercials were nothing new for Ray. Back in the mid-Sixties he'd endorsed Pepsi's rival Coca-Cola in a series of radio ads he'd produced himself at RPM, some of them with Aretha Franklin. Then from 1975 to '77 he did a series of spots for Olympia Beer, and in '77 also appeared on TV breaks extolling the virtues of Scotch recording tape. 1982 saw him urging viewers to "get that good to the last drop feeling" while soulfully crooning the virtues of Maxwell House coffee, and he appeared as an animated "claymation" raisin singing 'I Heard It Through The Grapevine' in a 1988 TV commercial for California Raisins.

Ray's popularity as a familiar figure was boosted in 1991 when Pepsi renegotiated his original one-year contract for an estimated $3 million, launching what would be rated the most memorable commercial of that year. With a Raelette-like trio, the ads involved Ray singing a catchy jingle to the ladies, and then in various mock scenarios, always ending with the hook "You got the right one baby, uh-huh" which soon had the nation joining in. And for those that missed it, photo "opportunities" were available with life-size cut-out figures of Ray Charles and The

Raelettes at selected supermarkets, followed in some shopping malls by personal appearances.

Importantly the "Uh-uh" campaign appealed to Americans across the board, young and old alike. In its own way as potent a part of his broad repertoire as 'America The Beautiful', the Pepsi ditty suddenly elevated Ray Charles – now completely white-haired and into his sixties – to the status of a national treasure. When writer Robert Gordon mentioned a friend's kid who saw Ray on TV and said, "There's the Pepsi cola man," Ray agreed that the ads gave him cross-generational appeal. "The name of the game, man, is keeping people into you in whatever you do. Right now the Pepsi thing is very, very popular. You say just kids, but the old folks dig it too. But these youngsters, when they get to be 20, and God knows if I'll be around, they'll be saying, 'Mr Charles, I remember that Pepsi commercial. My mama had all your records, I've been hearing you all my life.'"

In 1994 the TV commercials would take an even more bizarre twist, when Ray was signed up as the star of a series of car adverts. Here he was, a smiling, blind man in a bright red convertible, confidently making his driving debut at the age of 63 – although it *was* shot on the deserted landscape of the Great Salt Lake in Utah.

While the first series of Pepsi ads were amusing viewers across America, on February 21, 1990, Ray Charles' contribution to the evolution of modern popular music was acknowledged by the National Academy of Recording Arts and Sciences, when 'I Got A Woman' was inducted into the Hall of Fame at the 32nd Grammy Awards ceremony. Then on May 5 he took part in recognition of another musical giant, performing The Beatles' 'Let It Be' at a John Lennon Tribute Concert held on Liverpool's Pier Head. The open-air event on the banks of the River Mersey involved an all-star line-up that also included Paul McCartney, Ringo Starr, Elton John, Billy Joel, Joe Cocker, Hall & Oates, David Bowie, Roy Orbison and Cyndi Lauper.

Touring with the band from the summer of '90 took Ray through the usual venues across America and Europe, ending with a week at the prestigious Blue Note jazz club on West 3rd Street in New York's Greenwich Village. And immediately after the Village gig, starting September 29 he laid the band off for a few weeks while he joined B.B. King in the Phillip Morris Superband on a five continent world tour taking in places as far flung as Milan and Tokyo. The tour, sponsored by Phillip Morris cigarettes and also including jazz luminaries Gene Harris, Jeff Clayton,

Roy Brown and trumpet legend Harry "Sweets" Edison, ended up on November 10 at the Apollo Theater in Harlem.

And as the Superband was jetting around the world, in October Warner Brothers released their first album by Ray Charles, a collection of the tracks he'd been working on at RPM since early in 1989 with in-house writer Jimmy Lewis. Right at the start of the project Lewis had brought in Richard Cason, a synthesiser virtuoso who exploited the possibility of creating brass, strings, guitar, percussion – all the sounds you might need – on the electronic keyboard. Ray, as ever fascinated by the recording process and how he could use new innovations in his music, was intrigued.

The music on the resulting album, *Would You Believe?*, consisted of just Ray (plus soul singer Peggy Scott on one track) and Cason's computerised accompaniment. Co-produced by Ray and Lewis (who wrote half of the songs), despite the contemporary Nineties backing the collection features Ray's usual mix of R&B, ballads and the odd novelty song. Although Ray delivers his vocals with gritty panache, the contrast with the hi-tech sounds is refreshing on first hearing but ultimately rather bland.

The liveliest track, the Lewis-penned 'Child Support, Alimony', is a humorous tirade against money-grabbing ex-wives with sentiments that are *very* Ray. Equally the Peggy Scott duet 'Let's Get Back To Where We Left Off' works as a soulful slice of modern R&B, but too many offerings like the gospel-based 'I Can't Get Enough' and 'Living Without You' (shades of 'Drown In My Own Tears') come over as gimmicky rehashes of previously successful formulae. Having said that, one track – 'Ellie, My Love' – had already topped the charts in Japan before the album was released.

However, a Japanese hit notwithstanding, the album sank without trace as soon as it hit the shops. The executives at Warners weren't exactly surprised, they had not been enthusiastic about the material since first hearing it, but Ray was calling the shots so they had to put it out anyway. An interesting side-note to the album's release was the cover photography; it was the work of Vincent Kotchounian, who was Ray's son by his Parisian lover Arlette Kotchounian, a songwriter (also known as Ann Grégory) who he'd first met in 1967.

As the "Uh-huh" series of Pepsi ads started rolling at the beginning of 1991, Ray's media presence was increasingly positive despite the dearth of album successes. "Everywhere I go in the world, people are very, very familiar with my music. Look at my name like a household word," he'd say in 1992. "You mention Ray Charles anywhere in the world, people gonna know who the hell you're talking about. I hope you don't think that the only reason I can still go out and fill houses is because I do Pepsi commercials. I was doing that long before the commercial ever came out."

So, lucrative though the commercials were, in order for regular money to come into the organisation Ray (although individually a very rich man) continued to rely on live concert dates. And in any case, as he would always stress, live performance was at the heart of the music that was his life — always had been, always would be. The only difference between gigging around the chitlin' circuit one-nighters and the way he played dates now, he insisted, was the size of the band and entourage, and the often exotic locations visited on worldwide touring.

One such visit came in February, when Ray and the band were booked for a couple of gigs in New Zealand. Australian promoter Glenn Wheatley, then working for the IMG company, told me how their arrival nearly ended in disaster.

"I had to meet Ray at the airport to help him in case there were any problems getting him and the band through customs. It was just as well I did, because unfortunately one of the band members was carrying a very small amount of marijuana in his jacket." New Zealand, with its strict rules about importing foodstuffs, always has sniffer dogs at points of entry, and this time it was more than a packet of biscuits that excited them.

"So of course the police dogs could smell it, and one dog absolutely pounced on this guy's crutch. Joe Adams went crazy — 'Who's in charge here?' — and I put my hand up. 'Get that dog off my . . .' — he was going absolutely nuts about this dog. The policeman said, 'Well sorry sir, he's obviously carrying something, you'll have to let me go through the process.' So the customs came up, and the guy *was* carrying a little bit — not enough to get anybody in real trouble, it was obviously for personal use. But the police in New Zealand took a very dim view of this, and they're saying, 'We're going to have to deport him,' and I'm thinking, 'Oh God, this is going to become an international incident, it's going to be on CNN and all over the place.' So I had to go back to them, and said, 'Please let's try and hose it down a little bit. It's a very small amount and clearly for the guy's own personal use.'"

By this time however, more trouble was about to erupt. Ray, it seems, had a habit of eating pork rind, and he had with him a little plastic bag of pork rinds. "To the dogs he smelled like a bacon rasher, so they're going crazy with Ray as well. Ray's not carrying any substances, he's just smelling like bacon! By this time Joe Adams is going *berserk*, shouting at me, 'You get that dog off Mr Charles now!'

"Imagine when he was going through customs, not sure of what's going on, all he can hear is dogs barking, then there's dogs crawling all over him. That's got to be scary. He was sitting there holding his braille copy of *Playboy*, then it began to gel for him – 'What's going on man, what's going on?'– it must have been terrible for him."

Fearing the worst, Wheatley calmed things down. "I thought, 'We just don't need an international incident. I've got a show tomorrow night.' Anyway, we all calmed everything down, and I had to sit down and negotiate through this very carefully, signing a guarantee that these people wouldn't be doing any more substances, and there would be good behaviour while they were in New Zealand."

Wheatley got them out of the airport and to the hotel, after which they went on to do a magical open-air show during a beautiful night in Auckland, the next day flying in a small plane for a gig at the Mission Estate on the picturesque Hawke's Bay near the town of Napier. Not that Ray could appreciate the scenery, as Wheatley wryly recalled, having booked him a couple of times after that first trip: "He'd just arrive right at the deadline and do the show, and then go. Ray had a nasty habit of always turning up at the last minute, and when I mentioned this his famous line to me was, 'What am I gonna do, go sightseeing?'"

Into the Nineties, and the world was now truly Ray's stage. Individual musicians might come and go, but the band, as an instrument of Ray Charles' whole *raison d'être*, would continue the treks between airport, hotel, concert hall and the next airport, just as long as its leader chose to do so. "There are plenty of people who will show up at any Ray Charles event and don't care about genius or perfect tempos or creative fire," wrote Bob Porter, blues presenter on New Jersey's WBGO jazz station, in 1996. "They will show up because Ray Charles means more to them than mere music. It's as though he were teaching Sunday School and attendance was required."

David Hoffman joined the band in the early part of the decade, and stayed for more than a dozen years both as trumpet and flugelhorn player, and arranger. That was longer than a lot of the jobbing musicians that Ray recruited, who would stick at it for a couple of seasons before moving on. But, in common with many of those players, he first got the gig on a last-minute call from Ray himself, leaving little time for either formal audition or even rehearsal, as he would explain to me: "A friend of mine, Jeff Helgesen – a great trumpet player who played with Ray from about 1987 – he left the band, and before he went he let me know he was leaving, and that if I wanted to try to get the gig I should send a tape. So I sent a tape, and a few months went by, and I thought nothing was going to happen – then Ray called me on the phone.

"The first gig was at the Hollywood Bowl in Los Angeles, for the Playboy Jazz Festival. I got there in time for just one proper rehearsal, because he called me on the Tuesday and I got there by Thursday, and the gig was on the Friday. And so there we were on stage at the Hollywood Bowl."

Hoffman was handed his set list just minutes before the start of the show, and had to search for the numbers in a chart book he'd never seen before. Then as the stage revolved into position, a gust of wind caught his stand and the sheets of music started to fly away, the new boy catching most of them but now having the charts in serious disorder. To add to his problems, he'd been hurriedly issued with an ill-fitting band suit, with a jacket too small and pants several sizes too big. He had a couple of solos on that first date which involved him walking to the front of the band to take them; suddenly he considered the very real prospect of his pants falling down in front of 10,000 people at the Hollywood Bowl – "so it was a bit stressful".

But his pants stayed on, and so did he, embarking immediately on a six month tour during which he soon became acquainted with Ray's working style. "He could be touchy . . . which musically was okay, because it was nice to know what he wanted. And actually there were some times when he'd try to explain something – like the way he played ballads, which was just unlike anyone else would play them – and it took a while getting into. And he'd get real touchy if you didn't do it the way he wanted to do it. Then sometimes personally, he was just . . . a little bit difficult."

Like so many before him, Hoffman also had to get used to Ray Charles' timing. He remembered how it sometimes took new musicians weeks to understand how to play at the ultra-slow tempos. "The time would be so elastic, and it was so slow, he'd style it so slowly, that you couldn't do any-thing except just *feel* how he was doing it. You couldn't just subdivide it like you can with most bands. You couldn't think of, say, eight counts, you just had to think of these *long* stretches of time.

"It was especially hard on rhythm sections that way. The drummer used to say the only way he could really follow was to watch Ray's feet, because his feet and his whole body would be conducting. It did affect the brass section too, because sometimes we were playing something that had to be right with him, some of the shout choruses especially, and at first you *do* watch his feet, and then you start just kind of getting it, and you don't have to. It's still good to reference that, but basically you're just kind of feeling it the way he's feeling it."

On his website, David Hoffman describes how he often witnessed Ray's creative process in action. "He would hear a tune he liked, and decide to perform it. You would catch him doodling around on the piano, trying to come up with something different in the chord structure or the melody. Again, making the tune personal to him. He decided that he wanted to sing Paul Simon's tune 'Still Crazy After All These Years'. I thought this was an odd selection for him, and the first few nights that he sang it, it sounded awkward. But gradually it began to sound like Ray Charles. It took many performances, and it took him knowing the tune so well he could just let go and be himself. And at that point, it was terrific. Ray has been termed a genius, but to me this does not describe him. It was workmanship, it was persistence, and more than anything it was a way of personalising a song."

Soon after he joined the band Hoffman became aware that Ray would show his approval of something as clearly as he would indicate disapproval, just by his physical reactions at the piano. "On 'Just For A Thrill' there's a very nice improvised flugelhorn solo. One night Ray said that he wanted me to play that solo. I played that night, and Ray seemed happy enough, although I could tell he wasn't ecstatic with my performance. He called me into his dressing room after the gig. He wasn't unhappy, but wanted to give me a bit of direction on how to play the tune . . . he just played it for me on the piano, the way he wanted it.

"He called the tune again the next night. I followed his direction, and he reacted by squirming so enthusiastically on his piano bench that he appeared to be in danger of falling off. This, along with grunt-like vocalisations, was how he indicated his approval.

"You never really knew for sure what would make Ray squirm, but I think I can speak for all of us in the band that it was something we wanted to see happen. So when I played that solo, I would try different things, gauging Ray's reaction to them. Sometimes he would react to something simple and bluesy, sometimes to a short display of virtuosity, sometimes to one held note. In time, by watching his reactions, I began to get a sense of what excited him musically, and within a few weeks had him squirming just about every time I played that solo.

"Ray had other methods of getting what he wanted, including out and out screaming at the rhythm section, or the sound man, or to anyone that happened to displease him even in the slightest. But the most effective way was his profound joy at hearing something that moved him musically. This is ultimately how he moulded his band into an extension of himself, and why at its best the band moved with Ray, breathed with Ray, and swayed to the beat with Ray. Those moments made the difficult life on the road meaningful for me."

Among the many memorable dates that Hoffman would play with Ray Charles was one during that first year of his tenure with the band, on September 19, 1991. As if to confirm Ray's status as a venerated member of the American music establishment, with fortunes revived by the increased recognition he was enjoying as a result of the Pepsi ads, his 61st birthday was celebrated with a gala concert at the Civic Auditorium in Pasadena, just east of Los Angeles. Entitled "Ray Charles – 50 Years in Music", the spectacular event featured a host of well-wisher participants including Stevie Wonder, Willie Nelson, Gladys Knight, Michael Bolton, Bill Cosby, Gloria Estefan, MC Hammer, James Ingram, Quincy Jones, Randy Travis, and even Paul McCartney with a videotaped greeting from London. Not always the case in such events – which was filmed and broadcast as a TV special in October – the music was magnificent, the high point being a stunning duet with Ray and Stevie Wonder on the latter's 'Living For The City', though for many home viewers across the United States it was probably the emotional finale with the whole cast joining Ray on 'America The Beautiful'.

Just as Ray was embracing the world, it seemed like the world – or his world of America at least – was embracing Ray. Towards the end of 1991 Atlantic Records released a box set, *Ray Charles: The Birth Of Soul*, which featured all his Atlantic singles on three CDs with copiously detailed liner notes. Its very title marked a recognition of what Ray's legacy really represented in terms of the history of popular music. Then, in January 1992 the Public Service Broadcasting network in America aired the first comprehensive warts-and-all documentary about his life and career, called *Ray Charles: The Genius Of Soul*. Written, directed and narrated by Yvonne Smith, it pulled few punches when talking about his drug habit, his womanising and so on, but at the same time reinforced the notion of Ray Charles as a seminal figure in modern American culture.

He was presented with the Distinguished Service Medal as the 1992 Black History Month recipient by the County Board of Supervisors in

February 1992, in recognition of his "outstanding contributions". And in the same month he was inducted into the Florida Artists Hall of Fame, joining Ernest Hemingway and Tennessee Williams, among others. Ray Charles wasn't just a venerated musician any more, or everybody's cuddly Uncle Ray from the Cola ads. He was fast becoming a national institution.

To many industry watchers the choice of Richard Perry, who Warners had mooted to co-produce Ray's next album, was intriguing to say the least. Having cut his teeth on left field projects such as Captain Beefheart's debut album and the bizarre Tiny Tim, his chequered track record included work with Ella Fitzgerald and Barbra Streisand, a comeback album for Fats Domino, Ringo Starr's most commercially successful work and projects with retro-vocal stylists Manhattan Transfer and disco divas The Pointer Sisters. Like Ray, he had an eclectic taste and the hand of a time-served professional. Whether the two could work together, given Ray's aversion to "outside" interference in his music, was another question.

In the event, as the album *My World* developed through the latter half of 1992, the two worked largely apart, Perry putting together backing tracks based on charts provided by Ray, Ray then overdubbing the vocals. Three elements on the resultant collection guaranteed its success, artistically if not commercially – very strong material, most of it hand-picked by Perry (with Ray's final approval, of course); some big-name session players and guest stars; and Ray simply at his latter-day best.

The two most familiar numbers are among the strongest tracks. A marvellous only-Ray-could-do-it interpretation of Leon Russell's 'A Song For You' reveals the strength in a previously bland-sounding item, and his solid R&B take on Paul Simon's 'Still Crazy After All These Years' complements rather than competes with the original. The studio musicians, including drummers Steve Gadd and Abe Laboriel, keyboard ace Greg Phillinganes and guitarist Paul Jackson Jr, keep everything at high-octane level, from the gospelly 'So Help Me God' to the funky 'Let Me Take Over'. Star names include Billy Preston on organ, who is unfortunately often lost down in the mix, and Eric Clapton. The blues guitar supremo solos tellingly on 'None Of Us Are Free', the main "message" song on the album written by soul diva Brenda Russell and songwriting veterans Barry Mann & Cynthia Weill.

The vocal guests backing Ray are similarly distinguished, with Mavis Staples adding to the drama of 'Love Has A Mind Of Its Own' and the

Family Stone's Rose Stone shining on 'Let Me Take Over'. Instrumentally Ray hardly plays a note, apart from a synthesiser break on 'Still Crazy', but his vocals more than compensate for that on an album that sets his customary mix of ballads, R&B and gospel in a highly contemporary context. There's even a touch of light hip-hop in the title track and 'I'll Be There'.

The album received some glowing reviews, many of them significantly in the hip end of the music press. Giving it three stars, *Rolling Stone* enthused that it "takes the sound of Charles' best Sixties records and discreetly updates it by underlining the swelling gospel choruses with crisp, techno-improved beats." Q magazine wrote, "The old champion still has it in him to inject feeling and human spirit into the most startling of covers," while *Entertainment Weekly* gushed, "When Richard Perry loosens things up and goes for the funk, Brother Ray really starts testifying." And in a move taking himself even closer to the rock mainstream, early in 1993 Ray made an appearance on the album *Full Moon, Dirty Hearts* by INXS. His not-to-be-ignored presence on the track 'Please (You've Got That . . .)' did much to bring out the basically soul-driven sound of the band.

When *My World* was released in March '93 it failed to impact on record buyers in the way WB had hoped. Even a taster single featuring 'A Song For You' – which peaked at number nine on the Adult Contemporary charts and went on to win a Grammy award for Best Male R&B Vocal Performance – didn't generate sufficient airplay to kick-start the album. Ray Charles might have become a national institution to the country at large, but in the youth-driven world of the music industry he was in danger of being perceived as a museum piece, fashionable production and trendy backings notwithstanding.

Seemingly confirming his insistence that appearances with Republican presidents were not motivated by party preference, in January 1993 Ray joined other invited celebrity performers in the pre-inaugural concert at the Lincoln Memorial honouring President Bill Clinton. Entitled "Call for Reunion", the two-hour free concert attracted a crowd of several hundred thousand, who crowded onto the mall to see a line-up of celebrities including Aretha Franklin, Michael Bolton, Tony Bennett, Bob Dylan, Diana Ross and rapper L.L. Cool J. Plus Ray, who – perhaps inevitably – sang 'America The Beautiful'.

Later in the year, in October, Ray attended a dinner at the White

House at which President Clinton presented him with the National Medal of Arts. The other 11 recipients of the honour that evening included playwright Arthur Miller, painter Robert Rauschenburg, veteran film director Billy Wilder and the 85-year-old jazz singer and bandleader Cab Calloway. Saxophone-playing Bill Clinton was obviously something of a fan; when, on MTV's *A Town Hall Meeting With President Clinton*, he was asked to name his favourite song, his answer was Ray's version of 'A Song For You'.

Meanwhile, between the concert halls, European dates, TV chat shows and life at RPM, less grandiose but equally meaningful accolades were bestowed upon Ray. On June 2, 1993, Billy Joel (a lifelong fan who named his daughter after Ray Charles) had presented him with the Lifetime Achievement Award at the 24th annual Songwriters Hall of Fame dinner at the Sheraton Hotel in New York. And in December he was one of 15 artists that got a star at the inaugural "Sidewalk of the Stars" outside New York's Radio City Music Hall.

And the honours and awards kept coming into 1994. In March Ray received a Lifetime Achievement Award as part of the Black Achievement Awards television show, sponsored by the Johnson Publishing Company. Then, on May 12, he was presented with the Helen Keller Personal Achievement Award from the American Foundation for the Blind.

By this time Ray Charles had probably accrued more citations and tributes than almost anyone in popular music, but ironically he was yet again without a record label. After the expense, ballyhoo and subsequent failure of *My World*, Warner Brothers had decided to pass on any further albums with the ageing star. And, as was his nature, Ray doggedly got down to his next studio project, this time with his Parisian friend Jean-Pierre Grosz.

The two had started working on an album in 1992, Grosz submitting songs by various songwriters, then making instrumental tracks in France for the ones Ray chose. The whole project was put on hold when Jean-Pierre's father was diagnosed with cancer, and overtaken for the time being by *My World*. But now they were committed once again, furiously editing and mixing vocal and backing tracks through the months of 1994 when Ray wasn't out on the road.

The resulting *Strong Love Affair* turned out to be one of the unsung high points of his Nineties' output. With Ray's usual pot pourri of moods from modern R&B to graceful ballads, there's an elegant charm to the album which undoubtedly owes much to Grosz's hand in the majority of tracks.

Ray's voice has a well-rounded, softer edge to it, gelling smoothly with the part-orchestral, part-synthesised backings. On first hearing some of the songs, like 'I Need A Good Woman Bad' and the title track, sound a little trite. But there's an underlying strength to the whole collection – particularly on the emotion-wrenching 'Angelina' and Ray's closing duet with soul singer Peggy Scott-Adams, 'If You Give Me Your Heart' – that permeates every number.

Though the album was wrapped up production-wise by the end of '94, it took another year to see it on sale in America. Grosz had fixed a release for it on an Italian label, but a major deal eluded them despite efforts by both him and Ray to come up with a contract. Eventually Ray's most loyal and longest-standing ally in the music business, Quincy Jones, stepped into the breach. Not specifically for *Strong Love Affair* – he just couldn't see Ray without a label for his next album, so signed his old buddy to his Qwest label – but it was *Strong Love Affair* that he got. As Columbia and Warners had found out, and Atlantic second time round, when you signed Ray, you got what Ray wanted you to have.

When the album was eventually released in January 1996, too late to hit the Christmas holiday market, Warner-owned Qwest also got the kind of results that Ray's other recent labels had experienced: good reviews followed by bad sales figures. It would be Ray's last new album to come out for over six years.

All the time he and the Frenchman were wheeling and dealing through 1995 – and there was more wheeling than dealing until Quincy came into the frame – Ray's life was otherwise as hectic as ever.

On March 2, 1995, he received another Lifetime Achievement citation, this time at the 6th annual Rhythm & Blues Foundation Pioneer Awards. Then the band were back on the road by the early summer, but Ray made sure he had time to collect the Horatio Alger Award in June, an honour particularly close to his heart. Founded in 1947, the Horatio Alger Association of Distinguished Americans describes its mission as "Honouring the achievements of outstanding individuals in our society who have succeeded in spite of adversity, and encouraging young people to pursue their dreams through higher education".

Between gigs across the Midwest, dates in South America and cabaret in Las Vegas he even squeezed in an appearance on TV's *Sesame Street*, though not for the first time. All in all he appeared in several episodes of the kid's programme that featured the Muppets along with celebrity guests. One memorable appearance was when he sang 'Georgia On My Mind' to the assembled puppets, on another he gave them 'Oh What A Beautiful Morning'. But the strongest bond with the show came after he had adopted Kermit the Frog's anthem 'It Ain't Easy Being Green' as part of his repertoire, including it on his 1975 *Renaissance* album.

The Shrine Auditorium in Los Angeles was the venue for a lavish 80th birthday bash in honour of Frank Sinatra on November 19, taped and subsequently broadcast by ABC television on the singer's actual birthday on December 12. The 30-plus line-up of celebrities included movie stars Angela Lansbury, Robert Wagner and Gregory Peck, while the music world was represented by artists as diverse as Bruce Springsteen, Natalie Cole, Bono, Tony Bennett, Little Richard, Bob Dylan and many more. Ray, appearing right after TV star Roseanne Barr, sang a show-stopping version of 'Ol' Man River'.

The opening weeks of 1996 saw the inauspicious release of *Strong Love Affair*, but this time, as yet another album floundered, Ray wasn't busying himself with the next one. He was always fooling around at RPM with new material of course, he'd spend hours there tinkering with this, mixing down that, but there was no grand plan now, no new album around the next corner. It was almost as if he realised it was time to pause and take stock of things.

Outside the cream walls of the 30-year-old RPM building life continued much as normal. On February 27, Ray performed 'Let The Good Times Roll' at the 27th annual Image Awards of the civil rights organisation, the National Association for the Advancement of Colored People (NAACP) in honour of Quincy Jones. Then in May, Ray received an Honorary Doctorate in Performing Arts from Occidental College, just before the band got back on the road after a longer-than-usual early year break. The itinerary was as worldwide as ever, as well as winding across the United States, taking in European festivals – including a date on the same bill as Van Morrison at London's Wembley Arena in June – South America, and at the end of the year, Japan.

Increasingly over the last few years, however, Ray's performances were conducted with just a regular rhythm section and orchestras put together for the occasion by the promoter. The drummer with Ray through most of the Nineties was Peter Turre, with John Bryant (who'd left the band in '75) deputising from time to time: "His regular drummer was Peter Turre, who I think can probably claim that he played more gigs with Ray than any other drummer. Peter had to take off a few times, and he spoke with Ray about who he wanted to sub, and they called me to substitute for him. So then I would fly out to these gigs – they were mainly symphony gigs."

These dates were often grand civic or corporate affairs – arts festivals, business conferences and so on. Typical of these far better paid engagements (and where Ray didn't bear the expense of transporting and paying a band) was one on May 8, 1997, when Ray was booked to play at the opening of the luxurious Crown Casino complex in Melbourne, Australia.

Glenn Wheatley, who'd rescued Ray's arrival in New Zealand from disaster back in 1991, was promoter of the whole event. Wheatley had flown to Los Angeles weeks before to go through things with Ray, who would only be required to perform for 20 minutes but also join in a finale number with two of the show's other stars, Kylie Minogue and John Farnham, a big name in Australia whom Wheatley managed. Ray was happy with the arrangement, and Glenn suggested the three might sing John Lennon's 'Imagine' as their trio spot. Ray agreed.

"So I thought, 'Well this is working out very nicely.' And it was all set up – very nervously – and when he arrived on the day of the show, everyone's heart was in their mouth because we'd been rehearsing for a week with the orchestra, but without Ray Charles. So he arrived at the show and I said, 'And are you ready to do "Imagine", Mr Charles?'

"And then Joe Adams stepped in and said, 'No, he's not doing "Imagine".'"

Wheatley was stunned, he'd understood it was all part of the deal.

"Kylie had learnt it, John had learnt it, and I didn't have any charts because I expected Ray to have all the charts ready . . ."

Adams blunt reply was, "No, we don't have the charts, we're not doing that song."

"That was a very tense and awkward moment because Lloyd Williams, the chairman of the casino company at the time the venue opened, was not very happy; he was a very demanding, very particular man. He knew exactly what he wanted and I'd told him about the running order and how we'd be doing this one song together, so of course it was very tense there for a while."

Wheatley eventually got Ray and Joe Adams to agree to go ahead with the number as planned. "But I had to have Chong Lim, John Farnham's music director, stay up all night, because although I got them to agree to do it, we didn't have the charts, and it was the night before the show."

Once the matter of 'Imagine' was settled, Ray threw himself into

263

rehearsal as if there'd never been a problem. Wheatley, a lifelong fan, was in awe. "Just to be able to see him walk up and find everything, how he knew where it was – he'd instinctively know where the microphone was – and work the way he did. They called him a genius and I think he was – he was just one of those great voices of our time, one of the great songwriters. I guess the most memorable thing, and this is the most fortunate side of being a manager or promoter, was to be at his side at the piano while he was doing his rehearsals with John and Kylie and [Australian opera star] Anthony Warlow – how extraordinary was that? That just sent shivers down your spine. And he required very little rehearsal. Because he improvises every time he sings, he had to discipline himself when he was singing with the other people, but they've got the ability of being able to watch and get a feel, but he's got to do it largely by himself, and expect the others in some respect to follow, because he can't follow any leads . . .

"But it turned out an extraordinary night, and one of the great nights of my life, to see Ray up there singing, and singing with John Farnham and Kylie Minogue – something I was very proud of doing."

In retrospect, Glenn Wheatley didn't have such fond memories of dealing with Joe Adams: "It was always a chore, because although Ray was always delightful, Joe always had to be difficult, and if there wasn't a problem I felt that Joe would create one."

He felt that Ray's relationship with Adams was somehow strained, particularly on that visit: "It always appeared to be edgy, but you stayed away from it. I could feel it was tense between him and Joe, and the second time he came I wasn't talking to Joe very much, I was talking to this young Frenchman who seemed to come in to the picture. I seem to think he was going to be the new management, and putting Joe out of the picture, but Joe quickly got back in control somehow, there was a bit of a coup I thought, that seemed to be happening at the time."

The Australian's instincts were spot-on. Over the preceding few months Ray hadn't just been taking stock of his recording, but thinking about the way his overall career was being managed. Like himself, Joe Adams wasn't getting any younger – he was 73 in 1997 – and Ray was thinking about replacing him. It got to the point where, on a European tour, Ray offered Jean-Pierre Grosz the job. There was already intense rivalry between the Parisian and Joe as far as the latter was concerned, but Grosz had carefully kept his distance over the years. Now Ray was offering him the job he probably dreamed of, even giving him a desk in the RPM offices, but things couldn't be changed that easily.

As soon as Adams got wind of the situation, he characteristically dug his heels in, and outmanoeuvred his challenger in the first round, making access inside the organisation and contacts outside as difficult as possible. Very soon things were back as they'd always been, Grosz in his Paris office, and Joe Adams in his at RPM.

One thing that did come out of the brief power struggle was Ray's version of 'Imagine', which Grosz produced and released as a single in France on the Qwest label. Recorded for the soundtrack of a commercial for a French bank, it featured the Harlem Gospel Singers in a sanctified-sounding version of Lennon's highly secular anthem ("Imagine there's no heaven, it's easy if you try"). With lush synth-strings rising under Ray's electric piano and a bluesy guitar, the choir magnificently omnipresent, it's a classic example of Ray putting his instantly recognisable stamp on a universally familiar song – and this was just for a TV ad!

The rest of 1997 was very much business as usual, with a clutch of European dates highlighted by an appearance at the Montreux Jazz Festival in Switzerland. Ray played Montreux on a number of occasions – including a famous collaboration with Dizzy Gillespie in July 1978 – but probably his finest concert there was the one that year, captured on a live CD and DVD released in 2002. The band, under the direction of alto player Al Jackson, sound stunning as Ray handles everything from light-hearted numbers like 'Busted' and 'Mississippi Mud' to intense ballads 'Angelina', 'People Will Say We're In Love' and 'Just For A Thrill'. Described by one reviewer as "a stellar performance", it demonstrates that although Ray often appeared to be just going through the motions on many gigs during his later years, when he rose to the occasion he was still a unique – and now revered – voice in the world of popular music.

It was a world that had changed much during the course of Ray's career, changes which he had very definite opinions about – as he would tell a journalist in September 1997 when asked if he could begin a music career in the present-day industry: "No. When I was coming up, the record people looked at the talent. I made about four records at Atlantic before I got a hit. Ain't no way I could be with a big company today and make four records that was not hits and they'd still keep me."

His comments on rap music were just as uncompromising: "You can't even print what I think. Just to *talk* to music, I did that years ago on 'It Should've Been Me' and 'Greenbacks'." And it wasn't the first time he'd made the point, he'd been saying it back in 1992: "I can't see how I can get anything out of rap music. I really can't. I've been talking ever since I was two! People say, 'Well look at it from a poetic point of view.' The poetry – for me – ain't that great."

On September 2, 1997, Ray signed a five-year agreement with Rhino Records for them to package his back catalogue, the first release in October being a magnificent 5-CD boxed set containing over 100 titles spanning his whole career. The subsequent re-releases of whole albums (usually with "bonus" tracks), plus various compilations, were studiously presented with facsimile covers and detailed liner notes. When the deal expired in 2003, Ray renewed the contract for a further five-year term.

Also in October, an honour that probably satisfied him more than most was bestowed upon Ray Charles, when he was inducted into the Jazz Hall of Fame.

And as if to confirm once again his across-the-board profile, he had a guest role on *The Nanny*, a weekly sitcom on CBS Television, in which he played Sammy, the fiancé of the heroine's twice-married 86-year-old grandmother, Yetta.

On March 14, 1998, Ray made a television appearance of a very different kind, a live broadcast on the QVC shopping channel to promote and sell a book and CD set entitled *Ray Charles: My Early Years (1930–1960)* for $25.97. But more in the world of conventional record retail, the Rhino programme of reissues paid off in April with *Ray Charles And Betty Carter/Dedicated To You*. Comprising his two ABC-Paramount albums from 1961, the CD peaked at number 13 on the R&B charts.

The touring continued through '98, albeit a little more intermittently. Everywhere he went, people wanted to talk to Ray, now more often as a respected father figure, a wise elder who would hand out some home-spun philosophy to the local media. "Do it right or don't do it at all," he opined in the Fort Lauderdale *Sun-Sentinel*. "That comes from my mom. If there's something I want to do, I'm one of those people that won't be satisfied until I get it done. If I'm trying to sing something and I can't get it, I'm going to keep at it until I get it where I want it."

Thirteen years after he had been one of the original inductees to the Rock'n'Roll Hall of Fame, on March 15, 1999, Ray presented Billy Joel with the same honour, at the 14th annual ceremony at the Waldorf-Astoria Hotel in New York.

As well as special dates like this, when he would usually sing at least one number if not a set, there were the occasional charity events, which seemed to increase in proportion to the rest of his gigs as Ray got older and his status nearer to that of a cultural institution. That same year he played a concert for the Miami Lighthouse for the Blind which was later released on a DVD, a sparkling set which included two duets with the Grammy-winning jazz singer Diane Schuur, another blind performer. Otherwise, apart from these ceremonials and gala functions, the road rolled on as usual.

The rest of touring was, as always for Ray, a job – it was what he *did* – as well as being a vocation – he couldn't for a minute contemplate giving it up. David Redfern photographed Ray Charles at more concerts than he can accurately quantify, 30 or more, from the days of the first British tours in the early Sixties through to the last times Ray visited Europe. He always had access backstage, and over the years saw a lot of Ray though never really made personal contact. Offstage Ray was screened from most people, be it venue employees, photographers or even fellow artists on the bill.

Asked as to whether he considered himself a loner, Ray had this to say: "Maybe that's not the word I'd use, let's just say I'm not going to have a lot of people around me unless it involves what I do, and by that I mean my work. It doesn't matter if we've got thousands of people out there in the audience, that's fine by me, but when it comes to more personal contact, I'm more low-key. And if you get more than four or five people around me, I call that a crowd."

Redfern recalls that apart from official press calls, you'd see little of Ray till showtime. At these of course, there was a modicum of contact afforded the media folk: "One time in the Nineties he gave a very intimate press conference in a small room in Juan-les-Pains, and those French journalists were asking the stock questions; 'Why do you like it here? . . .' What do you say? – there were no serious questions. He was very affable, and had a glass of wine with everybody, but I can't say I ever actually talked to him. Conversely, I was never given a hard time by anybody. I always got to photograph Ray Charles when I wanted to, and was never told I couldn't."

Keeping the press happy, ensuring venues had everything ready as requested before Ray arrived, juggling big band dates with intimate trio gigs, dovetailing this charity event with that symphony extravaganza, running through new numbers with the band, making sure the diary was open for the next awards ceremony or tribute concert, hiring (and occasionally firing) musicians as became necessary, slotting in television appearances; this was the week-by-week, month-by-month pattern of life for Ray Charles and Ray Charles Enterprises. Between which Ray pottered in the studio, listening to new songs and laying down basic tracks – even though, as the 20th century came to a close and the 21st became a reality, there was no new record deal or album project on the horizon.

19

Brother Ray

"I've been a very, very fortunate and blessed human being. The things that I genuinely wanted to do in my career I've been able to do."

– Ray Charles

I'm sitting at the bar of Pete's Tavern, one of the oldest pubs in New York City. There's a baseball game about to start on the TV, the second game of the World Series, broadcast live from the Bank One Ballpark in Phoenix, Arizona. The Arizona Diamondbacks are playing the New York Yankees, so there's a lot of local interest and the bartender's got the sound up a little louder than usual.

A familiar trumpet fanfare grabs my attention. There in the middle of the vast field, surrounded by a stadium-full of sports fans, is Ray Charles sitting alone at a grand piano, in close-up looking old, grizzled even, and somehow serene. As he breaks into 'America The Beautiful', stars and stripes flutter amid the crowd under the bright Arizona sunshine. The bar-room hubbub descends into a reverential silence, a cold Manhattan wind whispering gently outside. It's October 28, 2001, and less than two months since the most traumatic event in modern American history.

Ray's version of the unofficial anthem resonated across the country that autumn when he resumed one-nighters, just six days after the nation had ground to a halt on September 11. Unlike many of his countrymen, he didn't feel inclined to stop flying, though in cases like this the decision was made as much out of necessity as choice.

When a 12-date European tour kicked off in the middle of November, however, some of the team chose not to make the trip. Also taking in Germany, Switzerland, France, Denmark and Belgium, Ray performed with a trio when I saw him at London's Hammersmith Apollo on

November 23. He had, however, featured a big band on some of the earlier continental dates.

From the vantage point of the front row of the 3,600-seater auditorium, formerly the Hammersmith Odeon where Ray had played several times over the years, I got the feeling I was almost in an intimate cabaret room as Ray came on, sitting at a tiny electric keyboard just a few feet away, with only guitar, bass and drums as accompaniment.

The trio's short opening set had been fairly lacklustre, but once Ray sat down the atmosphere changed completely. The place positively crackled with energy as he opened with an instrumental, and his voice – mellower now, and pitching slightly less spectacularly since a 1999 throat problem – still wove magic into songs like no other could on earth. When he sang a blues, without the multi-textured arrangements of a big band behind him, the music was stripped down to its bare essentials, at the core of which was Ray Charles' soul. As he was led off the stage at the end of his one-hour set, stooping slightly and looking his 71 years, a tangible aura left with him, the stage not just emptier but colder without his presence. It was the last time he would play in the UK.

After the European dates, Ray rested over the Christmas holiday – "resting" usually including hours spent at RPM of course – then it was back to one-off engagements while the full band was still off the road in the New Year. One such booking involved two gigs in Australia in February 2002, one at the magnificent Sidney Myer Music Bowl in Melbourne, followed by a concert at a winery in the New South Wales countryside outside Sydney.

The first date was with the Australian Pops Orchestra, and supporting Ray on both concerts was the Australian soul singer Renée Geyer. Primarily influenced by Aretha Franklin, Geyer was nevertheless thrilled at getting the support slot: "His management hired me because they'd heard of me, and heard my stuff and wanted me to support him, and he'd okayed it. It was wonderful, him being the legend that he is. All through my life, while being inspired equally by other people, some more so, I've had times when he's touched me, and coming in close contact with Ray Charles and his music was incredible."

Like most fellow performers on Ray's gigs, Geyer didn't get to see a lot of him backstage. "He was kept away from people, mainly because they were just intent on getting him on and off stage and making sure he was comfortable. So there wasn't a whole lot of socialising . . ." But when she did meet Ray, Geyer was struck by one thing in particular. "When he came to greet me on the second night, he was just charming. When he asked for me and shook my hand, I loved the intoxicating smell of beautiful cigars and aftershave, it was regal, it was the smell of wealth. I just remember smelling my hands for about an hour after shaking his hand. I remembered that more than anything; apart from the fact that he was amazing, sounded great and looked wonderful, he smelt great . . ."

The off-duty days and weeks Ray had spent in the RPM studios over the past four or five years hadn't been time wasted – Ray knew that, even if the rest of the world didn't. With 2002 offering hope and anxiety in equal measure after the dark days of the previous year, in the spring Ray was ready to unveil his latest project. Co-produced with Billy Osborne, who also wrote most of the songs, *Thanks For Bringing Love Around Again* was released in June on a now *totally* independent Crossover label.

Keyboard player Osborne, with his vocalist-drummer brother Jeffrey, had been a member of Seventies funk outfit L.T.D. (Love, Togetherness and Devotion). After three US Top 40 hits they disbanded in the early Eighties, Billy creating a niche for himself as a songwriter and producer on the Los Angeles studio scene. His assiduous work with Ray over the months before the album's completion certainly paid dividends, artistically if not financially. *Thanks For Bringing Love Around Again* is nothing less than the *magnum opus* of Ray's final years.

A blues-driven work with an uncompromisingly contemporary edge, Ray marks out its territory right at the start with a bold (many would say foolhardy) restatement of his unassailable classic 'What'd I Say'. With some crisp trumpet and sax parts, supported by swooshing synth and chunky hip-hop beats layed down by a drum machine, it's best to forget the original and take this at face value. The spirit of the 1959 hit's still there, albeit expressed in some distinctly modern language. Ray even cross-references vocally with female counterparts – this time credited as The Waters rather than Raelettes.

Billy Osborne's 'Can You Love Me Like That' is hot R&B in a classic Ray mood. The humorous observations of comparable lovers through the ages name-check Samson & Delilah, Liz Taylor & Richard Burton, Antony & Cleopatra et al. The abdicated British monarch Edward VIII's even in there – "Edward left the throne for Wallace, Said he did not want to be no king" – as Ray trades vocals with Brenda Lee Egar in true Charles-Hendricks style.

A lazy, loping blues also from the pen of Osborne, 'How Do You Feel

The Morning After' has Ray's multi-tracked voice riding on a cushion of warm sweeps of synthesised sound. The female voices on the funky, spunky 'I Love You More Than I Ever Have' are likewise from a single source, one of the current Raelettes, Katrina Harper-Cooke.

A strident synth horn section brings in 'Really Got A Hold On Me', Ray super confident with the hi-tech world he'd clearly immersed himself in the years since his last album. The title track has a more traditional feel to it, the kind of modern ballad Ray had made his own on albums in the Nineties, with Brenda Lee Egar and Billy Osborne providing the backing vocals.

The closest thing on the album to down-home R&B comes with the magnificent 'Save Your Lovin' Just For Me', a tough up-tempo rocker complete with punchy horns, and Ray celebrating lovemaking ("I just want to be the one you give it to" he choruses with the girls) as only Ray can. Still looking over his shoulder from his comfortable place at the synth keyboard, 'I Just Can't Get Enough Of You' harks back to the honky-tonk sound of some of Ray's classic country records, confirmed by a no-nonsense blues guitar solo from Jack Wargo.

Ray's French lover for 35 years, Arlette Kotchounian contributed the lyrics on the languid 'Ensemble', in which Ray shares vocals in English and French. Recorded in Paris with strings laid down in Chicago, it's the only track on the album made outside LA, all the others apart from 'What'd I Say' emanating from RPM. And there's a complete change of mood and pace with 'New Orleans' – though the French touch is still there – with a taste of Louisiana R&B and some gumbo-flavoured keyboard from Ray that would do Dr John proud.

Still in the Crescent City, 'Mr Creole' is a laid-back blues written by Ray's one-time trumpet player Renald Richard, who famously co-wrote 'I Got A Woman' in 1954. Ray's spoken vocal tells how "When you're broke, in comes a friend with a buck or two" – that's Mr Creole. And the closing track is 'Mother', a multi-voiced Ray intoning lyrics that, though written by Osborne, are clearly close to his heart. "Mother could be stern, but you knew that she loved you" echoes precisely his own early life, Ray's melancholy delivery bringing a most remarkable album to a poignant close.

Although the album fared disappointingly in overall sales, it got generally enthusiastic reviews, and in retrospect has been hailed as a high point of the final years of Ray's career. At the time of its release, 'I Just Can't Get Enough Of You' went on to make a clear impression with "beach music" fans, staying in the Top 40 Beach Music Chart for over 20 weeks, peaking

Volcanic action: Ray Charles at the piano in the early Seventies. *(Photofest/Retna)*

Ray with exotically dressed Raelettes on a Cher-hosted TV special taped in Los Angeles on August 7, 1975. *(Hulton Archive/Getty Images)*

Ray and British vocalist Cleo Laine during a recording session for the *Porgy And Bess album*, 1976. *(Photofest/Retna)*

Blues Brothers: Ray with comic actors Dan Ackroyd (left) and John Belushi on the set of the John Landis movie in early 1980. *(Photofest/Retna)*

Ray at the tape decks of his RPM studios in Los Angeles in the Eighties. *(LFI)*

At the induction ceremony for the Rock and Roll Hall of Fame, 1986, with fellow inductees Jerry Lee Lewis (left) and Chuck Berry. *(Ebet Roberts/Redferns)*

Ray performing with L'Orchestre National d'Ile de France at the 6th Banlieues Bleues Jazz Festival, 1989. *(Guy Le Querrec/Magnum Photos)*

Ray in the early Nineties with frequent collaborator Quincy Jones. *(LFI)*

'I Can't Stop Loving You': throughout his career, Ray never stopped performing live. *(David Redfern/Redferns)*

Snapped on a New York street in the summer of 1992, Ray's "Uh Huh" Pepsi ad campaign. *(Mike Evans)*

Clarinet legend Artie Shaw – here with Ray in 1994 – was an early musical influence. *(Jacques Lowe/Retna)*

Ray's "hug" (here in 1997) had been a trademark of his live appearances since his early days on tour. *(Steven Tackeff/ZUMA/Corbis)*

Into the 21st century, Ray at the Verizon Music Festival, New York City, August 9, 2001. *(LFI)*

Ray accepts an Atlanta Heroes Award from contemporary R&B star Usher, July 2002. *(Rick Diamond/WireImage)*

Ray with his Atlantic mentor and good friend Ahmet Ertegun in the studios in July 2003. *(Valerie Goodloe/WireImage)*

A still from the *Ray* movie, depicting Ray receiving his honour from the state of Georgia. *(LFI)*

Brother Ray: a studio publicity shot from the latter years of Ray's sixty-year career in music. *(LFI)*

at number 12 at one stage. And with 'Mother' Ray got his first single on the charts in almost 10 years when it reached 72 on the Hot R&B/Hip-Hop listing.

Ray was never averse to a commercial tie-in, and during 2002 was in on the start of a link-up between the Hear Music label and the Starbucks coffee shop chain; a business relationship which would later feature in the distribution and marketing of the final album of his career, *Genius Loves Company*, in 2004.

When Hear Music launched its *Artist's Choice* series of CDs, Ray was one of the initial names to be featured. The idea was for a compilation album that would present an artist's all-time favourite records – what in the UK would have been dubbed their "desert island discs" – with, in their own words, the reasons behind their choice. *Ray Charles Artist's Choice* is a concise summary of, in the words of the CD liner blurb, "the music that changed his life".

The collection opens with the kind of boogie-jazz that little Ray Robinson would have listened to on Mr Pit's jukebox back in Greenville, with trumpeter ace Harry James showcasing the great boogie-woogie pianist Pete Johnson on 'Boo Woo'. In the liner notes, Ray talks about the sheer technical challenge of the left hand doing something totally different to the right – the heart of much of his piano playing.

Duke Ellington – here with 'Solitude' – "voiced" the instruments of his orchestra like no other bandleader; with results that Ray would use as a template of perfection. Then we have one of his major influences, Artie Shaw, whose records helped persuade Ray to take up the clarinet – and music generally – seriously: "It makes you want to cry, man, so much feeling in that thing." Shaw's 'Stardust' is the definitive rendering of Hoagy Carmichael's classic tune.

Nat "King" Cole's 1940 version of 'Sweet Lorraine' was undoubtedly a model for Ray's vocalising in his early days, and part of his regular repertoire – but, as he points out, Cole was "a hell of a piano player" too. Whenever asked about "genius" Ray would always dismiss his own qualification for the tag, citing Art Tatum, along with Charlie Parker, as a true genius. Tatum's formidable technique – here on a live take of 'How High The Moon' – leaves every piano player who's walked the planet, before or since, out in the cold.

Charles Brown, Ray's other big influence during his early days on the road, had his biggest hit with 'Driftin' Blues'. As Ray says, he was far more bluesy than Nat Cole. Of alto giant Charlie Parker, playing a sparkling version of the standard 'Melancholy Baby' with Dizzy Gillespie, Ray reflects "by the time you think you've learned what he played, he went to some other place. You understand? That's creativity." Quizzed in 1992 as to what the last thing was that really caught his attention, Ray cited the same bebop era Parker. "Some of the last stuff that I listened to that made me sit up, and still makes me sit up and take notice, that's Charlie Parker, or the old Charlie Parker and Dizzy Gillespie duet thing. How accurate the stuff that they used to do together is. It was done maybe 40 years ago and even today it's still the most fantastic thing you ever want to hear in your life."

Jimmy Rushing – known as "Mr Five-By-Five" because he was five foot high and the same round the waist – was a great Kansas City-style blues shouter who worked for years with the Count Basie Band. "These really were the cats, man," says Ray, and 'Sent For You Yesterday And Here You Come Today' proves his point.

The great Hank Jones was another pianist hero of Ray's, a cool player in the modern tradition who glides through 'We're All Together' with a beguiling feel of effortlessly being in charge. And Miles Davis, of course, is an icon to anyone who loves jazz, and 'My Funny Valentine' one of his favourite themes. Ray tells how, when he was just a teenager, he'd hang round clubs, Miles urging him to get up on the stand – "C'mon, man, they tell me you can play. Let me see what you can do."

The Ella Fitzgerald track is the famous live take in Berlin when she forgets the lyrics to 'Mack The Knife'. "It will be another hundred years before you find another Ella Fitzgerald come through here," Ray reflects. The soul-jazz favourite 'Moanin'' is the Quincy Jones track, and opportunity for Ray to pay tribute to his oldest friend. And Oscar Peterson completes Ray's pantheon of piano giants on the album with 'Brotherhood Of Man'.

Significantly, it's track 14 before Ray's choice moves away from jazz and blues. The Swing Silvertones sing perfect close-harmony gospel, and 'Mary Don't You Weep' epitomises the sacred side of Black American music. Meanwhile, the synthesis of gospel and R&B forged by Ray and exemplified in Sixties soul was never better illustrated than in the records of Aretha Franklin, and 'Respect' is as good as it gets.

Ray's old friend Willie Nelson is the collection's acknowledgement of a country influence, though the track – a cover of Elvis' 'Always On My Mind' – is very much crossover material. Perhaps appropriate, and Ray's comment about Nelson could be equally applied to him – "What you see is what you get."

The album casts a fascinating light on what formed the basis of Ray Charles' musical taste. A consummate musician, his biggest admiration was for the true giants of American popular music; by the 21st century this might have seemed conservative and backward-looking, but it *was* with the Art Tatums, the Duke Ellingtons and the Charlie Parkers, the giants of jazz, that the creative heritage of that music lay. "They are the creators," Ray would say. "They are the artists who helped form the backbone of our country's popular music. When you talk about, say, classical music, you're talking about a form that came from Europe and European composers and musicians from an earlier time. But, *we* basically created jazz in this country, we own that form of music."

Early in 2003, Ray's winter schedule involved another trip to the welcoming summer climate of Australia, again under the auspices of Glenn Wheatley. This time the event was the Melbourne International Music and Blues Festival, and the routine, Wheatley recalled, was as before. "Again he was true to form, he arrived on the day and turned up at the gig. You could set your clock to the hour that he's going to perform, because that's it – not a minute more, not a minute less, every night. You booked for an hour, and that's what you got. He was always kept to himself. Joe kept him under wraps, bringing him out about two minutes before he goes on."

But for a lifelong fan like Wheatley, working with Ray on three occasions is a memory he cherishes. "They were three great memorable nights, from someone who I started liking as a kid and grew up with. And I played all his licks – I used to play 'Hit The Road Jack' in a little band when I was 18, playing bass guitar. We were called Masters' Apprentices, and used to do this elongated version of 'Hit The Road Jack' that went on for 20 minutes. So it was a thrill to work with him."

Around the same time, another long-standing fan was finally achieving an ambition involving working with Ray Charles. Movie director Taylor Hackford had first approached Ray about making a feature film of his life story back in 1988. Ray was generally sympathetic to the idea, but the various elements didn't fall in place for a decade – development money, studio support and ultimately Ray's signature on the dotted line. By mid-2002 things were looking better – he had Ray on side, and a young actor, Jamie Foxx, earmarked for the lead role. All the necessary deals were finally clinched in the early weeks of 2003, and Hackford was ready to shoot.

First on location in the South, then in the studios in LA, over the coming months the director's patience was justified. As with all the projects that had his stamp on them, once involved Ray threw himself behind the film 100 per cent. By the summer Ray and the young actor reprising his early life on film were rehearsing together at RPM, the elder statesman showing the other the nuances of a piano lick here (Foxx was a classically trained pianist), a movement of the head there. Ray would approve Braille drafts of the script, suggesting corrections where appropriate, and supervise musical elements, including recording material for certain scenes. The shooting and editing of the movie – at that stage called *Unchain My Heart* – carried on through the rest of the year.

The film would continue in production into 2004 but, while attending to it as and when required, Ray still had gigs to do and records to make. His touring schedule for 2003 was as varied as ever – blues festivals, orchestral concerts, casino seasons, jazz festivals, TV specials, corporate functions and the rest; some with the entire band, some without.

On Saturday, April 26, Ray headlined the White House Correspondents Dinner in Washington, DC, attended by the President, George W. Bush and his wife, Colin Powell and Condoleeza Rice. In a set that included 'Hit The Road Jack', 'Your Cheatin' Heart', 'Just For A Thrill', 'Every Time It Rains (I Think Of You)', 'Stranger In My Own Hometown' and '3/4 Time', some observers reported that he seemed a bit slower than usual, displaying a certain amount of vocal difficulty. A Nashville television special saluting country music's top 100 hits, on which Ray appeared with Vince Gill, George Jones and Glen Campbell, saw his performance of 'Behind Closed Doors' receiving the evening's biggest standing ovation. And early in the summer, Ray Charles performed what he calculated to be the 10,000th concert of his career at the Greek Theater in Los Angeles.

June 26 saw the whole team playing Montreal, Canada, where a journalist managed to catch The Raelettes backstage. Renée Collins Georges, at 36 into her fourth season with Ray, gave the lady interviewer an insight into dressing for a Ray Charles show: "Stella (Estelle Yarbrough) decides what we're wearing, usually depending on the venue. If we are outdoors she'll decide on something strapless, or if we're indoors and it's a symphony, she goes for that sort of look. Then she lets them know what we're wearing. They don't tell us what he's wearing. He (Ray) can coordinate that with his personal assistant, and then the band has to be told what we are wearing."

And early in July he took part in the major TV series *The Blues*. Under the overall guidance of Executive Producer Martin Scorsese, seven movie directors had been commissioned to explore the blues through their own personal styles and perspectives, making seven documentary films in all. Clint Eastwood, a committed jazz and blues fan, directed 'Piano Blues', and invited Ray to become an integral part of the programmes' structure. Sitting at a piano in the RPM studios, Ray and Eastwood talked on camera about the blues, Ray giving musical examples as they chatted, the interview forming a link throughout the feature-length film.

A month or so earlier, on June 12, Ray had inducted Van Morrison into the Songwriters Hall of Fame at an awards ceremony held at the Broadway Ballroom of the Marriott Marquis Hotel in New York. After the presentation Morrison and his idol duetted on 'Crazy Love', the performance being recorded by Phil Ramone for a cable TV programme of the ceremony, *The Songwriters Hall Of Fame*. And more importantly, the live recording would appear as the closing track (though the first recorded) on what would prove to be Ray's final album, *Genius Loves Company*, released over a year later.

Ramone, whose Grammy-winning track record included producing for artists as varied as Frank Sinatra, Bob Dylan, John Coltrane and Billy Joel, didn't get involved in the album project until November, after Ray had hammered out a deal with John Burk, Executive Vice President and producer for Concord Records. It was originally Burk's brainwave that Ray Charles should record an album of duets with big-name artists, many of them old friends. After months of careful negotiation, Burk finally sold Ray on the idea. Then, just a couple of weeks after he laid down the first studio track with his old friend and blues superstar B.B. King, at the end of July Ray was taken ill.

The first the band knew about it was when all tour dates through August were cancelled. Ray had looked tired from time to time, but that seemed par for the course for a musician still gigging busily at nearly 73 years old. Apparently he had to go into hospital to undergo hip replacement surgery after suffering what a press release described as "acute hip discomfort". "It breaks my heart to withdraw from these shows," he was quoted as saying at the time. "All my life, I've been touring and performing. It's what I do. But the doctors insist I stay put and mend for a while, so I'll heed their advice."

But when the temporary lay-off was extended, the rest of the tour dates through the year being cancelled, it became obvious that something more serious was wrong. It transpired that after performing a successful hip replacement procedure, in September the doctors had diagnosed that Ray was suffering from a failing liver.

In an interview published in the August edition of *Esquire* magazine, Ray said: "I remember one night we did a thing with Duke Ellington. He was on an oxygen tank until they called him to come out onstage. But he went out there and you'd never have known there was anything wrong with the man. That's what music can do. If you're sad, you can go home and play some records and make yourself feel better. If you're in the hospital and you're sick, music can be soothing."

Whether or not he felt that time was running out after he learned how seriously ill he was, and this might be his final creative project, no one can be sure. But when Phil Ramone came on board in November, with the recording of *Genius Loves Company* already well under way, Ray threw himself into finishing it with every ounce of energy his weakening body could muster. "The duets project has been a tremendous experience," Ray said. "I am working with some of the best artists in the business, as well as some of my dearest friends." The album, completed at a session with Elton John in March 2004, stands as a moving testament to Ray Charles' passion and creativity.

Acclaimed as the biggest new voice in jazz singing, Norah Jones nevertheless, like Ray, shines in a variety of musical environments. On the opening 'Here We Go Again', which Ray first recorded on 1967's *Invites You To Listen*, she's down that country road that Ray likes to travel so much, and, in Ray's words "she's singing the hell out of it". With Billy Preston's bluesy Hammond organ swelling underneath, there's a mutual warmth of purpose in every breath they take.

The only theme to the album, if there is one, is the power of contrast as exemplified in so much of Ray's work over the years. And a complete contrast from Ray's Nashville excursion with Norah comes in the second track, a duet with singer-songwriter James Taylor on a funkified version of Taylor's 'Sweet Potato Pie' with jazz-edged horns and cutting guitar. Ray would describe it as James Taylor's "unique style of sweet soul".

Canadian Diana Krall was another contender in the "biggest new voice in jazz" stakes when she made her debut in the early Seventies. Again, a country-tinged song seems a surprise choice, but her rich tones alongside Ray's lived-in baritone lift the Eddy Arnold classic 'You Don't Know Me' (which Ray recorded on *Modern Sounds In Country & Western Music*) to another level again. It's one of the five tracks produced by Phil Ramone, who described how Ray made the singer immediately at ease: "Ray had a very engaging way with her, and Diana, being a wonderful perfectionist about the way she works, was so humble. She started out very nervous, but I told her that she had reached that stature in her career so that if she was uncomfortable, say so or I'd say it. Ray had a radar that was his own and he could tell . . . he'd say, 'That's okay daawling.' He was very endearing."

Ray called Elton John's 'Sorry Seems To Be The Hardest Word' "probably his best song". Certainly the John/Bernie Taupin hit comes over as a dramatic *tour de force* in this collaboration, from the opening strings to the closing notes on the piano. Recorded on the final session for the album, Ramone would comment that Ray was looking quite fragile at that point, in March 2004. Yet he injects the emotional lyrics with the same passion that he delivered to songs throughout his career.

"Elton got there a hour and a half before the session!" Ramone would recall. "They had tea, and talked about other stuff . . . he was preparing. I think artists have a way of preparing, I have my own way of preparing. He was always aware of how Ray would come into the room and he wanted him to feel the love and respect in the room. How exciting it was. Ray always knew what he was going to do, Elton knew what he wanted to do. I prepared the crew to make sure that if anything was going to happen . . . the cameras would be outside. The crowd in the studio was huge, which is unusual for me."

Written by Raelette Mable John's brother Little Willie John, and famously recorded by Peggy Lee, Ray tackles the steamy 'Fever' with Natalie Cole, daughter of his original role model, Nat. Starting with the same bass and finger-clicking intro as the Lee classic, Ray puts a bluesy edge on the vocal that's more akin to the original. The laid-back but swinging backing allows Cole to trade verses with Ray as the temperature rises, subtly, chorus by chorus.

Country meets the blues in perfect synthesis when Ray and singer-guitarist Bonnie Raitt get together for what must now be the definitive version of Billy Burnette's 'Do I Ever Cross Your Mind', previously recorded by Ray during his "Nashville" period in 1984. Bonnie's slide guitar weeps appropriately, with the vocal harmonies evoking the reflective melancholy of broken dreams.

A grandiose string intro brings in Ray's country outlaw buddy Willie

Nelson for 'It Was A Very Good Year'. Produced by John Burk, the treatment of the youth-to-old-age narrative long associated with Frank Sinatra is an exercise in contrast, the vocals sounding essentially unsophisticated against the ambitious arrangement. When Ray sings "Now the days grow short, I'm in the autumn of my years" you know he's actually singing about a very good life. "We're looking back and loving everything we see," he would comment about the track.

Utilising the same 63-piece orchestra as the previous track, the Sixties feel-good factor of Carole King's 'Hey Girl' is given a slower, more reflective feel by Ray and Michael McDonald. But the arrangements, by Victor Vanacore (Ray's orchestral arranger in his last years) are still imbued with the the sunny optimism of the original. And then again in complete contrast, it's time for the blues. Ray takes turns with his old friend and master of the blues guitar B.B. King on an effortlessly dynamic version of 'Sinner's Prayer', written by his old boss Lowell Fulson. From B.B.'s intro, this is simply the real thing, with Ray on piano, Billy Preston on Hammond and one of the world's finest, Jim Keltner, on drums.

Admitting that it was his favourite song from 1972's *A Message From The People*, Ray chose 'Heaven Help Us All' for his "gospel" track on the album. In an uplifting version with a full-on gospel choir and jazzy horns, Gladys Knight's singing sanctified with Brother Ray as her inspiration. The third number to be recorded with the big string ensemble – on the soundstage at Warners Brothers' film studio rather than RPM – was the old Harold Arlen stand-by 'Over The Rainbow'. Here Ray's with balladeer Johnny Mathis, who, it has to be said, is outsung by the older man in terms of his sheer emotional input into the song.

'Crazy Love', Phil Ramone's live track with Ray and Van Morrison closes a remarkable album. It's pure undiluted soul on the Morrison song, with churchy organ, gospel-chords from the horn section and a Raelettes-alike vocal group that Ramone often worked with when in New York. On the liner note to the CD, Morrison said of Ray: "He is a soul brother in every sense of the word."

Through his time on the album, from November 2003 to March 2004, Ramone noticed how Ray was getting more frail by the day – "right after Christmas he looked weaker," he would reflect later. When first conceived, a year before its release, *Genius Loves Company* was intended to be a tribute to America's greatest living popular musician. When it came out, in August 2004, it would be his final legacy.

20

Exodus and Epitaph

"Music's been around a long time, and there's going to be music long after Ray Charles is dead. I just want to make my mark, leave something musically good behind. If it's a big record, that's the frosting on the cake, but music's the main meal."

– Ray Charles

Over the opening months of 2004, as he laid down the final tracks for *Genius Loves Company*, those around him began to realise just how serious Ray's condition might be. Ray being Ray, however, meant that he got on with things with his usual gusto.

Between the recording sessions, it seemed like the honours being showered upon him were accelerating by the day. Early in the year the president of the Grammy Award organisation (NARAS), Neil Portnow, presented Ray with the President's Merit Award at the RPM studios, while around the same time he was also a recipient of a Kennedy Center Honour and the Presidential Medal of the Arts. Also in February he attended a ceremony at which he was named a City of Los Angeles "Cultural Treasure" by Mayor James Hahn during an African American Heritage Month. And on March 6 the National Association for the Advancement of Colored People (NAACP) Image Awards honoured him with a Hall of Fame Award.

Following on from initial endowments announced by Ray and Joe Adams in 2002 to Morehouse College in Atlanta and Albany State University in Ray's birthplace of Albany, Georgia – with contributions exceeding $1 million each – Ray approved plans for the building of the Ray Charles Performing Arts Center at Morehouse College, which were set to be unveiled in September. But before that, another unveiling took place in April which would be Ray Charles' last appearance in public.

Built in 1960 on the design and instigation of Joe Adams, Ray's beloved RPM studios was designated as an historic landmark by the City of Greater Los Angeles, and on April 30, 2004, a plaque proclaiming the studios an official landmark was unveiled. The area outside the studio had also been renamed Ray Charles Square. Many of those who attended the ceremony – including Clint Eastwood, actress Cicely Tyson, Ray's biographer David Ritz, former Raelette Mable John and the City Council President Alex Padilla – were shocked when Ray appeared in a wheelchair, clearly in some pain, and had to be lifted to the podium where he uttered a few almost incoherent words of thanks. In an already prepared statement marking the ceremony, Ray said, "I love this place, it's the only home I've truly had for most of my professional career and I would never leave it, and I thank Councilman Martin Ludlow and his team and City Council president, Alex Padilla, for their special efforts to make the studios a special part of Los Angeles history."

The deterioration in his condition continued over the next month, at the end of which family and friends gathered at his home as Ray went into a final rapid decline. On Thursday, June 10 his publicist Jerry Digney, of Solters & Digney, announced to the world that Ray Charles had "died of acute liver disease at 11.35 am, at the age of 73". Cause of death was officially attributed to hepatocellular carcinoma – cancer of the liver. Among those assembled at the house were many of the 12 children, 20 grandchildren and five great grandchildren that survived him.

The impact of the news was immediate, as was the reaction from around the world of music. That same day Aretha Franklin issued a statement while travelling to Chicago, describing Ray as "The voice of a lifetime", while Billy Joel said from New York, "Ray Charles was a true American original who many artists tried to emulate, among them myself, Rod Stewart, Joe Cocker, Steve Winwood and countless others."

Singer Lou Reed was on an aeroplane when he learned of Ray's death; in an email quoted in the *San Diego Union-Tribune* he said he was brought to tears, "Ray Charles changed my life forever, for the better, and I owe him a debt that cannot be paid."

Lifetime fan and disciple Van Morrison was told of Ray's death while onstage at Hampton Court Palace in London: "I'm deeply shocked. I've lost a dear friend. Ray will be sadly missed." Then he sang 'I Can't Stop Loving You'.

Elton John, who was the last person to record with Ray, said, "The death of Ray Charles is an incredible loss to the world of music. He inspired so many people, and his music will live forever."

"People remember the big hits and the visual image of him, but they forget what an innovator he was in the Fifties as a jazz musician," said country music singer Marty Stuart. "He made inroads for all of us when he did 'I Can't Stop Loving You'. It took country music to places it hadn't been before."

"There was just no one like Ray Charles," was Tony Bennett's reaction. "It broke my heart today when I heard he had left us."

And Ray's longest-standing friend and frequent collaborator Quincy Jones issued a statement which could only hint at the loss he must have felt: "I truly have no words to express the deep sadness I have today. Ray Charles was my oldest friend, my brother in every sense of the word, and bigger than life. We first met when I was 14 years old and he was 16 in Seattle, and we had the blessing of God to realise all those boyhood dreams together. Ray used to always say that if he had a dime, he would give me a nickel. Well, I would give that nickel back to have him still here with us, but I know heaven has become a much better place with him in it."

In an official press statement issued on behalf of Ray Charles Enterprises, Joe Adams said: "Although he was very successful and owned a home in Beverly Hills, his first home was always his treasured studio, recently named a city landmark. Ray Charles was a true original, a musical genius and a friend and brother to me. He pioneered a new style and opened the door for many young performers to follow. Some of his biggest fans were the young music stars of today, who loved and admired his talent and independent spirit."

A week later, at 10 am on June 18, a memorial service was held at the First African Methodist Episcopal Church in central Los Angeles, before Ray's body was taken for interment at Inglewood Cemetery. At the service, described as a celebration of Ray's life, 1,500 invited guests packed the church to hear a series of eulogies and musical tributes led by Ray's son, Rev. Robert Robinson. "If you would do something for my family today, why don't you stand on your feet and give God some praise — because we're here to celebrate God today, and thank God for this man," he told the congregation.

As well as the big names from music and show business, people like B.B. King, Glen Campbell and Willie Nelson — many of whom had been close friends of Ray as well as musical colleagues from time to time — the congregation included civic leaders from the City of Los Angeles and elsewhere. These included the LA mayor Major James Hahn, and Chief of Police William Bratton, while former President Bill Clinton, who couldn't attend, sent a message expressing his affection for Ray and his music.

A disciple of Ray since childhood, Stevie Wonder told how he didn't realise Ray Charles was also blind, when he first heard his records. "Long before I knew how much we had in common I knew there was a man that had a voice that touched my heart. I knew that his voice made me feel like I wanted to love deeper, to care more and reach out and embrace the world." Wonder went on to highlight Ray's contribution to race relations: "What pains me equally as much as knowing that we have in the physical state lost a genius, a king of song, is that Ray was not able to outlive hate and injustice."

The Rev. Jesse Jackson delivered an emotional address, painting a picture of Ray among the other musical maestros like Basie and Ellington who'd passed on in recent years. "Ray, when you first get there, before you meet Count, before you meet Duke, before you meet family and friends, there's a man over there, across the river who is giving sight to the blind!"

Willie Nelson delivered a musical tear-jerker with a heartfelt version of 'Georgia On My Mind', then lightened the mood when he told of his last chess game with Ray (who always beat the country star) when he asked him: "Next time we play, can we turn the lights on?"

And another close buddy, Clint Eastwood, drew attention to Ray's broad taste in music which made everybody's lives that much richer. "He worked so hard to be a perfectionist and entertain us all . . . He was a teacher who taught us about the blues, to people who didn't understand the blues. He taught us about country music. He re-instilled our interest in patriotic songs. Anything he touched was just good."

Alongside the memorial tributes came the obituaries, in newspapers and magazines across the world. *The New York Times'* headline described him as "Musician Who Defied Easy Definition", while the ABC 7 television channel in Chicago recalled when he was in the city in 1996, promoting his pre-paid phone card, the first-ever such card to be produced in Braille. "I mean I am blind, true, but my life has to go on. I must tell myself, 'OK, I am blind so what?'," Ray told the station. "What we're doing here, we're saying OK here's a person that's blind – there's a lot of blind people around the world. Why shouldn't they be able to know the numbers too?"

In Britain, describing his music as "pan-American", Tony Russell wrote in *The Guardian* of "a hugely expressive voice, and fingers that knotted the emotional ambiguities of the blues with the incessant beat of gospel music." George Varga in the *San Diego Union-Tribune* waxed equally lyrical: "Gruff or aching one moment, poignant or playful the next, his voice was an instrument of remarkably expressive power, rising from a growl to a falsetto swoop and back again with seemingly effortless ease."

The response to Ray's death brought into focus his true place in the evolution of modern music, something that had been lost in the mediocre reception for even his best albums over the last 30 years of his career. Suddenly the world was reminded, via the obituaries and then more extensive tributes in print and the broadcasting media, of what was really meant by Ray Charles' "genius".

Naming *Modern Sounds In Country & Western Music* one of his all-time favourite albums, the singer Tom Waits would recall how Ray's music had touched him from way back. "I knelt at the altar of Ray Charles for years. I worked at a restaurant, and that's all there was on the jukebox, practically, that and some Patsy Cline. 'Crying Time', 'I Can't Stop Loving You', 'Let's Go Get Stoned', 'You Are My Sunshine', 'What'd I Say', 'Hit The Road Jack'. I worked on Saturday nights and I would take my break and I'd sit by the jukebox and I'd play my Ray Charles. It was just amazing what he absorbed and that voice, for years it was just 'the Genius of Ray Charles'. I also love a record called *Listen*. He did 'Yesterday' on electric piano and it just killed me, to hear that voice, it was like he crossed over a bridge, because he remained in R&B territory, yet there was something so timeless about his voice, and hearing him do a Beatles song was just indescribable."

"There was music before Ray Charles and there's music after Ray Charles," Bonnie Raitt reflected in a tribute edition of *Rolling Stone*. "It's that stark a difference. I don't think anyone did more to bring soul music into popular American music than Ray Charles did."

Billy Joel's assessment was equally to the point: "This may sound like sacrilege, but I think Ray Charles was more important than Elvis Presley."

"Ray Charles defines soul," said organ player Paul Shaffer, who worked with Ray on several occasions. "In the battle of the soul giants, he is the undisputed king. Everyone moves up one now, because the king is dead."

Keith Richards described Ray as "the first true crossover artist"; "Ray was rock'n'roll. He was rhythm & blues. He was jazz. He was country. He had such reach – and far-reaching effect."

The posthumous spotlight remained on Ray Charles throughout the summer and into the autumn of 2004, after *Genius Loves Company* was released to almost universal acclaim.

Appearing at the end of August, the album went straight to the top of the *Billboard* chart, after generally garnering favourable – though by no means ecstatic – reviews. Even the most doubtful reception that was afforded some tracks was balanced by the acknowledgement that overall it was a fitting last album from a man who'd given so much to music. As Adam Sweeting conceded in *The Guardian*, "Even if his voice is a croaking shadow of its former greatness, the tracks give some idea of the scope and scale of his career."

While recognising "it may not be weighty enough to be a career-capping masterpiece," *All Music Guide*'s Stephen Thomas Erlewine called it "a step up from his previous studio album, since it puts Ray Charles in a comfortable, relaxed situation that plays to his strengths."

And, as one website reviewer put it, "Even a reduced Ray Charles is far superior to many stylists at the top of their game."

But the muted praise of some critics did little to harm the public's response. By the end of the year *Genius Loves Company* had received Gold, Silver and Platinum certifications across North America, Europe and elsewhere, making it quite possibly the best-selling recording of Ray Charles' six-decade career. Since the late Forties Ray had made records on no less than 250 occasions, some of them huge sellers, but certainly the sheer speed of his final album's sales couldn't be matched, having sold in excess of 1.2 million copies by December 2004 in the United States alone.

And that performance was complemented on December 7 by the announcement that *Genius Loves Company* had been nominated for 10 Grammy Awards. In the event, when the 47th annual Awards ceremony was held at Los Angeles' vast Staples Center on February 13, 2005, Ray and the album won in eight of the nominated categories: Best Album of the Year, Best Pop Vocal Album, Record (single) of the Year for 'Here We Go Again' with Norah Jones, the Best Gospel Performance with 'Heaven Help Us All' with Gladys Knight, Best Vocal Collaboration for 'Here We Go Again', Best Instrumental Arrangement Accompanying Vocals (Victor Vanacore's charts for 'Over The Rainbow' with Johnny Mathis), Best Engineered Album (non-classical) and the Best Surround Sound Album. The other two nominations were for Best Traditional R&B Vocal Performance for the track with B.B. King, 'Sinner's Prayer', and a second Best Vocal Collaboration nomination for 'Sorry Seems To Be The Hardest Word' with Elton John.

At the ceremony 80-year-old Joe Adams accepted on behalf of Ray, saying, "We love you Ray, and I wish you were here for all the attention," while producer John Burk of Concord Records called Ray, "A true American icon."

By the time of the Grammy Awards ceremony the album had sold in excess of two million copies in the US, where its success was undoubtedly due in part to a distribution and marketing relationship between Concord Records and Starbucks' Hear Music. Hear Music is an offshoot of the giant coffee chain, and Starbucks stores were reckoned to be responsible for selling 580,000 copies of *Genius Loves Company* by February 2005. As well as a newly conceived chain of Hear Music outlets which double as coffee shops and traditional record stores, the name also applies to a record label which had already had a link with Ray Charles in 2002. That was when he had an album of his personally selected favourites by other artists featured in their *Artist's Choice* series.

But before the Grammy Awards were even announced, and not long after the album's initial release, in October 2004 an even more significant epitaph to Ray's life and music would appear, when Taylor Hackford's cinema biopic – now simply entitled *Ray* – was finally released.

Taylor Hackford (whose directing credentials included *An Officer And A Gentleman* in 1982, and the 1985 Chuck Berry documentary film *Hail Hail Rock'n'Roll*) and producer Stuart Benjamin first had the idea of a movie telling Ray Charles' life story in 1988, when they were approached by Ray's son Ray Jr. At the time, however, Ray was preoccupied with other, more immediate, matters. Although he wasn't averse to the idea, he didn't give it much thought. But the movie men persevered, lobbying various studios over the years, though the picture still never got off the ground. Benjamin remembers one meeting at RPM with himself and Hackford, studio executives, lawyers and Ray, that broke up "somewhat acrimoniously" after the thorny issue of creative control came up.

However, by 2000 things were looking up. Benjamin was now an executive at Crusader Entertainment (later Bristol Bay Productions), and his partners in the company, Phil Anscutz and Howard Baldwin, were equally keen on the long-standing Ray Charles project. They soon had a studio's interest lined up, and now – crucially – Ray was ready to come on board.

The issue of creative control didn't raise its head this time around. Hackford had written a treatment for the movie years before, and they gave it to screenwriter James White to work on. As White produced drafts they would get them translated into Braille for Ray to approve or amend as he saw fit. Now he was officially involved in the movie, Ray made sure things were accurate, talking to White at length about his life, filling in a detail here, checking a date there. But this was going to be no whitewash job – and Ray (as with his autobiography back in the Seventies) was anxious to have it that way. Talking on the BBC's *Film 2005*, Hackford told Jonathan Ross how he had warned Ray from the start: "Ultimately, if I'm gonna tell the story, I want to tell it warts and all, I want to tell the real Ray Charles. He laughed and said, 'Well you'll find out I'm no angel.' I said, 'Yes, I want to put it on film.'"

Hackford's biggest challenge, he always knew, would come in casting the role of Ray Charles himself. He'd liked Jamie Foxx's work in *Any Given Shadow* and *Ali*, and had seen the actor's comedy series *The Jamie Foxx Show* on TV, and tentatively offered him the part. He told Foxx immediately that it was one thing getting Ray's physical mannerisms and voice nuances right – difficult enough in itself – but he was more worried about the actor mastering Ray's piano movements, and synching it with the piano playing on the soundtrack.

To his amazement, it turned out that Foxx was a formally trained pianist. Hackford was elated, and couldn't wait to introduce him to Ray. However, when the two first met on July 12, 2002, it was an encounter that the director feared for a moment might blow up in his face, when Ray challenged the young actor to follow him at the piano on a tricky Thelonius Monk piece. Classically trained Foxx didn't get with it immediately, and Ray was urging him, "C'mon man, it's right under your fingers, c'mon man . . . it's just eight bars." But Foxx kept at it till he'd mastered the quirky phrasing, at which point Ray jumped up with excitement. "You could see Jamie just kind of glow, he'd won the role right there from Ray Charles," Hackford would recall.

The initial plan was then to have Jamie spend some time with Ray, to get to know him, but to Hackford's dismay the actor didn't show up. "I called Jamie and said, 'Go down' – and he didn't do it. I kept calling back and said, 'Have you been down?' and he said, 'No.'" Foxx then explained why he wasn't showing up to meet Ray: "I'm like a sponge – if I get the old Ray, then I won't be able to make the transition . . ." As an actor, he knew he had to think in terms of the young Ray.

They found the solution with Quincy Jones. Quincy gave Foxx an old cassette tape of Ray goofing around on Dinah Shore's TV talk show. The actor took the tape home, and made that chunk of Ray talking, laughing, moving around and joking, all those Ray Charles mannerisms, his "DNA" of Ray. He then painstakingly applied that DNA to every line of the whole script – "Sometimes you gotta be higher, sometimes you gotta be lower, so you take that DNA and you go through it, to change that voice, to change the spirit of the character . . ."

"It's the nuances . . ." Foxx explained to Jonathan Ross. "How does he talk to his women, how does he do this and that . . . in this way the impersonation starts to disappear, and you actually become the man." Once he'd crossed that barrier, he spent time with Ray just talking. "I would ask him about the women and the drugs, and he would open up and say this is what you have to tell, if you don't don't . . . then it won't be interesting. Everything that Ray did, he said it helped him . . . and it hurt him at the same time.

"So everything he did, and everything that happened to him, was necessary . . ."

Ross asked whether this would include Ray's blindness. "It probably would make him play a little longer," thought Foxx, "because if he had sight he'd probably be out seeing the world more. But he had to stay in with that music, and I think it helped him in that sense."

In terms of his physical movements, many of Ray Charles' familiar idiosyncracies – his peculiar gait, his feet and shoulder movements at the piano and so on – were based on the fact that he was sightless. This was something he had to get right, so Foxx decided that for a large amount of the time when shooting the film he would be blind.

In order to look exactly like Ray, particularly when he wasn't wearing his dark glasses, Foxx's eyes were covered with prosthetics, and also silicon, based on close-up photographs of Ray's eyes taken by Hackford. "It was tough on the eyes, but at the same time it was necessary because in his life it was uncomfortable . . . you get angry because you can't see. You want to take them off, but you know you have to keep them on. I had to keep them on even during lunch . . . so I couldn't see for 12, 14 hours a day. Which really, really worked on me." Hackford recalled that, when Foxx saw the rushes, he would be literally seeing some of the costumes and sets for the first time.

Everybody who knew Ray closely, when they saw the movie all agreed that Jamie Foxx was uncanny in the accuracy of his portrayal. "You know Ray Charles is part of my soul, for the last 57 years or so," Quincy Jones enthused, "and sometimes I couldn't tell the difference between Ray and Jamie."

Talking about how long the movie took to come to fruition, Taylor

Hackford reflected, "I'm lucky that I didn't make it for 15 years, because I wouldn't have had Jamie Foxx in the leading role." As Stuart Benjamin would later comment, Foxx was the only person on the planet who could have played the role.

And Ray Charles Jr, who had an active role as a co-producer of the film, was particularly moved by the portrayal of his father: "It was very emotional for me to watch him on set, because it was too real – the way he looked, and if he turned in a different way, and moved a certain way. It was like he'd stepped into a skin . . . and I think he had to truly dig deep to do that."

The rest of the casting was done with equal care, with consideration given to the main theme – which *was* Ray Charles. Jamie Foxx was hardly a household name, so Hackford knew he couldn't have better-known faces "competing" with the Ray character on screen. He consequently chose relatively unknown actors, but a cast that equipped themselves magnificently all the same. Ray's women were particularly well represented by Kerry Washington as Della, Regina King as Margie Hendricks and a stand-out performance from Sharon Warren as Ray's mother Aretha.

One criticism that came from several quarters when the film was released was that some of the other characters like Jerry Wexler, Jeff Brown and Fathead Newman were dealt with two-dimensionally, as supporting players in the Ray Charles story. Be that as it may, and that was down to the screenplay rather than the actors per se, but the casting itself – particularly Curtis Armstrong as Ahmet Ertegun, Clifton Powell as Jeff Brown and C.J. Sanders as the childhood Ray – was in the main spot-on.

Music of course played as important a part in the film as any of the characterisations, and for this it was decided early in the project to use, in the main, Ray's original recordings. Although Jamie Foxx could have carried off a good impersonation of Ray's voice – and indeed did in a couple of instances where Ray is pictured in his "Nat Cole" period – there was nothing like the real thing.

"In the end we decided Ray's voice was just too great not to use," said music supervisor Curt Sobel. "There just isn't anybody who could sing like him."

Likewise, the sheer instrumental impact of Ray's records couldn't be duplicated by studio musicians, however accurate the arrangements and expert the playing. And with modern reproduction and digital "cleaning" of the older recordings, the results were startlingly lifelike.

The age of some of the recordings posed a particular problem for Jamie Foxx. Laid down without the luxury of multi-tracking, many of the records from the Fifties were recorded "live", vocals and instruments in one take. When it came to "miming" to the soundtrack, Jamie had to perfect lip-synching the voice and visually synching the piano-playing movements at the same time, without the benefit of separate tracks to listen to. For the actor it meant often working through the night to get the songs right, even with a 6.30 call on the set. "If I hadn't been a musician, there was no way I could have done 96 cues of Ray Charles' music." In the end, with the added benefit of some seamless editing, the result was sensational, and as Hackford acknowledged it was largely down to Foxx: "When you see this film you are watching Ray Charles perform, because Jamie Foxx has made you believe that."

Likewise with the other actors playing the musicians. Some had special coaching to mime their parts correctly while others − like ex-sax player Bokeem Woodbine, who played Fathead Newman but also played sax − were also musicians, so found the synching far simpler to achieve. And Ray himself contributed some new music to the soundtrack, specifically for scenes where he's shown practising at home or working something out in the studio.

When working on his original treatment for the film, Taylor Hackford had decided to cover Ray Charles' career up until the middle Sixties, covering the years of his creative development, its enormous impact on music in general, and his ultimate superstar success. Those years, through the Forties, Fifties and early Sixties, were also the most volatile period of Ray's personal life, involving his relationships with women and his inter-related struggle with heroin. With that in mind, rather than dealing with Ray's traumatic childhood as a straightforward prelude in the narrative, Hackford used it as a cipher throughout the film, to present (though not to excuse) the singer's personal demons and foibles in the context of his all-round personality.

The main problem with the film finishing where it does, Ray's triumph over drugs giving a neat upbeat ending, is that it almost implies that what-ever he did after that time − i.e. without the heroin − was hardly worthy of mention. A brief montage of record covers from 1965 to 2001, and a scene at the Georgia State House when 'Georgia On My Mind' was designated state song in 1979, are all we see of the entire second half of Ray Charles' amazing life.

If anything the film comes over as a little glossy at times − the childhood sequences in particular might have benefited from a more "monochrome" look – but having said that, the early musical sequences in juke joints and nightclubs have a genuinely smoky, authentic feel. And while most of the "support" characters aren't developed as they might be, this *is* primarily a film about Ray Charles, and a celebration of his music. On the latter count it succeeds magnificently; everyone I spoke with agreed, including those who knew Ray closely, that the impact of the music, from the opening piano intro of 'What'd I Say', did justice to Hackford's ambitious brief.

Most reviewers agreed that what the film lacked in substance – both in terms of the broader characterisations and the somewhat perfunctory ending – it made up for in Foxx's stunning performance and the sheer richness of the music. Angie Errigo in *Empire* magazine gave it four stars out of five, calling Foxx's performance "nothing short of amazing", while *Box Office* spoke of "the kind of joyous movie experience that can make you see the light".

For the BBC, Stella Papamichael called it "a tear-jerking, toe-tapping biopic that serves as testament to the man's passion and resilience – despite a join-the-dots approach to his psychology." *The Independent* on the other hand, regretted that "a powerhouse title performance and a soundtrack that almost blisters the screen with its energy . . . is so very far from being great that you could weep for all its wasted effort." And *The New York Times* review, headlined "Portrait Of Genius, Painted In Music", concluded: "*Ray*, while not a great movie, is a very good movie about greatness, in which celebrating the achievement of one major artist becomes the occasion for the emergence of another. I'm speaking of Ray Charles and Jamie Foxx, of course, though at this point I'm not entirely sure I can tell them apart."

From a visual point of view, photographer David Redfern felt the movie did justice to a subject he'd shot many times over the years. "Ray was one of those artists, like a lot of the big jazz names, and James Brown, and Ike & Tina Turner, where you'd never miss an opportunity of photographing them, it doesn't matter how many times you've done them. I think the movie did that justice, all the live stuff. I'd like to have seen more of it, that atmosphere was captured extremely well. Because I'm a freak on all of that, I'd like to just have had less story and more music, but I suppose for Joe Public it's probably about right. You can go and see that movie and you'd learn an awful lot about Ray Charles, and also you don't have the music shoved down your throat."

Did Redfern agree that you don't have to be a music fan to enjoy the film? "No you don't. But if you know him, and have seen him like I have close up, then I think it's just amazing, amazingly well done, and I'm delighted that they didn't re-record everything. And of course because Ray was involved in it, that was the magic."

Those closest to Ray, who were played by actors in the film, inevitably have a very different and unique perspective on the movie. David Newman, for one, had reservations about the balance of the movie: "I thought that Jamie Foxx did an incredible job, he actually became Ray, and Bokeem Woodbine played the Fathead part very well. However the Fathead character was a little inaccurate in my estimation, it wasn't *exactly* like me, a little brash compared to what I was in real life. I also felt – although the whole movie was a success – I personally felt it dealt with too much emphasis on sexual escapades and the drugs, as opposed to more emphasis on Ray's music. It was all about music [at the time], I felt it should have dealt a lot more with that. But a lot of people said, 'Well, that's what sells movies, the sexual escapades and the drugs,' so I have to go along with that. But that still doesn't stop me having my personal opinion about that."

And Jerry Wexler felt certain characters – including his own – could have been filled out more. "The film is terrific in many respects, but principally for the music, which stands alone, it's imperishable. And Jamie Foxx's fantastic performance. But I'm not a big fan of the script, or the way it played out, I especially don't like the way Ahmet Ertegun and I are portrayed in the film as flat, non-dimensional people, we're only incidental characters, peripheral. I wouldn't expect them to work on very complex characterisations, but if the writer and the director had given us a little more attention with a few more strokes . . .

"I'm vainglorious enough to feel that Ahmet and I were sort of different, initially, from the usual run of independent R&B record promoters and producers. I'm not going to enlarge on that, because this is a matter of personal hubris, but I believe that with a few deft strokes they could have indicated – I'm not going to name the others – that we were in some sense different from the others. We were all college graduates, we were all literate, we were all readers, we wrote, and so on. I felt that he just presented us as stick figures to advance the story."

Ahmet Ertegun on the other hand was sorry that the film's narrative finished in the Sixties, if only because it missed the fact that Ray returned to Atlantic Records in the Seventies: "That's not in the film – it shows how he left us, but doesn't show that he came back. Somebody asked me, 'Is the film truthful, is it absolutely factual?' Now if it was *absolutely* factual, it would be a documentary, and nobody would go and see it. They take dramatic licence, which they have to . . . but the overall effect of the film is truthful. It shows in a dramatic way actually what happened in Ray Charles' life. And Jamie Foxx must surely win an Oscar – although of course the people who give the Oscars didn't necessarily ever see Ray Charles – because his personification of that character is just incredible . . ."

Jamie Foxx did get that Oscar. After winning a Golden Globe award in January 2005 for Best Actor in a Musical or Comedy for his performance in *Ray*, he was a hot favourite for the Academy Award a month later. The Globes have long been considered an indication of what might happen at the Oscars, and Jamie's case was to prove the rule. And when the Oscar nominations were announced in January, *Ray* appeared in another five categories – for Best Picture, Director, Editing, Costume Design and Sound Mixing – as well as citing Foxx for Best Actor. In the event, at the Oscar ceremony on Sunday, February 27, *Ray* scored twice – for Jamie Foxx as widely predicted, and for Best Sound Mixing.

And *Ray* scored at the box office too. By the beginning of November 2004, in its first week of release it grossed an estimated $20 million in 2,000 cinemas across the United States, with its distributor Universal claiming it to be the biggest ever debut for a musical biopic. By February this had climbed to $74 million, with another $80 million from DVD/ video sales and rentals – this including $40 million on the first day of the DVD's release alone. And these figures were just for the US, the movie not seeing a release elsewhere until January 2005 – by April 2005 its worldwide gross amounted to over $96 million, not bad for a film made on a "limited" budget of less than $40 million.

Not long before his death Ray got to "see" a final cut of the film, when Taylor Hackford and Stuart Benjamin took a videotape of the movie to his office. As they played the tape Taylor described the settings and locations to Ray. "For about 25 minutes he didn't even move, and then he started talking back to the screen . . . not looking at the screen of course, but talking back saying, 'That's it, that's the truth.' He ultimately said, 'Taylor I'm really happy, I'm very pleased . . .' – that's like the best review that I could ever have."

Three weeks before the film's Hollywood premiere and a month before its general release, a tribute event was held at the Beverly Hills Hotel to help raise money for the newly opened $15 million Ray Charles Performing Arts Center at Morehouse College, Atlanta. Ray had already given the black liberal arts college $2 million to fund the complex, which he hoped would help to inspire a new generation of creative musicians.

The gala banquet was hosted by comedian Bill Cosby, who recalled that during a jazz festival at the Hollywood Bowl, Ray appeared on stage with a band of all white musicians. "I said to Ray, 'Your band is all white.' He said, 'That's funny. They don't sound white.'" Cosby went on to rerun his old gag that he'd first aired in the Sixties, about Christopher Columbus crossing the Atlantic "to discover Ray Charles".

An eclectic gathering of music stars performing some of Ray's hits included Stevie Wonder, country singer Travis Tritt, former Doobie Brother Michael McDonald and R&B artists James Ingram and Patti Austin. The actor Samuel L. Jackson was on hand to pay his respects, calling Ray Charles, "A guy of grace who reunited religions. He had a great heart. All the world loved him. Everyone is here to honour his life, this is not a sad day. We were fortunate to have him, he brightened up everyone's life." Quincy Jones also stressed that this was about celebration not mourning: "Make no mistake about it, this will be no pity party."

Jamie Foxx and action star Steven Segal were among the 500 invited guests who heard a message being read out from Bill Clinton, who was set to co-host the gala but had to pull out following recent heart surgery. "Ray Charles was America's national treasure," Clinton wrote. "His songs are a major part of America's musical heritage, and his life story was a testament to the power and promise of the American dream." Joe Adams' words were closer to home, when he remembered Ray's indomitable spirit. "He used to always say, the difficult he would do immediately. The impossible would take a while."

And just a few days later, an even more ambitious evening dedicated to Ray was staged at LA's Staples Center. Broadcast by CBS television on October 22, the show was called *Genius: A Night For Ray Charles, A Night To Remember*, and featured another raft of big-name performers including Mary J. Blige, Kenny Chesney, Al Green, Elton John, Norah Jones, B.B. King, Reba McEntire, Usher and Stevie Wonder. Hosted by Jamie Foxx, the stars, singing the songs that Ray made famous, were introduced by Tom Cruise, Mos Def, Quincy Jones and Bruce Willis.

Among the musicians backing the vocalists were Ray's old sideman Fathead Newman, and a group of Raelettes specially reunited for the occasion. Quincy, Fathead and B.B. also reminisced about their friendship with Ray. Celebrities spotted in the audience included the British jazz pianist and vocalist Jamie Cullum and Taylor Hackford and his wife, actress Helen Mirren. Proceeds from the glitzy bash went to the Ray Charles Robinson Foundation, set up by Ray to aid research into helping those with hearing problems.

With the success of both his final album and the movie that bore his name, by the close of 2004, just six months after his passing, Ray Charles' public profile was higher than it had been for many years. And early in 2005, on Friday, February 11, *Daily Variety* reported that the RPM studio in Los Angeles was to become a museum honouring his memory.

The paper said that there were plans for an education centre for inner-city children to be built next door to the complex, which had only once before been open to the public when it was used to help celebrate the release of *Genius Loves Company* in August 2004. Under the direction of Joe Adams, the staff at RPM had begun to collect items for display at the planned museum – due to open in 2007 – and, just the day before the news item, Ray's 12 Grammys – which have been restored – were unveiled at the studio. "Ray's kids used to play with those things like they were choo-choo trains and they were all busted," Adams told *Variety*.

The plan unveiled was to convert the 20,000-square-foot, three-storey building into a museum housing recordings, awards and even a tour bus, but which would also function as a working recording studio and education centre with classrooms, a rooftop café and a retail shop. "We didn't want it in Beverly Hills or a monument to Ray Charles anywhere but right where it is," Joe Adams told the press, stressing the museum would be "a working monument in this community, the community he was proud of, the community that was proud of him." A series of fund-raising events were planned for the summer of 2005 to meet the cost of the conversion under the auspices of the Ray Charles Museum Foundation.

Museum plans aside, the honours and tributes bestowed upon Ray Charles through his life, and now in the aftermath of his death, were many and generous.

On February 15, 2005, a Bill was introduced to Congress in the House of Representatives in Washington, DC, "To award a congressional gold medal to Ray Charles in recognition of his many contributions to the Nation". A list of Congressional Findings covering Ray's musical achievements, his battle to succeed despite poverty and blindness, and his contribution to race relations, ended with the following sentence: "Whether plaintive or rousing, the music of Ray Charles transformed the everyday lives, pain, and joy of the common people into songs that resonated with and inspired people of all nationalities, races, and classes."

Ray Charles embodied all the unique traditions of Black American popular music – jazz, gospel, blues – and brought them together as soul music. But when he broadened his vision, recognising a commonality of spirit that extended to country music, show tunes and myriad pop songs, he touched on something bigger again, the pure music of the soul, *his* soul. That was what he shared with the world, and for that the world is forever in his debt.

Source Notes

Listed below are specific sources used, over and above general reference sources indicated elsewhere. In addition to the titles indicated below, two books in particular proved an invaluable reference resource: Ray Charles' much-acclaimed autobiography, *Brother Ray*, by Ray Charles & David Ritz, and Michael Lydon's meticulously researched *Ray Charles: Man & Music*. Details of both are to be found in the general Bibliography. Quoted material also appears throughout from interviews conducted by the author as listed in the Acknowledgements.

CHAPTER 1
Fort Lauderdale *Sun-Sentinel*, 1998
Ray Charles interview, BBC *Omnibus*, 1986
raycharles.com
Ray Charles interviewed by Robert Gordon, 1992
Ray Charles interviewed by Ben Fong-Torres, *Rolling Stone*, Jan 1973
Rolling Stone
Whitney Balliett, *American Singers*, Oxford University Press [US] 1988

CHAPTER 2
raycharles.com
Rolling Stone

CHAPTER 3
Seattle Times
Quincy Jones interviewed by the American Academy of Achievement, June 3, 1995 and October 28, 2000
Quincy Jones, *Q: The Autobiography Of Quincy Jones*, Hodder & Stoughton [UK] 2001
raycharles.com
Rolling Stone
Billboard

CHAPTER 4

raycharles.com

Billboard

Lowell Fulson interviewed by Stephen Rosen for *Guitar Player*, 1976

Ahmet Ertegun, *What'd I Say: The Atlantic Story*, Orion [UK] 2001

Ray Charles interviewed by Robert Gordon, 1992

CHAPTER 5

Stuart Grundy, John Tobler, *The Record Producers*, BBC Books [UK] 1982

Jerry Wexler & David Ritz, *Rhythm And The Blues: A Life In American Music,* Jonathan Cape, [UK] 1994

Justine Picardie & Dorothy Wade, *Atlantic And The Godfathers Of Soul,* Fourth Estate [UK] 1993

Ray Charles interviewed by Robert Gordon, 1992

Charlie Gillett, *Making Tracks: The Story Of Atlantic Records*, WH Allen [UK], 1975

Ahmet Ertegun, *What'd I Say: The Atlantic Story*, Orion [UK] 2001

Ray Charles Story Vol 1, liner notes, Jerry Wexler [Atlantic] 1962

Arnold Shaw, *Honkers And Shouters: The Golden Years Of Rhythm And Blues*, Collier Books [US] 1978

Gerri Hirshey, *Nowhere To Run: The Story of Soul Music*, Macmillan [UK] 1984

Fathead/Ray Charles Presents David Newman liner notes, Gary Kramer, [Atlantic] 1959

Salt Lake Tribune

CHAPTER 6

San Jose Mercury News, 1994

Rolling Stone

Ray Charles interviewed by Robert Gordon, 1992

Ray Charles interviewed by Steve Turner, 1982

Nelson George, *The Death Of Rhythm & Blues*, Omnibus [UK] 1988

Ray Charles At Newport liner notes, Kenneth Lee Karpe [Atlantic] 1958

Tony Heilbut, *The Gospel Sound*, Simon and Schuster [US] 1971

Ray Charles: Genius & Soul – The 50th Anniversary Collection CD notes, [Rhino] 1997

CHAPTER 7

Rolling Stone

Billboard

Tony Heilbut, *The Gospel Sound*, Simon and Schuster [US] 1971

The Great Ray Charles liner notes, Gary Kramer [Atlantic] 1957

Arnold Shaw, *Honkers And Shouters: The Golden Years Of Rhythm And Blues*, Collier Books [US] 1978

Geoffrey C. Ward, *Jazz: A History Of America's Music*, Pimlico [UK] 2001

Gerri Hirshey, *Nowhere To Run: The Story of Soul Music*, Macmillan [UK] 1984

Roy Carr, *A Century Of Jazz*, Hamlyn [UK] 1997

The Genius Sings The Blues liner notes, Billy Taylor [Atlantic] 1961

Ray Charles liner notes, Guy Remark [Atlantic] 1957

The Best Of Ray Charles liner notes, Ralph J. Gleason [Atlantic] 1970

Soul Brothers liner notes, Bill Randle [Atlantic] 1958

Ray Charles At Newport liner notes, Kenneth Lee Karpe [Atlantic] 1958

Whitney Balliett in *The New Yorker*, December 7, 1957

Ray Charles: Genius & Soul – The 50th Anniversary Collection CD notes, [Rhino] 1997

Bill Millar, *The Drifters: The Rise And Fall Of The Black Vocal Group*, Studio Vista [UK] 1971

Martha Bayles, *Hole In Our Soul*, The Free Press [US] 1994

Stuart Grundy, John Tobler, *The Record Producers*, BBC Books [UK] 1982

Liner notes, *Jazz On A Summer's Day*, DVD, 2002

John S. Wilson in *The New York Times*

Fathead/Ray Charles Presents David Newman liner notes, Gary Kramer, [Atlantic] 1959

Melody Maker

CHAPTER 8

Ray Charles interview, BBC *Omnibus*, 1986

Ray Charles: Genius & Soul – The 50th Anniversary Collection CD notes, [Rhino] 1997

Stuart Grundy, John Tobler, *The Record Producers*, BBC Books [UK] 1982

Martha Bayles, *Hole In Our Soul*, The Free Press [US] 1994

Tony Russell in *The Guardian*

Nelson George, *The Death Of Rhythm And Blues*, Omnibus [UK] 1988

The Beatles, *The Beatles Anthology*, Cassell & Co [UK] 2000

Bill Wyman, *Rolling With The Stones*, Dorling Kindersley [UK] 2002

The Genius Hits The Road CD notes, Billy Vera [Rhino] 1997

Rolling Stone

John J. Goldrosen, *Buddy Holly: His Life And Music*, Charisma Books [UK] 1975

CHAPTER 9
The Genius Of Ray Charles liner notes, Nat Hentoff [Atlantic] 1959
Ray Charles Story Vol 2 liner notes, Jerry Wexler [Atlantic] 1962
Ray Charles In Person liner notes, Zenas Sears [Atlantic] 1960
Jerry Wexler & David Ritz, *Rhythm And The Blues: A Life in American Music*, Jonathan Cape, [UK] 1994
Ray Charles: Genius & Soul – The 50th Anniversary Collection CD notes [Rhino] 1997
Ray Charles interviewed by Mike Sagar, *Esquire*, August 2003

CHAPTER 10
Rolling Stone
Billboard
Ray Charles interviewed by Whitney Balliett, *The New Yorker*, March 28, 1970
Justine Picardie & Dorothy Wade, *Atlantic And The Godfathers Of Soul*, Fourth Estate [UK] 1993
The Genius Hits The Road CD notes, Billy Vera [Rhino] 1997
Melody Maker
Down Beat
Genius + Soul = Jazz liner notes, Dick Katz [Impulse!] 1961

CHAPTER 11
Melody Maker
Andria Lisle & Mike Evans, *Waking Up In Memphis*, Sanctuary [UK] 2003
Stanley Booth, *Rhythm Oil*, Vintage [UK] 1993
Ray Charles And Betty Carter liner notes, Sid Feller [ABC–Paramount] 1961
Jimmy Scott, *Mojo*, 2001
Mike Zwerin, Paris 2003
Nik Cohn, *Pop From The Beginning*, Weidenfeld & Nicholson [UK] 1969
New Departures No 4, 1962
Ray Charles: Genius & Soul – The 50th Anniversary Collection CD notes, [Rhino] 1997
Indianapolis Times, November 1961

CHAPTER 12
Ray Charles interview, BBC *Omnibus*, 1986
What'd I Say liner notes, Ren Grevatt [Atlantic] 1959
Rolling Stone
Ray Charles interviewed by Robert Gordon, 1992
Modern Sounds In Country And Western Music CD notes, Todd Everett [Rhino] 1988
Al Aronowitz, *The Blacklisted Journalist*
l'Humanité, June 12, 2004
Melody Maker
Nelson George, *The Death Of Rhythm And Blues*, Omnibus [UK] 1988
The Observer
Ingredients In A Recipe For Soul CD notes, Steve Hoffman [Actual] 1990

CHAPTER 13
Los Angeles Times, 1986
Ray Charles interviewed by Robert Gordon, 1992
Melody Maker
Mersey Beat
Henri Henroid interviewed by Bill Harry, 1997, www.triumphpc.com/mersey-beat
Billy Preston interviewed by Wayne Robbins, *Creem* magazine
Boston Globe
Los Angeles Times

CHAPTER 14
raycharles.com
Billboard
Gerri Hirshey, *Nowhere To Run: The Story Of Soul Music*, Macmillan [UK] 1984
Ray Charles: Genius & Soul – The 50th Anniversary Collection CD notes [Rhino] 1997
Robert Gordon, *It Came From Memphis*, Secker & Warburg [UK] 1995
Jerry Wexler & David Ritz, *Rhythm And The Blues: A Life In American Music*, Jonathan Cape, [UK] 1994
San Jose Mercury News, 1994
Life magazine, 1966
A Man And His Soul liner notes, Stanley Dance [ABC-Tangerine] 1967
Ray Charles Invites You To Listen liner notes, Chris Wilson [Tangerine] 1967

Down Beat
Rolling Stone

CHAPTER 15
Rolling Stone
Ray Charles interviewed by Whitney Balliett, *The New Yorker*, March 28, 1970
Raelettes interviewed by Mary Ann Lacey, June 26, 2003, montreal.com
Esquire magazine
BBC interview, 1986
My Kind Of Jazz liner notes, Quincy Jones [Tangerine] 1970
Ray Charles interviewed by Robert Gordon, 1992

CHAPTER 16
Ray Charles interviewed by Robert Gordon, 1992
John Bryant in *Dallas Morning News*, October 2004
The Genius Of Soul DVD, directed and written by Yvonne Smith featured in the Masters of American Music Series
Ray Charles interviewed by Michael Hobson, *Classic Records* newsletter, 1999
Porgy And Bess liner notes, Norman Granz/Benny Green [RCA] 1976

CHAPTER 17
Rolling Stone
Genius Loves Company liner notes, various [Concord/EMI] 2004
Mick Brown in *The Guardian*, 1984
Barney Hoskins in *Mojo*
Harry Belafonte and Quincy Jones interviewed on *Today*, NBC TV, February 5, 2005
Ray Charles interviewed by Johnny Carson, *Tonight* show, 1986
Billboard
Ability magazine
DrumBeats magazine, June 2004
Calvin James, calvinjames.com

CHAPTER 18
Los Angeles Times, 1986
Billboard
Ray Charles interviewed by Robert Gordon, 1992

Berlin 1962 CD notes, Bob Porter [Pablo] 1996
Rolling Stone
Q magazine
Entertainment Weekly
A Town Hall Meeting with President Clinton, MTV 1993
Ray Charles interviewed by Marc Silver, *US News And World Report*,
    September 22, 1997
Fort Lauderdale Sun-Sentinel
Ray Charles interview, BBC *Omnibus*, 1986

CHAPTER 19
Ray Charles interviewed by Robert Gordon, 1992
Ray Charles: Artist's Choice liner notes, Ray Charles [Hear Music] 2002
Taylor Hackford, *Ray: A Tribute To The Movie, The Music And The Man*,
    Newmarket Press [US] 2004
Raelettes interviewed by Mary Ann Lacey, June 26, 2003, montreal.com
Ray Charles interviewed by Mike Sagar, *Esquire*, August 2003
Genius Loves Company liner notes, various [Concord/EMI] 2004
Phil Ramone interviewed by Paula Edelstein, JazzUSA.com

CHAPTER 20
Washington Post
Press release on behalf of Ray Charles Enterprises, Solters & Digney
San Diego Union-Tribune
The New York Times
ABC 7 TV, Chicago
Tony Russell in *The Guardian*
George Varga in the *San Diego Union-Tribune*
Tom Waits in *The Observer* blog
Rolling Stone
Billboard
Adam Sweeting in *The Guardian*
Stephen Thomas Erlewine in *All Music Guide*
Taylor Hackford interviewed by Jonathan Ross, *Film 2005*, BBC TV
Jamie Foxx interviewed by Jonathan Ross, *Film 2005*, BBC TV
Ray DVD [Universal] 2005
Taylor Hackford, *Ray: A Tribute To The Movie, The Music And The Man*,
    Newmarket Press [US] 2004
Angie Errigo in *Empire* magazine

BBC Television News
The Independent
The New York Times
Seattle Times
Genius: A Night For Ray Charles, A Night To Remember, CBS TV, October 22, 2004
Daily Variety
Report of 1st Session of the 109th Congress of the House Of Representatives/ theorator.com

Bibliography

BOOKS

Balliett, Whitney, *American Singers*, Oxford University Press [US] 1988

Balliett, Whitney, *The Sound Of Surprise*, Pelican [UK] 1963

Bayles, Martha, *Hole In Our Soul*, The Free Press [US] 1994

Beam, Alex, *Gracefully Insane: The Rise And Fall Of America's Premier Mental Hospital*, Public Affairs [US]

Beatles, The, *The Beatles Anthology*, Cassell & Co [UK] 2000

Booth, Stanley, *Rhythm Oil*, Vintage [UK] 1993

Broven, John, *Walking To New Orleans*, Blues Unlimited [UK] 1974

Carr, Roy, *A Century Of Jazz*, Hamlyn [UK] 1997

Charles, Ray & Ritz, David, *Brother Ray*, Macdonald and Jane's [UK] 1979

Cohn, Nik, *Pop From The Beginning*, Weidenfeld & Nicholson [UK] 1969

Ertegun, Ahmet, *What'd I Say: The Atlantic Story*, Orion [UK] 2001

Evans, Mike, *NYC Rock: Rock'n'Roll In The Big Apple*, Sanctuary [UK] 2003

George, Nelson, *The Death Of Rhythm & Blues*, Omnibus [UK] 1988

George, Nelson, *Where Did Our Love Go?: The Rise And Fall Of The Motown Sound*, Omnibus [UK] 1986

Gillett, Charlie, *Making Tracks: The Story Of Atlantic Records*, WH Allen [UK] 1975

Gillett, Charlie, *The Sound of the City*, Pantheon Books [US] 1970

Goldrosen, John J., *Buddy Holly: His Life And Music*, Charisma Books [UK] 1975

Gordon, Robert, *It Came From Memphis*, Secker & Warburg [UK] 1995

Grundy, Stuart and Tobler, John, *The Record Producers*, BBC Books [UK] 1982

Guralnick, Peter, *Last Train To Memphis: The Rise of Elvis Presley*, Abacus [UK] 1995

Guralnick, Peter, *Sweet Soul Music*, Virgin Books [UK] 1986

Guralnick, Peter (contributor), *The Rolling Stone Illustrated History Of Rock'n'Roll*, Random House [US] 1976

Hackford, Taylor, *Ray: A Tribute To The Movie, The Music And The Man*, Newmarket Press [US] 2004

Heilbut, Tony, *The Gospel Sound*, Simon and Schuster [US] 1971

Hirshey, Gerri, *Nowhere To Run: The Story Of Soul Music*, Macmillan [UK] 1984

Jones, Quincy, *Q: The Autobiography Of Quincy Jones*, Hodder & Stoughton [UK] 2001

Leigh, Spencer, *Baby, That Is Rock'n'Roll*, Finbar International [UK] 2001

Lewens, Alan, *Walk On By: Soundtrack Of The Century*, HarperCollins [UK] 2001

Lisle, Andria & Evans, Mike, *Waking Up In Memphis*, Sanctuary [UK] 2003

Lydon, Michael, *Boogie Lightning: How Music Became Electric*, Perseus Books [US] 1980

Lydon, Michael, *Ray Charles: Man & Music*, Routledge [UK] 2004

Mahal, Taj with Foehr, Stephen, *Taj Mahal: Autobiography Of A Bluesman*, Sanctuary [UK] 2001

Millar, Bill, *The Drifters: The Rise And Fall Of The Black Vocal Group*, Studio Vista [UK] 1971

Palmer, Robert, *Deep Blues*, Macmillan [UK] 1981

Picardie, Justine & Wade, Dorothy, *Atlantic And The Godfathers Of Soul*, Fourth Estate [UK] 1993

Rosenthal, David, *Hard Bop*, Oxford University Press [US] 1992

Silvester, Peter, *A Left Hand Like God: The Story Of Boogie-Woogie*, Omnibus [UK] 1990

Shaw, Arnold, *Black Popular Music In America*, Schirmer [US] 1986

Shaw, Arnold, *Honkers And Shouters: The Golden Years Of Rhythm And Blues*, Collier Books [US] 1978

Turner, Steve, *Hungry For Heaven*, Virgin [UK] 1988

Ward, Geoffrey C., *Jazz: A History Of America's Music*, Pimlico [UK] 2001

Wexler, Jerry & Ritz, David, *Rhythm And The Blues: A Life In American Music*, Jonathan Cape, [UK] 1994

Williams, Richard, *The Man In The Green Shirt: Miles Davis*, Bloomsbury [UK] 1993

Wyman, Bill, *Bill Wyman's Blues Odyssey*, Dorling Kindersley [UK] 2001

Wyman, Bill, *Rolling With The Stones*, Dorling Kindersley [UK] 2002

NEWSPAPERS AND PERIODICALS

Balliett, Whitney, *Profiles: It's Detestable When You Live It*, The New Yorker, March 28, 1970

Bibliography

Bryant, John, *Dallas Morning News*, October 2004
Courrier, Kevin, Review of *Ray, Box Office*, 2004
DrumBeats Magazine, June 2004
Entertainment Weekly, Review of *My World*, March 12, 1993
Errigo, Angie, Review of *Ray, Empire*, January 2005
Life magazine, July 29, 1966
Mendelssohn, John, *Joe Cocker: With A Little Help From My Friends'*
Q magazine, Review of *My World*, March, 1993
Quinn, Anthony, Review of *Ray, The Independent*, January 21, 2005
Renzhofer, Martin, *The Salt Lake Tribune*
Rolling Stone, August 23, 1969
Sagar Mike, *Esquire*, August 2, 2003
Scott, A.O., Review of *Ray, The New York Times*, October 29, 2004
Silver, Marc, *Still Soulful After All These Years, US News And World Report*,
    September 22, 1997
Rolling Stone, Review of *My World*, May 13, 1993
Snow, Mat, *All Together Now: Joe Cocker, Q*, May 1992
Tobler, John, *The Joe Cocker Story [Part Three], Blank Space*, May 1979
Robins, Wayne, *Creem*, May 1974
Wexler, Jerry, *What It Is – Is Swamp Music – Is What It Is, Billboard*,
    December 1969

Also: *Ability, All Movie Guide, Billboard, Boston Globe, Daily Telegraph, Disc, Down Beat, Ebony, Entertainment Weekly, The Guardian, Guitar Player, Fort Lauderdale Sun-Sentinel, Indianapolis Recorder, Melody Maker, Mersey Beat, Mojo, New Musical Express, New York Times, New Yorker, Q, Rolling Stone, San Diego Union-Tribune, Uncut*

WEBSITES

amazon.com, David Sprague review of *The Spirit Of Christmas*
barnesandnoble.com
bbc.com, Stella Papamichael review of *Ray*
calvinjames.com, *Light a Candle for Ray Charles*, June 10, 2004
classicrecords.com, Ray Charles interviewed by Michael Hobson, 1999
cmt.com
culturekiosque.com, Mike Zwerin, *International Herald Tribune*
davidhoffmanjazz.com

harvardmagazine.com
montreal.com, Mary Ann Lacey, *An interview with The Raelettes*, 2003
msnbc.msn.com
nybluesandjazz.org
pauladams.org, Paul Adams Music
Reuters/Billboard/entertainment-news.org (Jerry Wexler interviewed by
    Bill Holland)
triumphpc.com/mersey-beat, Henri Henroid interviewed by Bill Harry
westcoastmusic.com

BROADCASTING AND OTHER MEDIA

Belafonte, Harry and Quincy Jones interviewed by Jamie Gangel, *Today*
    show, NBC TV, February 5, 2005
Bowes, Peter, BBC News, June 18, 2004
Charles, Ray, interviewed by Charlie Gillett, *Omnibus*, BBC TV, 1986
Genius Of Soul, The, DVD/*Masters Of American Music* series
Jones, Quincy, interviewed by the American Academy of Achievement,
    June 3, 1995 and October 28, 2000
Review of *Ray*, Channel 4 TV
UPI News Service, February 11, 2005

LINER NOTES

Charles, Ray, *Ray Charles: Artist's Choice* [Hear Music] 2002
Cooper, Carol, *The Definitive Otis Redding* [Rhino] 1993
Dance, Stanley, *A Man And His Soul* [ABC-Tangerine] 1967
Everett, Todd, *Modern Sounds In Country And Western Music* CD notes
    [Rhino] 1988
Feather, Leonard, *The Genius After Hours* [Atlantic] 1961
Feller, Sid, *Ray Charles And Betty Carter* [ABC-Paramount] 1961
Gleason, Ralph J., *The Best Of Ray Charles* [Atlantic] 1970
Granz, Norman and Green, Benny, *Porgy And Bess* [RCA] 1976
Grevatt, Ren, *What'd I Say* [Atlantic] 1959
Hentoff, Nat, *The Genius Of Ray Charles* [Atlantic] 1959
Hoffman, Steve, *Ingredients In A Recipe For Soul* CD [Actual] 1990
Jones, Quincy, *My Kind Of Jazz* [Tangerine] 1970

Karpe, Kenneth Lee, *Ray Charles At Newport* [Atlantic] 1958
Katz, Dick, *Genius + Soul = Jazz* [Impulse!] 1961
Kramer, Gary, *Fathead/Ray Charles Presents David Newman* [Atlantic] 1959
Kramer, Gary, *Soul Meeting* [Atlantic] 1961
Kramer, Gary, *The Great Ray Charles* [Atlantic] 1957
Kramer, Gary, *Yes Indeed!* [Atlantic] 1958
Porter, Bob, *Berlin 1962* CD [Pablo] 1996
Randle, Bill, *Soul Brothers* [Atlantic] 1958
Remark, Guy, *Ray Charles* [Atlantic] 1957
Sears, Zenas, *Ray Charles In Person* [Atlantic] 1960
Taylor, Billy, *The Genius Sings The Blues* [Atlantic] 1961
Unknown, *Ray Charles: Genius & Soul – The 50th Anniversary Collection* CD [Rhino] 1997
Various, *Genius Loves Company* [Concord/EMI] 2004
Vera, Billy, *The Genius Hits The Road* CD [Rhino] 1997
Ward, Rick, *Sweet And Sour Tears* [ABC-Paramount] 1964
Wexler, Jerry, *Ray Charles Story Vol 1* [Atlantic] 1962
Wexler, Jerry, *Ray Charles Story Vol 2* [Atlantic] 1962
Wilson, Chris, *Ray Charles Invites You To Listen* [Tangerine] 1967

SONG CREDITS

Alfred, Ray – lyrics from *I've Got News For You*, Cecil Lennox, 1961
Arlen, Harold/Mercer, Johnny – lyrics from *Blues In The Night*, Chappell Music, 1942
Axton, Durden/Presley, Elvis – lyrics from *Heartbreak Hotel*, Tree Music, 1956
Bates, Katharine Lee – lyrics from *America The Beautiful*, Oliver Ditson Company, 1917
Brown, Cadena, Herman – lyrics from *The Right Time*, M.C.P.S., 1958
Burnette, Billy/Smotherman, Michael – lyrics from *Do I Ever Cross Your Mind*, Chrysalis Music/Dorsey Music/EMI April Music, 2004
Charles/Harper – lyrics from *Them That Got*, Tangerine Music, 1960
Charles, Ray – lyrics from *A Fool For You*, Progressive Music, 1955
Charles, Ray – lyrics from *Don't You Know*, Progressive Music, 1953
Charles, Ray – lyrics from *Hallelujah I Love Her So*, Progressive Music, 1955
Charles, Ray – lyrics from *I Believe To My Soul*, Progressive Music, 1959
Charles, Ray – lyrics from *Questions*, Tangerine Music, 1980

Charles, Ray – lyrics from *Tell All The World About You*, Progressive Music, 1958

Charles, Ray – lyrics from *What Kind Of Man Are You?*, Progressive Music, 1957

Charles, Ray – lyrics from *What'd I Say*, Progressive Music, 1959

Charles, Ray and Mayfield, Percy – lyrics from *But On The Other Hand Baby*, Tangerine Music, 1961

Drake, Ervin – lyrics from *It Was A Very Good Year*, Lindabet Music, 1961

Jenkins, Gordon – lyrics from *New York's My Home*, Leeds Music, 1956

Lennon, John – lyrics from *Imagine*, Lenono Music, 1971

Mayfield, Percy – lyrics from *At The Club*, Tangerine Music, 1962

Mayfield, Percy – lyrics from *Hide 'Nor Hair*, Tangerine Music, 1962

Mayfield, Percy – lyrics from *The Danger Zone*, Tangerine Music, 1961

Miller, Ronald – lyrics from *Heaven Help Us All*, Stein & Van Stock Music, Inc., 1970

Oliver, Sy – lyrics from *Yes Indeed!*, Campbell Connelly, 1943

Osborne, Billy – lyrics from *Can You Love Me Like That*, Racer Music, 2002

Osborne, Billy – lyrics from *Mother*, Racer Music, 2002

Osborne, Billy – lyrics from *Save Your Lovin' Just For Me*, Racer Music, 2002

Richard, Renald – lyrics from *Mr. Creole*, Tangerine Music, 2002

Seals, Troy – lyrics from *Two Old Cats Like Us*, Two Sons Music, 1994

Theard, Sam and Moore, Fleece – lyrics from *Let The Good Times Roll*, Pic Music, 1976

Tormé, Mel – lyrics from *A Stranger In Town*, Blue Ribbon Music, 1954

Appendix 1

ALBUM DISCOGRAPHY

Ray Charles (aka *Hallelujah I Love Her So*) (*compilation*)
Atlantic (6/57)
Ain't That Love / Drown In My Own Tears / Come Back Baby / Sinner's Prayer / Funny (But I Still Love You) / Losing Hand / A Fool For You / Hallelujah I Love Her So / Mess Around / This Little Girl Of Mine / Mary Ann / Greenbacks / Don't You Know / I've Got A Woman

The Great Ray Charles
Atlantic (8/57)
The Ray / My Melancholy Baby / Black Coffee / There's No You / Doodlin' / Sweet Sixteen Bars / I Surrender Dear / Undecided

Soul Brothers – with Milt Jackson
Atlantic (6/58)
Soul Brothers / How Long Blues / Cosmic Blues / Blue Funk / 'Deed I Do

Ray Charles At Newport
Atlantic (10/58)
The Right Time / In A Little Spanish Town / I Got A Sweetie (I Got A Woman) / Blues Waltz / Hot Rod / Talkin' 'Bout You / Sherry / A Fool For You

Yes Indeed! (*compilation*)
Atlantic (10/58)
What Would I Do Without You / It's All Right / I Want To Know / Yes Indeed! / Get On The Right Track Baby / Talkin' 'Bout You / Swanee

River Rock (Talkin' 'Bout That River) / Lonely Avenue / Blackjack / The Sun's Gonna Shine Again / I Had A Dream / I Want A Little Girl / Heartbreaker / Leave My Woman Alone

What'd I Say (*compilation*)

Atlantic (9/59)
What'd I Say / Jumpin' In The Mornin' / You Be My Baby / Tell Me How Do You Feel / What Kind Of Man Are You? / Rockhouse / Roll With Me Baby / Tell All The World About You / My Bonnie / That's Enough

The Genius Of Ray Charles

Atlantic (10/59)
Let The Good Times Roll / It Had To Be You / Alexander's Ragtime Band / Two Years Of Torture / When Your Lover Has Gone / 'Deed I Do / Just For A Thrill / You Won't Let Me Go / Tell Me You'll Wait For Me / Don't Let The Sun Catch You Cryin' / Am I Blue / Come Rain Or Come Shine

Ray Charles In Person

Atlantic (5/60)
The Right Time / What'd I Say / Yes Indeed! / The Spirit-Feel (Hot Rod) / Frenesi / Drown In My Own Tears / Tell The Truth

The Genius Hits The Road

ABC-Paramount (7/60)
Alabamy Bound / Georgia On My Mind / Basin Street Blues / Mississippi Mud / Moonlight In Vermont / New York's My Home / California, Here I Come / Moon Over Miami / Deep In The Heart Of Texas / Carry Me Back To Old Virginny / Blue Hawaii / Chattanooga Choo-Choo

Dedicated To You

ABC-Paramount (1/61)
Hardhearted Hannah / Nancy / Margie / Ruby / Rosetta / Stella By Starlight / Cherry / Josephine / Candy / Marie / Diane / Sweet Georgia Brown

Soul Meeting – with Milt Jackson

Atlantic (2/61)

Hallelujah I Love Her So / Blue Genius / X-Ray Blues / Soul Meeting /
Love On My Mind / Bag Of Blues

Genius + Soul = Jazz

Impulse! (2/61)

From The Heart / I've Got News For You / Moanin' / Let's Go / One
Mint Julep / I'm Gonna Move To The Outskirts Of Town / Stompin'
Room Only / Mister C / Strike Up The Band / Birth Of The Blues

The Genius After Hours

Atlantic (6/61)

The Genius After Hours / Ain't Misbehavin' / Dawn Ray / Joy Ride /
Hornful Soul / The Man I Love / Charlesville / Music, Music, Music

Ray Charles And Betty Carter

ABC-Paramount (7/61)

Ev'ry Time We Say Goodbye / You And I / Intro: Goodbye/We'll Be
Together Again / People Will Say We're In Love / Cocktails For Two /
Side By Side / Baby, It's Cold Outside / Together / For All We Know /
Takes Two To Tango / Alone Together / Just You, Just Me

The Genius Sings The Blues (*compilation*)

Atlantic (9/61)

Early In The Mornin' / Hard Times (No One Knows Better Than I) / The
Midnight Hour / The Right Time / Feelin' Sad / Ray's Blues / I'm Movin'
On / I Believe To My Soul / Nobody Cares / Mr Charles' Blues /
Some Day Baby (Worried Life Blues) / I Wonder Who

Do The Twist! (aka The Greatest Ray Charles) (*compilation*)

Atlantic (11/61)

Tell Me How Do You Feel / I've Got A Woman / Heartbreaker / Tell The
Truth / What'd I Say / Talkin' 'Bout You / You Be My Baby / Leave My
Woman Alone / I'm Movin' On

Modern Sounds In Country & Western Music

ABC–Paramount (4/62)

Bye Bye, Love / You Don't Know Me / Half As Much / I Love You So Much It Hurts / Just A Little Lovin' / Born To Lose / Worried Mind / It Makes No Difference Now / You Win Again / Careless Love / I Can't Stop Loving You / Hey, Good Lookin'

Ray Charles Greatest Hits *(compilation)*

ABC–Paramount (7/62)

Them That Got / Georgia On My Mind / Unchain My Heart / I'm Gonna Move To The Outskirts Of Town / The Danger Zone / I've Got News For You / Hit The Road Jack / Ruby / I Wonder / Sticks And Stones / But On The Other Hand Baby / One Mint Julep

The Ray Charles Story *(compilation)*

Atlantic (7/62)

The Sun's Gonna Shine Again / Losing Hand / Mess Around / It Should've Been Me / Don't You Know / Come Back Baby / I've Got A Woman / A Fool For You / This Little Girl Of Mine / Mary Ann / Hallelujah I Love Her So / Lonely Avenue / Doodlin' / Sweet Sixteen Bars / Ain't That Love / Rockhouse / Swanee River Rock (Talkin' 'Bout That River) / Talkin' 'Bout You / What Kind Of Man Are You? / Yes Indeed! / My Bonnie / Tell All The World About You / The Right Time / What'd I Say / Just For A Thrill / Come Rain Or Come Shine / Drown In My Own Tears / Let The Good Times Roll / I'm Movin' On

The Ray Charles Story, Volume One *(compilation)*

Atlantic (7/62)

The Sun's Gonna Shine Again / Losing Hand / Mess Around / It Should've Been Me / Don't You Know / Come Back Baby / I've Got A Woman / A Fool For You / This Little Girl Of Mine / Mary Ann / Hallelujah I Love Her So / Lonely Avenue / Doodlin' / Sweet Sixteen Bars / Ain't That Love

The Ray Charles Story, Volume Two *(compilation)*

Atlantic (7/62)

Rockhouse / Swanee River Rock (Talkin' 'Bout That River) / Talkin' 'Bout You / What Kind Of Man Are You? / Yes Indeed! / My Bonnie /

Tell All The World About You / The Right Time / What'd I Say / Just For
A Thrill / Come Rain Or Come Shine / Drown In My Own Tears / Let
The Good Times Roll / I'm Movin' On

Modern Sounds In Country And Western Music, Volume 2
ABC-Paramount (10/62)
You Are My Sunshine / No Letter Today / Someday (You'll Want Me To
Want You) / Don't Tell Me Your Troubles / Midnight / Oh, Lonesome
Me / Take These Chains From My Heart / Your Cheating Heart / I'll
Never Stand In Your Way / Making Believe / Teardrops In My Heart /
Hang Your Head In Shame

The Ray Charles Story, Volume Three (*compilation*)
Atlantic (6/63)
Sinner's Prayer / Funny (But I Still Love You) / Feelin' Sad / Hard Times
(No One Knows Better Than I) / What Would I Do Without You / I Want
To Know / Leave My Woman Alone / It's All Right / Get On The Right
Track Baby / That's Enough / I Want A Little Girl / You Be My Baby /
I Had A Dream / Tell The Truth

Ingredients In A Recipe For Soul
ABC-Paramount (8/63)
Busted / Where Can I Go? / Born To Be Blue / That Lucky Old Sun / Ol'
Man River / In The Evening (When The Sun Goes Down) / A Stranger In
Town / Ol' Man Time / Over The Rainbow / You'll Never Walk Alone

Sweet & Sour Tears
ABC-Paramount (1/64)
Cry / Guess I'll Hang My Tears Out To Dry / A Tear Fell / No One To
Cry To / You've Got Me Crying Again / After My Laughter Came Tears /
Teardrops From My Eyes / Don't Cry Baby / Cry Me A River / Baby,
Don't You Cry (The New Swingova Rhythm) / Willow Weep For Me /
I Cried For You

Have A Smile With Me
ABC-Paramount (6/64)
Smack Dab In The Middle / Feudin' And Fightin' / Two Ton Tessie /

I Never See Maggie Alone / Move It On Over / Ma (She's Making Eyes At Me) / The Thing / The Man With The Weird Beard / The Naughty Lady Of Shady Lane / Who Cares (For Me)

The Great Hits Of Ray Charles Recorded On 8-Track Stereo (*compilation*)

Atlantic (6/64)
Tell Me How Do You Feel / I Had A Dream / Carrying That Load / Tell All The World About You / I Believe To My Soul / What'd I Say / I'm Movin' On / You Be My Baby / The Right Time / Yes Indeed! / Tell The Truth / My Bonnie / Early In The Mornin'

The Ray Charles Story, Volume Four (*compilation*)

Atlantic (6/64)
Blackjack / Alexander's Ragtime Band / I Believe To My Soul / A Bit Of Soul / Greenbacks / Undecided / When Your Lover Has Gone / It Had To Be You / Early In The Mornin' / Heartbreaker / Music, Music, Music / Tell Me How Do You Feel / In A Little Spanish Town / You Won't Let Me Go

Ray Charles Live In Concert

ABC-Paramount (1/65)
Opening / Band: Swing A Little Taste / I've Got A Woman / Margie / You Don't Know Me / Hide 'Nor Hair / Baby, Don't You Cry / Makin' Whoopee / Hallelujah I Love Her So / Don't Set Me Free / What'd I Say / Finale

Country And Western Meets Rhythm & Blues (aka Together Again)

ABC-Paramount (8/65)
Together Again / I Like To Hear It Sometime / I've Got A Tiger By The Tail (Swingova) / Please Forgive And Forget / I Don't Care / Next Door To The Blues / Blue Moon Of Kentucky (Swingova) / Light Out Of Darkness / Maybe It's Nothing At All / All Night Long / Don't Let Her Know / Watch It Baby

Crying Time

ABC-Paramount / TRC(1/66)

Crying Time / No Use Crying / Let's Go Get Stoned / Going Down Slow / Peace Of Mind / Tears / Drifting Blues / We Don't See Eye To Eye / You're In For A Big Surprise / You're Just About To Lose Your Clown / Don't You Think I Ought To Know / You've Got A Problem

Ray's Moods

ABC-Paramount / TRC(7/66)

What-Cha Doing In There (I Wanna Know) / Please Say You're Fooling / By The Light Of The Silvery Moon / You Don't Understand / Maybe It's Because Of Love / Chitlins With Candied Yams / Granny Wasn't Grinning That Day / She's Lonesome Again / Sentimental Journey / A Born Loser / It's A Man's World / A Girl I Used To Know

A Man And His Soul (*compilation*)

ABC (1/67)

I Can't Stop Loving You / What'd I Say / Ol' Man River / One Mint Julep / Crying Time / Makin' Whoopee / Busted / Takes Two To Tango / Ruby / Let's Go Get Stoned / Cry / Unchain My Heart / Georgia On My Mind / Baby, It's Cold Outside / Worried Mind / I Chose To Sing The Blues / I Don't Need No Doctor / Born To Lose / Hit The Road Jack / You Are My Sunshine / From The Heart / Teardrops From My Eyes / No Use Crying / Chitlins With Candied Yams

Ray Charles Invites You To Listen

ABC / TRC (6/67)

She's Funny That Way (I Got A Woman Crazy For Me) / How Deep Is The Ocean (How High Is The Sky) / You Made Me Love You (I Didn't Want To Do It) / Yesterday / I'll Be Seeing You / Here We Go Again / All For You / Love Walked In / Gee, Baby Ain't I Good To You / People

A Portrait Of Ray

ABC / TRC (3/68)

Never Say Naw / The Sun Died / Am I Blue / Yesterday / When I Stop Dreamin' / I Won't Leave / A Sweet Young Thing Like You / The Bright Lights & You Girl / Understanding / Eleanor Rigby

I'm All Yours, Baby!

ABC / TRC (2/69)
Yours / I Didn't Know What Time It Was / Love Is Here To Stay / Memories Of You / Till The End Of Time / I Had The Craziest Dream / Someday / Indian Love Call / I Dream Of You (More Than You Dream I Do) / Gloomy Sunday

Ray Charles Doing His Thing

ABC / TRC (5/69)
The Same Thing That Can Make You Laugh (Can Make You Cry) / Finders Keepers, Losers Weepers / You Ought To Change Your Ways / Baby Please / Come And Get It / We Can Make It / I'm Ready / That Thing Called Love / If It Wasn't For Bad Luck / I Told You So

The Best Of Ray Charles (*compilation*)

Atlantic (1/70)
Hard Times / Doodlin' / Rockhouse / How Long Blues / Sweet Sixteen Bars / Blues Waltz

My Kind Of Jazz

Tangerine (4/70)
Golden Boy / Booty Butt / This Here / I Remember Clifford / Sidewinder / Bluesette / Pas-Se-O-Ne Blues / Zig Zag / Angel City / Senor Blues

Love Country Style

ABC / TRC (6/70)
If You Were Mine / Ring Of Fire / Your Love Is So Doggone Good / Don't Change On Me / Till I Can't Take It Anymore / You've Still Got A Place In My Heart / I Keep It Hid / Sweet Memories / Good Morning Dear / Show Me The Sunshine

Volcanic Action Of My Soul

ABC / TRC (4/71)
See You Then / What Am I Living For / Feel So Bad / The Long And Winding Road / The Three Bells / All I Ever Need Is You / Wichita Lineman / Something / I May Be Wrong (But I Think You're Wonderful) / Down In The Valley

A 25th Anniversary In Show Business Salute To Ray Charles
(*compilation*)

ABC (11/71)

Hit The Road Jack / Hallelujah I Love Her So / Mary Ann / Unchain My Heart / Don't Let The Sun Catch You Cryin' / Georgia On My Mind / What'd I Say / I've Got A Woman / One Mint Julep / I Can't Stop Loving You / If You Were Mine / Busted / Crying Time / Yesterday / Let's Go Get Stoned / Eleanor Rigby / Born To Lose / Don't Change On Me / It Should've Been Me / Mess Around / Don't You Know / A Fool For You / You Are My Sunshine / Drown In My Own Tears / Ain't That Love / Lonely Avenue / Swanee River Rock (Talkin' 'Bout That River) / I Believe To My Soul / Ruby / Rockhouse / Just For A Thrill / The Right Time / Yes Indeed! / Understanding / Booty Butt / Feel So Bad

A Message From The People

ABC / TRC (4/72)

Lift Every Voice And Sing / Seems Like I Gotta Do Wrong / Heaven Help Us All / There'll Be No Peace Without All Men As One / Hey Mister / What Have They Done To My Song Ma / Abraham, Martin And John / Take Me Home, Country Roads / Every Saturday Night / America The Beautiful

Through The Eyes Of Love

ABC / TRC(8/72)

My First Night Alone Without You / I Can Make It Thru The Days (But Oh Those Lonely Nights) / Someone To Watch Over Me / A Perfect Love / If You Wouldn't Be My Lady / You Leave Me Breathless / Never Ending Song Of Love / Rainy Night In Georgia

Jazz Number II

Tangerine (1/73)

Our Suite / A Pair Of Threes / Morning Of Carnival / Going Home / Kids Are Pretty People / Togetherness / Brazilian Skies

Ray Charles Live (double album re-issue)

Atlantic(5/73)

The Right Time / In A Little Spanish Town / I've Got A Woman / Blues

Waltz / Talkin' 'Bout You / Sherry / Hot Rod / A Fool For You / The Right Time / What'd I Say / Yes Indeed! / Hot Rod / Frenesi / Drown In My Own Tears / Tell The Truth

Come Live With Me

Crossover (1/74)
Till There Was You / If You Go Away / It Takes So Little Time / Come Live With Me / Somebody / Problems, Problems / Where Was He / Louise / Everybody Sing

Renaissance

Crossover (6/75)
Living For The City / Then We'll Be Home / My God And I / We're Gonna Make It / For Mama / Sunshine / It Ain't Easy Being Green / Sail Away

My Kind Of Jazz, Part III

Crossover (10/75)
I'm Gonna Go Fishin' / For Her / Sister Sadie / 3/4 Time / Ray Minor Ray / Samba De Elencia / Metamorphosis / Nothing Wrong / Project "S"

Ray Charles Live In Japan

Crossover / London (Japan) (1976)
Introduction / Metamorphosis / Pair Of Threes / Spain / Blowing The Blues Away / Introduction MC Ray Charles / Let The Good Times Roll / Then I'll Be Home / Till There Was You / Feel So Bad / Georgia On My Mind / Busted / Am I Blue / Living For The City / I Can't Stop Loving You / Take Me Home, Country Roads / Don't Let Her Know / What'd I Say

Porgy And Bess – with Cleo Laine

RCA (11/76)
Summertime / My Man's Gone Now / A Woman Is A Sometime Thing / They Pass By Singing / What You Want With Bess? / I Got Plenty O' Nuttin' / Buzzard Song / Bess, You Is My Woman Now / Oh, Doctor Jesus / Crab Man / Here Come De Honey Man / Strawberry Woman / It Ain't

Necessarily So / There's A Boat Dat's Leavin' Soon For New York / I Loves You, Porgy / Oh Bess, Where's My Bess? / Oh Lord, I'm On My Way

What Have I Done To Their Songs *(compilation)*

Crossover / London (01/77)
What Have They Done To My Song Ma / The Long And Winding Road / I Keep It Hid / A Perfect Love / Eleanor Rigby / Wichita Lineman / Never Ending Song Of Love / Something / Take Me Home Country Roads / See You Then / Yesterday / Sweet Memories

True To Life

Crossover / Atlantic (10/77)
I Can See Clearly Now / The Jealous Kind / Oh, What A Beautiful Mornin' / How Long Has This Been Going On / Be My Love / Anonymous Love / Heavenly Music / Game Number Nine / Let It Be

Love & Peace

Crossover / Atlantic (9/78)
You 20th Century Fox / Take Off That Dress / She Knows / Riding Thumb / We Had It All / No Achievement Showing / A Peace That We Never Before Could Enjoy / Is There Anyone Out There? / Give The Poor Man A Break

Ain't It So

Crossover / Atlantic (9/79)
Some Enchanted Evening / Blues In The Night / Just Because / What'll I Do / One Of These Days / Love Me Or Set Me Free / Drift Away / (Turn Out The Light) And Love Me Tonight

Brother Ray Is At It Again

Crossover /Atlantic (1980)
Compared To What / Anyway You Want To / Don't You Love Me Anymore? / A Poor Man's Song / Now That We've Found Each Other / Ophelia / I Can't Change It / Questions

Wish You Were Here Tonight

Columbia (3/83)

3/4 Time / I Wish You Were Here Tonight / Ain't Your Memory Got No Pride At All / Born To Love Me / I Don't Want No Stranger Sleepin' In My Bed / Let Your Love Flow / You Feel Good All Over / String Bean / You've Got The Longest Leaving Act In Town / Shakin' Your Head

Do I Ever Cross Your Mind

Columbia (7/84)

I Had It All / Do I Ever Cross Your Mind / Woman Sensuous Woman / Then I'll Be Over You / (All I Wanna Do Is) Lay Around And Love On You / Love Of My Life / They Call It Love / If I Were You / Workin' Man's Woman / I Was On Georgia Time

Friendship

Columbia (2/85)

Two Old Cats Like Us / This Old Heart (Is Gonna Rise Again) / We Didn't See A Thing / Who Cares / Rock And Roll Shoes / Friendship / It Ain't Gonna Worry My Mind / Little Hotel Room / Crazy Old Soldier / Seven Spanish Angels

The Spirit Of Christmas

Columbia (11/85)

What Child Is This / The Little Drummer Boy / Santa Claus Is Comin' To Town / This Time Of Year / Rudolph The Red Nosed Reindeer / That Spirit Of Christmas / All I Want For Christmas / Christmas In My Heart / Winter Wonderland / Christmas Time

From The Pages Of My Mind

Columbia (9/86)

The Pages Of My Mind / Slip Away / Anybody With The Blues / Class Reunion / Caught A Touch Of Your Love / A Little Bit Of Heaven / Dixie Moon / Over And Over (Again) / Beaucoup Love / Love Is Worth The Pain

Just Between Us

Columbia (9/88)

Nothing Like A Hundred Miles / I Wish I'd Never Loved You At All / Too Hard To Love You / Now I Don't Believe That Anyone / Let's Call The Whole Thing Off / Stranger In My Own Hometown / Over The Top / I'd Walk A Little More For You / If That's What'Cha Want / Save The Bones For Henry Jones

Would You Believe?

Warner (10/90)

I'll Take Care Of You / Your Love Keeps Me Satisfied / Ellie, My Love / I Can't Get Enough / Let's Get Back To Where We Left Off / Child Support, Alimony / Fresh Out Of Tears / Living Without You / Where're The Stairs / Leave Him!

My World

Warner (3/93)

My World / A Song For You / None Of Us Are Free / So Help Me God / Let Me Take Over / One Drop Of Love / If I Could / Love Has A Mind Of Its Own / I'll Be There / Still Crazy After All These Years

Strong Love Affair

Qwest (1/96)

All She Wants To Do Is Love Me / Say No More / No Time To Waste Time / Angelina / Tell Me What You Want Me To Do / Strong Love Affair / Everybody's Handsome Child/ Out Of My Life / The Fever / Separate Ways / I Need A Good Woman Bad / If You Give Me Your Heart

Berlin, 1962

Pablo (06/96)

Band Intro / Strike Up The Band / One Mint Julep / I Got A Woman / Georgia On My Mind / Margie / The Danger Zone / Hallelujah I Love Her So / Come Rain Or Come Shine / Hide 'Nor Hair / Alexander's Ragtime Band / I Believe To My Soul / Hit The Road Jack / The Right Time / Bye, Bye Love / Unchain My Heart / What'd I Say

Thanks For Bringing Love Around Again

Crossover (6/02)

What'd I Say / Can You Love Me Like That / How Do You Feel The
Morning After / I Love You More Than I Ever Have / Really Got A Hold
On Me / Thanks For Bringing Love Around Again / Save Your Lovin' Just
For Me / I Just Can't Get Enough Of You / Ensemble / New Orleans /
Mr. Creole / Mother

Live At The Montreux Jazz Festival

Pioneer / Geneon (7/02)

Opener / I'll Be Home / Busted / Georgia On My Mind / Mississippi Mud /
Just For A Thrill / You Make Me Love You / Angelina / Scotia Blues (Blues
For Big Scotia) / Song For You / Do It To Me Slow / Watch Them Dogs /
Shadows Of My Mind / Smack Dab In The Middle / I Can't Stop Loving
You / People Will Say We're In Love / What'd I Say

Genius Loves Company

Concord / EMI (8/04)

Here We Go Again / Sweet Potato Pie / You Don't Know Me / Sorry
Seems To Be The Hardest Word / Fever / Do I Ever Cross Your Mind /
It Was A Very Good Year / Hey Girl / Sinner's Prayer / Heaven Help Us
All / Somewhere Over The Rainbow / Crazy Love

Ray!: Original Motion Picture Soundtrack *(compilation)*

Rhino (10/04)

Mess Around / I Got A Woman / Hallelujah I Love Her So / Drown In My
Own Tears / Night Time Is The Right Time / Mary Ann / Hard Times /
What'd I Say / Georgia On My Mind / Hit The Road Jack / Unchain My
Heart / I Can't Stop Loving You / Born To Lose / Bye Bye, Love / You
Don't Know Me / Let The Good Times Roll / Georgia On My Mind

Compilation Albums

In addition to major compilation albums included above, the following is a
selection from the many released over the years:

The Original Ray Charles, Hollywood (1962)

The World Of Ray Charles, Crossover / London (1974)
The World Of Ray Charles, Vol.2, Crossover / London (1975)
The Right Time, Atlantic (1987)
A Life In Music, 1956–59, Atlantic (1982)
Greatest Hits Volume 1, 1960–67, Rhino (1988)
Greatest Hits Volume 2, 1960–72, Rhino (1988)
Anthology, Rhino (1989)
The Collection: ABC Recordings, Castle (1990)
Blues Is My Middle Name, 1949–52 Recordings, Double Play (1991)
The Birth Of Soul: The Complete Atlantic R&B, '52–'59, Rhino/Atlantic (1991)
The Living Legend, Atlantic (1993)
The Best Of The Atlantic Years, Rhino/Atlantic (1994)
Classics, Rhino (1995)
Genius & Soul (5-CD box set), Rhino (1997)
Standards, Rhino (1998)
The Complete Country & Western Recordings, 1959–1986 (4-CD box set), Rhino (1998)
Ultimate Hits Collection, Rhino (1999)
The Very Best Of Ray Charles, Rhino (2000)
The Very Best Of Ray Charles, Volume II, Rhino (2000)
The Chronological Ray Charles, 1949–1950, Jazz Classics (2001)
The Definitive Ray Charles, WSM (2001)
Ray Charles Sings For America, Rhino (2002)
The Chronological Ray Charles, 1950–1952, Jazz Classics (2003)
Mess Around, Proper (2004)

Appendix 2

SINGLES DISCOGRAPHY

Down Beat/Swing Time:
I Love You, I Love You/Confession Blues (3/49)
How Long Blues/Blues Before Sunrise (4/49)
A Sentimental Blues/You'll Never Miss The Water (4/49)
Alone In This City/Can Anyone Ask For More? (5/49)
Let's Have A Ball/Rockin' Chair Blues (6/49)
I've Had My Fun/Sittin' On Top Of The World (7/49)
Ain't That Fine/Don't Put All Your Dreams In One Basket (7/49)
See See Rider/What Have I Done? (8/49)
Honey Honey/She's On The Ball (8/49)
Th' Ego Song/Late In The Evening Blues (9/49)
Someday/I'll Do Anything But Work (10/49)
I Wonder Who's Kissing Her Now/All To Myself (1/51)
Lonely Boy/Baby Let Me Hold Your Hand (1/51)
I'm Glad For Your Sake/Kissa Me Baby (3/52)
Baby Won't You Please Come Home/Hey Now (7/52)
Baby Let Me Hear You Call My Name/Guitar Blues (8/52)
Misery In My Heart/The Snow Is Falling (2/53)

Atlantic:
The Midnight Hour/Roll With Me Baby (9/52)
The Sun's Gonna Shine Again/Jumpin' In The Mornin' (1/53)
Mess Around/Funny (But I Still Love You) (7/53)
Feelin' Sad/Heartbreaker (9/53)
It Should've Been Me/Sinner's Prayer (3/54)
Losing Hand/Don't You Know (8/54)
I've Got A Woman/Come Back Baby (12/54)
A Fool For You/This Little Girl Of Mine (6/55)
Blackjack/Greenbacks (10/55)

Mary Ann/Drown In My Own Tears (1/56)

Hallelujah I Love Her So/What Would I Do Without You (5/56)

Lonely Avenue/Leave My Woman Alone (8/56)

I Want To Know/Ain't That Love (1/57)

It's All Right/Get On The Right Track Baby (6/57)

Swanee River Rock/I Want A Little Girl (8/57)

Talkin' 'Bout You/What Kind Of Man Are You? (1/58)

Yes Indeed!/I Had A Dream (4/58)

You Be My Baby/My Bonnie (8/58)

Rockhouse Part 1/Rockhouse Part 2 (10/58)

Tell All The World About You/The Right Time (11/58)

That's Enough/Tell Me How Do You Feel (4/59)

What'd I Say Part 1/What'd I Say Part 2 (6/59)

I'm Movin' On/I Believe To My Soul (10/59)

Let The Good Times Roll/Don't Let The Sun Catch You Cryin' (12/59)

Just For A Thrill/Heartbreaker (2/60)

Sweet Sixteen Bars/Tell The Truth (7/60)

Doodlin' Part 1/Doodlin' Part 2 (1960)

Tell Me You'll Wait For Me/Come Rain Or Come Shine (11/60)

A Bit Of Soul/Early In The Morning (2/61)

Am I Blue/It Should've Been Me (5/61)

Hard Times (No One Knows Better Than I)/Ray's Blues (I Wonder Who) (9/61)

Carrying The Load/Feelin' Sad (1/63)

Talkin' 'Bout You/In A Little Spanish Town (6/64)

Come Rain Or Come Shine/Tell Me You'll Wait For Me (12/67)

ABC–Paramount/Impulse!/Tangerine:

My Baby! (I Love Her, Yes I Do)/Who You Gonna Love (1/60)

Sticks And Stones/Worried Life Blues (5/60)

Georgia On My Mind/Carry Me Back To Old Virginny (8/60)

Them That Got/I Wonder (8/60)

Ruby/Hardhearted Hannah (11/60)

One Mint Julep/Let's Go (2/61)

I've Got News For You/I'm Gonna Move To The Outskirts Of Town (6/61)

Hit The Road Jack/The Danger Zone (8/61)

Unchain My Heart/But On The Other Hand Baby (11/61)

Baby, It's Cold Outside/We'll Be Together Again (1/62)

At The Club/Hide 'Nor Hair (3/62)
I Can't Stop Loving You/Born To Lose (4/62)
You Don't Know Me/Careless Love (7/62)
You Are My Sunshine/Your Cheating Heart (11/62)
Don't Set Me Free/The Brightest Smile In Town (2/63)
Take These Chains From My Heart/No Letter Today (3/63)
No One/Without Love (There Is Nothing) (5/63)
Busted/Making Believe (8/63)
That Lucky Old Sun/Ol' Man Time (11/63)
Baby, Don't You Cry/My Heart Cries For You (2/64)
My Baby Don't Dig Me/Something's Wrong (5/64)
No One To Cry To/A Tear Fell (6/64)
Smack Dab In The Middle/I Wake Up Crying (9/64)
Makin' Whoopee (Part 1)/Makin' Whoopee (Part 2) (11/64)
Cry/Teardrops From My Eye (1/65)
I Gotta Woman (Part One)/I Gotta Woman (Part Two) (3/65)
Without A Song (Part 1)/Without A Song (Part 2) (4/65)
I'm A Fool To Care/Love's Gonna Live Here (6/65)
The Cincinnati Kid/That's All I Am To You (9/65)
Crying Time/When My Dreamboat Comes Home (10/65)
Together Again/You're Just About To Lose Your Clown (3/66)
Let's Go Get Stoned/The Train (5/66)
I Chose To Sing The Blues/Hopelessly (8/66)
Please Say You're Fooling/I Don't Need No Doctor (10/66)
Something Inside Me/I Want To Talk About You (2/67)
Here We Go Again/Somebody Ought To Write A Book About It (4/67)
In The Heat Of The Night/Something's Got To Change (8/67)
Yesterday/Never Had Enough Of Nothing Yet (10/67)
That's A Lie/Go On Home (1/68)
Understanding/Eleanor Rigby (5/68)
Sweet Young Thing Like You/Listen, They're Playing My Song (8/68)
If It Wasn't For Bad Luck/When I Stop Dreaming (11/68)
I Didn't Know What Time It Was/I'll Be Your Servant (2/69)
Let Me Love You/I'm Satisfied (4/69)
We Can Make It/I Can't Stop Loving You (8/69)
Claudie Mae/Someone To Watch Over Me (11/69)
Laughin' And Clownin'/That Thing Called Love (1/70)
If You Were Mine/Till I Can't Take It Anymore (8/70)
Don't Change On Me/Sweet Memories (2/71)

Booty Butt/Sidewinder (3/71)
Your Love Is So Doggone Good/Feel So Bad (7/71)
What Am I Living For/Tired Of My Tears (11/71)
Look What They've Done To My Song, Ma/America The Beautiful (6/72)
Hey Mister/There'll Be No Peace Without All Men As One (12/72)
Every Saturday Night/Take Me Home, Country Roads (1/73)
I Can Make It Thru The Days/Ring Of Fire (4/73)

Crossover/Atlantic:
Come Live With Me/Everybody Sing (10/73)
Louise/Somebody (3/74)
Living For The City/Then We'll Be Home (7/75)
America The Beautiful/Sunshine (2/76)
I Can See Clearly Now/Anonymous Love (11/77)
Game Number Nine/A Peace That We Never Before Could Enjoy (3/78)
Riding Thumb/You Forgot Your Memory (10/78)
Christmas Time/There'll Be No Peace Without All Men As One (11/78)
Some Enchanted Evening/You 20th Century Fox (8/79)
Just Because/Love Me Or Set Me Free (11/79)
Compared To What/Now That We've Found Each Other (8/80)

RCA:
Oh Lawd, I'm On My Way/Oh Bess, Where's My Bess (w/Cleo Laine)
   (10/76)

Qwest/Warner:
Beers To You/Cotton-Eyed Clint (w/Clint Eastwood) (10/80)
I'll Be Good To You (Part 1)/I'll Be Good To You (Part 2) (10/89)
A Song For You/I Can't Get Enough (3/93)

Columbia:
Born To Love Me/String Bean (11/82)
3/4 Time/You Feel Good All Over (3/83)
Ain't Your Memory Got No Pride At All/I Don't Want No Strangers
   Sleepin' In My Bed (8/83)
We Didn't See A Thing/I Wish You Were Here Tonight (w/George Jones)
   (11/83)
Do I Ever Cross Your Mind/They Call It Love (3/84)
Woman Sensuous Woman/I Was On Georgia Time (6/84)

Rock And Roll Shoes/Then I'll Be Over You (w/B.J. Thomas) (7/84)

Seven Spanish Angels/Who Cares (w/Willie Nelson ★ w/Janie Fricke) (11/84)

It Ain't Gonna Worry My Mind/ We Are The World / Grace (USA For Africa w/Lionel Richie, Stevie Wonder, Tina Turner, James Ingram, Michael Jackson, Diana Ross, Dionne Warwick, Al Jarreau, Paul Simon, Kenny Rogers, Billy Joel, Willie Nelson, Bruce Springsteen, Kenny Loggins, Steve Perry, Daryl Hall, Huey Lewis, Cyndi Lauper, Kim Carnes, Bob Dylan ★ by Quincy Jones) (2/85)

Crazy Old Soldier (w/Mickey Gilley ★ w/Johnny Cash) (4/85)

Two Old Cats Like Us/Little Hotel Room (w/Hank Williams, Jr. ★ w/Merle Haggard) (8/85)

The Pages Of My Mind/Slip Away (6/86)

Dixie Moon/A Little Bit Of Heaven (10/86)

Baby Grand/Big Man On Mulberry Street (w/Billy Joel) (3/87)

Seven Spanish Angels / It Ain't Gonna Worry My Mind (w/Willie Nelson ★ w/Mickey Gilley) (1988)

Warner Brothers:

I'll Take Care Of You (9/90)

Living Without You (7/91)

Fresh Out Of Tears (8/91)

A Song For You (3/93)

I'll Be There/Still Crazy After All These Years (7/93)

Crossover:

Mother/New Orleans (8/02)

Concord / EMI:

Here We Go Again (w/Norah Jones) (3/05)

Appendix 3

VIDEOGRAPHY

Live 1991 (Atlantic 1991)
Live At The Montreux Jazz Festival (Pioneer 2002)
Live At Montreux 1997 (Eagle Vision 2004)
Ã-Genio: 1963 Live In Brazil (Warner Music Vision 2005) DVD
The Genius Of Soul (Metrodome 2005) DVD
Ray (Universal 2005) DVD

Appendix 4

GRAMMY AWARDS

Ray Charles won 20 Grammy Awards, as follows:

1960 Best Vocal Performance Single Record or Track, Male, 'Georgia On My Mind'

1960 Best Performance by a Pop Single Artist, 'Georgia On My Mind'

1960 Best Rhythm & Blues Performance, 'Let The Good Times Roll'

1960 Best Vocal Performance Album, Male, 'The Genius Of Ray Charles'

1961 Best Rhythm & Blues Recording, 'Hit The Road Jack'

1962 Best Rhythm & Blues Recording, 'I Can't Stop Loving You'

1963 Best Rhythm & Blues Recording, 'Busted'

1966 Best Rhythm & Blues Recording, 'Crying Time'

1966 Best R&B Solo Vocal Performance, 'Crying Time'

1975 Best R&B Vocal Performance, Male, 'Living For The City'

1990 Best R&B Performance By a Duo or Group with Vocal, 'I'll Be Good To You' (with Chaka Khan)

1993 Best R&B Vocal Performance, Male, 'A Song For You'

2005 Best Album of the Year, *Genius Loves Company*

2005 Best Pop Vocal Album, *Genius Loves Company*

2005 Record (single) of the Year, 'Here We Go Again' with Norah Jones

2005 Best Gospel Performance, 'Heaven Help Us All' with Gladys Knight

2005 Best Vocal Collaboration, 'Here We Go Again' with Norah Jones

2005 Best Instrumental Arrangement Accompanying Vocals (Victor Vanacore's charts for 'Over The Rainbow' with Johnny Mathis)

2005 Best Engineered Album (non-classical), *Genius Loves Company*

2005 Best Surround Sound Album, *Genius Loves Company*

Index

Single releases and individual songs are in roman type. Albums are in italics. The recording artists are in parentheses.

1 2 3 4 5 6 7 8 9